Skulls and Skeletons

ALSO BY CHRISTINE QUIGLEY
AND FROM McFARLAND

*Conjoined Twins: An Historical, Biological and Ethical
Issues Encyclopedia* (2003; paperback 2006)

*Modern Mummies: The Preservation of the Human Body
in the Twentieth Century* (1998; paperback 2006)

The Corpse: A History (1996; paperback 2005)

*Death Dictionary: Over 5,500 Clinical, Legal,
Literary and Vernacular Terms* (1994)

Skulls and Skeletons

*Human Bone Collections
and Accumulations*

by
CHRISTINE QUIGLEY

McFarland & Company, Inc., Publishers
Jefferson, North Carolina, and London

"Bones are all that survive of the body. They are keys to our collective past and reminders of our own mortality, so it is no mystery that they have a magic aura for artists, for the faithful of many religions, for collectors, for all of us."—Barbara Norfleet, 1993

GN
70
Q6s
2001

The present work is a reprint of the illustrated case bound edition of Skulls and Skeletons: Human Bone Collections and Accumulations, *first published in 2001 by McFarland.*

LIBRARY OF CONGRESS CATALOGUING-IN-PUBLICATION DATA

Quigley, Christine, 1963–
Skulls and skeletons : human bone collections
and accumulations / by Christine Quigley.
p.   cm.
Includes bibliographical references and index.

ISBN 978-0-7864-3888-4
softcover : 50# alkaline paper

1. Human skeleton — Identification.   2. Human skeleton — Analysis.
3. Human skeleton — Collectors and collecting.
4. Museums — Collection management.
5. Human remains (Archaeology) — Repatriation.
6. Human remains (Archaeology) — Law and legislation.
7. United States. Native American Graves Protection and Repatriation Act.
I. Title
GN70.Q54   2008
599.9'47 — dc21   2001030340

British Library cataloguing data are available

Manufactured in the United States of America

On the cover: human skull (Art Today),
skeleton (Photospin), and a wall of skulls
on an 1897 stereoscopic viewing card.

McFarland & Company, Inc., Publishers
Box 611, Jefferson, North Carolina 28640
www.mcfarlandpub.com

Acknowledgments

The seeds of this book were sown in childhood in the 1970s when my parents took me to visit Dickson Mounds. I carried away lasting memories and a brochure that I have kept all these years. The seeds remained dormant in the late 1980s, as I stood in front of the Hyrtl skull collection at the Mütter Museum, and finally germinated after my *Modern Mummies* was published in 1998. My thoughts kept returning to the skeletal hands of Civil War soldiers I had seen stored neatly in shallow drawers at the National Museum of Health and Medicine (NMHM).

I went back to Dickson Mounds, the NMHM, and the Mütter Museum during the research for this book. I would like to thank their curators for their hospitality and help, along with those of the many laboratories and institutions I was grateful to have the invitation and opportunity to visit: Tony Falsetti, C.A. Pound Human Identification Laboratory; Judith Franke, Dickson Mounds Museum; David Hunt, National Museum of Natural History; Bruce Latimer and Lyman Jellema, Cleveland Museum of Natural History; Paul Sledzik and Lenore Barbian, National Museum of Health and Medicine; James Starrs, George Washington University; Rose Tyson, San Diego Museum of Man; Michael Wiant, Illinois State Museum; and Gretchen Worden, Mütter Museum.

Thanks are also owed to the many researchers and other individuals who shared information so generously: Paul Anderson, Susan Anton, John Auchard, Arthur Aufderheide, Bill Bass, Geraldine K. Bell, Eric Bentley, Michael Blakey, Father Bonaventura, Capt. Harvey Lee Boswell, J.S. Brink, Kathleen Butler, Simon Chaplin, Eve Christoffersen, Eve Cockburn, Joan Carroll Cruz, Dennis C. Curry, Steven de Clerq, Chris Fellner, H. Garner, Georgina Gratacós i Teixidor, Gloria Greis, Gisela Grupe, Lorena M. Havill, Maciej Henneberg, Patrick Horne, Jane Hughes, Eric Humphries, Lydia Icke-Schwalbe, Bill Jamieson, Flemming Kaul, Martin Legassick, Inmaculada Lopez, Niels Lynnerup, Francis P. McManamon, Ann McMullen, Charles Merbs, Edward Meyer, Janet Monge, Mohammed Mouna, Walter Neves, Michael O'Brien, Gregor Oezelt, Rosine Organ, Colin Pardoe, Joseph Powell, Karen Reeds, Susan Sacharski, Paul P. de Saint-Maur, Ana Luisa Santos, Shelley R. Saunders, Tom Serafin, Giuseppina Spadea, James Taylor, Vittoria Villani, Jay Villemarette, Ronn Wade, Joachim Wahl, Phillip Walker, Julia Walton, P. Willey, Larry Zimmerman, and anyone I have inadvertently left out.

Thanks to the following for permission to reproduce photographs and illustrations: Lenore Barbian, National Museum of Health and Medicine; Jasmine Day; Heather Ercilla, The Wellcome Trust; Charlie Fellenbaum; Melody Galen, Missouri Archaeological Society; George Higham; Hildegard Hnatek,

Rollettmuseum; Eric Humphries, Skulls Unlimited; Jutta Lange, Museum für Sepulkralkultur; Bruce Latimer, Cleveland Museum of Natural History; Kristan Lawson; Laurie Richardson Marx, University of Michigan; Susan M. Sacharski, Northwestern Memorial Hospital; Thomas J. Serafin, ICHRusa; Ann Silvers, Institute of Human Origins; Craig Wilkie, The University Press of Kentucky; and Norman Woods, Parish of St. Leonard. And thanks to the following individuals for translating material in German, Italian, and French: Mark Benecke, Sebastiano Brida, Claudia Brown, and Amy Sepinwall.

As always — many thanks to my family and friends for their support and indulgence, particularly those who have accompanied me in my travels or were kind enough to read the manuscript: Jody Arlington, Maddy Biggs, Heidi Crayton, Donna and Del Gritman, Cris Hastings, Melissa and Nicholas Heilweil, Janice Lane, Jim Miller, James and Sarah Quigley, Katina Stockbridge, Dorothy Sutton, Chris Sweeters, and my colleagues at Georgetown University Press. And a special salute to Edward Johnson (June 29, 1914–December 25, 2000), who gave me so much encouragement while writing this book.

Contents

Preface

Among the various components of the human body, the bones have a unique durability that lends itself to collection. Provided a body has not completely disintegrated, the skeletal remains can be recovered even millions of years after death, cleaned of flesh or debris, studied at length, and stored indefinitely without the maintenance that wet specimens require. But that is not why bones are collected. It only makes their collection easier.

Human skeletal remains have been collected by scientists to provide anthropological data banks: drawers and cabinets full of carefully catalogued specimens. Ancient bones reveal our evolutionary and biological history. Contemporary bones provide standards against which newly discovered remains can be compared, assessed, and possibly identified. Doctors have also assembled collections of skulls and skeletons. Medical collections include standard specimens for the teaching of gross and comparative anatomy, but are also punctuated by the anomalous: famous skeletons of giants and dwarfs, conjoined twins, and "elephant men."

Other skeletons have been saved for their ethereal qualities, rather than their physical characteristics. The bones of saints and martyrs are imbued with special religious significance, exhibited singularly and often fragmentarily in ornate reliquaries and shrines. While the skeletal relics of the saints have been scattered far and wide through commerce and cooperation, the bones of their early Christian followers were allowed to repose in the Roman catacombs for centuries until medieval looters and a belief in the bones' magical properties left little but dust.

Elsewhere — through disease or natural attrition — bones simply piled up, resulting in such proliferation that they were used as building blocks in the formation of chapels. The scapulae and vertebrae of their brothers became the pebbles with which monks formed elaborate mosaics on the walls and ceilings. The skulls and bones of tens of thousands of victims of the Great Plague line the walls of churches in Eastern Europe. Charnel houses and ossuaries became necessities as graveyards filled up and the old bones had to yield to the newly deceased. This occurred in nineteenth-century Paris, where the skulls and long-bones of 6 million people were removed from overcrowded cemeteries and relocated underground in carefully arranged stacks dozens of feet thick. But it also occurs regularly in twentieth-century New Orleans, where bones are swept periodically from the above-ground tombs into pits below to make way for new occupants.

Cemetery relocation is not the only reason bones are excavated. Archaeological digs reveal ancient populations whose skeletal remains tell us how they lived and died. Forensic anthropologists excavate mass graves

1

whose victims plead silently for justice or historical accuracy. Though they may require cleaning, skeletal remains do not always require excavation. Human bones may litter the surface of the ground at a massacre site. Skulls may be harvested at the time of death by last century's headhunters or this century's soldiers, being added to a community skull rack or a private mantel. Or skulls, bones, and complete skeletons may simply be purchased legally — retail, wholesale, or mail order.

Motivations for collecting human skeletal material have ranged from practical to ritualistic, but whatever the reason, the resulting assemblages tend to remain intact even if no longer used for the intended purpose. For phrenologists, skulls were the raw material for attempts to link the physical characteristics of the cranium to personality traits; while their theories were debunked, some of their collections have survived. Over the centuries, many collections have moved from private hands to the public trust, being acquired by the world's museums, educational facilities, and scientific institutions. Now portions of those collections are at risk of being removed as a result of increased cultural sensitivity reflected in federal legislation. Compliance with the Native American Graves Protection and Repatriation Act (NAGPRA) causes mixed feelings, since the law puts emotional attachment to even remotely related bones ahead of the intellectual ground that could be gained from continued respectful study. The remains are human, as are the sensitivities — but so is the inquisitiveness about them.

Bones are ancestors. Bones are fossils. They are saints, specimens, and victims. Bones are merchandise and trophies. Bones are art.

Bones are the subject of this book. May the reader enjoy, and be edified.

Introduction

The skull is the most recognizable part of the human skeleton and is laden with symbolism, most of it negative. A single skull is a reminder of our individual mortality. Skulls in proliferation remind us that we all share the same fate. It was great numbers of skulls during the Great Plague that standardized the memento mori symbolism (Henschen 1965) and some of those very accumulations — for instance Kostnice, the bone church in the Czech Republic — can still be seen. But to anatomists and physical anthropologists, they are more than tableaux to be observed subjectively. They are distinct assemblages from which to glean objective data about populations past and present. This information includes age, gender, race, stature, and a number of other characteristics about each individual. But it is also important to determine the minimum number of individuals (MNI) represented by a group of bones, whether it represents a moment in time (a massacre) or many generations (a cemetery population). The larger the sample, the more powerful its message, both anthropologically and symbolically.

The whole is more than the sum of its parts, however, and collections and accumulations are not ranked according to size. A number of other factors contribute to their importance. Some collections, such as those associated with John and William Hunter, are notable for their history and still serve as the teaching aids intended by their namesakes. Others are noted for their documentation, for instance the Terry Collection and the Hamann-Todd Collection, and allow forensic anthropologists to estimate height based on the length of certain bones, among other things. Other assemblages of human remains represent culture and ritual in the form of religious relics and decoration of and with bones. The remains of early hominids, taken as a whole, offer a debated view of the past and our prehistory. And, yes, some groups of bones are known for their overwhelming numbers, such as the remains of millions in the Paris catacombs.

At a time when the technology to analyze these collections is evolving rapidly, continued curation has been discontinued in many cases or may be in jeopardy. This book will look at the repatriation issue from several angles, using as examples the contentious Kennewick Man and Mount Vernon Mound in the United States and Aboriginal remains worldwide. The number of precontact Aboriginal remains currently held by museums, historical societies, universities, and private collectors is conservatively estimated to be as many as 600,000 individuals (Price 1991). In the face of compliance with current legislation in the U.S., scientists in some cases have no choice but to gather as much data as they can from their collections in the event that they have

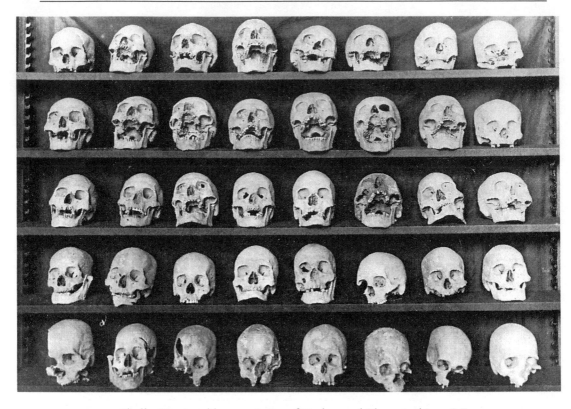

Skulls. Reprinted by permission of Underwood Photo Archives, S.F.

to give them up. Some series have already been reburied or returned to Native American groups. Collections that are not at risk include those acquired through body donation, such as the skeletal remains being curated by the University of Tennessee Forensic Anthropology Center those harvested from the dissection of unclaimed bodies, or skeletons that remain unidentified, such as pending cases at the C.A. Pound Human Identification Laboratory at the University of Florida.

Many collections and accumulations have resulted from unfortunate acts and events like war, for instance the Civil War collections at the National Museum of Health and Medicine, but have resulted in beneficial research. Some are the result of archaeological excavations that have allowed scientists to better understand historical events like the Battle of Little Bighorn. More recent excavations, such as those overseen by Clyde Snow in troubled parts of the world, allow forensic anthropologists to identify the remains of victims of genocide buried in mass graves. Other collections are the result of deliberate, positive intentions rather than the byproduct of war. Certain of these are the result of the foresight of a single individual, such as the Cobb Collection at Howard University in Washington, D.C., which remains an important resource and the only large collection of African-American remains in the country. Cobb and other medical men straddled the line between anatomy and physical anthropology and left lasting legacies that serve as raw material for continuing research. These legacies, if curated appropriately and handled carefully, will remain intact for future researchers to learn from and to leave their own marks in far-ranging fields: "[R]esearches on human skeletal collections have yielded, and continue to yield, results of

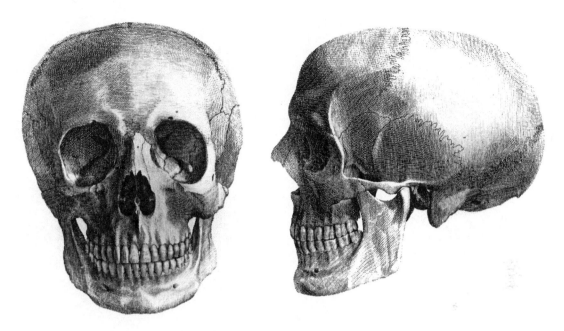

The human skull, front and side view. Reprinted from *Albinus on Anatomy,* by Robert Beverly Hale and Terence Coyle (New York: Dover, 1988).

value in human and primate anatomy, human biology and physical anthropology, human population biology, growth and development, odontology and dentistry, orthodontics, pathology, forensic medicine, epidemiology, orthopedics, obstetrics, neurosurgery, pediatrics, and other clinical disciplines" (Tobias 1991).

Some collections, like the bones that decorate the Capuchin cathedral in Rome, are tourist attractions and show determined care and creativity. Others, like the neatly stacked bones at the English and European ossuaries, show more practicality than creativity, but serve as osteological "libraries" of their respective times, some tapped and some as yet untapped, but still the objects of attention. Rather than requiring a "Christian burial," these bones have spared room in the churchyard or are meant, as in the case of Christian relics, to serve a higher purpose. Bones are many things to many people. These are just a few of those bones and those things.

SYMBOLIC SIGNIFICANCE

Man's cranium is a very singular object. If one were to ask why it is so frequently represented in art, the answer would almost certainly be: because of its obvious significance as a symbol of death and mortality. And indeed this has come to be true to so great an extent that many may find it impossible to think of the skull in any different connotation or to free their thoughts from what the skull had once been.
— *Folke Henschen [1965]*

There has been much symbolism over the centuries attached to the bones of the human skeleton, most notably those of the skull. The skull holds our interest because it houses many of the senses in a living individual (including sight, as reinforced by those empty sockets) and because it also holds the brain. The shape of the skull also gives us our facial appearance, so from the skull alone the face may be reproduced well enough to allow identification, if it is in

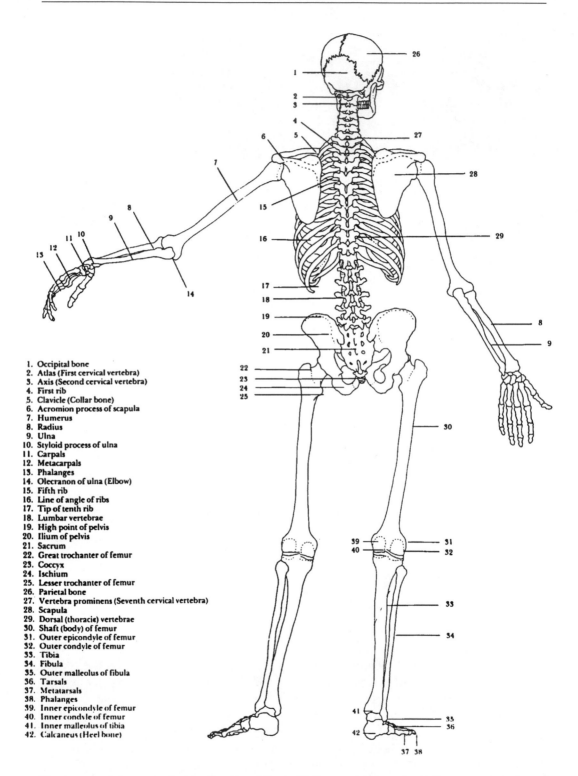

1. Occipital bone
2. Atlas (First cervical vertebra)
3. Axis (Second cervical vertebra)
4. First rib
5. Clavicle (Collar bone)
6. Acromion process of scapula
7. Humerus
8. Radius
9. Ulna
10. Styloid process of ulna
11. Carpals
12. Metacarpals
13. Phalanges
14. Olecranon of ulna (Elbow)
15. Fifth rib
16. Line of angle of ribs
17. Tip of tenth rib
18. Lumbar vertebrae
19. High point of pelvis
20. Ilium of pelvis
21. Sacrum
22. Great trochanter of femur
23. Coccyx
24. Ischium
25. Lesser trochanter of femur
26. Parietal bone
27. Vertebra prominens (Seventh cervical vertebra)
28. Scapula
29. Dorsal (thoracic) vertebrae
30. Shaft (body) of femur
31. Outer epicondyle of femur
32. Outer condyle of femur
33. Tibia
34. Fibula
35. Outer malleolus of fibula
36. Tarsals
37. Metatarsals
38. Phalanges
39. Inner epicondyle of femur
40. Inner condyle of femur
41. Inner malleolus of tibia
42. Calcaneus (Heel bone)

The human skeleton, back view. Reprinted from *Albinus on Anatomy*, by Robert Beverly Hale and Terence Coyle (New York: Dover, 1988).

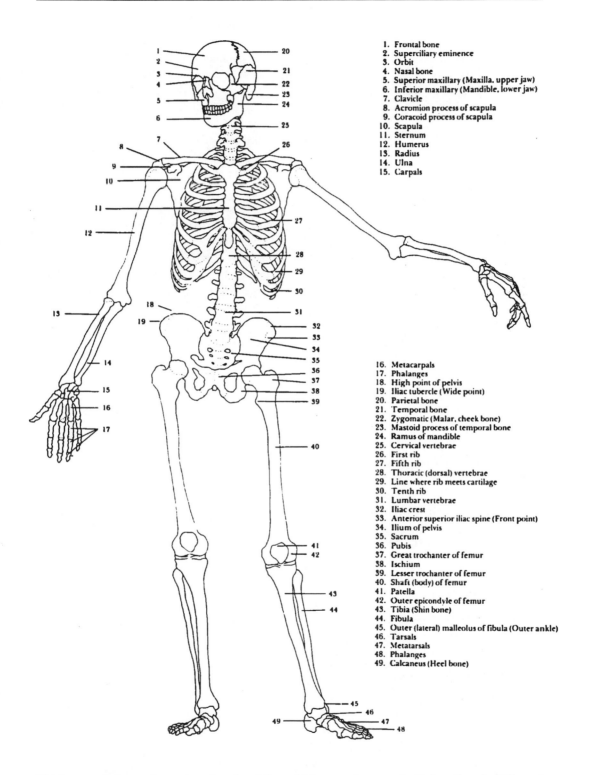

1. Frontal bone
2. Superciliary eminence
3. Orbit
4. Nasal bone
5. Superior maxillary (Maxilla, upper jaw)
6. Inferior maxillary (Mandible, lower jaw)
7. Clavicle
8. Acromion process of scapula
9. Coracoid process of scapula
10. Scapula
11. Sternum
12. Humerus
13. Radius
14. Ulna
15. Carpals

16. Metacarpals
17. Phalanges
18. High point of pelvis
19. Iliac tubercle (Wide point)
20. Parietal bone
21. Temporal bone
22. Zygomatic (Malar, cheek bone)
23. Mastoid process of temporal bone
24. Ramus of mandible
25. Cervical vertebrae
26. First rib
27. Fifth rib
28. Thoracic (dorsal) vertebrae
29. Line where rib meets cartilage
30. Tenth rib
31. Lumbar vertebrae
32. Iliac crest
33. Anterior superior iliac spine (Front point)
34. Ilium of pelvis
35. Sacrum
36. Pubis
37. Great trochanter of femur
38. Ischium
39. Lesser trochanter of femur
40. Shaft (body) of femur
41. Patella
42. Outer epicondyle of femur
43. Tibia (Shin bone)
44. Fibula
45. Outer (lateral) malleolus of fibula (Outer ankle)
46. Tarsals
47. Metatarsals
48. Phalanges
49. Calcaneus (Heel bone)

The human skeleton, front view. Reprinted from *Albinus on Anatomy*, by Robert Beverly Hale and Terence Coyle (New York: Dover, 1988).

question. We have a number of attachments to the skull and it has taken precedence over other bones among collectors ranging from physical anthropologists to headhunters. This was true in the nineteenth century, when interest in the shape of the skull was stirred by phrenologists, some of whose collections are still on display. And it was true in the early twentieth century, when Aleš Hrdlička collected skulls from the surface of the Peruvian desert that are still curated at the San Diego Museum of Man. Theories of prehistory are dependent on skull-centered research: "Traditionally, the skull is the single most studied bone in physical anthropology, and much of our knowledge of human evolution is based on cranial remains" (Krogman and Iscan 1986).

Attentions have been focused on the skull in most cultures and range from painting it to measuring it after death. Artificial cranial deformation of the developing skull has been practiced on every continent except Australia (White 1991). Headhunters collected the skulls of enemies, phrenologists collected the skulls of the famous, and archaeologists collected the skulls of our ancestors. Even the anonymous skulls that make up these groups claim their differences, while symbolizing our shared fate:

> The skull is man's final claim to individuality. After the fleshy features have disintegrated and each skeleton separated into anonymous bones only the cranium remains to distinguish one individual from another. Even in death, every head remains different: the three squiggly lines that mark where the cranium's sections join trace varying patterns, no two exactly alike [Weil 1992].

The prevalence of skulls, the quantity of information that can be obtained from them, and the predisposition in favor of them over the post-cranial remains led to the curation of only skulls in some museum collections. Douglas Ubelaker (1989) warns that this bias should be taken into account when studying skeletal collections: "Fragmentary remains, infants, and even post-cranial bones of well preserved adults have often been discarded, only the complete skulls being saved. No museum collection should be used for demographic reconstruction without investigating its history before and after its arrival at the museum." But well before the end of the twentieth century, preserving the value of discrete skeletons became a well-established principle in the sciences. Thus the "crossbones" were added to the skulls.

And yet some collections manage to retain their symbolic character without consisting of entire bones at all. A small splinter is all that is needed of a saintly relic to provide a focus for faith and belief. Native Americans feel a connection with the remains of their ancestors, regardless of whether those remains are partial or complete, and many are opposed to scientific testing that will destroy even a minute portion of the bones. Phillip L. Walker (In press) brings into focus the dichotomy between those who revere the bones and those who study them:

> Bioarchaeologists do not view human remains primarily as symbols. Instead they value them as sources of historical evidence that are key to understanding what really happened during the biological and cultural evolution of our species. This lack of concern with symbolic issues is in stark contrast to the richness of the symbolic connotations human skeletons have for most people. This conflict in worldviews is especially acute in areas of the world that were subjected to European colonization. In North America, Hawaii, and Australia, where the indigenous people suffered the greatest devastation at the hands of European colonists, ancient human remains have assumed great significance as symbols of cultural integrity and colonial oppression. In this post-colonial world, gaining control over ancestral remains is increasingly considered essential to the

survival and revitalization of indigenous cultures.

Bones evoke strong feelings that often conflict with the intellectual goals regarding them. But examination, analysis, and testing of both indigenous and saintly remains have been allowed in many cases where study is not seen as synonymous with disrespect — of a culture or its physical remnants. In fact, while they are able to set aside any emotional attachment to human skeletons, physical anthropologists do treat the bones with respect, but to them they symbolize not a spiritual attachment to the past, but an offering of knowledge from the past that it is their privilege to interpret.

PHYSICAL INTEGRITY

Bones have a structure that can be studied, compared, excavated, analyzed, curated, cast, and displayed. They can last millions of years beyond the lifespan of their original owners, as modern dating methods prove. They survive in diverse cultural and environmental conditions. In most of the indoor contexts, the bones remain clean and stable: stacked in ossuaries, trusted to museum drawers and cabinets, and studied in laboratories. But even outdoors, bones fare well, whether bleached by the sun or blanketed by the soil — unless that soil happens to be very acidic. Studies by William Bass (1984) indicate that skeletons may decay in as little as 25 years in hot, wet, acidic soil, but that neutral soil may not destroy the skeleton at all.

There are in fact more than a handful of threats to the preservation of bones. One of them is time itself, as bones eventually fulfill the "dust to dust" proverb. Fossil hominid remains are rarely found unbroken at paleontological sites, explains Tim D. White (1991), because the relatively few hominids rarely died in swampy or lakeside conditions that favor fossilization. "The processes of bone preservation are such that the farther back in time we go, the less there is," writes Jeffrey H. Schwartz (1998). "There are few species represented, fewer individuals representing this incomplete sampling of species, and fewer pieces of the skeleton of each of these individuals." Bones are subject to damage caused by rockfalls, freeze-thaw cycles, rapid evaporation, abrasion, fire, and the effects of sun and high heat. Weathering bones first display a network of fine, usually parallel surface cracks that progressively deepen and widen, deteriorating the bone surface at a rate dependent on temperature and humidity. Pitting, scoring, and puncturing of the bone surface (and particularly the ends of the long bones) may be the work of carnivores including hyenas, wolves, dogs, leopards, and crocodiles (White 1991). On a microscopic level, bones are subject to the effects of bacteria, algae, and fungi. Acids secreted by the roots of plants may etch the surface of buried bones and the roots themselves may cause damage: "Plant activity can have profound effects on skeletal preservation ... large roots can easily stave in a coffin or a skull or wind their way through the shafts of long bones, creating mechanical damage and dispersing the remains" (Nawrocki 1995).

The various ways that bones may be covered up after death affects their preservation. Clothing speeds up skeletal decay, while delayed decay of soft tissue will insulate bone from water, acids, and erosion (Nawrocki 1995). Being blanketed by a layer of sand, silt, mud, or volcanic lava may result in mineralization or complete fossilization over time (Kanowski 1987). Burial in various soils has differing effects on preservation: chalk soil may result in eroded and friable bones, cave soil may mineralize bones or cause them to become encrusted with precipitated carbonates, clay may cause corrosion based on pH levels, gravels — depending on whether they are acidic, permeable,

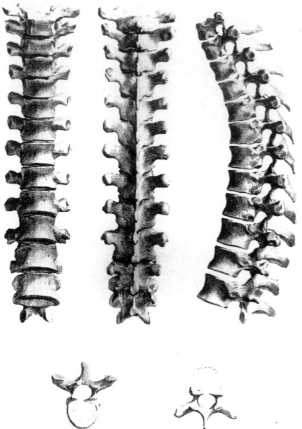

The thoracic vertebrae from the front, back, and side. Reprinted from *Albinus on Anatomy*, by Robert Beverly Hale and Terence Coyle (New York: Dover, 1988).

or waterlogged — may lead to good preservation, and sand may preserve bones well if the acidity and temperature are favorable (Brothwell 1981). Muck soil, rich in decaying organic matter, may cause the outer layers of buried bones to "peel off" in about 50 years (Krogman and Iscan 1986). Deliberately buried bones are affected by the depth of burial, the type of casket, the season of burial, and whether or not the body was embalmed (Ubelaker 1995). Other factors include delay between death and burial and the amount of body fat. And yet, interment favors preservation: "[T]he simple act of burial does more to preserve bones than any other phenomenon in the natural world,"

states Nawrocki (1995). Janet Henderson (1987) concurs, noting that humans are the most important factor in skeletal preservation, since they determine who is buried, when, how, and where.

Bones from which the calcium has leached out, leaving mainly collagen bundles (the main organic component of bone), have the unusual capability of being tied in knots, but demineralized bones can be easily destroyed by water and acid soil. Replacement of the minerals resolidifies, and eventually fossilizes, the bone (Schwartz 1998), but even this means of preservation is variable within the skeleton and within individual bones, depending on density (Wolpoff 1996). It has been determined that the preservation of bones is most apt to occur when they are either completely wet or completely dry, suggesting that the best places to find intact remains are lake and stream margins, delta formations, and protected areas such as caves and rock shelters. In their studies of bone distribution in several geological contexts, Diane Gifford, K. Behrensmeyer, and A. Hill observed that bone densities were greatest in delta environments and least on the floodplain, with channel deposits intermediate (Binsford 1981). Others including H. Toots have studied patterns of disarticulation, noting that the skull and some limbs become disconnected first, then the ribs loosen and fall off, followed by further disintegration of the limbs and the disarticulation of the vertebral column (Binford 1981). Articulation is maintained the longest with the bones of the foot, lower leg, and thoracic portion of the vertebral column (Ubelaker 1989). Insects also play a role in the dispersal of skeletal remains. As Nawrocki (1995) colorfully relates, "Large maggot masses can carry and scatter ribs much like a surfboard is carried by waves."

Another factor in the survival of skeletal remains is size. Male skeletons do not decay as quickly as female skeletons and adult skeletons of both genders outlast the skeletons of children. Within individual skeletons, the survival rate of the leg bones and heavier parts of the skull is greater than that of spongy bones which usually have thin walls and low specific gravity (Kanowski 1987). "Bone is one of the strongest biological materials in existence and is the main supporting tissue of the body," writes White (1991), who also notes that of the bones of the human skeleton, the femur is the longest, heaviest, and strongest. This would explain why thigh bones and other "long bones" are so common in assemblages, while smaller and more fragile bones are less commonly preserved. Even more prevalent than the bones of the limbs, in most archaeological contexts, are teeth, which are the most resistant part of the skeleton to decay. Because teeth even outlast bone, they have played a key role in the study of fossil humans (Bass 1987). And because of their unique characteristics, they serve to positively identify contemporary remains of individuals for whom dental records can be located.

While bones are of course subject to deterioration, it is less likely that they will crumble to dust than they will be dispersed by external forces, human and otherwise: "The melancholy of anatomy is that it keeps disintegrating on us. Scattered around the earth lie all manner of mortal remains — bones, limbs, skulls, relics, skeletons, mummies, corpses, fleshy fragments — honored or coveted by families, the devout, collectors, antiquarians, curiosity seekers and other connoisseurs" (Weil 1992). Nawrocki (1995) indicates that human cultural activities, rather than any environmental factors, are the most important accumulators of

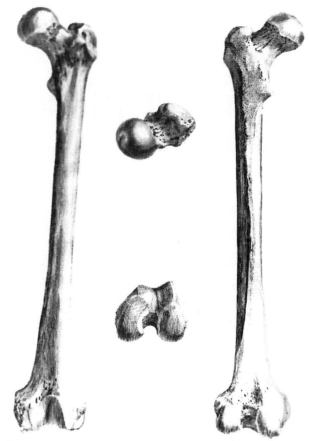

The femur from the front and back and from the top and bottom. Reprinted from *Albinus on Anatomy*, by Robert Beverly Hale and Terence Coyle (New York: Dover, 1988).

human remains. It would seem, conversely, that human activities are also responsible for a fair amount of dispersal. Secondary burials, in which the bones are redeposited after the flesh is gone, yield fragmentary and often commingled remains despite the care taken during reburial. Only 40 to 60 percent of cremated remains are likely to be found, since this is the proportion likely to have been recovered from the funeral pyre and buried (Pearson 1999). While cremation may cause bones to fragment, distort, and shrink, the process drives off moisture and the organic components, leading to favorable preservation (Mays 1998). Charring (resulting in white, gray, black, and blue hues) and transverse cracking are evidence of cremation, while patterns of burning, cutmarks, percussion, crushing, and other fracture on human remains are usually interpreted as signs of cannibalism (White 1991). Physical anthropologists have listed a number of criteria, all of which have to be met, before the sensitive subject of cannibalism is suggested. But ironically, cannibalism may lead to those damaged bones being found. As Henschen (1965) points out, "[I]f you are eaten, your bones have a better chance of being preserved for posterity than if your body is simply abandoned. Being tossed into a garbage dump is better from the archaeological point of view than being left for the wolves and hyenas on the lone prairie."

So some skeletons survive, some only partially, and some not at all. And yet what remains, while not encyclopedic, certainly provides solid reference for past ways of life. Because of their resistance to decay, bones and teeth form a lasting record that may reveal age, sex, stature, and pathologies. Analysis of a group of skeletons reveals population structure, biological affinities, cultural behaviors, and disease patterns. Study of the fossil record reveals evolutionary history of humanity (White 1991). During life, bone serves as a mineral reservoir that can be studied chemically after death, taking into account continued postmortem interaction with the environment (Sandford 1992). Since chemicals can be absorbed by the bones from percolating ground water, soil samples are taken from excavation sites so that the remains will not be misread. Physical and forensic anthropologists are also faced with the often challenging task of determining which characteristics of a skeleton tell us about the life of an individual and which tell us about his or her death or posthumous history. For instance, bones may be remodelled during life artificially (head-binding), they may have deformed due to pathological causes (tumor), or they

may have been altered after death by earth pressure (Brothwell 1981). Damage to a skull that appears to be posthumous may in fact be perimortem trauma and vice versa. Trauma may be mistakenly read into the normal effects of aging on the skeleton (Ubelaker 1989). Holes left by tree roots may be misinterpreted as caused by antemortem violence. Even taphonomic processes themselves, though, are used to the scientists' advantage. Damage caused by weathering, for instance, helps to estimate how long it took for some bone assemblages to accumulate on former land surfaces (White 1991). And soil silhouettes, created by the minerals in bones as they dissolve, are of value in reconstructing a site in the absence of the bones themselves. Once buried bones are exposed, however, they are subject to the decay caused by the new conditions and must be conserved carefully.

RESEARCH POTENTIAL

The skeleton, although mute as stone, speaks volumes concerning its former owner. It tells the person's age, sex, race, and stature, as well as the diseases and injuries suffered. The skeleton also often tells what happened to the bones following the owner's death. The bones may indicate that they were buried, chewed by wolves or nibbled by rodents, carefully curated or roughly handled. By shedding light on all these areas, bones provide a unique perspective on the person — in life and death.
— *Douglas D. Scott, P. Willey, and Melissa A. Connor [1998]*

Human skeletal remains are a unique source of information on the genetic and physiological responses our ancestors made to the challenges posed by past natural and sociocultural environments. Consequently, they provide an extremely valuable adaptive perspective on the history of our species.
— *Phillip L. Walker [In press]*

During life, the skeleton has been characterized as merely "something to hang meat on." Bones protect and support soft tissues; anchor muscles, tendons, and ligaments; produce blood cells and store fat; and serve as reservoirs of elements such as calcium (White 1991). After death, the skeleton encapsulates details about the life, the death, and the culture of the person whose musculature and organ systems it supported. A wealth of information can be learned from a single bone. That potential increases when an entire skeleton can be studied and multiplies when the skeletal remains of a cross-section of a population can be analyzed. This demography of the dead applies rates of growth and aging established for modern humans to the remains of past populations to determine their vital statistics (White 1991). Skeletal remains are essential in the teaching of osteology. It is also a necessity for paleontologists to study large skeletal collections to familiarize themselves with variation in modern humans and apes (White 1991). "The study of evolution essentially would be impossible if bones were eliminated as a source of data," writes Bass (1987). But in addition to making skeletal collections available to new scholars, access to previously studied skeletal material is required to test previous findings and to make use of scientific techniques that are continually being developed and refined (Bass 1987).

Phillip V. Tobias (1991) enumerates the ways that collections of human bones are of value. His list includes the following suggested or continued studies: a baseline for metrical and non-metrical variability of contemporary humans with which to compare early hominids; averages with which to estimate height based on the dimensions of isolated bones; comparison of traits and measurements to determine interrelationships, understand diversification, and study heritability; growth changes; sexual dimorphism; bone strength and structure; and anomolies and pathologies. Studies of human skeletal material are used to advance research in many fields, including physical and forensic anthropology, paleontology, anatomy, neurosurgery, clinical medicine, orthopedics, dentistry and odontology, orthodontics, obstetrics, population biology, pathology, and epidemiology. Skeletal collections are also utilized by those entering these and related fields, as Tobias (1991) notes: "The existence of human skeletons in such collections is crucial for the teaching of human anatomy, including dental anatomy, to students of medicine, dentistry, physiotherapy, occupational therapy, nursing and pharmacy; as well as students of comparative anatomy, primatology and general morphology.... Clearly the continued existence of human skeletal collections is of critical importance for purposes of education and research in a wide variety of medical, dental and pure scientific disciplines."

Each skeleton is its own collection of bones, the number of which decreases with age. From 806 distinctive ossification centers (Buikstra and Ubelaker 1994), there are about 450 centers of bone growth at birth (Krogman and Iscan 1986) and 206 bones in the adult human skeleton, including 22 in the skull. The vertebral column usually comprises 33 elements in the adult human, 24 of which are moveable and the others fused. The hands contain 27 major bones (White 1991). Adults have 32 teeth (including eight to 12 molars) and children have 20 (Bass 1987, 273). "When you have seen one skeleton, you have 'seen 'em all,'" writes Stanley Rhine (1998). "They all have the same bones, shaped the same ways, located in the same places and doing the same things. That is why a thoracic vertebra is a thoracic vertebra is a thoracic vertebra." And yet, once a student learns the basics, he or she learns that each skeleton has unique features, from size differences, to inherited anomalies, to pathologies. As an example, standard skeletal charts do not make note of the small sesamoid bones that may lie within the tendons or wormian bones that sometimes grow between the sutures of the skull. Many of the individual characteristics of a skeleton, such as the shape of the skull, have a strong inherited component (Mays 1998). Many variants — the numbers of bones or teeth, anomalies of bone fusion, differences in bony foramina, articular facet variations, hyperostoses, hypostoses, and variations in the form of the tooth crowns — cannot be measured and are thus termed nonmetric.

Osteologists and paleopathologists must use modern technology and close observation in examining skeletal remains because few diseases leave a mark on them and those that do may cause very similar skeletal reactions. In addition, the researchers must differentiate between deviations of the bones from the normal condition, those caused by pathological agents, and those caused by taphonomic agents. And to further complicate research efforts, conclusions must be based on a sample that is both large enough and that accurately represents the past population (White 1991). Research rests on assumptions, for instance, that disease that has not contributed to death mirrors the prevalence of that disease in the living (Waldron 1994). But bias can be introduced by a number of factors. The proportion of buried skeletons to deaths in a community as a whole may differ due to bodies being buried elsewhere, remaining undiscovered at the site, or completely disintegrating and leaving no trace (Waldron 1994). Post-depositional disturbance, differential burial, and post-excavation loss of human remains may also distort the data (Boddington 1987).

Forensic anthropologists face equally daunting tasks. Identification of skeletal remains depends on their age (since younger individuals can be aged more accurately than older individuals), the number and type of bones present (since certain bones are required to determine sex with certainty), and the reliability of the methods used to de-

termine age and sex (White 1991). Aside from testing methods, the most important factor is provenance of a set of remains, as Skinner and Lazenby (1983) reinforce: "Positive results are more likely to be forthcoming from a forensic anthropologist armed only with experience and presented with a complete skeleton from a documented and thorough recovery procedure than from a lab full of aparatus applied to a few scraps of bone of questionable context." For human osteologists, the primary questions to be answered upon encountering bones are whether they are human, how many individuals are represented, and of what antiquity they are (White 1991). For physical anthropologists, the "Big Four" are stature, age at time of death, sex, and stock or race. Accessory information includes weight and body build, duration of interment, cause of death (if it is registered in the bones), and other details including bone pathologies (Krogman and Iscan 1986). Unfortunately, most changes in bone density that would indicate pathologies cannot be seen on a clinical x-ray (Ortner 1991). Those that are observable may not necessarily have caused or contributed to the death (Powell 1991).

The dating technique heard mentioned most often is radiocarbon analysis, though this technique cannot be used to date older fossil remains, since the carbon atoms in dead organic material eventually lose all their radioactivity, or calcined remains, which do not retain adequate protein. Another option is to perform radiocarbon dating on wood or charcoal associated with the remains and thus arrive at a date indirectly (Brothwell 1981) or to arrive at a window of time based on the dated layers above and below which the remains were found. A relative date can also be arrived at by measuring the amount of fluorine the bones have absorbed and comparing with material from the same general area (Kanowski 1987).

Chronological (or biological) age of human remains is estimated by at least one — and usually the consensus of more than one — method. If long bones are used to estimate age, Douglas Ubelaker (1989) recommends averaging estimates from several bones, since growth rates vary widely among populations and even among individuals of the same racial group. Observations of eruptions of the teeth and uniting of the epiphyses may be plugged into a formula or applied to a table to arrive at an age for a growing individual, but observations of degenerative changes must suffice for individuals of about 25 or 30 years or older (Bass 1987). These include attrition, wear, and loss of the teeth (Brothwell 1981); metamorphosis of the pubic symphysis; closure and obliteration of skull sutures; alterations in the spine, joints, and skull; and resorption of cancellous bone (Ubelaker 1989). Other aging methods have also been developed that examine and compare changes to the sternal end of the fourth rib and certain sutures of the skull. Although aging by sutures has generally been proven unreliable, Owen Lovejoy and colleagues have found that the sutures on the sides of the skull can be used to estimate age with a margin of error of only a few years (Schwartz 1998). And while traditional methods of aging rely on the presence of teeth and other age indicators, a technique devised by Ellis Kerley in 1965 estimates age microscopically by counting osteons and osteon fragments (Rhine 1998).

There has been no parallel method developed for determining gender of a set of remains, although DNA testing may be used in the future to sex ancient skeletons (Mays 1998). Predictably, of primary importance when determining sex of a skeleton is the pelvis, with the obvious anatomical differences to allow childbirth. The difference between male and female skulls is less distinct, so rather than relying on determinations based on single specimens in a series, the entire population is seriated and sorted so that a pattern becomes clear. Research has shown that accuracy for sexing adult skeletal material varies with the combination of bones available for examination: 100 percent from the entire skeleton, 95 percent from the pelvis alone, 90 percent from the skull alone, 98 percent from the skull and pelvis, 80 to 90 percent from the long bones, 90 to 95 percent from the long bones and the skull, and at least 95 percent from the long bones plus the pelvis (Krogman and İscan 1986). In general, male skulls, pelves, and long bones are larger and heavier than those of females, with larger muscular ridges, impressions, and attachments. Other indicators of a male skull include thicker vault walls; larger cheek bones, mastoid process, sinuses, and palate; a more oval foramen magnum; more rectangular orbits; a squarer chin; and a more receding forehead (Skinner and Lazenby 1983). The teeth of men are also larger and measurements of the first and second permanent molars have been used to separate the sexes (Schwartz 1998). Among the skeletons of subadults, comparing the stage of calcification of the teeth with the stage of maturation of the post-cranial skeleton has been used to sort out the males from the females, based on the fact that the post-cranial skeletons mature more slowly in boys than in girls, but the rate of calcification of the teeth is about the same (Ubelaker 1989).

Unlike aging and sexing, geographic ancestry is most often estimated based upon observations of the skull and even so is less than certain:

> Whereas soft tissue characteristics such as skin color, hair form, and facial features often allow unambiguous attribution of geographic ancestry among living people, the hard tissues display less reliable signatures of affinity. There are, in fact, no human skeletal markers that correspond perfectly to geographic origin [White 1991].

Features of the skulls are grouped into three types. The crania of blacks (classified as

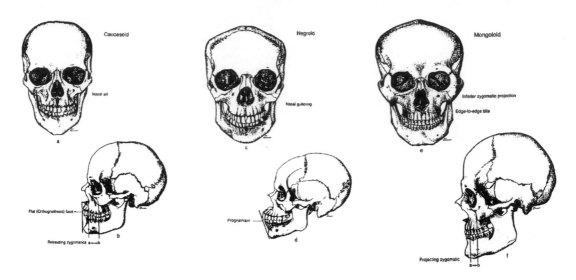

Front and side views of Caucasoid, Negroid, and Mongoloid skulls indicating anatomical features useful in evaluating racial origin. Reprinted with permission from *Human Osteology: A Laboratory and Field Manual*, by William M. Bass (Columbia: Missouri Archaeological Society, 1987).

Negroid) usually show relatively little projection of the malar bones, more rectangular orbits, wider interorbital distances, and a broad nasal aperture and palate. The crania of Asians and American Indians (classified as Mongoloid) have very forward-projecting malar bones and comparatively flat faces, more circular orbits, and a moderate nasal aperture with a slightly pointed lower margin. The crania of whites (classified as Caucasoid) are characterized by very receding malar bones that give the face a pointed appearance, a narrow nasal aperture with a prominent sharp lower border, and a relatively narrow and trianguloid palate (Ubelaker 1989). Determination of race, like other characteristics such as height, is helped by the development of formulas based on averages. Stature can be estimated pretty precisely using the charts that have been developed based on the major skeletal collections. The estimates are made from the long bones, preferably from the lower limbs.

Not only vital statistics but the behaviors of humans and some of the diseases to which we are subject can be learned from skeletal remains. "We would ... be unable to trace the history of many forms of disease — leprosy, syphilis, tuberculosis, cancers, and other forms of pathology which leave their traces in the bone — without the comparative and systematic study of skeletal remains.... At the same time, only through the study of human skeletal remains can we project the long-term impacts of altered diets on the human condition" (Buikstra 1981). The most common pathologies that leave signs on the skeleton are osteoarthritis, fractures, infections, and congenital disorders. In general, bones will become thicker and stronger if greater demands are made upon them, even into adulthood (Brothwell 1981), so skeletons will show signs of chronic physical stresses. Deviations from the normal shape of a bone in cross section may indicate level of activity (Buikstra and Ubelaker 1994). Pathologies in the teeth have been used to infer diet, dietary change, and social status. Bones will indicate in some instances long-term illnesses, major injuries, and possible causes of death (Scott 1998). And they show attempts to counteract or repair certain physical ailments with more or less success, including the setting of broken bones. Bones also provide evidence of early successful surgery, in the form of trephined skulls that show evidence of healing. The extent of remodeling in an injury to any bone can be used to estimate the length of time the individual survived the wound. Drawing scientifically based inferences from skeletons results in a more well-rounded picture of individual and community life than what most laypeople imagine could be learned from bones. Comparative analyses of osteological material provide important information about diets, levels of biomechanical stress, patterns of activity and occupation, disease loads, differential mortality, and quality of life (Crist 1995). The individual analysis of skeletons in large collections, followed by the compilation and comparison of that data, allows researchers to trace the frequency of disease and to assess population stress in correlation with cultural changes and pressures (Ubelaker and Grant 1989).

The information that a skeleton will reveal is not always easily accessible. Physical anthropologist Stanley Rhine (1998) writes, "The skeleton speaks in the softest of voices, but if one listens closely the bones do talk." Forensic anthropologist Clyde Snow adds, "Although they speak softly, they never lie and they never forget" (Joyce 1991). And paleoanthropologists Alan Walker and Pat Shipman (1996) remark, "[T]he skulls seem to talk to those who are sympathetic. When you search for them and sweat over them and love them, you begin to hear what they are saying." Bones may exhibit injuries of several types — blunt trauma, sharp trauma, projectiles, and rapid deceleration (Krogman and Iscan 1986) — but it is the skill, experience, and resources of researchers that allow what is hoped to be correct interpretation. Damage to the foramen magnum determined to be postmortem and accompanied by signs of weathering, for instance, may indicate that a skull has been placed on a stake or a skull rack (Buikstra and Ubelaker 1994). Determination of an individual's occupation relies on disease processes specific to that occupation (Waldron 1994). Findings are often approximate, such as the temperature to which bones were exposed based on their color (from the ivory of fresh bone to the blue-gray or white of bone cremated at high temperatures). But they are other times more certain, for instance checked cracks on burned bone indicates it was "green" or fresh and parallel cracks indicate it was dry (Buikstra and Ubelaker 1994). Deeply charred or blackened bone also indicates that flesh was present during burning (Brothwell 1981).

The means to determine many facts about a person's life and death have been developed, the more recent of them highly sophisticated. Bones of all ages have yielded to a number of examinations and analyses, including macroscopy, endoscopy, microscopy, scanning electron microscopy, radiology and radiography, computerized axial tomography (CT-scan), magnetic resonance imaging (MRI), DNA testing, x-ray emission spectroscopy, and mass spectrometry. All this in an effort to better understand ourselves and our past, as Phillip L. Walker writes (In press):

> Encoded within the molecular and histological structure of skeletal tissues is a detailed record of the person's childhood development and adult history of metabolic responses to the challenges encountered in his or her natural and sociocultural environment. This information can be supplemented by an equally rich record of ancestral relationships and the evolutionary history of our species recorded in the structure of the DNA molecules preserved within a skeleton. The information about historical events encoded in the skeletons of our ancestors can be thought of as a complex message from the past that we can decode through bioarchaeological research.

In fact, bones and teeth protect the DNA within from ultraviolet light, microorganisms, and chemical breakdown (Parsons

1997). Skeletal remains allow dietary reconstruction through trace element ratios and concentrations (strontium and calcium for meat) and stable isotopes (nitrogen and carbon for grasses) that accumulate in bone tissue (White 1991). As Thomas A.J. Crist explains, "The basic premise underlying bone-chemistry studies is that the elements found in human bone reflect the types of foods ingested during life, since elemental levels vary widely among different classes of goods. While no single element is indicative of an individual's diet, multielemental analysis can reveal trends suggesting dietary preferences or limitations." Examination of stable strontium isotope ratios allows the reconstruction of migration patterns, since new bone formed after a geographic move will differ in isotopic composition (Buikstra and Ubelaker 1994). Other aspects of behavior may be suggested by levels of bone minerals such as lead.

A number of wide-reaching sets of facts can be learned through such testing and techniques. Subsistence patterns, nutrition, disease patterns, and even ages of infant weaning are being learned from chemical approaches. Histological and biochemical investigative techniques can provide information about age at death, diet, health status, residence patterns, genetic relationships, environmental reconstructions, and antiquity of remains. Health status can be determined by assessing bone remodeling rates and extracting noncollagenous proteins that are synthesized in response to infections (Buikstra and Ubelaker 1994). Other analyses, including a fluorescent antibody method

developed by I. Lengyel, have been devised to determine blood type from bones (Krogman and Iscan 1986). Most analyses, like most interpretations, have some limitations. Radiocarbon analysis, for instance, is only successful on relatively recent remains and requires a sample of at least 100 grams. DNA testing is a very efficient way of determining genetic relationships, but is at present an expensive procedure, though requiring a very small sample.

The averages that allow anthropologists to estimate age at death, stature, sex, and race are based on surveys of large skeletal collections that are continually being improved upon. In order to build on current statistics, research, and observations about skeletal remains, scientists need continued access to collections over time: "Accurate age and sex estimates in human skeletal remains are basic to studies of past adaptations and demographic histories. Age and gender-based differences in diet, disease, activity patterns, and mortuary practices are all accessible through investigations of human skeletal materials. Skeletal studies can also provide temporal perspectives on human demography that are available from no other source" (Buikstra and Ubelaker 1994). Future research will certainly be affected by the availability of skeletal material, making it all the more important to keep accurate records and complete as many analyses as possible on currently curated remains that are subject to repatriation. Carefully collected data about the remains before they are lost will at least succeed them.

1

Accumulations

Bones accrete, accrue, and accumulate. In addition to remains that occurred due to normal death rates, large assemblages of human bones have resulted from mass deaths: the victims of disease such as plague buried in communal graves, the casualties of war left to disintegrate on the surface, and victims of religious persecution deposited in underground galleries. Whether scattered, mingled, or stacked, bones may represent an event in time (like the Crow Creek massacre) or many generations (like most other Native American ossuaries). When a combination of time and disease or disaster filled the cemeteries, they were emptied and the bones placed, for the most part, in existing structures. Though not as deliberately decorated as the bone churches and galleries discussed in a later chapter, many of the resulting ossuaries were toured in the past and are still open to the public, now having centuries-old histories attached to them, along with attendant myths and legends.

CATACOMBS

There are many words for bone galleries: charnel houses, ossuaries, crypts, but only one common term for extensive underground galleries: catacombs. The word summons images of arm and leg bones piled in dark tunnels and chambers. This is not far from the mark when referring to the Parisian catacombs to this day, but many are surprised to learn that the Roman catacombs — associated with the bones of centuries of saints, martyrs, and other early Christians — are now mostly empty of human remains. The relics of the holy, at first visited and venerated, were removed over time and used to consecrate new churches, augment existing collections of relics, or provide income for dealers in such things. Unlike the Christian saints, whose resting places in the catacombs were carefully marked, the individual identities of the catacomb populace of Paris have remained anonymous except for markers indicating which cemeteries the remains were removed from — a fact that has probably saved the bones of Rabelais (d. 1553) for instance, from becoming collector's items. Catacombs were intended to safeguard the dead. They were in some sense less successful in Rome, although many of the dispersed relics are still venerated elsewhere, but even while walking among the plentiful remains under Paris the urge to take a souvenir is only suppressed in some visitors by knowing that their bags will be checked upon exiting.

Although those of Rome and Paris are the most well-known, they are by no means the only catacombs. Others — some created by Christians and others by Jews — exist in Italy (in Naples, Syracuse, Catania, Agrigento, and Palermo), Greece (Klima), Malta (Rabat), Tunisia (Sousse), Syria (Emesa), and cities in Israel, Cyprus, Iran, and Peru. Of these, perhaps the most famous is the catacomb of San Gennaro in Naples, which served to house not only the bones of early Christians, but the remains of hundreds of plague victims who died in the eighteenth century and needed to be buried hurriedly and with a minimum of effort. Other catacombs were used for the deposit of dead family members, whose bones usually remained longer than those of the saints. In *Famous Caves and Catacombs* (Adams 1972), first published in 1886, the author describes the catacombs beneath Syracuse: "The niches are now empty, and the corpses have been removed, though in a few some bones are still preserved. At intervals, we meet in these catacombs with isolated chambers, which seem to have been appropriated as family vaults. In nearly all of these are deposited a trough-shaped coffin. Numerous tombs in these private vaults are covered with mosaics; some have not been opened." Rather than beginning as public burial places and being used to bury family groups, many Roman catacombs began as family tombs which were shared with members of the faith and maintained by donations from the church.

Many times tombs in catacombs were constructed so that they did not need to be opened either to admit another body or to access the existing remains in at least a limited way. The tombs in the catacombs at St. Paul's in Rabat, Malta, had a window through which bodies were inserted (Stevenson 1978). In the Roman catacombs loculi, or cavities carved into the walls to hold the bodies, were sealed except for an opening through which the faithful could insert a piece of cloth that after touching the relics would be considered a third-class relic itself (Adams 1972). The actual relics remained at considerable risk, however, and were eventually removed or stolen. But bones did not need to be saintly to risk disappearance, since they deteriorated and eventually disintegrated

under certain conditions. The remains of several thousand people were found in the catacomb of the Maltese Hal-Saflienni Hypogeum in 1902, but no bones remain in the second-century secular burial niches at Kom al-Shuqafa that were discovered one hundred feet below the ground in Alexandria, Egypt, two years earlier. Catacombs containing bones may provide assemblages for anthropologists and osteologists to study, but whether the bones are extant or not, their underground galleries draw visitors just like they have for centuries.

Catacombs of Rome

We ever and anon came into pretty square roomes, that seem'd to be Chapells with altars, and some adorn'd with very ordinary ancient painting. Many skeletons and bodies are plac'd in the sides one above the other in degrees like shelves.... Many of the bodies, or rather bones (for there appear'd nothing else) lay so intire as if plac'd by the art of the chirurgeon, but being only touched fell all to dust.
— *John Evelyn on a visit to the catacombs in 1645*

Catacombs often have a religious connotation and even smaller crypts containing human remains are dubbed catacombs by virtue of the fact that they are located beneath a church. In the case of the Roman catacombs, the association with the church is entirely justified. Although the tunnels weren't located beneath a single cathedral, they were themselves worshiped in, if common belief is to be trusted. Actually, research in recent years has indicated that the catacombs served merely as burial places. But the holding of services near the holy bones in the catacombs — or just the legend of their being held — is directly related to the fact that church altars for years were obligated to contain the relic of a saint. Popular belief also tells us that the Roman catacombs were one vast maze of tunnels in which the early Christians hid from their persecutors. In fact, the Roman catacombs consist of some forty unconnected sites in and around the city, and although there's no denying that the early Christians were persecuted, it has been shown that hiding among the rotting bodies in the catacombs would have been rather inhospitable. J. Stevenson (1978) refutes the idea that the early Christians worshipped and hid in the catacombs, explaining that there were no large rooms built in the centuries of persecution that were capable of holding many worshippers and that there is no proof that they were used as hiding places. Researcher Judith A. Testa of Northern Illinois University points out that the catacombs would have made poor hiding places because they were not in fact secret. Stevenson concurs that Christians did frequent catacombs, particularly to visit the tombs of martyrs and their own family members. So the primary use of the miles of tunnels, niches, tombs, and galleries was to deposit the dead and yet most of these earthly remains have vanished. Tom Weil (1992) writes, "Murals, reliefs, niches, grave markers, cisterns and other features are housed in the catacombs of Rome, but the ossuaries lack the one object most associated with them — bones."

Another irony about the Roman catacombs is that they were "lost" for centuries. Despite the attention they received from pious Christians and unscrupulous relic hunters beginning in the mid-second century and peaking in the fourth century, they were abandoned and forgotten. At the end of the eighth century, the relics of the martyrs and saints were ordered by the Pope to be taken to the city churches. The bones that had not been taken home by countless medieval pilgrims still amounted to several cartloads, a portion of which was deposited in the crypt of Santa Prassede by Pope Paschal I. The removal of the last of the relics in the ninth century doomed the catacombs to extinction by relocating the foci of the "cult of the martyrs." The translation of the relics to the churches of Rome was done to protect them from invasions of barbarians (Goths and Longobards), among other threats, but left no reason for pilgrims to visit the catacombs (Adams 1972). The entrances became overgrown and the catacombs remained unknown until the sixteenth century, when they were rediscovered and systematically investigated by Antonio Bosio (d. 1629). Scientific exploration of the catacombs was later carried out by G. Settele (d. 1840), G. Marchi (d. 1860), and Giovanni Battista de Rossi (d.1894), the "father of Christian archaeology" who mapped the passages (Stevenson 1978, Mancinelli 1981).

Amateurs also tried their hand at exploring the tunnels, with mixed results. Adams (1972) repeats a tale recounted by C. Macfarlane in *The Catacombs of Rome* in which a company of young officers in the French Republican army visited and explored the Roman catacombs in 1798. One man was separated from the rest and was unable to find them:

> [H]e fell, and his torch being extinguished, he found himself in total darkness. As he groped his way, he fell through a chasm. The fall was slight, for the chamber beneath was very full; but as he alighted among crackling, clattering, and crumbling bones, his nerves sustained another shock, and he could scarcely maintain his self-control. However, with an effort he released himself from his horrible position, regained the crypt above, and on his hands and knees crept slowly onward until he reached the oratory…. His thirst grew intolerable. Looking about, he caught sight of a bottle glittering in the moonlight, near the stone altar. The wanderer seized it, and drank eagerly of its contents. Instead of water it was filled with brandy, and in a few minutes, the potion acting with violence on a frame already burning with thirst and fever, he became delirious. Wild visions swept before him; dark spectres seemed to gather round him; the skulls lying on either hand seemed reanimated with ghastly eyes that penetrated to his

very soul; the bones of the dead became instinct with life; they rose, and clattered, and loud shrieks escaped from fleshless lips: it was a phantasmagoria of terror, in which the occasional sounds that reached him from without, and the flickering beams of the moonlight, became the agents of ever-new delusions.

The officer was discovered the following morning, spent several months in a military hospital, and had his faith restored by the experience. The catacombs have not since relinquished their power to inspire both faith and fear.

The Christians and the Jews of Rome had taken advantage of the softness of the tufa to excavate tunnels and chambers in order to continue the practice of burial rather than adopting cremation. But earlier Romans had made use of abandoned quarries for the same reason, thus the Roman catacombs contained the remains of many pagans among the estimated 194,000 individuals deposited there. Corpses were not embalmed, but merely wrapped in a sheet before being placed in either a tomb or a niche hollowed out of the wall. In either case, the name of the deceased and any inscription was painted, carved, or sculpted on the door or in the mortar with which the covering plaque was sealed. The hollows in the wall were sometimes made large enough to contain three or more bodies and even more than that could be accommodated in the occasional grave pits (Stevenson 1978). The use of catacombs saved on space in the city and continued until the early fifth century. Altogether, the early Romans dug over 750 miles of galleries on five levels and to a depth of 80 feet (Ragon 1983). The earthly remains of the beatified and sainted were a big draw. Many believers wanted to be buried near the body of a saint to guarantee their own salvation. Later believers thronged to Rome to pay their respects at these subterranean burial sites.

Today, there are some 60 miles of Roman catacombs, not all of which have been fully explored and some of which still do contain a bone or two. Journalist Eleanor Emerson (1998) writes, "The catacombs have a somber and reverential air, with random piles of anonymous bones left here and there for the visitor to contemplate." And they have been contemplated for a millennium. Describing the catacombs of St. Callixtus in *The Marble Faun*, Nathaniel Hawthorne (1889) writes, "On either side were horizontal niches, where, if they held their torches closely, the shape of a human body was discernible in white ashes, into which the entire mortality of a man or woman had resolved itself. Among all this extinct dust, there might perchance be a thigh-bone, which crumbled at a touch; or possibly a skull, grinning at its own wretched plight, as is the ugly and empty habit of the thing." Travelers Kristan Lawson and Anneli Rufus (1999) note the advantage of visiting the lesser known of the five sections of catacombs in Rome that are open to the public. The catacombs of Sant'Agnese fuori le Mura are the least famous "and consequently the best preserved and least crowded, with more skeletons and bones than you care to count and a general air of hushed mortality."

Catacombs of Paris

The decoration of this subterranean City of the Dead ... consists of a regular and symmetrical arrangement of the bones. The apophyses of the great bones of the legs and arms are brought forward in such a manner as to exhibit an almost level surface, which, at intervals, is traversed by a row of skulls, above which is placed another layer of great bones; the severe monotony of these dreary walls being sometimes interrupted by a couple of tibias arranged in the form of a cross. Some of the crypts, or mortuary chambers, appropriated to the bones of a particular cemetery, are decorated with a fantastic coquetry: with garlands or wreaths of skulls, and tibias and cubitus intertwining as the more or less felicitous framework of the

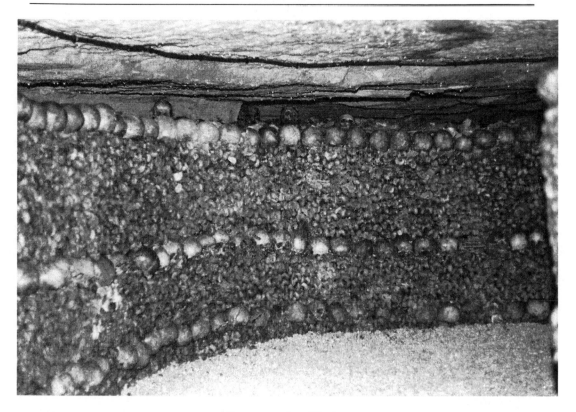

The catacombs of Paris.

pyramids outlined on the background of the wall by another arrangement of skulls. These strange attempts at embellishment do not add to the serious reflections which the spectacle is so well calculated to awaken in the mind of every thoughtful visitor.
—*William H. Adams [1972]*

What in 1786 was a spent quarry is today a tourist attraction, accessible on the Metro (Place Denfert-Rochereau), with regular hours (Tuesday through Friday from 2 to 4 P.M. and Saturdays and Sundays from 9 to 11 A.M. and 2 to 4 P.M.), a small admission fee (33 francs), and visitors in excess of 200,000 annually. But people have been coming to see the catacombs since they were opened to the public in 1874. They came, and still come, to see the bones. To walk the galleries stacked with tibias, dotted with skulls. To ponder over countless indistinguishable remains that include those of Robespierre (d. 1794), Danton (d. 1794), Mon-

tesquieu (d. 1755), Pascal (d. 1662), Lavoisier (d. 1794), La Fontaine (d. 1695), and Madame de Pompadour (d. 1764). Visitors are struck by the anonymity of the remains in addition to their quantity. The individuals represented in the catacombs outnumber the living inhabitants of the city three to one (de Montclos and Willesme 1994). The overwhelming effects of the great numbers of remains are only mitigated by the electric light and the company of the others with whom the visitor has jostled to get in the door.

The catacombs have always been popular with tourists. It is unclear whether this was the cause or the effect of changing the visitors' entrance in the late eighteenth century from the rue des Catacombes (now rue Dareau) to the west wing of the barrière d'Enfer (Hell's Gate), one of the most well-traveled of Paris's 40 toll gates. In the earliest public visits, patrons were conducted

The catacombs of Paris.

tria in 1814 and by the Russian regiments bivouaced nearby. In 1860, the catacombs were toured by Napoleon III and his son. Chancellor Bismarck descended into the catacombs in 1867 and shortly thereafter Crown Prince (later king) Oscar of Sweden left his mark by scratching graffiti: "Toute vie a sa mort/Toute mort a sa vie" (All life has its death/All death has its life).

Félix Nadar was drawn to underground Paris in 1861 to practice photography, which had been discovered only 25 years earlier. The infancy of the medium and the irony of practicing what was considered a sun-based technique in the dark posed a number of challenges that Nadar overcame, proving both his own merits and those of photography. He may have been inspired to document the catacombs on film because of the activity there at the time, but in *Le Paris Souterrain de Félix Nadar* (1982), Philippe Neagu speculates that Nadar also found the location strangely beautiful and ideal for experimenting with electric light, which he generated with magnesium and reflectors. Reproduced in *Le Paris Souterranian* are numerous images of the catacombs, including a pile of skulls, a heap of long bones, a façade of tibias ornamented with a row of skulls, walls of bones noted for their height and ornamentation, squared and rounded corners of the bone galleries, geometric arrangements of long bones and skulls, several of the tombs and inscriptions accompanying the skeletal material, and a self-portrait of Nadar sitting in front of a wall in one of the bone galleries. Using mannequins because of the lengthy exposure times required, Nadar illustrated workers

through the underground passages by the foremen from the quarry workshops. Later visitors took self-guided tours — following a painted black line that is still visible on the ceiling — or paid an additional fee for a guide. Whether for a guided tour or an occasional special event, many notable figures visited and enhanced the popularity of the catacombs. In 1787, the Count of Artois (later Charles X) toured the catacombs with the ladies of the Court. The following year, the galleries were visited by Madame de Polignac and Madame de Guiche. They were seen by the Emperor Françis I of Aus-

The catacombs of Paris.

manipulating the tumble of bones at the bottom of the well, pulling a cart filled with bones, unloading the bones in the galleries, and negotiating through piles of loose bones. With the help of special laborers, the book explains, the complete menu of bones is piled in more or less cubic heaps, ornamented by the skulls that are in the best condition. Thus the bones of both saints and sinners are rendered visually pleasing. Mixed together are the bones of the famous and infamous, and former generations of French families — all anonymous whether their names would be recognized or not.

The catacombs proved inspirational to many, both directly and indirectly. The texts on the plaques were published by Abel Lemercier in about 1878. Earlier that century, Viktor Mussorgsky (d. 1881) composed a piece devoted to the Paris catacombs inspired by a drawing of his friend Victor Hart-mann amidst the skulls. And the Paris catacombs continue to be popularized around the world through the writings of Victor Hugo (d. 1885). In spite of their inherent symbolism and because of their abstract numbers and sculptural shapes, the walls and piles of bones run the risk of becoming "detached from all human meaning, disconnected from life, like man-made artifacts rather than man-making anatomical components" (Weil 1992). It is left up to the visitors to make sense of this mass of bones and how it has affected them individually and collectively. Even recent visitors wax poetic: "The remains present themselves as if they were part of some vast coral reef, a slow accretion of minerals in a tideless sea of time" (Gup 2000).

The catacombs therefore served not only as a mere repository, but as a sight to see and a place to investigate. Diverse cultural activities and exhibits have been carried out in the catacombs over the centuries. An experiment was conducted in 1813 in which Chinese bream fish placed in the Fountain of the Samaritan survived, but became blind and were unable to reproduce. In the late 1800s, a museum was opened but didn't last. On April 2, 1897, a two-hour concert was held in the catacombs at midnight; the clandestine event, attended by about 100 members of high society, featured Chopin's "Marche Funébre," Saint-Saëns "Danse Macabre," and the "Marche Funèbre" from Beethoven's *Eroica*, and led to the firing of the complicit workers. In 1898, a laboratory was set up by the Natural History Museum, but soon closed due to the difficulty of its location. During World War II, the catacombs became the headquarters for the French Resistance.

Celebrations are still held in the underground galleries and clandestine activities are still carried out. During the first week of December each year, some 200 students from the École des Mines are allowed to throw a massive party on the day that honors St. Barbe, patron of engineers and miners. Other visitors, who call themselves "cataphiles," do not obtain permission for their visits. They share information about successful entry points and celebrate their exploits on their websites. While most simply explore and congregate, playing games or music, some have tagged or painted the walls (Gup 2000). In spite of occasional vandalism — and regularly retrieved from the bags of exiting visitors — the bones remain. The stacks of bones loom taller than the average human and are many meters thick. The excavation of gypsum used to make plaster, and limestone used to construct many of Paris's buildings and churches including Notre Dame, left tunnels and spaces punctuated by square pillars that had been carved and left in place to support the roof. These spaces were filled bone by bone, cartload by cartload, cemetery by cemetery, generation after generation. The floors of

the galleries are now layered with gravel to help absorb humidity and slow the accelerated decay that the breath of the living brings to the bones of the dead.

The Paris catacombs encompass 120,000 square feet of passages. The tunnels no longer follow the public streets above, but the galleries currently open to the public — concentrated in an area of 800 meters — are for the most part contained in the fourteenth arrondissement and are bordered by the rue Hallé, the Arcueil aqueduct, the rue Rémy-Dumoncel, and the avenue René-Coty. Bones that had taken more than a thousand years to accumulate in the cemeteries and churchyards had taken almost the next hundred to remove and redeposit in these extensive underground galleries. The task was carried out under cover of darkness, with solemnity, and with priests in attendance including the three — Fathers Mottret, Maillet, and Asseline — who consecrated the catacombs for burial in 1786. The cartloads of bones were covered with black veils and the burial service was recited. The progress of the transfer is marked by the plaques in the galleries of the catacombs, which name the cemetery and the date its remains were moved to this second tomb some sixty-five feet below the ground: Cimetière des Innocents (1786), Saint-Etienne-des-Grés (1787), Saint-Eustache (1787), Saint-Landri (1792), Sainte-Croix-de-la-Bretonnerie (1793), Saint-André-des-Arts (1794), Saint-Nicolas-des-Champs (1804), Saint-Laurent (1804), Hospital of la Trinité (1814), and Carmes convent (1814).

Other removals not chiseled in stone include Saint-Julien (1792), the college of the Bernardine monks (1793), Saint-Jean-en-Grève, Saint-Honoré, the church of the White Friars (1804), Saint-Louis-en-l'Isle (1811), Saint-Benoît (1813), Bonne-Nouvelle, Cimetière de Vaugirard (1826), Sainte-Geneviève (1845), Saint-Jacques-du-Haut-Pas (1850), Saint-Jean-Porte-Latine, Sainte-Madeleine-de-la-Ville-l'Eveque, Saint-Leu,

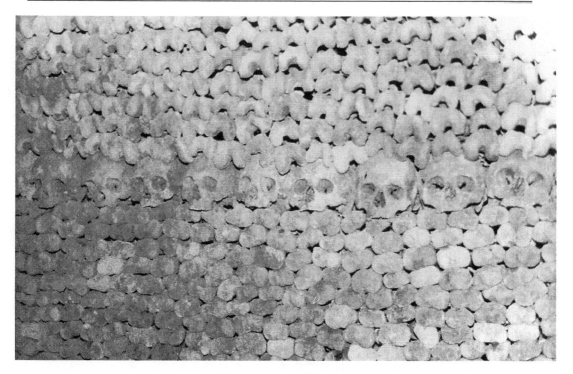

The catacombs of Paris.

Saint-Gilles, and Saint-Jacques-de-la-Boucherie (1859).

The time span belies the urgency that prompted the use of the quarries by the city as a municipal ossuary. In fact, the overburdened Cimetière des Innocents collapsed. The charnel house that had been built around the perimeter in the fourteenth century to receive the bones from overflowing graves was itself overflowing by the mid-eighteenth century. In May 1780, a communal grave along the rue de la Lingerie cracked open and spilled its gruesome contents into the cellars of neighboring houses. In December of that year, future burials were prohibited by parliamentary decree. When King Louis XVI decided to have the remains transferred to the outskirts of town, he charged General Inspector of the Quarries Charles-Axel Guillaumot with finding a suitable site. Guillaumot chose the quarries of the Montsouris plain, which until 1860 were outside the boundaries of the city.

The actual transfer of remains was an efficient operation. At Saints-Innocents, a recorded thousand cartloads of skeletal remains were removed between December 1785 and January 1787. In preparation, the quarry tunnels were reinforced with masonry, a staircase was excavated, and a stonework well was constructed "into which the bones could be thrown," according to the English guidebook (de Montclos and Willesme 1994). Some of the bones merited more attention than others in providing support or aesthetics: "The workmen built an actual rampart made up of the large bones, meticulously laid out, and lined up the skulls for decorative effect. Behind this wall, the bones were thrown haphazardly, reaching thirty meters at times" (de Montclos and Willesme 1994). The bones remain where they were placed two centuries ago, as Ted Gup (2000) describes: "[O]n either side of a narrow passageway, rises a solid wall of human remains — femurs, tibias and skulls — stacked neatly like cords of firewood, six feet high and stretching interminably into the darkness.

Behind the orderly walls is a chaotic mass of decayed and undifferentiated human rubble consisting of fragments and shards, broken skulls and pelvises. Here lies what little is left of victims of the plague, the guillotine and the French Revolution." The victims of several riots that foreshadowed the French Revolution had been transported directly to the catacombs. They included those killed outside the Hôtel de Brienne and in the place de Grève following the minister's downfall in August 1788, those who died during the looting of the Réveillon factory in April 1789, and those massacred during the events in the Tuileries in August 1792. The Revolution itself provided an abundance of remains and the anonymous dead of the catacombs include Robespierre, Danton, and Lavoisier (all executed in 1794). Long after the Revolution, during the Paris Commune of 1871, troops blocked the exits and killed a number of insurrectionists who had sought refuge underground, though it is unknown whether their remains are among the bones today.

The catacombs were an appropriate place for remains that turned up in places other than the churchyard or guillotine. The remains of the victims of leprosy from the Rue de Douai were deposited in 1857; in 1859, the catacombs received bones uncovered during the course of major urban development work; the contents of 813 tombs found in the foundations of the quarter surrounding the new market hall of Baltard were placed underground in 1860; and in 1871, the catacombs became the final resting place of thirty skeletons discovered in the crypt of the church of Saint-Laurent. As more bones were deposited, more visitors came to see them. Guillaumot's successor, Héricart de Thury, even placed a guest book at the exit of the catacombs to collect opinions. Not all of the visits were supervised, though, and not all of the visitors survived their morbid sidetrip. In 1793, for instance, Philippe (or Philibert) Aspairt, a porter at the Val-de-Grâce hospital, descended alone and got lost, presumably when his torch went out. His skeleton was not found until 11 years later by members of a topographical crew, who buried it where it was found — only a few yards from an exit. The horror and the danger of the catacombs was real, but often exaggerated for effect. Nineteenth-century travel writer Augustus Hare warned that any visitor left behind in the catacombs would soon be eaten alive by rats (Weil 1992). Other potential dangers included cave-ins, such as the one that killed a man named Décure (also known as Beauséjour) after he finished carving a small replica of Port-Mahon (the Balearic Island fortress where he had been imprisoned) into the catacomb wall. The bas relief sculpture can still be seen.

The lobby and exhibition rooms provide an illustrated history of the catacombs, but most patrons are too eager to see the bones to pay the exhibits much attention. More impact is made by an anteroom, whose masonry pillars are decorated in stark architectural shapes in black and white, and the verse (by a Father Delille) above the next door that reads, "Arrete! C'Est ici l'Empire de la Mort!" (Halt! This is the Empire of Death). Other quotes spaced throughout the galleries are taken from Racine, Homer, Virgil, Horace, Rousseau, and the Bible. The catacombs retain some of their original features, including a small pool used by the quarriers as a foot-bath, a larger pool known as the Fountain of the Samaritan, and the "Sepulchral Lamp," a stone dish flanked by truncated obelisks in which a fire was kept burning by the quarrymen. A few larger monuments housed in the galleries include an ancient altar discovered on the banks of the Rhône in 1807 and the empty sarcophagus of a poet named Gilbert inscribed with a few of his lines. As visitors leave through a long tunnel that runs beneath the rue Dareau, they encounter three large bell-shaped hollows in the ceiling created when the quarry roof subsided and was reinforced with thick masonry, another reminder of past danger.

Despite such proven dangers, despite closure of the catacombs at times due to vandalism, and despite the deterioration of more than two centuries, the catacombs remain open to visitors. In 1983, after 200 years of conservatorship, the Inspectorate of Quarries handed over the management of the catacombs to the Cultural Affairs Department of the Ville de Paris. The current director of the catacombs is Jean-Pierre Willesme, who sees himself as a curator (Gup 2000). The entrance was again moved, this time to the other side of the avenue at 1, place Denfert-Rochereau. "We pass through a tiny doorway, where row upon row of skulls, bones and skeletons stretch unbelievably away, into the far reaches of darkness. Acre upon acre of browning tibias, femurs and grinning, empty-socketed skulls form decorative columns and designs, piled high in every corner.... Immense, endless broad boulevards of the departed stretch beyond imagination. On, it appears, forever," describes Mikelbank (1988). The exit at 36, rue Rémy-Dumoncel, is 1.7 kilometers — and a world — away.

OSSUARIES

Catacombs, crypts, ossuaries, charnel houses, memento mori chapels and other such funerary sites usually contain nothing more than bare bones. Some house only a skeletal sampler—just a few bony fragments or a scattering of skulls and other pieces of disused anatomy.
— Tom Weil (1992)

Secondary burial, the deposit of bones recovered after allowing the flesh to decay, has been a custom in many countries and cultures. In some of them it is believed that the soul does not enter the realm of the dead until the flesh is gone. Preparation of the skeleton after the initial burial period also signifies the end of the mourning period (Huntington 1979). And secondary burial may simply be a practical necessity. Bones have therefore been cleaned by family members in Greece and placed in community charnel houses. They have been evicted from their graves in Europe and the southern United States and swept into communal pits. Bodies have been exposed to the elements in the Middle East and the American Midwest and the bones afterward gathered up and interred in pits. This two-part treatment of the dead results in collections of skeletal remains that may reveal the details of a battle or the vital statistics of a population over many generations. Careful analysis of the bones in an ossuary may sort out whether they did in fact result from a massacre, as often claimed, or were simply placed in the church crypt en masse when the churchyard became overly crowded. Contemplation, rather than analysis, will yield the same symbolism as the catacombs but on a smaller scale.

In the Middle Ages, all cemeteries had charnel houses, sheds, or chapels in which long-buried bones would be piled. According to Philippe Ariès (1982), the transfer of the bones from burial ground to ossuary had no symbolic meaning, but only served to make room for other graves. The bones remained close to the church and therefore to the saints under whose protection they had been placed. The lucky (or influential) benefited by having their remains transferred to the church rather than the charnel: "Although the Christian preference was for separate burial, intermingling of the bones of the dead was often the practical reality.... Exhumed bones were usually collected together and placed in a charnel house, or ossuary. On rare occasions exhumed bones were taken into the body of the church and have thus survived to the present day" (Wilkins 1991). Ariès (1974) points out, though, that the remains of the wealthy, buried under the flagstones, eventually followed the path to the charnel houses also.

In rural Greece, the bones of the dead are exhumed by their family members after a period of five years. Loring Danforth (1982) describes their placement in the village ossuary:

> Beyond a small floor-space a ladder led down to a dark, musty-smelling area filled with the bones of many generations of villagers. Near the top of the huge pile the remains of each person were bound up separately in a white cloth. Toward the bottom of the pile the bones — skulls, pelvises, ribs, the long bones of countless arms and legs — lay in tangled disarray, having lost all trace of belonging to distinct individuals with the disintegration of the cloth wrappings. Stacked in one corner of the building were metal boxes and small suitcases with names, dates, and photographs identifying the people whose bones lay securely within.

Among the villagers, the charnel house remains a symbol of death, but also of the unity of the living. Depositing the skeletonized and cleaned remains allows them to repose and allows survivors to emerge from their mourning period.

Ossuaries in India and Iran also stem from religious convictions. The Zoroastrians or Parsees exposed their dead to scavengers in order to avoid polluting the earth, air, or water. In communities large enough to maintain them, "towers of silence" (*dakhmas*) were used for this purpose. The towers were made of stone with an unroofed interior and only the unclean would enter. Only a few hours after a shrouded body was unwrapped and laid out by the outcast funeral servants, vultures reduced the body to bone. The attendants entered the tower at intervals to gather the bones and drop them into the central pit (Habenstein and Lamers 1994). In most places, the vultures have vanished and it has been a generation since the towers have been used, but they maintain a long history. A tower in Bombay was described in 1876 as being nearly 14 feet high, 40 feet in diameter, with a well five or six feet across in the center and a ten- to 12-foot parapet around the upper surface. The surface traditionally contained three concentric rings of open stone coffins, the outer for the bodies of men, the middle for women, and the inner for children. The well contained four drains filled with charcoal, which filtered the rainwater that washed the bones (Iserson 1994).

Skeletons do not remain long in the tombs of New Orleans, Louisiana, before their bones are mingled with those of previous occupants in a central pit or *caveau*. A city ordinance states that a casket must remain entombed for a minimum of "a year and a day" (Florence 1996), the brevity of which is necessitated by the space demands of a high water table that precludes underground burial. The remains in a wall vault may simply be pushed to the back or the sides after removal of the casket, but the bones in a family or society tomb are swept into a chamber in the tomb's foundation. This caveau represents a bottomless cup of bones: "It is unlikely that the caveau would ever run out of room, for bones do break down rather quickly" (Florence 1996). Still, they last long enough to provide a treasure trove for the occasional artist desperate for a model skull or the relic hunter willing to go to such unprincipled lengths to obtain material. The bones from which they pick and choose may prove to be somewhat homogeneous within each tomb. St. Louis Cemetery #1 contains tombs owned and used by people of African origin (the Dieu Nous Protege Society tomb), Spanish descent (the Cervantes Society tomb), French descent, and Italian ancestry. The tomb of the Italian Mutual Benevolent Society, although no longer used, was built in 1857 and contains 24 vaults:

> Its caveau is on the interior, a massive cylinder which can easily hold thousands of

remains. Consider that within a century nearly 2,400 people — the headcount of a decent-sized cemetery in many other places — could conceivably be buried in this one tomb, and the efficiency of land usage in this burial practice becomes apparent [Florence 1996].

Louisiana law has seen to it that tombs remain in the family through "forced heirship," thus a caveau can house countless branches of a family tree. Society tombs can more easily change hands. The tomb of the defunct Portuguese Society, for instance, is now owned by the St. Vincent de Paul Society, which provides free burial for the poor.

Many bone collections arise from practices put in place to allow for grave turnover in churchyards and secular cemeteries. Cemetery overcrowding was a problem in Victorian England, where tons of skeletal remains were removed from the public burial grounds each year and charnel houses had been common since the Middle Ages. Bones that were not ground up for use as fertilizer were installed in the "bone house," sometimes fairly soon after death, since there was a profit motive to accept as many burials as possible (Morley 1971). Even today cemeteries in Portugal, Spain, Italy, and other countries in continental Europe are leased for a period of usually not more than 25 years. At the expiration of the lease, a card is sent to the family requesting instructions. Many choose to have the remains transferred to a wall mausoleum, in which case the bones are washed, placed in a small box, and installed in a niche that may be fronted with engraved marble or curtained glass. If there is no response from the family, the bones are disinterred and placed in a common bone pit. (Muslims and Jews do not follow this practice.) In Switzerland, bodies in public graveyards were exhumed about every 30 years. The bodily remains were cremated, but the skulls were arranged in rows in chapels (*tokenkapelle*) especially built for the purpose. Each skull was numbered and the name of the deceased was entered in a register (Haestier 1934).

As time went on, the charnel houses themselves began to fill up. In sixteenth-century England, more than a thousand cartloads of bones from charnel houses were dumped at a site that inevitably became known as Bone Hill, later metamorphosed into Bunhill, and was itself used as a cemetery (Weil 1992). The great quantities of remains from charnels have provided fodder for generations of physical anthropologists. The nearly 1,000 skeletons removed from the crypt at Christ Church, Spitalfields, have been of great benefit to researchers because more than one third of the remains were associated with legible coffin plates bearing their names, ages, and dates of death, which ranged from 1729 to 1852. The information, making this an important documented archaeological collection, has allowed scientists at the Natural History Museum in London to reconstruct social backgrounds in addition to assessing medical histories.

Bones in the safekeeping of churches and monasteries had both more security and a better class of visitors than graveyard charnel houses. Like the Roman catacombs, church crypts drew both the faithful and the curious:

> It was important to see. The charnels were exhibits. Originally, no doubt, they were no more than improvised storage areas where the exhumed bones were placed simply to get them out of the way, with no particular desire to display them. But later, after the fourteenth century, under the influence of a sensibility oriented toward the macabre, there was an interest in the spectacle for its own sake. The bones and skulls were arranged around the courtyard of the church so as to form a backdrop for the daily life of those sensual times [Ariès 1982]

Most of the churches with bone-filled crypts still make arrangements to accommodate tourists. The crypt in Vienna's St. Michael's church may be toured during the week from May through November (Lawson 1999).

Churches often accommodate both visitors and researchers. Physical anthropologist Douglas Ubelaker shed light on the central ossuary within the church of the Convento de San Francisco in Quito, Ecuador, in 1990. Large quantities of human remains (mixed with soil, decayed wood, clothing, and mold and fungus) were found in three subterranean chambers, some believed to date from the foundation of the church in 1535 (Ubelaker 1995). Other ossuaries are off limits even to the few visitors who may know of their existence. Most who walk the paths of Paris's Père-Lachaise cemetery are unaware of the vast ossuary beneath them that was created in 1950 to contain the remains of dilapidated perpetual plots. There is a similar ossuary underneath Montparnasse cemetery and a move to use it to store the contents of several communal graves in Paris (de Montclos and Willesme 1994). The dozens of Aboriginal ossuaries in the U.S. — underground charnels that can only be accessed by excavation — are also the subject of many studies.

St. Catherine's Monastery, Sinai

At Santa Caterina monastery in the Sinai, the skulls and bones of some 3,000 monks — most of them anonymous — are contained in a white ossuary outside the walls. Santa Caterina, one of the oldest active monasteries in existence, was established in the sixth century on the traditional site of Moses' burning bush. Treatment of the skeletal remains is based on rank, with the bones of archbishops and bishops placed in small wooden caskets and stored in niches. Weil (1992) describes, "Just inside the charnel house entrance, in the first compartment to the left, stand stacks of skulls piled high like interchangeable assembly-line products

stored for later use. Along the right wall stretch nine rectangular alcoves filled with sets of bones that belonged to the higher ecclesiastics, and to the rear of the house stand four-foot-high stacks of mixed bones supplied by lesser mortals. A nearby cove holds a taller bank of bones taken from the extremities."

A visit made more than 150 years earlier is recounted by John Lloyd Stephens (1970):

> From this the door opens into the cemetery, which was so different from any I had ever seen, that I started back on the threshold with surprise. Along the wall was an excavation about thirty feet in length, but of what depth I could not tell. It was enclosed by a fence, which was three of four feet above the ground, and filled with human skulls; and in front, extending along the whole width of the chamber, was a pile of bones about twenty feet high, and running back I could not tell how far. They were very regularly disposed in layers, the feet and shoulders being placed outward alternately, and by the side of the last skeleton was a vacant place for the next that should be ready.... There was something peculiarly and terribly revolting in this promiscuous heaping together of mortal relics; bones upon bones; the old and young; wise men and fools; good men and bad; martyrs and murderers; masters and servants; bold, daring, and ambitious men — men who would have plucked bright honor from the moon, lying pell-mell with cowards and knaves. The superior told me that there were more than thirty thousand skeletons in the cemetery — literally an army of dead men's bones.

A full-scale study of the monastery was conducted by Professor George Forsyth of the University of Michigan during an expedition to the Near East in 1956. The monastery is said to have the skeletons of two male murderers and of St. Stephanos (d. 580), but the dispersal of the relics of St. Catherine to Europe has left the monks with only her skull and hand (Bentley 1985).

Bone House, Ripon Cathedral, England

In Volume IV of his *Curiosities of Natural History* (1873), Frank Buckland conveys his impressions upon visiting Ripon Cathedral for the purpose of examining the collection of human bones which he had heard was preserved in the crypt. With deference to the remains, he is curious about their history. He is shown into the crypt by a verger:

> Unlocking the massive door, we at once beheld a "Golgotha." Bones, bones, bones everywhere; skulls, arm-bones, leg-bones; skulls of old men, young men, men in the prime of life, and of women and children; they were not, I am pleased to say, huddled together in an unseemly and incongruous mass, but all stacked and arranged with decency and order. So many bones are there that the visitor cannot see the walls of the crypt, for against them is piled a wall of bones about six feet high, and four feet in thickness.

Buckland learned that the bones, which had once been scattered about the vault, had been neatly arranged (and some of them reburied) by sexton Dennis Wilson in 1843 and describes his handiwork: "He placed a row of skulls on the floor; then a thick row of arm and leg-bones with the round ends protruding; them another layer of skulls, and so on, till the space from the floor to the roof of the crypt was entirely occupied. I counted these skulls in their several compartments, and found that there were, from the wall to the outside of the stack, thirteen skulls in a row, and twelve in a row lengthways."

Buckland was very intested in making an estimate of the number of individuals represented by the bones:

> Each person must of necessity have had a skull, so that, by counting the skulls, I conceived I might get at an approach to the number of people whose remains were deposited in this crypt. We accordingly counted the skulls in their length, breadth, and thickness; measured the compartments, length of the crypt, et cetera, and, by a calculation, we made out that there were the skulls of about 9,912 in the bone-stacks in this crypt. Not all the bones of these individuals were, of course, there, as there would not have been room for them.

To piece together the history of the ossuary, Buckland interviews Mr. Harrison, the local repository of archaeological information. Harrison tells him that the bones had been found in a jumbled mass between two buttresses of the cathedral, having accumulated during the digging of graves in the churchyard, and were moved into the crypt. Buckland notes that the bones were in good condition, with the exception of signs of wear (a polished surface) on accessible skulls caused by the touch of visitors to the crypt. He found the shape of the skulls to range from delicate to massive and found the condition of the teeth to vary. Buckland examined signs of fractures in the remains and doubted that the breaks had been set correctly.

Pleased with his findings, Buckland is told by the verger that the room contains another crypt just below them, also full of bones. Buckland relents, writing, "What a vast assemblage of the mortal remains of human beings are, therefore, collected together! I leave it for the reader to calculate the sum...." He then adds a P.S. to his readers, should they desire to make their own observations in person, that the crypt had been closed to the public in 1867 by order of the local authorities.

Capuchin Crypt and Invention of the Cross Church, Brno, Czech Republic

This crypt in Brno, Czech Republic, is maintained by five members of the Friars Minor Capuchins. The church contains the relics of St. Clementine-the-Martyr, but the crypt attracts more visitors than the church, writes Father Bonaventura (personal correspondence, October 23, 1999). The bones accumulated from halfway through the seventeenth to nearly the end of the eighteenth century, during which the friars took advantage of the natural conditions and ventilation to allow the bodies of their brothers to mummify naturally in the crypt. The crypt was originally located down a narrow staircase, but in 1928 a new entrance was introduced. "The crypt includes skeletal remains in addition to mummified remains," writes Father Bonaventura, "but not entire skeletons. One altar is decorated with skulls and crossed long bones and various bones are stacked in the crypt of the friars."

Capuchins allowed others to be buried there and the secular bodies fare better than the religious. Of the more than 150 Capuchins buried in the crypt, only 24 of them were preserved. Many of the remains retain their identity and include nearly 50 benefactors: Baron Trenck (d. 1749), Austrian colonel and adventurer; Jakub Kunes of Rosenthal (d. 1658), city counsel; Martin Stiller (d. 1677), burgess; Dolesanský (d. 1753), Polish nobleman; Kaspar of Šternek (d. 1748), court pharmacist; Frantisek Preisler (d. 1780), doctor; Mořic Grimm (d. 1757), architect; and Barnabás Orelli (d. 1757), master chimney sweep and donor of several rare eighteenth-century reliquaries.

Catacombs at St. Stephan's Cathedral, Vienna

> In my life, I was abbot, bishop, prince.
> Now I am dust, shadow and nothing.
> — epitaph of the first Prince Bishop,
> Anton Wolfrath [d. 1639], entombed
> in St. Stephan's Cathedral

The catacombs beneath St. Stephan's Cathedral have many notable associations. In a chapel at their entrance a plaque marks the spot where Wolfgang Amadeus Mozart's body was consecrated in 1791. In the cata-

combs proper, the Ducal Vault contains the sarcophagus of Rudolph IV, Empress Maria Theresa (d. 1780), and more than a dozen other members of the royal family. Another vault was built in 1953 to house the exhumed remains of 14 of Vienna's bishops and a separate tomb designated for the church canons. The remains of the approximately 11,000 people buried in the catacombs beneath the cathedral include notables such as architect Johann Bernhard Fischer von Erlach, humanist poet Conrad Celtis (d. 1508), and doctor, historian, and diplomat Johannes Cuspinian (d. 1529) and family.

The catacombs were a popular resting place, but not just because of its inhabitants. The cemetery that had encircled the cathedral was closed in the late 1730s. By 1744, the complex of passageways and chambers beneath the cathedral had to be expanded. The cellars of surrounding houses to the northeast beneath Stephansplatz were incorporated into the system of vaults. Subterranean space was no longer at a premium after Emperor Joseph II prohibited church burials in 1783. One hundred years later the human remains were walled in and remained for a time inaccessible. The corridors lined with casketed remains and chambers filled with stacked bones can now be toured Monday through Saturday (Lawson 1999). One visitor writes, "Beneath Vienna, under the cathedral, the tour guide leads us through the catacombs. I wish I could come down here alone. Without the group clattering through the stone corridors, this could be a genuinely unnerving place: thick stone walls, silent and dank, with the weight of St. Stephen's pressing down overhead. There are one or two plague pits, into which they've opened small, barred windows. These were big holes in the ground, into which they dug an opening from the street and shoveled in the corpses while the Plague raged.... Old gray bones litter the floor of the pit, a foot or two deep.

We crowd around the tiny window with our cameras" (Reich 1995).

Medieval Ossuary at Wamba, Valladolid, Spain

The Monastery of Santa Maria, in the town of Wamba in northern Spain, has had an ossuary since the Middle Ages. Wamba, located in Valladolid, was a visigothic village abandoned for nearly 200 years after defeat by the Muslims. The monastery was refounded in 928. Somewhere between the fifteenth and seventeenth centuries, the need for room in the surrounding cemetery prompted the opening of the oldest tombs and placing the bones in an ossuary. Theories that the bones resulted from battle are belied by the fact that the little trauma found in the bones can be related to accidents. In fact, the ossuary contains the remains of centuries of villagers and has revealed much about their daily life. Initial analysis of the remains was carried out in the 1950s, when part of the ossuary's contents were removed to the School of Medicine of the Complutense University of Madrid. The bones were (and still are) used by students of anthropology and were moved to the Department of Biology more than 25 years ago. Once well-preserved, the bones have suffered somewhat from their use over the years, but have served many useful purposes. One drawback of the collection is that it does not consist of discrete skeletons, but commingled bones, since the ossuary consisted of independent series of bones, such as hip bones, skulls, and long bones. Still, much about disease and activity patterns has been learned by a team directed by Dr. Gonzalo Trancho.

Inmaculada López-Bueis (et al. 1996) has studied ulnar osteoarthrosis in the Wamba population using a sample of 197 ulnae and found the frequency of exostosis to be 60 percent of the adults, with the occurrence higher in males than females. Beat-

riz Robledo (Trancho et al. 1994) has examined the sexual differences in the ilium, ischium, and pubis of 1,155 adult specimens from Wamba and compared the morphological differences with those of five other skeletal series. A sample of 561 tibiae from Wamba provided the means for López-Bueis (et al. 1994) to assess stress factors in the medieval community — attributable to hormonal factors, diet, aging, physical activity, and hereditary frailty — by examining exostosis, which was found in 45 percent of the samples. For her 1998 doctoral dissertation, López-Bueis examined a sample of 516 humeri, 186 radii, 198 ulnae, 671 femora, and 561 tibiae to study the frequency and distribution of osteoarthritis, periostitis and trauma in the long bones. She also studied sexual dimorphism in a total of 501 humera, 173 radii, 185 ulnae, 635 femora, and 538 tibiae in an attempt to counter the long-standing notion that sex cannot be determined from isolated bones (personal communication, May 26, 2000).

Most recently, López-Bueis and Trancho (1999) studied the paleopathology of the Wamba population. They examined 2,200 long bones (516 humeri, 186 radii, 198 ulnae, 671 femora, and 561 tibiae), all in an excellent degree of preservation. They determined the sample to be 60 to 70 percent male. Half of the bones examined (radii, ulnae, and femora) showed lipping at the joints, the first sign of degenerative joint disease. The frequency of periostitis was assessed at less than 10 percent in the arm bones, but more than 50 percent in the legs, possibly due to riding horses, but most lesions were fully healed. The pattern of fractures in the long bones supports the idea that the ossuary originated as a reutilization of the nearby cemetery rather than being due to violence. López-Bueis and Trancho (1999) point out the advantages of the Wamba skeletal series: large sample size, good degree of preservation, and correlating historical documentation about the degree of sexual dimorphism and life-long exposure to stress in this farming community. They do note that the isolation of the bones (rather than being complete skeletons) hampers comparison with other populations and affects the diagnosis of disease. The Wamba skeletal series will continue to reveal information to scientists, while the rest of the bones will inspire tourists to the Monastery.

Crypt of St. Leonard's Church in Hythe, Kent, England

> When the guide opened the oak doors I saw an immense stack of human bones, piled up in regular order and evidently with the care always due to the sacred remains of our fellow creatures. The walls of the pile are formed by the rounded ends of arm and leg bones ... while every here and there a skull is built into the stack.... On one of these skulls I found some short hair still remaining, which, when examined with a glass, I found to be of a red fox-like colour.... The teeth remaining in the skulls are in excellent order; and I observed but very few symptoms of disease about them.
> — Frank Buckland's firsthand account [1865] of a visit to Hythe

Wamba has what might be considered a sister ossuary in Kent, England. The crypt of St. Leonard's Church in Hythe holds thousands of bones exhumed from local burial grounds in the late Middle Ages. As with Wamba, scientific analysis has put to rest the popular notion that the remains were amassed as a result of a battle. History at Hythe had been entirely lost, as indicated by Chaplain James Brome, who writes in 1679 about "the charnel house adjoining to the church, or the arched vault under it, wherein are orderly piled up a great stack of dead men's bones and skulls, but which appear very white and solid.... But how or by what means they were brought to this place the townsmen are altogether ignorant and can give no account of the matter" (Barker 1998). Edinburgh anatomist and physiolo-

gist Alexander Walker examined the bones in 1834, noting two different skull shapes: the first long and narrow and the second short and broad. He identified the first as Celtic and the second as Roman and concluded that a great battle had taken place. The remains were observed in 1884 by Dr. Robert Knox, who disagreed with earlier racial attributions, but found the bones to be all male and thus assumed the individuals to have fallen in battle and been buried in a mass grave. A magazine article from the turn of the twentieth century in fact refutes the idea of the remains having come from a cemetery because they do not include the remains of women and children. The article puts forth the idea that the bones are the legacy of a great battle between the Britons and Saxons in 456 and were recovered from the battlefield, complete with evidence of cutmarks and other signs of violence (McGregor 1898/99). A few years later, examination by Professor F.G. Parsons in 1908 indicated earth in the eye sockets, nose, and ear cavities. Observations by Professors Brenda N. Stoessiger and G.M. Morant in 1932 found no flesh, but did note the existence of traces of brain and of wood fibers from coffins.

The accumulation of bones at St. Leonard's, while determined not to be the result of plague or battle, has a long and speculative history. Many of the bones may have been uncovered during new burials or churchyard excavations, as occurred in 1881 outside the north door of the crypt and in 1985 and 1992 during work in the cemetery. Some remains may have been exposed during a great storm that flooded the area in 1287. Many bones were brought to Hythe, for instance from ruined churches in the area. Bones that may have been disturbed during renovations in the twelfth century remain under the high altar. During excavations in 1959, 70 sacks of bones were recovered from the building's foundations and were reburied behind the vestry. A wooden

Skulls in the crypt of Hythe Church. Photo courtesy of the Parish of St. Leonard, Hythe.

charnel shelter was used to house recovered bones until it fell into ruin.

Altogether, the crypt at St. Leonard's contains about 2,000 skulls and 8,000 thigh bones believed to represent more than 4,000 people. "So great a quantity as I never saw elsewhere in one place," wrote Rye town clerk Samuel Jeake in 1678 (Barker 1998). The bones are mentioned in Parish Vestry records three times between 1725 and 1870, one of these an 1828 proposal to adopt measures for their preservation. They have been protected for the most part since, but have been utilized by more than scientists. One of the skulls in the collection has been nested in by a bird, most recently in 1992. Historian Jack F. Barker writes, "Honesty compels me reluctantly to admit that research indicates that this happened after death! The truth is that the doors of the crypt are not always bird-tight and the birds are often able to fly in and out" (Barker 1998).

Most of the deposited bones have been preserved despite many threats. "Some 8,000 thighbones dating back to before the Norman Conquest are stacked like canned goods on the shelves and in the crypt. They're accompanied by 2,000 skulls. Do the math. That leaves another 2,000 people's heads and sundry body parts unaccounted for," quip Lawson and Rufus (1999). Reverend T.G. Hall, vicar of Hythe from 1873 to 1899, suspected during his tenure that some chamberlains had raised money on the side by selling skulls from the collection, and he took measures to stop the practice. Six skulls from Hythe made their way into the hands of Barnard Davis and were later acquired by the Royal College of Surgeons. In 1931, Reverend H.D. Dale, Vicar of Hythe from 1899 to 1926, wrote about his reluctance to allow dentists into the crypt unsupervised because of the temptation to pull teeth from the skulls, which he countered by placing the teeth in glass cases. It was Reverend Dale who posted the notice reading, "Visitors are requested to respect the dead and not to write on the bones"—a sign that was still hanging in 1982. The bones are fragile and visitors are still reminded not to touch them. Sturdier femurs outnumber the fragile skulls, although more than half of the skulls survive complete. The majority of them (1,138) are displayed on shelves, a practice first begun in 1851. The rest are placed with smaller bones in a pile measuring some 25 feet long by 5½ feet wide by 7½ feet high. The pile is documented to have existed in the seventeenth century and has been rearranged several times since then: order was created from the "utter confusion" that existed on the floor of the crypt in about 1846, bricks were put in to allow the air to circulate in 1908, and the south end of the pile was restacked in 1965.

The bones have also received a lot of attention from researchers. In 1889, an account of the bones was published by Vicar Hall after examination by a Mr. Prideau, who believed them to be Celtic and Anglo-Saxon, with a few execptions. At about the same time, the skulls were analyzed by Dr. Randall Davis and Professor Owen. In 1908, the collection was studied by Professor Parsons, lecturer in anatomy at St. Thomas's Hospital, who wrote in 1914 that the remains were townspeople of the twelfth, thirteenth, fourteenth, and fifteenth centuries. While measurements of the skulls were used to hesitatingly assign not only race, but nationality, a difference in measurements of skulls from the north and south bays of the crypt does imply that the collection built up over time rather than being a sudden accumulation. Early researchers may be forgiven for misinterpreting a sword wound on one of the skulls that modern physical anthropologists recognize as showing signs of healing and therefore of having survived the blow.

Today the remains are believed to have come from a Saxon cemetery dating to 1000 A.D., but may have accumulated up to 200 years earlier or 500 years later. All but a few of the bones date from prior to 1500 A.D. The individuals in the collection are believed to have died before the age of 50. The height of the males, based on measurements of the femurs, averaged 5'4" to 5'5" and the height of the females 5'1". The results of scientific examinations over the years were recorded on labels that were kept with the skulls, but were modified when necessary, for instance to correct gender if it was reassessed. More specific observations and studies have also been conducted. When the teeth were examined, researchers agreed with Frank Buckland's nineteenth-century assessment that most showed few signs of decay, but noted among the skulls several examples of malformed dentition, including missing molar sockets and impaction. The skull of an older man showed the wear that would have been caused by eating rough food. The man's teeth, though, were probably the least of his worries. Analysis shows that he had survived a fracture of the skull and had, probably subsequently, undergone a trephination which he also survived. Another unusual component of the collection are two skulls noted for their small size, but believed to be adults because of the closure of the sutures. The apparent contradiction would be explained by dwarfism. The Hythe collection also includes examples of osteomyelitis and osteoporosis, a bone tumor believed to have been benign, and unset fractures that left the broken limb shorter when healed.

The Hythe crypt is one of only two church ossuaries in England that can still be toured, the other being at Rothwell. The bones at Hythe have the distinction of having been shown to the public for at least the last 400 years. Historian Jack Barker suggests that the collection of bones was maintained to attract thirteenth-century and later pilgrims on their way to the tomb of St.

Thomas à Becket at Canterbury (d. 1170). Recent interest has been more scientific than religious, but either way the bones and their caretakers benefit:

> There has, from time to time, been some criticism that the bones should be exposed to the public, but it would be a pity to deny the historic and scientific interest of the collection. In addition, since the income derived is of great assistance to the parish, the people represented in the crypt continue to serve their church in death as they did in life [Barker 1998].

Visits to the crypt were led by the chamberlain or sexton, who received an additional annual sum for his privileged task of exhibiting the bones. One of the visitors was a young George Borrow, who writes in 1851 about the skulls in the crypt: "It was half filled with substances of some kind, which at first looked like large gray stones. The greater part were lying in layers. Some, however, were seen in confused and mouldering heaps, and two or three, which had perhaps rolled down from the rest, lay separately on the floor." Today, the bones are always shown reverence and the church thinks of its visitors as modern-day pilgrims (Barker 1998).

Northeastern extremity of Nanjemoy (Juhle) Ossuary #2. Reprinted from *Reconstruction of Demographic Profiles from Ossuary Skeletal Samples,* by Douglas H. Ubelaker (*Smithsonian Contributions to Anthropology 18,* 1974).

Native American Ossuaries in the United States

The U.S. is dotted with ossuaries dating from the third century to the seventeenth century. These Native American communal graves continue to be found, sometimes through diligent searching, but more often accidentally during construction of previously undeveloped land. Bones have also been exposed by erosion and other natural processes. These bones may be Huron if found in the midwest or Algonkian if found in the mid–Atlantic region. Depending on their cultural affiliation and the circumstances under which they were found, the remains may be repatriated. But the more time allowed for scientific appraisal, the more pieces the bones will contribute to the puzzle of prehistory. Secondary burial itself, which necessitates close contact with bones and renders them more portable, tells a lot about the spiritual beliefs and ancestral ties of its practitioners.

While the particulars varied by culture, the use of ossuaries in prehistoric America followed a pattern. The dead were disposed of by defleshing, cremation, or exposure (allowing the body to decay), followed by periodic gathering and cleaning of the remains, bundling of the bones, and deposit in pits or mass graves. Evidence that remains buried in ossuaries were first exposed above ground includes a skull found in Virginia that contained the nest of a mud-dauber wasp. The practice of secondary burial was documented among the Huron of Ontario in 1636 by French Jesuit missionary Jean de Brébeuf. The dead were buried temporarily or exposed on a scaffold. Every decade or so the natives of the area would convene for a final interment ceremony, an event that may have been triggered by the death of a leader. The remains were collected, cleaned of any remaining flesh, and prepared for reburial in a communal pit. The pit was lined with skins and outfitted with burial gifts before the bones were emptied into the grave (Curry 1999). The Huron and other related people in the St. Lawrence area were known for their spectacular ossuaries. In the Hopewell and Mississippian cultures, secondary burial was carried out in log tombs inside earthen mounds. In the Southeast and Middle Atlantic area of the U.S., reburial was in sand mounds. In some communities, the bones remained articulated. In others, they were cremated.

Native American ossuaries in the Northeast are less common than to the south and west, but include the Indian Neck site on Cape Cod, Massachusetts, and the Archery Range site in Bronx County, New York. Other ossuaries have been found in Pennsylvania and Florida. Most are linked to groups that spoke related Algonqkuian languages (Roylance 1999). Ossuaries in the tidewater region of Maryland include both genders and all ages. They number nearly

three dozen and contain as many as 600 individuals (Curry 1999). The mound cultures of the East and Midwest were prodigious in their efforts. Cahokia Mounds in Illinois includes the largest mound in the United States and 68 smaller mounds. The mounds at Kolomoki Mounds State Park in Georgia are between 6 and 20 feet high and up to 50 feet in diameter.

Secondary burial has been practiced at many times and by many Native American cultures. The Broad Reach site in North Carolina dates to 1280 A.D. (±80 years). Most of the Virginia ossuaries are believed to date from 1550–1650, A.D. although a burial mound complex in the Blue Ridge Mountains containing the remains of hundreds of individuals of the Lewis Creek Mound Culture may be 600 years older than that. As late as 1792, Nanticoke Indians in Pennsylvania were still returning to the Eastern Shore to collect their ancestors' bones. But by 1700, most remnant Indian groups in Maryland were burying their dead in the European style (Roylance 1999). Centuries of tradition left cultural and biological remnants of great quantity. The coast of North Carolina includes five Algonkian ossuaries, four of which (Hatteras Village, Piggot, Hollowell, and Baum) contain the remains of between 30 and 60 individuals. The McLean Mound on the Cape Fear River in North Carolina contained 242 bundle burials and 25 cremations representing a total of 438 individuals.

Many ossuaries are uncovered by bulldozers. "It is always a macabre and chilling sight — hundreds of densely packed human bones, tumbling out of a shallow pit, unexpectedly exposed by a backhoe or erosion," describes Frank D. Roylance (1999). When construction work began in 1936 at Bolling Field (now Bolling Air Force Base) along the Anacostia River in Maryland, the bones of at least 56 individuals were found below less than twelve inches of sandy soil (Curry 1999). More careful excavation of the site (known as Nacotchtanke–1) revealed a pit measuring about 10 by 12 feet and containing a 12–inch layer of bones. A second site (Nacotchtanke–2) was located approximately 50 meters to the east and contained the bones of at least 63 individuals in an irregularly-shaped bed 15 feet wide and up to 18 inches thick. A small ossuary was disturbed by water line work at the University of Maryland's Eastern Shore campus in 1992, but was left in place under the grass, which may allow for later unhurried excavation.

Other ossuaries were found "in the back yard." Alice Leczinska Lowe Ferguson practiced her archaeology skills at her family's Hard Bargain Farm, located at the confluence of the Piscataway Creek and the Potomac River in Charles County, Maryland. With the help of volunteers, high school students, and her farm hands, Mrs. Ferguson exposed a few individual burials and other features of a sixteenth-century village during her first two seasons. Beginning in 1937, a series of ossuaries was found:

- Moyaone Ossuary #1: This first ossuary was discovered at Accokeek Creek. It measured 16 × 10 feet and was about 4 feet deep. Based on skull counts, including fragments of three cremated skulls, the number of individuals represented were 288.

- Mayaone Ossuary #2: This ossuary was only partially excavated, then covered by a small concrete block building and exhibited to the many visitors to the site until 1976 when it was demolished. The pit measured 10 by 24 feet wide and was up to 3 feet deep. While 155 skulls were actually removed, the ossuary was estimated to contain a 250 individuals.

- Mayaone Ossuary #3: From this ossuary, measuring 8 by 18 feet wide and 3½ feet deep, 248 skulls were removed. Cremated remains of four individuals were also found.

- Mayaone Ossuary #4: This was the largest (23 by 21 feet) and the deepest (3 to 5 feet) of the ossuaries found by Mrs. Ferguson. The upper sides of many of the bones had been scorched by a large fire lit on top of the bone bed. In addition to cremated bones representing 30 individuals, 618 skulls were excavated. One of the female skulls enclosed a shell necklace and contained a large shell bead deep in each eye socket. The site was dated to between the fifteenth and the seventeenth centuries.

- Susquehannock Fort: In her search for this 1675 Colonial fort, Mrs. Ferguson found a small ossuary containing 42 burials, including the remains of seven young children, that was believed to have accompanied the Susquehannocks when they occupied the site briefly.

- Mockley Point: Also during her search for the Susquehannock Fort, Mrs. Ferguson found an ossuary containing 11 skulls, but did not record its exact location.

- Ferguson Ossuary/Piscataway Fort: Here Mrs. Ferguson removed a reported 254 skulls from an oval deposit later determined by T. Dale Stewart to contain 207 individuals ranging in age from two years to adult. The skeleton of an infant was found in a leather pouch and some of the skulls contained beads and small bones.

Some sites suffered from uninformed techniques, but may not have been discovered at all if not for amateur enthusiasm. Whether discovered by accident or amateur, many sites were excavated or at least studied by experts. Native American ossuaries offer many avenues for research, given the opportunity to pursue them. Aboriginal remains offer ancient examples of pathologies, including dental caries, periostitis, and fractures. The bones may confirm their multigenerational status and refute the theory of a battle or epidemic. Douglas Ubelaker and

Dale Stewart excavated an ancient ossuary in southern Maryland that was discovered in 1971 when a fence line was being erected. They recovered the skeletal remains of over 150 individuals. Using microscopic analysis of bones and x-rays of teeth, they reconstructed the ages of death of everybody in the sample. Determining that the ossuary had been in use for four years allowed them to estimate the total number of people in the population at 1,000 (Ubelaker and Scammell 1992). According to Curry (1999), ossuaries are a key to reconstructing prehistoric populations and demographic profiles, to addressing Aboriginal health and nutritional issues, and to deciphering Native American social, political, and belief systems. Study reveals changes that a culture has undergone and confirms or corrects earlier assumptions. The teeth in many of the skulls found in Maryland were riddled with cavities, leading to the conclusion that they were damaged by the starchy sugars in the diet after the change to corn agriculture. There are also signs of disease that earlier investigators had assumed was syphilis, but is now believed to have been yaws, a chronic skin and bone infection caused by a microorganism and poor sanitation.

The current status of the bones from the many American ossuaries and native cemeteries varies. The bulk of the skeletal material from those found by Mrs. Ferguson remains in the collection of the Smithsonian, except for the remains with a less well-established provenance, which were donated by the Alice Ferguson Foundation to the Maryland Geological Survey in 1971 and are now curated by the Maryland Historical Trust (Curry 1999). Dennis C. Curry, archaeologist at the Maryland Historical Trust, reports that most of the human remains from Maryland ossuaries are held in either the Smithsonian Institution or the Maryland Archaeological Conservation Laboratory in Calvert County. Study has been blocked on some of the bones by modern Piscataway Indian groups seeking their return. Other remains have already been repatriated and Curry notes that this was an early impetus for the research that resulted in his book about the ossuaries of Maryland, *Feast of the Dead.*

MASS GRAVES

Churchyards, with their shallowly buried corpses, were often used as pasture and the cattle would sometimes uncover human bones. Many graveyards had so-called 'charnel houses' in which were collected any skeletal remains that had been dug up. In times of plague it was not always possible to bury the dead, and these were piled up in heaps in the open instead. If one searched near gallow mounds and other execution places or on old battlefields, one could find crania denuded of all the soft tissues by decay or the ravages of carrion birds or as a result of deliberate skeletonization. It was at such places that the great anatomists of the Renaissance, who were often artists as well, discovered the material they required.
— Folke Henschen [1965]

Mass graves by definition contain the remains of many people. The reasons these typically unrelated remains have accumulated range from accidental (the prey of carnivores) to political (the victims of genocide) to economical (evicted tenants of leased cemetery plots) to judicial (recipients of the death penalty). The number of bodies to be disposed of after a massacre necessitated depositing the dead in a single large grave. The decay of a succession of gibbeted prisoners resulted in a scattering of skeletal elements, as noted by Henschen (1935):

> Bodies were … left hanging for a long time after execution, and at the beginning of the nineteenth century, after a fresh wind, it was possible to pick up crania which had fallen to the ground from the gallows in London.

In the simplest forms of gibbeting, the

bodies of criminals who had been hung in chains were left in place as a warning to others. They remained until they fell to pieces or the gibbet was blown down, although humane persons have been known to gather the desolate bones together and lay them in a grave (Hartshorne 1841). A more efficient structure was used on Montfauçon in Paris at the end of the twelfth century: a monumental gibbet from which fifty-two criminals could be hung and strangled. The gibbet was four-sided with a platform running around three sides of its interior. The bones and fragments that resulted from its use were swept periodically into a vault formed in the center, as described by Albert Harshorne in 1841: "[T]he ossuarium, or charnel-house, being cleared out, as necessity dictated, through a doorway level with the outside ground on the further or sinister side of the building. It must have been a thing quite unique in the world, somewhat recalling the Towers of Silence of the Parsees."

In addition to criminals, those guilty only of being poor or friendless were also disposed of en masse. Paupers' graves at the Cimetière des Innocents in nineteenth-century Paris were left open until their 1,500–body capacity was filled, a span of as many as three years. The cemeteries of continental Europe still maintain bone pits used to dispose of remains after the specified occupation of a grave or tomb and in the absence of instruction from the families. The casualties of war also required efficient disposal in the form of mass interment. During the American Civil War some 13,000 prisoners died at Andersonville, Georgia. Up to 160 bodies a day were buried in trenches that held 100 bodies apiece. During World War II, Russians executed more than 4,000 Polish officers in the Katyn Forest near Smolensk and buried them in a mass grave. Perhaps the most prone to mass burial are the victims of mass execution or massacre. The 146 victims of the Black Hole of Calcutta were buried together in a ditch.

After the liberation of the German concentration camps, Allied troops had no alternative but to collectively bury the tens of thousands of prisoners who had not survived (Iserson 1994).

Some battles are so bloody that there are no resources left to bury the dead. In one of the earliest recorded incidents of unburied battlefield casualties, three Roman Legions were killed with their general Publius Quinctilius Varus in the forests of Germany in 9 A.D. Tacitus records that Germanicus and his command went to bury the dead six years later and found the bones of the men and their horses scattered throughout the area, with skulls fastened to nearby trees by the victorious Germans. They gathered the bones and raised a proper burial mound to their memory (Scott 1998, 338). During the French and Indian Wars, General Edward Braddock and his command were defeated in July 1755 along the Monongahela River. Five years later, Colonel Jehu Eyre recorded his impressions of the site, noting that the bones of the 450 English and Colonial troops killed were "lying about as thick as leaves" (quoted in Scott 1998). Large collections of war dead are powerful symbols and can be made to serve psychological purposes. After the mansion of Robert E. Lee — now on the grounds of Arlington National Cemetery — was seized by the Union Army and converted into a military headquarters at the beginning of the Civil War, the individual graves of over 16,000 federal soldiers and the collective grave of 2,111 unknowns were placed around the home to prevent Lee from returning to it.

Exhumation of mass graves by forensic anthropologists allows a country to address its human rights violations. Fredy A. Peccerelli is part of a team investigating civil war atrocities in Guatemala, a politically explosive endeavor, since many of those responsible remain in power in the government or military. Abuses — documented by crushed skulls, machete-severed spinal columns, and

M-16 rifle wounds — are being cataloged, but will never be comprehensive. The three teams of anthropologists can only respond to a fraction of the requests they receive to unearth potential sites: "If graves were mines, we would be afraid to walk in Guatemala," says Peccerelli (Moore 1998). Human rights organizations estimate that 100,000 people (the majority of them noncombatants) were killed. One site in Rio Negro contained the remains of 159 women and children killed by army and paramilitary troops. Many of the mass graves are relatively easy to locate because survivors have been visiting them and leaving memorials (flowers, crosses, and candles) for 20 years. Relatives also assist with the identification of the dead by recognizing fragments of clothing clinging to the bones and by giving samples of their DNA with which the remains can be compared (Moore 1998).

When the bones of military personnel litter the ground, traffic in human remains inevitably results. After the Vietnam War, much of this traffic has been routed through the U.S. MIA Office in Hanoi, which had examined more than 7,400 bones or bone fragments as of 1992. While some are legitimate reports by Vietnamese citizens who find them while working in the fields or accidentally stumble on a crash site in a remote area, others are animal or Vietnamese remains turned in by bone dealers who believe rumors that in exchange for the remains of a missing U.S. service member, American authorities will pay for the finder's family's passage to America. The misinformation has misdirected efforts (difficult and costly as they are) to find, identify and repatriate American MIA remains (Mann 1998). The role of anthropologists in identifying war dead is well-established. After World War II, Charles C. Snow and Mildred Trotter were chief physical anthropologists at a central identification laboratory established in Hawaii. After the Korean conflict, the Memorial Division of the Office of the Quartermaster General established laboratories in Kokura, Japan, staffed by T.D. Stewart, Ellis R. Kerley, and Charles C. Warren. Over a five-month period, Stewart analyzed 450 skeletons, of which 375 were positively identified (Thompson 1982).

Killing Fields of Cambodia

Genocide under the rule of Pol Pot (d. 1998) left skeletons strewn across Cambodia. Four years after the country had been taken over by the Khmer Rouge in 1975, between 1 and 2 million people (a quarter of the population) had died of starvation, exhaustion, torture, and execution. Anyone who had refused his orders to flee Phnom Penh into the countryside was shot. Monks, artists, and intellectuals were rounded up, killed, and buried in mass graves at sites now known as "Killing Fields." Thousands more Cambodians died of starvation and exhaustion in forced labor camps. And thousands of Pol Pot's enemies were systematically tortured and murdered. When Pol Pot revealed himself publicly as the leader of the Khmer Rouge in 1977, his army then slaughtered hundreds of Vietnamese villagers, causing Vietnam to invade Phnom Penh. Pol Pot was forced out, the camps were closed, and killing fields throughout the country were revealed before Vietnam withdrew. Despite more than sufficient skeletal and other evidence, Pol Pot never showed any remorse and was never tried for his crimes against humanity because it could not be decided which country would host the tribunal.

The crimes are documented and Pol Pot's victims commemorated in a museum housed in what was, until 1979, the main prison of Phnom Penh, a way station for tens of thousands executed in the Killing Fields nine miles away. In what John Auchard (1999) calls "the inevitable packaging of genocide," a donation is requested at the entrance to the block buildings at the Tuol

Sleng museum that contain implements and images of torture, the names and photographs of victims, and a large map of the country entirely covered with human crania. "At Tuol Sleng there is something ghastly yet vulgar about the map covered with skulls. The photos of the dead, photos taken just before their death, are much more disturbing, and there is something grotesque about the way someone, somehow, arranged skulls of different sizes and shapes to just cover the borders of the country on the map," writes Auchard (personal correspondence, October 20, 1999). The skulls rarely fail to move visitors, as Phillip Walker attests (In press): "[T]he racks of skulls from the Cambodian killing fields at Tuol Sleng prison ... speak volumes about real historical events that ended the lives of real people." In fact, the symbolic value of displaying the remains outweighed Buddhist religious beliefs that mandate cremation, although monks anoint and pray over the skulls. After the government announced in 1994 that the skulls and bones would be cremated, and King Sihanouk pledged $20,000 for the ceremony and a stupa for the ashes, a plea from the central committee of the Cambodian People's Party caused the idea to be abandoned in January 1995. The majority of Cambodia's population wanted to keep the bones as witnesses of Khmer Rouge atrocities. Although some of the skulls have been removed to the museum, plenty remain on the surface of the Killing Fields. In addition to the most famous one outside Phnom Penh, in which long bones and skulls are stacked behind glass in a tower and the grassy field is dotted with multilingual markers to assist the many tourists, there is another less well-known site outside of Siem Reap near Angkor.

Battle of Towton in York, England

While an overwhelming number of victims over a four-year period can relay a strong message about the misuse of power, careful investigation of the casualties of a single battle can illuminate history. The Battle of Towton was a definitive battle of the Wars of the Roses (1453–1487) because it confirmed Edward IV's claim to the throne of England. The battle was fought between the villages of Towton and Saxton near York in northeast England on March 29, 1461, as church bells rang because it happened to be Palm Sunday. Statistics show that more than 3 percent of Britain's population of 3 million fought at Towton and the casualties they suffered made it the bloodiest battle ever fought on British soil. With snow blowing in their faces, King Henry's archers could not see and their arrows fell short, only to be used against them by the Yorkists, led by 18-year-old Edward IV. Having destroyed the bridge to block enemy escape, the Lancastrians were unable to retreat across the river and many drowned in the attempt.

As Anthea Boylston explains (personal correspondence, July 1, 1999), the mass grave containing the Towton casualties was discovered during excavations to put a garage extension on the side of a house located a half mile from the battlefield. Burials were found to extend under the house and the front garden. The excavation of the site — one of only two excavations in the twentieth century of medieval battles in Europe (the other being the mass grave from the Battle of Visby in 1361) — was carried out by the University of Bradford and the West Yorkshire Archaeology Service. To avoid damage to the bones, most of the digging was done lying on a plank. The entire grave was exposed before any of the burials were lifted. The bodies had been stripped, so there were few artifacts found in the grave, but most of the skeletons were recovered in an articulated state, apart from some of the bones of the hands and feet. The skeletons were sketched in situ, photographed, and surveyed with an electronic distance meter.

They were then removed and bagged for transport to the laboratory.

The remains from the Battle of Towton were analyzed by a forensic anthropologist, a geophysicist, a medieval historian and anthropologist, and three paleopathologists. Immediately apparent was damage to many of the skulls, indicating head injuries, although evidence of healing showed that some of these wounds had been survived from previous battles. Three types of trauma — projectile, blunt force, and sharp force — are represented, including a radiating fracture from a penetrating injury and a square perforation possibly caused by the point of a pole-axe. There is very little post-cranial trauma, but changes to the left elbow (a greatly expanded articular surface and avulsed medial epicondyle) testify to the physical demands of the British longbow. Signs of extreme stress placed on the spine at a young age are evidenced by intervertebral osteochondrosis in one of the soldiers' lumbar vertebra. It was determined that the assemblage included 37 individuals, 29 of whose skeletons were complete. The youngest individual was about 17 years old, with ten others also under 25 and 11 over 35. The average age was calculated at 30 and the average stature between 5'7" and 5'8". A special computer program allowed digital reconstruction of the grave and a later exhibit at the Royal Armouries in Leeds paired battle wounds on selected skeletons with vintage examples of the weapons that may have killed them.

Crow Creek Massacre in Chamberlain, South Dakota

Crow Creek is the largest archaeologically recovered massacre series in the world. Because all of the people died virtually simultaneously, they represent a living group better than cemetery samples, which reflect accretional deaths over several or many generations. Studying the Crow Creek remains is similar to examining members of a living village.
— P. Willey [1990]

The Crow Creek Massacre is notable for many reasons, not the least of which is its presence on the World Wide Web (www.uiowa.edu/~anthro/paleopathology/). Mindful of the sensitivies that were encountered during the discovery, excavation, and analysis of these Native American remains, the website warns the viewer not to continue if he or she is bothered by pictures of human skeletal remains. An additional disclaimer states that the photographs are intended for educational purposes; that they are used with the permission of the Arikara people (who are their descendants), the Crow Creek Sioux Reservation (on whose land the remains were discovered), and American Indians Against Desecration; and that they should not be downloaded without permission. With all of this said, the text explains that the bones at Crow Creek belong to several hundred victims of a fourteenth-century massacre.

The Crow Creek site, located 11 miles north of Chamberlain on the east bank of the Missouri River, was uncovered by severe erosion in May 1978. A visitor to the site (which is a National Historic Landmark) noticed bones washing out of the side of a bluff. The U.S. Army Corps of Engineers was asked by the state archaeologist to remove and reinter what were then believed to be a few isolated burials. Permission from federal officials to do so took two weeks, during which time a relic hunter used a mattock or crowbar to gouge a hole 4½ feet high, 6 feet wide, and 3 feet deep — and containing nearly 50 skeletons — into the bank where the bones had been exposed. This caused an avalanche of hundreds of bones to trail down the slope (Zimmerman and Alex 1981). To forestall the looting that had already begun, plans were initiated for the human remains to be excavated by the University of South Dakota under an agreement with the Arikara, the Crow Creek Sioux Reservation, and the U.S. Army Corps of Engineers. The agreement stipulated that study be done within the state of South Dakota, completed within one year, and followed by prompt reburial. Fears that bones removed from the reservation would be mishandled in the laboratory were put to rest when procedures for analysis were spelled out. During the period of scientific study, native ceremonies were conducted by Lakota holy man Bill Schweigman and Native Americans worked as both excavators and guards at the site, which was watched around the clock.

The massacre, possibly a territorial dispute, occurred around 1325 A.D. and wiped out an estimated 60 percent of the villagers, ending the functions of the village as a social unit, fortress, and home (Willey 1990). Archaeologists estimate that between 744 and 831 people lived in the fortified Crow Creek village when it was attacked. The bones recovered indicate a minimum number of individuals of 486, based on the petrous portion of the right temporal bone. The remains of perhaps fifty others still lie — unexcavated — where survivors piled them. The number slain include few women of child-bearing years and few children, suggesting that they escaped, were killed but not recovered, or that the raiders absorbed them into their own villages. The bodies lay exposed for some time (likely several weeks) after the massacre, as evidenced by punctures in many of the long bones that have been interpreted as chewing marks made by dogs, coyotes, or wolves. The lack of insect remains makes time between death and burial difficult to estimate, but may suggest that the bodies were only exposed during cold weather (Willey 1990). Survivors apparently returned some time later and hauled clay up from the river bottom to cover the remains, which they buried in the fortification ditch that surrounded the village (Zimmerman and Alex 1981, P. Willey 1990).

The Crow Creek skeletons evidence the health and well-being of Aboriginal natives before the arrival of Columbus. Physical anthropologist P. Willey (1981) writes,

"The massacre offers an extremely rare opportunity to study the sample of a population at one point in time. Few other collections exist that are so potentially revealing as the one from Crow Creek concerning the diseases a prehistoric people lived with daily (contrasted with afflictions which killed people), population structure and prehistoric mutilation patterns. Crow Creek is also a crucial site for studies of prehistoric stress and biological affinities with other populations." Willey was contracted to analyze the looted bones before reburial. He took the fragments to the University of South Dakota laboratories in Vermillion, washed and examined them. Willey determined the minimum number of individuals represented in the sample to be 44. He found cut marks indicative of scalping on most of the skulls, two of which had prior healed cutmarks. Other signs of violence pointed toward decapitation and possible dismemberment.

Members of the University of South Dakota Archeology Laboratory, under the direction of Larry Zimmerman and under contract with the Corps of Engineers, excavated the Crow Creek site beginning in August and continuing into early December. They began by cleaning and superimposing a horizontal grid system over the ditch containing the remains. The bone bed (consisting of an upper thinner deposit and a lower cone-shaped deposit) covered almost the entire area of the excavation and was up to 3 feet deep. Both bone layers were photographed and mapped. Articulated units of two or more bones, of which there were more than 700, were numbered and collected. The lower bone bed had proportionately more articulations (1,784 among 17,380 bones and bone fragments) and the upper bed had a greater number of skull fragments, suggesting that the upper layer was collected and deposited subsequent to the initial interment (Willey 1990). Publicity about the excavation drew a thousand people a day to the site, a number that dwindled to a few hundred a week. The reservation posted guards from its Bureau of Indian Affairs police force and five Sioux from the reservation were assisting in the excavation by September. When the question of whether a malevolent spirit who guarded graves was being disturbed, a Sioux holy man held a ritual in which he communicated with the spirit world through a skull from the site. After an all-night vigil, he announced that the spirit had been released long ago, that the bones were merely bones, and that the work should continue (Zimmerman and Alex 1981).

Of first priority were cranial measurements and nonmetric observations, postcranial measurements, and age and sex assessments (Willey 1990). An inventory of bone elements present was performed to determine the minimum number of individuals, with the understanding that some of the skulls may have been taken as souvenirs by the raiding tribe. All relatively complete Crow Creek skulls were reconstructed by Mark Swegle and P. Willey in January 1979. Measurements were taken on 104 skulls by Willey. A total of 67 of the skulls, for which a full complement of measurements were possible, was analyzed. The measurable skulls all appear to belong to a homogenous group, that of the village inhabitants. "No craniometric patterning based on location is present, so apparently the skulls were placed in the ditch without regard to cranial morphology and presumably without regard for kinship affiliation," Willey (1990) concludes. Age distributions show that the young males outnumber the young females, while the old females outnumber the old males. Femurs were measured to determine the number of each sex represented in the sample and resulted in a slight majority of males. The measurements were also used to analyze sexual dimorphism and compare Crow Creek with other sites, indicating that its value falls near the mean and that the statures of both sexes were average, but shorter than later Arikara.

A concerted effort was made to identify perimortem trauma that might indicate cause of death or mutilation (Willey 1990). In examining the bones, changes were considered in the following categories: congenital and developmental; degenerative processes; dental diseases; infectious and inflammatory; metabolic and nutritional; obstetric and gynecological; traumatic; and tumors. Skulls and mandibles were inspected for cuts, fractures, and evulsions. Cutting of the cranial vault was generally interpreted as scalping, from which no age group or sex was exempt. Nearly 90 percent of the skulls show indications of scalping, and since it has been shown that scalping without leaving marks on the bone is possible, the frequency may have approached 100 percent. If each scalping took two minutes, the 360 scalps taken at Crow Creek would have required at least 12 work-hours to remove. The Crow Creek specimens also show evidence of evulsion (removal of the teeth), cutting out of tongues, and decapitation (possibly of a quarter of the victims). Of the more complete skulls, 40 percent showed depressed fractures, some with as many as five depressions. Postcranial mutilations were also recorded and the missing ends of the long bones listed as being whole, chewed, splintered, or lost postmortem. Mutilations include dismemberment, cuts on the face, chewing (by scavengers), and charring. There were few projectile points associated with the bones and punctures left after the points were removed may have been easily overlooked.

Aside from the obvious trauma, the paleopathology of the skeletons reveals much about their lives and another possible reason for their deaths. Analysis shows that the inhabitants of the village were undernourished. They may have been raided by equally hungry neighbors desperate to get at stored food (Folsom and Folsom 1994). Ironically, the fact that the Crow Creek natives were cooperative and compassionate is inferred from the skeleton of a seven-year-old child with a badly dislocated hip, which suggests that those who became handicapped later in life were given communal support (Zimmerman and Alex 1981). Research into the health of past generations may lead to newer and better methods of treatment and prevention of these problems in the regional native population. "Examples of the applications of our analyses include determinations of biological relationships which support Indian land claims and understandings of prehistoric disease which could alleviate suffering among present-day Native Americans," explain Zimmerman and Alex (1981).

The limitations imposed on the Crow Creek excavation were criticized by scientists. Willey notes that the deadline imposed by the Sioux Tribal Council allowed only five months for analysis of the bones, sharply limiting the amount of data that could be gleaned from them. The analysis that was done raised questions which could not be answered in the short time frame. And yet Willey points out that two years after return of the remains, they still had not been reinterred, but during that period were unavailable to scientists. "When we all stand to benefit, the interests of one ethnic group should not be permitted to stand in the way. We must be able to do the most complete and comprehensive study of all human skeletons of all human groups," he writes (Willey 1981).

At the time of the Crow Creek find, the state was formalizing its guidelines regarding the dead. In 1976, the Council of South Dakota Archaeologists was formed and adopted a policy that only human remains endangered by factors such as construction activity or erosion could be excavated. Once removed, they would be analyzed and then reburied. Burials accidentally encountered would receive the same treatment. Ten years later, the Administrative Rules of South Dakota (ARSD) were implemented, requiring that recovered human skeletal remains be analyzed within five years of their discovery by a qualified expert who is compensated by the state. While the ARSD may be modified and further restrictions imposed, it has a provision for retaining skeletal materials beyond this five-year time limit if the remains are from mass burials or of extreme importance (Willey 1990), a clause written too late to benefit the Crow Creek researchers. The Crow Creek remains were repatriated by the established deadline of May 31, 1979. They were reburied on August 10, 1981, in six concrete burial vaults on the land where they had lived. Public and private Christian and traditional Lakota ceremonies were conducted. A memorial plaque marks the site, which is administered by the U.S. Army Corps of Engineers.

2

Excavations

Much has been learned about the recent and distant past through the analysis of excavated human skeletal material. As excavation techniques improve, the recovery of remains is more thorough and more contextual information is preserved. Concurrently, technological innovations allow more detailed inferences to be made from bones and provide less labor-intensive means to locate them underground. And continued land development reveals cemeteries which offer anthropologists and archaeologists the opportunity — in such cases often hurried — to study past populations. Sometimes time puts a constraint on the recovery of human bones. Other times excavation is compromised by looting or a lack of funds. But in a great number of cases, excavation and study of human bones are subject to political pressures exerted by the biological, cultural, or spiritual descendants of the remains or members of the racial or geographical group to which they have been assigned. These pressures may result in repatriation at the expense of research.

Some excavated series, such as that at Dickson Mounds, have built up a long and impressive history of research prior to the passage of NAGPRA and mandated repatriation. Prehistoric and protohistoric Native American remains have been examined for patterns of nutrition, infant death rates, and pathologies including degenerative changes. Neandertal remains are compared with those of other hominids to properly place them within our evolutionary history. Nineteenth-century remains have shown differences in the lives of the underprivileged (as indicated by the health status of a poorhouse population) and in their deaths (as evidenced by the casual discard of dissected remains). Excavations of historic battlegrounds, such as that of Little Bighorn, shed light on the past that can be cross-checked with the written record to arrive at a more three-dimensional recreation. Excavations of modern mass graves by forensic anthropologists provide disturbing reconstructions of human rights abuses, but also serve the important purposes of bringing the abusers to justice and answering the long-asked questions of survivors through establishing identities of the remains.

The interpretation of skeletal remains is in many ways dependent on the care with which they are recovered, as Stephen P. Nawrocki (1995) points out: "Anyone with experience in the excavation of human remains knows that the skeleton rarely looks as good in the lab as it did just before it was removed from the ground. The simple act of opening the burial exposes the bones to the above-ground environment, where sun-baking and precipitation can create more damage in just a few hours than the skeleton suffered in all of its years beneath the soil. Scratches, nicks, and cuts from trowels frequently occur and can later be mistaken for

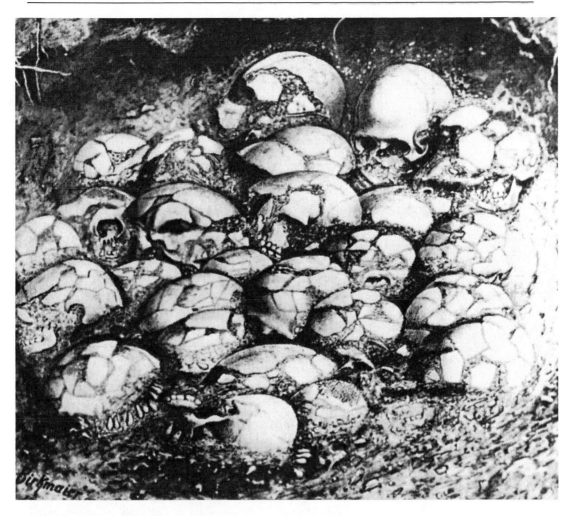

A drawing of a nest of prehistoric skulls found in the Ofnet cave between Augsburg and Nuremberg, Germany, in 1908. Reprinted with permission of Thames & Hudson from *The Human Skull: A Cultural History,* **by Folke Henschen (New York: Frederick A. Praeger, 1965).**

perimortem trauma. Packaging, transport, and cleaning all may negatively affect the remains." Rather than probing the soil until bone is struck, scientists today use much more sophisticated methods to locate underground skeletons. These include ground-penetrating radar, the proton magnetometer to measure soil resistivity, and the proverbial probe — but one with a metal sphere on the end to detect a change in soil resistance (Ubelaker 1995). Vapor detection and remote sensing, such as infrared aerial photography, have also been used and principles of botany, geology, and entomology applied to the search.

The recovery of human remains should follow the best practices of the field. After any necessary permits are obtained and any preliminary research, testing, and clearing of underbrush conducted, all surface bone should be collected from a potential site. Signs that may reveal subsurface features should be noted, particularly when the site is being sampled for selective excavation. Buried skeletons should be exposed entirely before removal (Bass 1987). The outline of the pit should be defined and recorded, then excavated slowly downward by removing soil inside the pit or clearing a large area around it (Ubelaker 1989). Right and left components of the skeleton should be placed in separate containers and the vertebrae should be bagged by type. The cranium and mandible should each be packed separately and any teeth that have become dislodged should be kept with the jaw that lost them. All containers (preferably paper bags in the short term) should be labeled with water-proof ink with the site name, burial or feature number, date, excavator, and contents (Bass 1987, Ubelaker 1989). Earth from the abdominal region of all skeletons should be screened to recover dietary or fetal skeletal remains, and the rest of the soil from the site should be screened to recover any missing small bones or fragments (White 1991).

Almost as important as the bones themselves is the context, evidence of which should be retained. A written record following recommended data collection standards should be kept. The exact location of each burial should be recorded in both horizontal and vertical dimensions after mapping or superimposing a grid over the site. Deposition (the overall configuration of the body in the ground, for instance on the left side) and position (the relationship of the parts of the body to each other, for instance flexed) should be described. Orientation (the direction in which the head lies, or faces if seated), depth from the surface, and all measurements that will aid in description or possible reconstruction should also be recorded (Ubelaker 1989). Polaroid photos should be taken as insurance against the loss of conventional photographs, with either type useful in later reconstructions of the scene. Photos should be taken in both black and white and color, and should include direction indicators and size scale. Water may be sprayed on the soil to heighten the contrast between it and embedded bones (White 1991). Any hair adhering to the skull should be removed and placed in an airtight container (Brothwell 1981). Soil samples should be gathered for later analysis. As much dirt as possible should be removed from bones at the time of recovery and dirt should never be left inside the skull (Bass 1987). Bones should be washed and then allowed to dry in the shade. They may be fanned, but should never be heated (White 1991). Bones should never be treated with a preservative in the field, although they may be recovered in situ by creating a plaster jacket around them (Bass 1987) or by undercutting the entire feature and removing it intact (Ubelaker 1989).

Earlier excavators were not as meticulous or methodical as contemporary ones. English wool merchant William Cunnington opened no fewer than 465 British burial mounds, sometimes several a day, to indulge his antiquarian interests (Fagan 1996). Skeletal excavations today — and the records kept as they are conducted, if the remains are reburied — allow scientists of many disciplines to assess whether an ancient society practiced human sacrifice or cannibalism; whether a society was matrilocal or patrilocal; whether members of a prehistoric society only a few generations or many centuries removed abused their children; and whether a modern society betrayed its citizens by indiscriminately taking their lives. The bones of those who died naturally, accidentally, or homicidally will often give up their secrets if excavated, handled, documented, and interpreted with care.

PREHISTORIC AND PROTOHISTORIC SITES

Many prehistoric skeletal finds seem familiar to us because they have been given nicknames: Lucy, Peking Man, Taung Child, Turkana Boy. In fact, how familiar the original owners of these remains were to our modern selves is still debated, with gaps filled in as new finds are made. In some cases, bones offer proof of such esoteric characteristics as the ability to speak and weaning age. In other cases, researchers contest whether damage to bones indicates cultural cannibalism or scavenging by animals. Fossil remains can be dated numerically, resulting in an age in years and an error range, or relatively, resulting in a sequence. Most important, in many ways, is to determine the relationships between and among peoples so that sense can be made from the sketchy skeletal evidence of the peopling of the planet. But these relationships must span not just centuries, but millennia: Phillip Tobias noted in 1982 that South African hominids were represented by 511 individuals spanning more than 3 million years — an average of one individual for every 5,871 years (Pfeiffer 1991). As Alan Walker and Pat Shipman (1996) put it, "The irony of paleoanthropology is that most of the links are missing."

The human fossil record constitutes a collection in itself, but one that is nowhere near complete and never assembled in a single location. Paleoanthropologists must make several stops worldwide to examine the specimens, and then only if they have been granted access. Eugene Dubois (d. 1940) was notorious for denying legitimate scientific access to the fossils he found in Java, leading to rumors that he had destroyed them, when in fact they were hidden inside cabinets in his dining room. His reluctance to share is understood, if not condoned: "Anthropologists who deal with human fossils tend to get very emotionally involved with their bones," offers Donald Johanson. "Fossils that you have found, particularly skulls, are like your children. That is why fossil finders guard them so jealously and love to give them new names," write Walker and Shipman (1996). Louis Leakey was very protective of his fossils, keeping them locked in a safe in his office and exhibiting them to researchers at his own discretion. After assuming directorship of the Kenya National Museums, his son Richard Leakey discontinued the practice of shipping the fossils

to qualified scientists for study and only allowed them out of the museum in extraordinary circumstances, forcing those scholars to travel to Africa. Tours taken to examine the original fossil evidence around the world are not common, but are persuasive. Wilfrid Le Gros Clark's examination of the full range of Australopithecine material in South Africa in 1947 left him doubting his own convictions (Tattersall 1995). But even researchers able to make such a pilgrimage may be thwarted. Milford Wolpoff boasts that a grant from the National Science Foundation in 1978 allowed him the opportunity to examine firsthand every hominid fossil that existed at the time of his four-year tour (Shreeve 1996). But on Christopher Stringer's earlier three-month trip around Europe in 1971 to examine ancient hominid fossils, he found that some important material was completely unavailable for study (Lewin 1993).

Fossil skeletal remains are most often curated at the institution with which the discoverer is affiliated. The fossils discovered by the Leakey family are housed in the National Museums of Kenya in Nairobi. Those that are not on display are kept locked in a vault known as the "chapel," which is thickly carpeted to protect any specimen that is accidentally dropped. The fossils are stored in labeled, foam-lined wooden boxes organized by site and locality. The skeleton of the *Australopithecus afarensis* specimen known as Lucy — the oldest, most complete, and best-preserved skeleton of any erect-walking human ancestor that has ever been found — was kept in a padded box in a safe in Donald Johanson's office at the Cleveland Museum of Natural History, with a cast of the fossil placed on display. "Lucy always managed to look interesting in her little yellow nest — but to a nonprofessional, not overly impressive," Johanson is quoted as saying (Lewin 1997). "There were other bones all around her in the Cleveland Museum. She was dwarfed by them, by drawer after drawer of fossils, hundreds of them from Hadar alone."

Milford Wolpoff of the University of Michigan Department of Anthropology pictured with prehistoric skulls. Photo courtesy of the University of Michigan.

In 1984, the American Museum of Natural History succeeded in bringing together a remarkable number of original hominid fossils, among them Lucy's skeleton and a group of more than a dozen skeletons discovered at the same site in 1975 and nicknamed the "First Family." The goal was ambitious, as Roger Lewin (1997) describes:

> The so-called *Ancestors* exhibition was years in the planning and deep in the agonizing, because it involved persuading museum curators the world over to part briefly with their priceless and fragile relics, which would be shipped to New York and placed on public view, some for the first time ever. Curators arrived at John F. Kennedy Airport, having carefully cradled their charges in first-class seats, to be met by a motorcade of limousines and police escort. No VIP had more attentive care and reception.

A dozen anthropologists at a time were allowed to examine the fossils during a workshop held before the exhibit opened to the public, from whom they were protected by bulletproof glass. To have had the opportunity to actually touch and hold the fossils was described as a very emotional experience, but to at least be able to examine them visually in a single location was unique.

As difficult as it is to discover hominid remains, it is even harder to recover complete skeletons, which is why so many curated specimens are fragmentary. Walker and Shipman (1996) point out that prior to deliberate burial, bodies were at the mercy of carnivores and natural destructive processes, with the ribs least likely to survive. Ian Tattersall (1995) explains, "As fossils erode out of the enclosing sediments they are attacked by the elements and begin to fall to pieces, however complete they may have been to begin with. And complete they will rarely have been, since most fossil bones represent the remains of some ancient carnivore's dinner or have otherwise had a checkered postmortem career." Theories of the evolution of *Homo sapiens* are therefore based mainly on small groups of incomplete skeletons, the interpretation and classification of which are contentious issues.

Paleoanthropologists debate whether human ancestry began in Africa or in China. They accuse each other of overinterpretation of the fossil evidence, for instance inferences about family structure and whether they purposely buried their dead. "There is and always has been far more fleshing out of the course and cause of human evolution than can fully be justified by the scrappy skeletons provided by the fossils," says Roger Lewin (1997). They argue over

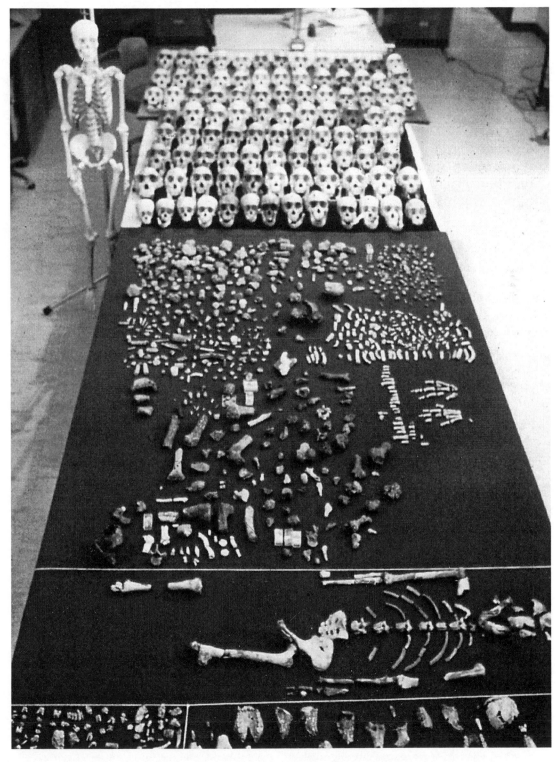

Fossils laid out at the American Museum of Natural History, including the "First Family" and "Lucy."
Reprinted with permission of the Institute of Human Origins.

whether distinct populations interbred, merely coexisted, or replaced each other by attrition or aggression. "It's often a question of who looks at the fossil material, and what they want to see," remarks Christopher Stringer (Lewin 1993). Judgment may be clouded by the relationship of the scientists to the fossils they are attempting to make sense of. Many of the disputes, though, have arisen over attaching dates to fossil hominid remains. The gaps left between the reliability of radiocarbon dating (to 30,000 to 40,000 years ago) and potassium-argon dating (1 million years or more), coupled with the poor provenance of some of the specimens, leave a lot of uncertainties, some of which are being clarified by new techniques such as thermoluminescence and electron spin resonance (Lewin 1993).

Neandertal remains are among the most prevalent and perhaps the most debated, from whether they practiced cannibalism to whether they interbred with other species. The bones of more than 200 members of this group, which thrived for about 100,000 years, have been found since their first discovery in 1856. It was the discovery of the skeleton of the "Old Man of La Chapelle" in 1908 that led to the characterization of Neandertals as hunched-over cavemen. While they did commonly seek shelter in caves, the stooped posture of that particular individual was later attributed to arthritis. Other pathologies diagnosed from Neandertal bones indicate healed injuries that would not have been survivable without help, indicating a caring community. Those who died appear to have been buried ritualistically, suggesting to some the beginnings of a spiritual or religious sense. And the Neandertals had the ability to speak, based on the discovery of the first complete hyoid bone and its comparison to modern humans.

While their species assignment is often disputed, raising questions of how "human" they are, ancient hominid remains have added immeasurably to the store of knowledge about prehistoric life. It is the fossils that usually capture the imagination, more than the theories about their origin and the technological intricacies of their analysis. Biochemists attempting to explain human lineage through analysis of the genetic makeup of the fossil record are characterized as relying too heavily on mathematical formulae that assume steady rates and their research is considered abstract and remote from the bones themselves. Thus the physical remnants of Lucy may be thought of as having more presence than the hypothetical "Eve" (technically the "mitochondrial DNA lineage coalescent point") who began the line of descent that stretches from more than 100,000 years ago to today.

Many sites yield quantities of skeletons with research potential that grows with time and opportunity. A limestone cave in Atapuerca, Spain, called the "Sima de los Huesos" ("Pit of the Bones") has produced more than 1,600 bones from at least 32 individuals of an archaic *Homo sapiens* species. The fossils — remarkable for their quantity, completeness, and marked variation in size and form — were found at the bottom of a shaft with layers dating from 200,000 to 300,000 years ago. An ancient cemetery outside Jerusalem dating to between 700 and 750 B.C. contained the skeletons of about 2,000 individuals, some of whose crania show blunt force trauma and three of which exhibit trephination. In the first half of the twentieth century, 3,051 burials dating between 1050 and 1650 A.D. were excavated from within mounds and from cemeteries outside the plaza at Moundville, Alabama (Pearson 1999). In La Chaussée-Tirancourt, France, a well-preserved megalithic tomb was found to contain more than 360 burials that had accumulated between 2800 and 2100 B.C. (Pearson 1999). During his excavations of the Royal Cemetery at Ur in Iraq from 1922 to 1934, Sir Charles Leonard Woolley (d. 1960) discovered dozens of male and female human skeletons dating from 2500 B.C. and exemplifying the practice of retainer sacrifice.

In modern times many excavations are conducted under salvage conditions, such as the large numbers of remains recovered in Nubia in advance of the construction of the Aswan Dam on the Nile. As important as careful digging in such hurried circumstances is the standardized data collection from the skeletal specimens so that they can continue to be of use even if the time allotted for their physical analysis is limited. The same thing is true of material excavated by previous generations, since there is no guarantee that fossils tens or even hundreds of thousands of years old will necessarily be around forever. For instance, some of the Neandertal skeletal evidence has been lost, including a collection of over 25 skeletons from the 26,000-year-old site of Predmosti that was destroyed by the Germans during World War II, despite Czech attempts to safeguard the specimens (Shreeve 1996). With the continued availability of many Aboriginal remains at stake, the data from those that can and have been examined are being recorded in minute detail. In 1983, P.J. Key produced an exhaustive synthesis of around 1,000 Plains Indian crania, leading to the formation of a comprehensive Plains craniometric data base. In spite of such tools, there are several populations that will probably remain untapped, including more than 200 undisturbed ossuaries in Ontario, Canada alone (Ubelaker 1989).

Peking Man at Zhoukoudien, China

One of the sites that has been productively excavated for decades is that of the caves in Zhoukoudien (previously Chou K'ou Tien or "Dragon Bone Hill") in China. This was the site where the fossils of "Peking Man" were found, but those remains were lost in unique circumstances during World War II. Luckily the bones were analyzed, photographed, and cast by Franz Weiden-

reich, and the find has been complemented by numerous subsequent discoveries of *Homo erectus* remains. At one point, between 100 and 200 people were working at two or three individual sites spread over two square kilometers (Walker and Shipman 1996).

Peking Man was found during excavations conducted between 1921 and 1937. The first find of human fossils was made in 1921 by Austrian paleontologist Otto Zdansky, who kept the find secret until 1926. A braincase was finally found in 1929 and work continued until 1937, by which time 14 skulls had been excavated (Tattersall 1995). Between 1930 and 1935, the dig was overseen by Weidenreich, who succeeded Davidson Black (d. 1934) of Peking Union Medical College (PUMC). Under Weidenriech's direction, the remains of more than 45 individuals (represented by 15 skulls or skull fragments, 14 lower jaws, numerous postcranial bones, and 147 teeth) were recovered from the rock shelter, which was inhabited some 400,000 to 600,000 years ago (although the age and span of the site still require clarification).

After the Japanese invaded China in 1937, only a skeleton crew continued working at the Zhoukoudian site and in the following year the site was left to a few local caretakers. Weng Wenhao, director of the Geological Survey of China, asked Weidenreich to take the Peking Man fossils with him when he left the country. The fossils were packed up by the only remaining member of the research team and a Chinese laboratory assistant. Over three days, the specimens were checked against an inventory list, wrapped, and placed in cardboard boxes. The boxes were packed in two redwood crates. One box contained fossils from the Upper Cave (including five skulls and the vertebrae of at least eight individuals) and the other contained *Sinanthropus* remains (including five skulls, approximately 150 jaw fragments and teeth, nine thigh bones and fragments, two upper arm bones, a collar bone, and a wrist bone). Both boxes were padlocked and transported by car to Marine Headquarters in Peking days before the Japanese took over the PUMC campus. The collection was transferred to regulation marine footlockers to await a transport train bound for the port city of Chinwangtao, 140 miles away. There they were to be stored at Camp Holcomb until they could be escorted to the Philippines aboard troop ship *U.S.S. President Harrison*, after which they were to be stored at the American Museum of Natural History in New York for safekeeping. On December 8, 1941, the 18 Americans at the camp were forced to surrender to the Japanese. Tragically, the ship was sunk en route to port, and the fossils — if, as many believe, they were on board — went down with it. The Upper Cave remains arrived in Tokyo in early 1942, but the Peking man remains were missing (Janus 1975).

In the 1970s, Chicago stockbroker Christopher Janus attempted to solve the mystery of the missing Peking Man fossils and wrote a popular book (Janus 1975) about his adventures. When Janus and colleagues were admitted into China in 1972, they were taken to the Peking Man Museum and shown the caves where the fossils had been found. After leaving China, Janus offered a $5,000 reward for information leading to the recovery of the fossils. He received a call from a widow who claimed that her husband, a marine, had left the fossils in their attic, and backed up her claim with a plausible photograph. Janus was also contacted by a Chinese man who told him that the fossils were in Taiwan and that their value was political as much as scientific. Others had led Janus to believe the fossils were in Tokyo, Hong Kong, New York, or still in China. In 1973, the F.B.I. issued a report to the State Department relaying the possibility that the Peking Man fossils were in the care of the wife of a Nationalist Chinese Army officer. Janus had become convinced that the whereabouts of the fossils was not known to the Chinese or the Taiwanese, but

he was equally sure that the fossils were not at the Nationalist Chinese museums. He found the idea that the fossils were lost in the confusion of the takeover of Camp Holcomb or were sunk in the Yellow Sea to be "too convenient" (Janus 1975). Janus pled guilty in 1981 to two counts of an indictment charging misuse of $640,000 he had raised to search for the missing fossils.

Perhaps the best course of action is searching the caves for any remaining fragments in the continued absence of the crania themselves. "Excavations at Zhoukoudian have been reopened and a few new pieces have been found that would clearly fit onto the original skulls, if only they could be found. I hope they rest somewhere, still intact, where they will be stumbled across and recognized" (Walker and Shipman 1996). The Zhoukoudian site consists of a number of caves clustered in a range of low hills 50 km southwest of Beijing. The excavated sample is one of the largest human collections from a single site and remarkable for its diversity. The site was occupied for some 250,000 years. The detailed notes recorded by Weidenreich make it one of the best described and analyzed fossil human collections (Wolpoff 1996).

Iron Age Remains in Denmark

As in other countries until relatively recently, Danish archaeologists did not always find it necessary to save excavated human bones and when they did, they usually recovered only the skull (Sellevold, Hansen, and Jørgensen 1984). Despite this practice, a large and well-documented collection has built up over the years. Most of the bones are housed in the Anthropological Collection at the University of Copenhagen, including skeletal remains transferred from the National Museum, with a smaller part of the material deposited in the National Museum and Danish provincial museums. A portion of the material dates from the Iron Age, from the beginning of the Pre-Roman period to the end of the Viking period (about 500 B.C. to 1050 A.D.), and includes 30 skeletonized bog bodies. In total, Iron Age skeletal finds total 1,016, of which 334 are males, 246 are females, and 436 are of undetermined sex. There are 844 adults and 172 children (Sellevold, Hansen, and Jørgensen 1984).

Examination of the skeletal material included macroscopic observations, measurements, and recording of nonmetric traits. Although few observations of nonmetric traits were recorded for material found before the 1950s, "The morphological differences found between the Iron Age groups are probably for the most part caused by differences in the environment. The nonmetric analyses show that the genetic differences are small between the Iron Age groups," conclude Sellevold, Hansen, and Jørgensen (1984). Among the 1,016 age-determined skeletons, 172 had not reached biological maturity. X-rays were taken in a few cases. Analysis has shown that the skeletal material is not representative of the population of the country as a whole, either geographically or chronologically due to varying preservation, the use of cremation, and weak representation in certain periods. But the collection does include some interesting specimens. Sixteen of the Iron Age skeletons were found face down. The Iron Age material includes three possible cases of artificially deformed skulls, three cases of trephinations, and four cases of anthropologically verifiable decapitations (Sellevold, Hansen, and Jørgensen 1984).

A several-volume reference work catalogs all of the Danish skeletal material, including provenance, excavators, associated grave goods, pathologies, and references in the scholarly literature. The collection includes the following Iron Age finds (Sellevold, Hansen and Jørgensen 1984):

- Fraugde: A cemetery with 79 graves, of which nine were inhumations and 50 urn cremations. Investigated by C. Neergaard and G.V. Blom in 1896–97 and dated mostly to the Late Roman period.

- Kannikegård: A large cemetery comprising about 800 cremation patches, 44 inhumations, and 120 other graves investigated by E. Vedel in 1870–76. Material from only two of the graves has been preserved.

- Lousgård: Fifty graves, of which all but one were inhumations, investigated in 1886 by E. Vedel and J.A. Jørgensen and in 1950 by C.J. Becker. Material from two of the graves is preserved.

- Mosede Fort: A large cemetery containing about 50 flat inhumation graves investigated in 1913 by H. Kjaer, G. Rosenberg, C. Neergaar, and G. Raklev. A total of 45 of the graves had preserved skeletal material.

- Slusegård: A large cemetery containing hundreds of inhumation graves from which 115 incomplete skeletons were recovered and additional cremation graves investigated in 1958–64 by O. Klindt-Jensen. A maxilla from one of the graves had an iron point embedded in it. Another skeleton shows signs of decapitation. Several skulls were deformed postmortem and one was microcephalic.

- Stengade II: A large cemetery comprising 122 inhumation graves and 12 cremation graves excavated in 1972–73 by J. Skaarup. Preserved skeletal material was found in 71 of the graves.

- Trelleborg: A cemetery containing at least 132 tightly spaced and shallow graves, some of which contained the remains of more than one individual. Investigated in 1934–42 by P. Nørlund, it was excavated in 1938 and 1939.

Analysis of the Iron Age remains has been broken down by period to indicate changing physical characteristics, demographic trends, and burial practices. In the Pre-Roman Period (500 B.C. to 0), cremation was the prevailing form of burial in Denmark and none of the skeletons were found in proper graves. The Early Roman Period (0 to 160–170 A.D.) is represented by 359 reliably-dated skeletons found in 86 different locations across the country. More than 41 percent of the skeletons were oriented with the head to the north. Of the 214 sex-determined Early Roman skeletons, 134 are males and 80 are females, with no immediate explanation for the imbalance. More than 16 percent are subadults. The Late Roman Period (160–170 A.D. to ca. 400 A.D.) is represented by 199 skeletons found at 93 sites. Of the 120 sex-determined skeletons, 66 are male and 54 female. More than 20 percent are subadults. Ninety skeletons could not be placed in either the Early or Late Roman Periods. Of the 42 sex-determined skeletons in this group, 57.1 percent are males and 42.9 percent are females. Subadults totaled 36.8 percent. Both Early and Late Roman Period skulls are pronouncedly long and narrow, of medium height, with high and narrow facial skeletons. The Late Germanic Period (ca. 550–575 to ca. 800 A.D.) is represented by 30 skeletons from 11 sites. The Viking Period (ca. 800–1050 A.D.) is represented by 320 skeletons with a male to female ratio of 116:100. The Viking skulls are short, broad, and round and two thirds of the Viking skeletons were oriented with heads to the west (Sellevold, Hansen, and Jørgensen 1984).

Early Hawaiians of Oahu

For many years, Hawaii's Bishop Museum curated ancient Native Hawaiian remains that had been found in the sand dunes of Mokapu both accidentally and through deliberate excavation. Most of these remains have been repatriated. Human skeletal material was first accessioned in 1921,

when Edward S.C. Handy brought to Bishop Museum a human skeleton that had been buried close to the sea near Mokapu Peninsula. The skeleton was in poor condition and was subsequently discarded. Human remains of five individuals from the Heleloa sand dunes on the Mokapu peninsula were donated to the Bishop museum by unknown donors between 1915 and 1932. In 1932, the museum acquired two skulls, and two mandibles that had been excavated by curator Edwin H. Bryan, Jr., and David F. Thrum after Mokapu resident Harold Kainalu Castle found burials in the Heleloa dunes near his house. A skull was found in a sand hummock near Heleloa by Fred E. Harvey in 1933 and additional material from the area was accessioned the following year.

In 1938, museum ethnologist Kenneth P. Emory accessioned eight skulls that had been discovered by Keith K. Jones, Jr., in the He'eia dunes on the Mokapu Peninsula. Emory made a three-day exploratory excavation at the site of the discovery that same year, recovering the remains of approximately 40 individuals. A more thorough excavation followed in October, for which Emory enlisted the help of staff and students at the University of Hawaii, including physical anthropologist Gordon T. Bowles. Over the next 15 months, a total of 401 remains were recovered (although the *Federal Register* of 1998 records that a total of 799 skeletons were excavated). A total of 64 of these were discovered as a result of commercial sand removal during preparations to build a naval air station on the peninsula. No excavation notes were published due to the outbreak of World War II, but summary reports indicate that the skeletons included men, women, and children and were found in both extended and flexed positions. The remains were housed in a safe mausoleum chamber provided by the Bishop Museum.

From 1939 to 1940, the undocumented remains of 184 individuals were brought to

Skulls of early Hawaiians. Reprinted with permission from *Early Hawaiians: An Initial Study of Skeletal Remains from Mokapu, Oahu,* **by Charles Snow (Lexington: University Press of Kentucky, 1974).**

Charles Snow and his assistant with the skeletal remains of early Hawaiians from Mokapu. Reprinted from the *Honolulu Star Bulletin*.

the museum by residents and visitors. In 1942, the remains of 222 unidentified individuals from Mokapu and other locations on Oahu were donated to the Bishop Museum by unknown donors. The skeletal material was stored at the museum and each bone marked with an identifying number and a letter indicating the location in which it was found, when known. In 1957, Robert N. Bowen of the University of Hawaii conducted a second major excavation under salvage conditions during the enlargement of the Marine Corps golf course in 1957. The one-month dig recovered the remains of 116 individuals (although the *Federal Register* of 1998 records that 186 skeletons were excavated), bringing the total in the Bishop Museum collection to more than 1,000. Unfortunately, half of the excavated burials had been partially or completely disturbed by bulldozers and could therefore not be recorded properly (Snow 1974).

Between 1957 and 1969, ten more museum accessions of skeletal material came

from Mokapu. In 1975, remains of 108 unidentified individuals were recovered during a construction project on Ulupa'u, Mokapu. From 1952 to1993, the remains of 78 unidentified individuals from unknown locations were donated to the Bishop Museum from unknown sources and curated as "isolated burials" within the Mokapu collection (*Federal Register* 1998). Until 1957, the bones were not stored as individual burials but were boxed by type of bone. After the bones were reassembled into individual burials, a census was taken. The result was a total of 1,171 individuals, some of which were represented by only a single skeletal element. Of the total group, 28 percent were under 20.6 years of age and 72 percent were 20.6 years or older. The life span was approximately 32 years for men and 29 years for women. The men averaged 5 feet 7 inches and the women 5 feet 3 inches. The population had relatively large heads and a distinctive curvature of the mandible called a "rocker jaw." The Mokapu bones and skulls are remarkably well-preserved, with only a few light, "chalky" bones (Snow 1974).

The skeletons had been recovered from dune areas, which were considered useless by the early Hawaiians for purposes other than burial, since they were incapable of food production. The dead were therefore buried in sandy coastal areas and inland areas having sufficient soil cover. These sites, usually some distance from residences, were often used for long periods of time. Popularly believed to represent war dead, the remains are now known to be the cumulative dead of coastal Hawaiian communities. Most of the burials were primary, but three secondary burials were found. "These secondary bones were not worked and show no signs of having been polished. They may have been parts of burials exposed by the wind, which were reburied; they may have been reburied by vandals; or they may have been keepsakes which were returned when affection waned" (Snow 1974). It was not uncommon for a relative to recover skeletal material, exhuming the body of a loved one and removing the leg bones and skull, washing them in water, and enclosing them in a pillow (Snow 1974).

Considerable variation in body position existed within the community and within extended families. Exact body positions were different in each case, with some found extended on their backs and sides and some found flexed on their sides. The remains of a heavily-muscled male show that colored pigments may have been used occasionally, either prior to burial or at the grave site. The entire surface of the skull was stained with a fine wash of red clay, which was most intense on the upper surfaces of the cranium and the mandible (Snow 1974). Many of the skulls (44 percent) showed signs of deliberate head-shaping, and other cultural practices are evident. Missing shafts from Mokapu bones may have been removed to make objects. The literature of Polynesian peoples include numerous ref-

erences to fashioning useful or ornamental objects from human bones and teeth. Bones were used to make fishhooks, for instance, and the lack of any skeletal fragments during excavation indicate that bones vandalized for artifact material were not broken up at the site (Snow 1974).

The result of burial in sand is that the preservation of the bones is excellent. They are easily excavated, despite apparent attempts to conceal the Mokapu graves by not marking them in any way. The only difficulty has been dating the remains, since the dune burials are intrusive and unstratified among themselves (Snow 1974). Charles E. Snow hoped to apply radiocarbon dating to the Mokapu sites to provide a basic chronological framework, but such testing has been precluded: "Northeast trade winds relentlessly expose burials to erosion, and human destruction, which began with Hawaiians themselves, continues." Because the sites are located on federal land, the remains are protected by federal laws and have been claimed for reburial by Native Hawaiian groups. While the Mokapu bones were in the custody of the Bishop Museum, they were studied intensively and compared to similar collections. The Mokapu series is extensive and valuable for being representative of a breeding isolate. Features that have been observed in the bones include large-sized bones, chipped and broken teeth, arthritis in the spine, and squatting facets at hips, knees, and ankles. Characteristics that are possibly genetic include nose bone anomalies, large-sized teeth, shovel-shaped incisors, and rocker jaws (Snow 1974). The skeletons form a large, statistically representative sample of an early Hawaiian population on windward Oahu. The absence of any European trade objects indicate that the burials precede any contact with white men and can therefore be dated prior to 1778 when Captain James Cook and crew arrived. Fluorine tests suggest a date of from 200 to 800 years ago (Snow 1974).

There will probably be little opportunity for analysis in the future. The National Park Service takes its legal responsibilities very seriously, as Geraldine K. Bell, Superintendant of the Pu'uhonua o Honaunau National Historic Park, explains (personal correspondence August 18, 1999):

> The treatment of human remains is definitely a major concern of Native Hawaiians.... Federal agencies routinely consult with two organizations, the Office of Hawaiian Affairs (OHA) and Hui Malama i na Kupuna o Hawaii Nei, both of which are named specifically in NAGPRA. The third organizations with which federal agencies in Hawaii usually consult is whichever of the State–appointed Island Burial Councils is appropriate to the particular case.... In recent years, and especially since the passage of NAGPRA, the National Park Service, like most agencies, firms, and private citizens, have made every effort to respect Hawaiians' wishes regarding the treatment of the remains of their ancestors. Accordingly, whenever possible, inadvertently discovered human remains are covered and left in place, and their locations are noted in confidential documents to reduce the likelihood of future disturbance. When it becomes necessary, remains are moved and reburied elsewhere with appropriate prayers and other ceremonial observances. The preparation, treatment, and ceremonies usually take place in private to show respect for the deceased. For this reason, whenever possible, we in the National Park Service customarily treat the information pertaining to such matters as confidential, to be used only in ways that are acceptable to the appropriate Hawaiian communities and organizations and in accord with our stewardship responsibilities under law.

The *Federal Register* (1998) records that a NAGPRA inventory of human remains at the Bishop Museum was conducted by the U.S. Marine Corps and museum staff in consultation with representatives of Hui Malama i na Kupuna O Hawai Nei and the Office of Hawaiian Affairs. Based on skeletal and cranial morphology, dentition, style and type of associated funerary objects, manner of interments, and recovery locations, the human remains were determined to be Native Hawaiian, although none of them could be individually identified. The inventory of a minimum of 1,582 individuals was distributed to representatives of several Native Hawaiian organizations, who were asked to submit their claims of cultural affiliation to the staff archaeologist at the Marine Corps Base at Kaneohe Bay by May 22, 1998.

Kolomoki Mounds in Blakely, Georgia

What is now Kolomoki Mounds State Historic Park in southwestern Georgia was once occupied by Swift Creek and Weeden Island Native Americans. Approximately 1,500 to 2,000 residents lived in the village. The three-hundred acre site includes "Unit 29," a fully excavated refuse pit, at the bottom of which was a burial. At the center of the site is "Mound D Midden," a deposit rich in ceramics and topped by a large burial mound. The most elaborate at the site, Mound D stood 20 feet high and was 100 feet in diameter. It included both primary burials and cremations covered with rocks and earth, resulting in a flat-topped mound. Cremation was quite thorough, with all bones altered to a bluish white color and a brittle texture. Three mass cremations were also found in Mound D, with disarticulated long bones and skulls present (Sears 1956).

An additional 40 skulls were discovered within the mound and may have been trophy skulls of enemies or the heads of important members of the community. The presence of facial ornaments lead researchers to believe that the heads were still fleshed when placed in the mound, since they could not have been kept in place without the flesh and hair. Seven skulls were found sitting on hands that had the forearms attached. The creation of Mound D was an ongoing process. A brochure explains, "The mound was built in one continuous operation to bury a leader along with sacrificed servants, trophy skulls, slaves, and wives. The remains of additional people, whose bodies had been stored in the temple awaiting burial, were included in the mound." It is estimated that a minimum labor force of nearly 1,000 people would have been required to deposit the existing amount of earth and to carry out the retainer sacrifices and partial cremations that went on concurrently. Radiocarbon dating in 1956 indicated that construction on the mound began in 30 A.D. (±300 years).

The Kolomoki Mounds excavations were conducted between 1949 and 1952 and directed by William H. Sears of the University of Georgia. The five seasons of digging yielded more than 85 burials. Each of the mounds appears to have been structured around a main burial which was then accompanied by a number of retainer burials. Some seventeen such retainer burials were uncovered in Mound D, which was restored to its original height after excavation. Three retainer burials and two possible trophy skulls were found in Mound E. The three major classes of secondary burials found at the Mounds therefore included single skulls, bundles of long bones, and deposits of thoroughly cremated and fragmentary bones (Sears 1956).

Mound E was the first of the mounds to be excavated and is now visible from inside the park's museum. A short film explains the burial ritual and the mound has been cut away so that the burial pit can be viewed from an observation deck. Radiocarbon dating in 1956 indicated that the mound was begun in 170 B.C. (±300 years). The original bones have been taken to the University of West Georgia in Carrollton for study and replicas put in their place, explains park manager Eric Bentley (personal communication, August 12, 1999).

Dickson Mounds near Lewistown, Illinois

To see Dickson Mounds was a moving experience. To study it was intellectually stimulating. To have the burial exhibition removed from display and permanently entombed in place was a victory for Native Americans, but a loss in the continued quest for knowledge about the human condition, past and present. Now the more than 200 skeletons are separated from the scientists who are able to unlock their potential by a cedar flooring. To the Native Americans they have been given the respect they deserve and instead of being violated by probing analysis, they are commemorated by a multi-dimensional presentation about their spiritual beliefs and the ongoing lives of their descendants. But the focus on life has not always been the case.

Dickson Mounds took its name from the Dickson Family, but the history of the site begins long before the excavation of the burials by Don F. Dickson. The mounds originally began as a cemetery, with graves dug into the hill surface of a blufftop northwest of the confluence of the Illinois and Spoon rivers. Burial mounds were added later, two of which were partially exposed by the Dickson excavation. It is suspected that most of the burials were placed in prepared graves and probably that individual mounds were built and then filled with graves. Burial activity at the site appears to have begun by 1000 A.D. and terminated by the middle of the fourteenth century (Harn 1980).

In the late 1860s, William Dickson cleared the burial area of brush and trees in preparation for the planting of an orchard. He reburied any human bones he found while working his land at a time when many of his neighbors simply tossed them aside as litter. In the late 1800s, local doctor and naturalist W.S. Strode dug in the mounds, but his findings are not reported. For nearly four

The Dickson Mounds excavation. Photo courtesy of the Illinois State Museum.

decades, the mounds were a popular source for collectors, whose uncontrolled digging, coupled with soil erosion, gradually reduced the skeletal population. Further destruction to the burial area occurred in 1900 due to the effects of previous excavations and the erection of an adjacent house by Thomas Dickson. These factors are responsible for the disturbance of at least 43 burials in the Dicksons' controlled excavation.

In many ways, Don Dickson was ahead of his time. Rather than being motivated by the prospect of digging for relics, his professional interest as a chiropractor was in pathology. Dickson was excavating during the infancy of modern archaeological methods. While not a professional archaeologist, he is to be commended for his extraordinary foresight in having exposed the remains and left them in place. At a time when most amateur archaeologists were fo-

cusing on objects, Dickson was interested in skeletal biology and pathology. His meticulous digging brought attention and admiration from academics and educational institutions, explains Illinois State Museum curator Michael Wiant (personal communication, December 23, 1999). Don F. Dickson and his uncle Marion Dickson began partial excavation of the Middle Mississippian burial ground on Don's father's land in 1927. He left the skeletal material in situ, which was both good and bad for researchers: "The greatest value may be that it affords all persons an equal opportunity to study the remains and arrive at their own conclusions. There are certain disadvantages, however, the major problem being the limitation for overall analysis imposed by the many skeletons which are only partially uncovered due to the presence of other burials directly over them" (Harn 1980).

To keep up his hobby and to satisfy the curious public, Don Dickson began publicly exhibiting his excavation in early 1927 after the discovery of three semi-flexed burials in a small test pit. The skeletons were protected by an A-frame shelter and grew in number until by April of that year more than 20 burials had been exposed by Dickson, his relatives, and chiropractor T.W. Routson. Dickson replaced the small canvas tent shelter with a wood frame structure. In the southwestern corner of the excavation a second frame building was erected. To help defray the expenses of these and other planned public facilities, Dickson began charging a modest fee in 1927, a practice that continued for nearly 20 years. Both buildings were replaced in January 1928 by a 46– by 76–foot tile block building. Excavation continued until the summer of 1929, when the last of the 234 burials were exposed

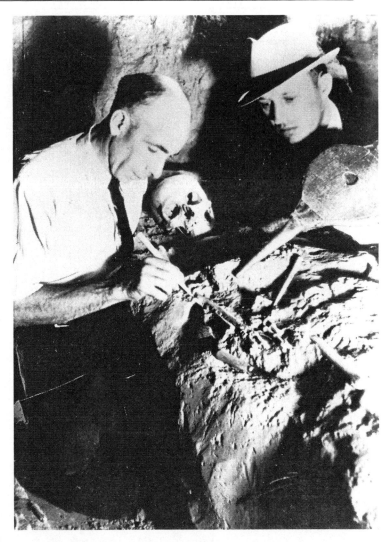

Marion and Don Dickson working at the Dickson excavation. Photo courtesy of the Illinois State Museum.

(Harn 1980). The site was promoted as the "Dickson's Moundbuilders Tombs," and the program distributed at the time focused on the quantity of skeletons that were visible. For decades, visitors stood behind a protective railing and listened to a lecture about the excavation while they observed it.

It proved to be impossible for the Dicksons to keep the burial exhibit in its pristine condition. The remains of three seven-month fetuses, possibly representing a multiple birth, were originally positioned in the Dicksons' walkway into the excavation, but were taken up and rearticulated on a board. During his research, Alan Harn (1980) has determined that burial goods had been moved from one grave to another, many of the artifacts appeared in wrong positions, and artifacts and one skull had been added to burials in the excavation. The changes may have been inadvertent, suggests Harn (1980): "Intraburial artifact movement probably took place during periodic cleaning of the exhibit. Badly damaged skulls and long bones were sometimes exchanged with less-viewable specimens

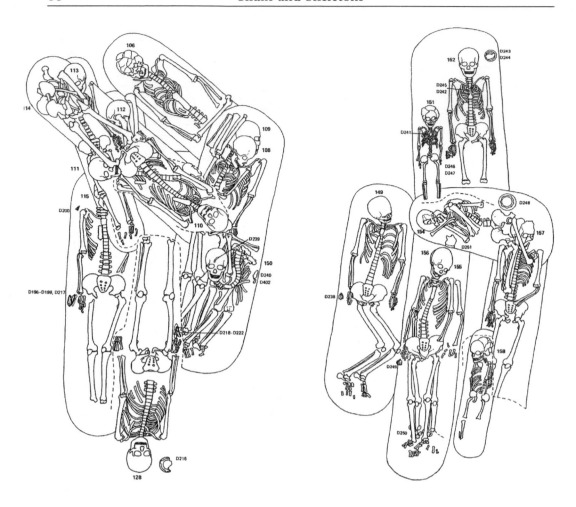

Drawings of the positions of burials in the Dickson excavation. Courtesy of the Illinois State Museum.

nearby to enhance the appearance of the exhibit." Some of the less presentable or more fragmentary remains were removed during the excavation process, according to Dickson's notes. Less fault should be found with his discriminatory practices when it is remembered that the Native American showed small regard for the bones they came across during the more than 18 intrusive burials at the site: "Little reverence was paid the burials encountered; while some disturbed bones were gathered and replaced in a stack nearby, many were thrown aside, and other bones and bone fragments were included in the fill over the newly placed bodies" (Harn 1980).

The excavation technique poses another issue associated with stratigraphy: "Because of the absence of good profiles and the removal of all earth down to the level of a given burial, it is difficult to determine the relationship of some burials to the original hill surface" (Harn 1980). Fault has also been found with the Dicksons' documentation of the site. But each burial and artifact was numbered, and all burials were described with regard to body position, association with other burials, and estimates of age, sex, and pathological conditions. Of the 248 exposed burials, only 234 have numbers, though occasionally a single number was assigned to a group of bones representing more than one person (Harn

1980). In spite of the criticisms and the Dicksons' self-taught techniques, the burial exhibits were informative and educational. To maintain the exposed skeletal remains, varnishes and shellacs were tested on bones eroded out of the mound, but were found to discolor and leave an unnatural sheen. Hot paraffin and other solutions were also unsuccessful. The paraffin was applied to the most porous bones (vertebrae and joints), but became cloudy and was discolored by dirt. It occasionally penetrated cracked bone and split it further. A mixture containing Alvar 7-70 and chemically pure acetone proved successful: it was easy to apply, penetrated well, and sealed out the air without producing an unnatural appearance, protecting indefinitely (Harn 1980).

The Dicksons continued their tours of the main excavation until 1945, when they were no longer succeeding financially due to the Depression. The museum and surrounding grounds were sold to the State of Illinois's Department of Conservation by the family, who continued to work at the site. The entrance fee was discontinued and a park, picnic grounds, and a nature trail were added. The museum continued under the immediate direction of the Dicksons as Dickson Mounds State Park and Dickson Mounds State Memorial. It was Don Dickson's serious archaeological avocation and collaboration with the scientists of the 1930s that had made the site valuable, and it suffered after his death in 1964: "His knowledge and personality made Dickson Mounds State Park successful for the Department of Conservation," writes Milton D. Thompson (1988). The museum kept in touch with Don Dickson's widow Fern until her death several years ago, after which her sister Louise Fike presented to the museum a large collection of black and white photographs of the excavation.

In 1965, a bill was passed authorizing the Illinois State Museum to hold title to the property at Dickson Mounds and the museum became the Illinois State Museum's second facility. A new museum building was planned, protective shelters were erected over three of the other excavations, and additional property to the north and south was acquired, increasing the grounds to just over 161 acres (Thompson 1988). The remains of 806 individuals were removed from Dickson Mounds in the mid–1960s in a meticulous excavation by archaeologists to prevent their destruction during construction of the new museum building, which was planned to include a main exhibits museum and buildings to cover and protect the excavated structures at the Eveland village site. The excavated remains are housed at the Research and Collection Division of the Illinois State Museum in the Human Osteology laboratory, which curates a total of about 6,000 human remains. They are currently being documented by two full-time employees. The museum, however, has a moratorium on invasive studies on human remains, so no DNA or other testing requiring samples will be performed. Instead, a systematic study of the skeletons is being conducted to include photographs, measurement, and analysis. The Illinois State Museum has invested in three-dimensional scanners, but time will not permit this sophisticated documentation of the entire collection unless the technology improves, since it takes about eight hours to digitize a human cranium to suitable resolution and the memory requirements to store the obtained electronic data are still overwhelming, explains Michael Wiant (personal communication, January 3, 2000).

When the new building to house the exhibits and the burial excavation was completed in 1970, the excavation display underwent major changes. Skulls and other bones illustrating pathologies and displayed in glass cases were removed and any loaned remains returned to their owners. Unfortunately, unauthorized brochures published by the Division of Tourism emphasized sensational pictures of Native American burials and skulls, the very images and aspects of the area that the Illinois State Museum was trying to change. Despite this temporary setback, the museum succeeded in changing Dickson Mounds' public image and modernizing its presentation (Thompson 1988). The 2,000-square-foot excavation site was enclosed in an exhibit hall, which visitors viewed from an elevated walkway. In fact, not all of the burials had been exposed. The Dickson Mounds cemetery is estimated to contain more than 3,000 burials, of which only about 1,200 were excavated or removed. Other mounds at the park remain intact.

Alan Harn (1980) has spent decades assessing and analyzing the Dickson excavation. According to his surveys of the site, 73 of the graves contain a single individual. A total of 82 percent of the burials were in the supine or extended dorsal position. Two burials were tightly flexed and six were semi-flexed. In addition to 17 bundle burials, at least 41 of the extended primary burials appear to have been originally wrapped. The skull is usually present with female burials, but absent in secondary burials of males. Nearly 60 percent of the burials were of individuals included in mass graves, including a single grave containing the remains of ten individuals. On the southern edge of the excavation, six graves contained about 20 people, later superimposed by a mass grave containing at least a dozen individuals.

Other researchers have devoted a similar amount of time to the study of this unique assemblage. Georg K. Neumann of Indiana University studied the Dickson Mounds remains for more than 40 years. His research revealed that of the 269 skeletons for whom age and sex could be definitely established, 78 are male, 85 female, 75 children under 13, and 31 are fetuses. The adult males average 42 years of age and 5'6" in height and the adult females

35.4 years of age and 5'2" in height (Harn 1980). Alan Harn's later analysis of Neumann's findings about the in situ remains determined that the average lifespan for adult males was 42 years and for adult females 35.4 years (Buikstra and Milner 1989). During the 1970s, the Dickson Mounds series (excluding the in situ remains) was loaned to the University of Massachusetts, where the remains were analyzed under the direction of Dr. George Armelagos, making the series one of the most intensively studied skeletal samples in North America and a reference standard for other regions. The Mounds have also been the subject of numerous studies, journal articles, and dissertations that have added to the body of knowledge.

The pathologies of the Dickson skeletons — which originally motivated Don Dickson's excavation — have been diagnosed. A collection of pathological specimens made by Don Dickson and housed at Dickson Mounds included examples of fractures, infectious lesions, bone tumors, degenerative osteoarthritis, ankylosing spondylitis, and other dental and osteological anomalies and pathologies. The average lifespan of the Dickson individuals was determined to be 24 years, due to high infant mortality, probably dietary deficiencies, and lack of sophisticated medical care. Bone pathologies also show evidence of osteomyelitis, rickets, and pyorrhea. The artificial deformation of many of the skulls may have been intentional, but could also have resulted from the application of pressure to the cranium stemming from the widespread use of the cradleboard. Osteoarthritis is the most prevalent of the bone diseases represented in the skeletal remains. Of the 56 males aged 21 and over, 47 cases were identified. The incidence was 100 percent after age 47. Eight individuals had a total of 17 injuries, all of them simple fractures with one possible compressed injury to the skull (Harn 1980).

Fulton County, in which Dickson Mounds resides, has long been known to have the greatest concentration of prehistoric archaeological sites in the state of Illinois, with almost 3,000 mound and village sites recorded as of 1980 (Harn 1980). The Dickson excavation was recognized for some time as being the first and most important in situ exhibit in the country. The loess soil of the Dickson Mounds site, which is located about three miles southeast of Lewistown, Illinois, and about 50 miles from the state capital of Springfield, has a high calcium oxide content and none of the acids that break down bone structure. Thus the skeletal remains are in a nearly perfect state of preservation. Some broken and displaced bones can be attributed to tree roots, the pressure of the overlying soil, and the tunneling of groundhogs. And in May 1933, a tornado partially destroyed the exhibit building, some of the archaeological material on display, and some of the artifacts from the excavation, but overall destruction of skeletal material was minimal (Harn 1980).

The bones at Dickson Mounds were therefore less at risk from the elements than they have been from the political pressures exerted on them. The exhibit had become increasingly controversial by the late 1980s. The possibility of closing of the museum was raised in public forums and debated in the media. The Department of Energy and Natural Resources (of which the Illinois State Museum is a part) recommended closure to Governor James Thompson, who had signed the Illinois Human Graves Protection Act in the 1980s, noting "that the mood of the nation, generally, had turned against displays of human skeletal materials. Decisions to remove such displays by the Smithsonian Institution in Washington, D.C., and many other museums in the nation, had left Dickson Mounds as one of the last museums in the country with such an exhibit" (Davidson 1991). Governor

Thompson put a hold on the proposed closing of the display until he had the opportunity to visit Dickson Mounds and form a personal opinion. After his visit and the receipt of a petition with more than 6,000 signatures that had been obtained to support continued public access to the burial site, Thompson announced that the exhibit would remain open.

In 1990, Native Americans raised the Dickson Mounds Museum issue before the U.S. Senate during congressional hearings. A public hearing was held in Peoria in January, after which the governor reversed his earlier anti-repatriation stance. Several viewpoints were put forward during state legislative hearings in March 1991. Professor Raymond Fogelson of the anthropology department at the University of Chicago compared the exposure of the Dickson Mounds burials to a form of "obscene pornography," because so many visitors had no background by which to interpret what they were seeing. In response to the justification that the display was educational, he said, "I'm not sure what one learns by staring into an unearthed pit of naked skeletons" (Davidson 1991). In contrast, William Sumner, director of the Oriental Institute of the University of Chicago, stated that such an exhibit "fires the imagination of school children and adults alike…. It inspires a striking recognition of how the past is a continuation with the present, and leaves a lasting impression that leads to an enriched, intellectual life" (Davidson 1991). In fact, Dickson Mounds was visited annually by about 13,000 to 14,000 school children on class field trips. In addition to whether the exhibit was an appropriate educational tool, economic issues and concerns over the affiliation of the remains with modern Native Americans were raised. Those opposed to the closing argued that the Indians represented by the excavated bones died out several hundred years ago and have no direct lineage to the contemporary Native Americans. Tribal affiliation to the remains at Dickson Mounds is hampered by significant gaps in the record. Even if scientists had been given the opportunity to assess genetic relationships through DNA testing, the lack of genetic databases available for existing tribes would have hampered comparison with the Dickson samples.

Opponents to skeletal display had turned to picketing and aggressive disruptions at Dickson Mounds. One of the most outspoken activists against the display of Native American remains is Michael Haney of McLoud, Oklahoma, who is of mixed Seminole-Sioux ancestry and an official of the United Indian Nations, which represents 26 Oklahoma tribes consisting of some 225,000 individuals. Haney turned his attention to the Dickson Mounds controversy, organizing a number of demonstrations. In October 1990, activists leapt over a railing from the viewing platform into the excavation and covered about ten of the skeletons with blankets. Director Judith Franke reported no damage to the skeletal remains. On April 6, 1991, eight protestors jumped into the pit at the Dickson Mounds Museum and shoveled dirt over two skeletons. They were led by Haney, accompanied by an additional 75 protesters, and observed by nearly 40 museum staff members and patrons. The protesters burned incense, sprinkled powder, sang to a drum beat, and chanted. State police and museum officials conferred with the governor's legal counsel and decided not to charge the protestors, most likely to avoid making them into martyrs (Davidson 1991).

The Native Americans left little room for compromise, with one group going so far as to insist on the destruction of associated field notes (Kerrigan 1990). Members of the Illinois Association for Advancement of Archaeology, who had made it clear in a published letter to Governor Edgar's office that they were opposed to the closing, recorded personal threats by Michael Haney

against them, their homes, their property, and their cemeteries. Other incidents clouded the issue. In May 1990, Mark B. Rich, age 25, of San Jose, Illinois, drove his car down the ramp into the central courtyard of the museum and ran into a wall bordering the gift shop and burial room. Thought at first to be an act of protest, since Rich is part Native American, it was revealed that he did not want the exhibit closed. The incident was blamed on his long history of mental illness and punished with a charge of reckless conduct. On September 15, 1990, several dozen people gathered at an old cemetery near the museum. Randall Riley, a Sauk representing the Quad Cities League of Native Americans, said, "Let me uncover Dr. Dickson's grave and bones.... Let me study his bones and learn what he learned from digging up my people's bones" ("Indians Continue to Protest Display at Dickson Mounds" 1990). Although Don Dickson is buried in another cemetery several miles away, the demonstrators made their point about the desecration of Native American burials.

Frustrated Native Americans persuaded State Representative Lee Preston (D-Chicago) to sponsor a bill in early 1991 that would outlaw the public display or sale of human remains in Illinois. On November 25th of that year, Thompson's successor, Governor Jim Edgar, announced that the Dickson Mounds burial exhibit would close to the public in April 1992. When the decision to close the exhibit was made, the Illinois State Museum cited policy statements of many major organizations and institutions, as well as legislation at the state and national levels regarding repatriation and reburial. When the Dickson Mounds Museum was excluded from a map of 303 American Indian sites published in the October 1991 issue of *National Geographic*, the burial exhibit remaining open was said to have played a role in the decision by the magazine's staff. Several years earlier in

1989, a World Archaeological Congress meeting in Vermillion, South Dakota, cited the Dickson Mounds exhibit as unacceptable museum practice (Pridmore 1992). Similar displays such as one in Moundville, Alabama, and the Indian Burial Pit near Salina, Kansas, had already been closed.

Governor Edgar recommended that the remains be entombed at the site in a vault-like structure. He promised to release about $275,000 and to recommend an additional $4 million for renovation and expansion of the museum building. The renovation would illustrate the culture of the Mississippians with special emphasis on their burial ceremonies and the sight of the skeletons would be replaced with a sophisticated sound and light show (Gardiner 1991). Negotiations with Native American groups and other constituents reached a compromise that allowed the museum to entomb the exposed remains by installing steel I-beams over the excavation area to support a cedar flooring that would seal it off completely from both the public and from scientists. But even the decision to entomb the remains in place was criticized: "The vault will preserve the scientific sanctity of the remains, although their cultural sanctity will be compromised by what amounts to a white man's tomb," complained James Krohe, Jr. (1992).

In anticipation of its closing, 15,000 people visited the exhibit in the final week, with 25 times the usual number arriving during the final weekend and 3,500 admitted on the last day. Many individuals and organizations regret the decision to close the excavation, some because they don't believe those buried in the cemetery would have objected to it. Anthropologists point out in the *ACPAC Newsletter* (November 1998) that the people of Dickson Mounds had no taboo about disturbing graves, regularly excavating through existing burials. Researchers continued to learn from the exhibit even as the plans to close it were underway. Before the exhibit was sealed off, Michael Wiant ascended the catwalk, from which spotlights had been hung to illuminate various graves during the original presentation, and took photographs from above. The photos revealed that the graves were arranged in a ring and supported the notion that the excavation included more than one mound. In 1989, Jane E. Buikstra and George R. Milner had written about the excavated Dickson assemblage, "As methods continue to be refined, particularly techniques for aging adult skeletons, we anticipate that the Dickson Mounds series will continue to be regarded as an important study collection, highly valued for its contribution to knowledge of the human condition. The series is a truly remarkable resource, because of its size, completeness of skeletons, good bone preservation, and accompanying information on cultural context." While the excavated series continues to be curated, the in situ burials are now off limits.

On April 3, 1992, the Dickson burial excavation closed to the public. On that day, a private Native American ceremony was conducted on Picnic Hill before the museum opened and another private ceremony was held near the entrance after closing at 5 P.M. Franke, who watched the afternoon ceremonies from the window with other museum staff and members of the Illinois State Police, explains, "As non–Indians interpreting a living culture for the generally non–Indian public, anthropologists are in a delicate position and must be sensitive to the customs, attitudes, and beliefs of that culture and flexible enough to adjust their attitudes and interpretation as those customs, attitudes, and beliefs change" (personal communication, January 7, 2000). Franke points out that the Dickson Mounds Museum's promotional efforts had not centered around the burial exhibit for about ten years. In 1993, the entire museum building closed for the planned renovations.

When it reopened in September 1994, it had an additional 7,000 feet of floor space, bringing the total to more than 50,000 feet, including almost 19,000 feet of exhibit space — none of which is devoted to the display of skeletons.

HISTORIC SITES

The historical data provided by skeletal studies are of such great value because the methodological problems inherent in extracting evidence from a skeleton are completely different from those historians face when they attempt to interpret the historical significance of the cultural products they work with.... Using a series of data sources that, standing alone, would be open to many different interpretations, it is in this way possible to triangulate on what really happened in the past.... In contrast to the symbolic problems inherent in historical reconstructions based upon written records and oral histories, human skeletal remains provide a direct source of evidence about the lives and deaths of ancient and modern people that is, at a fundamental level, free from cultural bias.
— *Phillip L. Walker [In press]*

The excavation of historic sites has been punctuated by difficulty. Cemeteries uncovered during the building of highways and structures halt construction for weeks or months, if the remains can be quickly reburied, years if the skeletons encountered belong to a group interested in asserting their rights or participating in the excavation. But even when the time frame is extended, the political processes usually leave little time for scientific analysis. On the other hand, scientists searching for the remains of a particular individual — even if they know where to look — face the possibility of not being able to find them. Or they may turn up more than they bargained for, such as when a German anatomist searching for the skull of Friedrich von Schiller (d. 1805) in the Kassengewölbe in

Weimar turned up no less than 70 possible candidates (Henschen 1965). Perhaps the most rewarding excavations are those that are commissioned by institutions to learn more about their history despite what may be revealed, or digs conceived by researchers to understand the trauma, pathology, and patterns of previous generations through recovery and study of human remains in war cemeteries, potters' fields, abbey graveyards, poorhouse plots, plague pits, and cadaver deposits.

It is not uncommon for human bones to be discovered during development, making excavation a necessary chore that may double as a research project. Human skeletal remains discovered during the building of a condominium in New Orleans in 1984 were determined to have been buried in the city's first cemetery dating to 1725, and included the bones of both blacks and whites (Florence 1996). Highway construction in the mid–1980s uncovered the skeletons of 700 individuals who had been buried in a German-Swiss cemetery in Pittsburgh associated with a nineteenth-century Evangelical church (Ubelaker 1995). Building activities do not always mandate thorough excavation, however. When the Holborn Viaduct was constructed in London, 12,000 skeletons were removed from St. Andrews Cemetery (Kanowski 1987). But when an unmarked burial ground was disturbed in Oneida County, New York, more than a dozen graves were left intact because they were not in direct line of construction activities, with the rest of the 81 burials transferred to Syracuse University for analysis (Nawrocki 1995).

The excavation of war cemeteries and mass graves gives archaeologists and physical anthropologists the opportunity to assess the damage that battle wreaked on individuals, armies, and communities. Some pioneering osteoarchaeological work of this sort was carried out in the early twentieth century, when grave pits containing casualties of the Battle of Visby were excavated. The battle, in which the Danish Army defeated an army of Swedish peasants in 1361 A.D., left thousands dead and required their disposal in mass graves. The first of these was excavated in 1905 by Oscar Wennersten and Nils Lithberg, who recovered 300 skeletons and identified many pathologies. Between 1909 and 1928, two more mass graves were excavated by Bengt Thordeman and Poul Nørlund, yielding 1,185 individuals whose injuries were studied by Swedish anatomist Bo Inglemark (Mays 1998). Another war cemetery was discovered and excavated between 1934 and 1937 by Mortimer Wheeler, Tessa Wheeler, and C.D. Drew. The remains of 38 Celtic defenders of Maiden Castle against the attack of Vespasian and his troops in 43 A.D. had been buried somewhat haphazardly, but with some ceremony. Of the 34 well-preserved skeletons, 23 were male and 11 female. The majority were between 20 and 40 years of age and most had severe head injuries that occurred perimortem. The bones show fractures, dislocations, and sword cuts, and in one case a Roman iron arrowhead was found still embedded in the thoracic vertebra (Kanowski 1987).

Like war, plague often necessitated mass interment in the past. Excavations of cemeteries in East Smithfield in London between 1986 to 1988 revealed the skeletal remains of 2,400 individuals, over 400 of which were interred in plague pits up to 410 feet long. The rough burial indicated by skeletons found in other locations in the United Kingdom may suggest a breakdown of funerary conventions due to disease such as plague, but some researchers believe hurried burials merely indicate the abandonment of long-established Roman burial customs (Kanowski 1987). Other individuals unlikely to have been given much attention after death were the residents of poorhouses and other public institutions, but their recovered remains have allowed scientists to compare them to the general population of the time. When contruction of a public facility at Highland Park in Rochester, New York, was begun by the Monroe County Parks Department in 1984, approximately 300 skeletons were uncovered. The 65 subadults and 77 females had been buried in a cemetery associated with a nearby building that had been at times an almshouse, workhouse, insane asylum, and penitentiary. By analyzing local death records, researchers were able to investigate to what extent the Highland Park skeletal collection is representative of the Monroe County Poorhouse residents and to assess the health status of poorhouse inmates relative to the general population of nineteenth-century Rochester. The study revealed that the causes of death experienced by poorhouse inmates did not differ considerably from the other residents of the Rochester area (Higgins and Sirianni 1995).

Other cemetery populations are more representative of the general population of the time. In Belleville, Ontario, human remains from approximately one third of a public cemetery adjacent to St. Thomas' Anglican Church were excavated in 1989 in advance of the construction of a parish hall. The well-drained and sandy soil allowed easy removal and had preserved the bones well. A total of 604 individuals, originally buried between 1821 and 1874, were excavated over four months and represented more than a third of the total number of interments during the period. In more than a dozen instances, infants were found buried with or above an adult female, although the infant mortality rate was determined to be moderate. Isotopic analysis of stable nitrogen allowed researchers to determine that the infants had been breastfed. During the year allowed for their study, the remains were examined, x-rayed, photographed, and tissue samples taken. The parish registers were consulted for demographic information, which included names, ages, death dates, burial dates, and — although much less reliable — causes of death. Other documentation consulted included censuses and municipal tax records. A sample of 282 subadult skeletons was analyzed and affirmed the accuracy of age estimates from tooth formation standards (Saunders et al. 1993). A sample of 276 adult skeletons was examined for caries, antemortem tooth loss rates, and the effects of age and sex on dental pathology, and compared with other American and British historical samples (Saunders, De Vito, and Katzenberg 1997). Another sample was analyzed to test the accuracy of methods used to determine sex from infracranial and long bone measurements (Saunders and Hoppa 1997). Each of the studies points to the value that existing records add to historical skeletal assemblages.

The occupants of a potter's field north of downtown Cincinnati did not show significant pathologies, but exhibited signs that their remains had been treated roughly during the century following their deaths. The public burial ground in which they were buried was owned privately until 1818, by the city until 1837, and by an orphan asylum until 1858. The property was then used as a public park for a time. When Sangerfest Hall was erected in 1870, bones encountered were packed into a barrel and stowed away in the building. Commingled bones exhumed during construction of a more permanent Music Hall in 1876 were packed into large dry-goods boxes and relocated to Spring Grove Cemetery, but not before curious crowds of children and medical students availed themselves of skulls and other souvenirs. Additional skeletal material that surfaced during the remodelling of the Music Hall in 1927 was entombed in a four-foot brick vault at the bottom of a new elevator shaft. It was the rediscovery of this vault in 1988 that led to detailed analysis. The remains were sorted by the Hamilton County Coroner's Office before being re-

leased to scientists for study. The remains were then cleaned, labeled, cataloged in a database, reconstructed, and conserved. Many of the bones had fragmented due to poor handling during the earlier and recent excavations. An inventory of 68 femora, 30 tibiae, 22 humeri, 20 ulnae, 18 radii, 11 fibulae, 11 metatarsals, 4 metacarpals, 16 crania, and numerous skull fragments indicated a minimum number of 30 adults, but may represent the remains of 65 or 70 individuals. The sample was determined to be two-thirds male and to include as many as 40 to 60 percent of African American ancestry. The majority were more than 40 years old and average stature was calculated at 66.7" for males and 62.2" for females. There was little significant or advanced pathology, most notably a limited amount of osteoarthritis and dental attrition, but medical students present during the earlier exhumation may have removed pathologic or anomalous bones (Murray and Perzigian 1995).

Like the victims of plagues and the tenants of poorhouses, the subjects of dissections were often the recipients of unceremonial burial. Examples have been uncovered during construction at two colleges. When the Berkeley Library at Trinity College, Dublin, was extended, the bones of at least 35 people, including many children, were found and believed to be the remains of cadavers dissected in the late eighteenth and early nineteenth centuries and then hastily buried in shallow graves. Renovations of the old Medical College of Georgia building were halted for a week in 1989 so that some 10,000 bones could be removed from beneath the dirt floor of the basement. The remains of 48 cadavers (as determined by the number of tibiae) had been covered with dirt and quicklime, presumably to dispose of them quickly, since dissection was illegal in Georgia until 1887. The bodies were often obtained from slave owners, which explains why the majority of the remains were African American. To gain further insight into the poorly documented dissection methods of the past, researchers planned to dissect a modern cadaver using nineteenth-century instruments and techniques and compare the cut marks on the bones to those in the archaeological sample (Harrington and Blakely 1995).

Two Danish excavations have given scientists the opportunity to assess the medical care and other characteristics of medieval populations. Æbelholt Abbey, a monastic hospital in Hillerød, Denmark, was excavated beginning in 1935 by Dr. Vilhelm Møller Christensen, a pioneer in the fields of osteoarchaeology and paleopathology. The abbey had been founded by Abbot Vilhelm (d. 1203), who was buried in the church, with his remains moved to the high altar upon his canonization in 1224. In 1561, King Christian III had ordered the abbey to be dismantled. The abbey complex included an extensive burial ground containing nearly 1,000 medieval skeletons, about 700 of which were analyzed. "By examining the skeletons, Dr. Christensen was able to identify many diseases that were prevalent in the Middle Ages, such as scurvy, rheumatoid arthritis, and tuberculosis. Some skeletons also show the results of surgery performed by the monks and attempts that were made to mend broken fractures. War wounds were also a common feature on the male skeletons. One case, showing 21 fresh incised wounds, provides a revealing example of the ferocity of close combat in the Middle Ages," reads the English Guide to the Æbelholt Abbey Museum, which has been open since 1957 and displays a large collection of the excavated skeletons, including the remains of a pregnant woman (Lawson 1999).

Excavations at Øm Abbey in Skanderborg, Denmark, began even earlier than at Æbelholt. Øm Abbey was in use by the Cistercian Order from 1172 to 1560, after which it was demolished as a result of the Lutheran Reformation. The abbey had a hospital with competent surgeons, a nursing home for the handicapped, a grammar school, and a scientific library. Excavations of the abbey ruins began in 1896 and approximately 1,000 tombs were uncovered in the abbey cemetery in the 1930s. The northern churchyard, containing the remains of hospital patients, was also excavated. The skeletal material provided the basis for a substantial amount of pathological and anthropological research conducted between 1912 and 1941, and has most recently been the subject of odontological studies. The Øm Kloster Museum currently curates about 900 skeletons, but most will soon be deposited at the Stno-Museum by the University of Århus to allow easier access byresearchers. A subset of the collection comprises bones showing the marks of disease and of operations conducted by the monks. Some of the bones will remain on exhibit at the museum — which focuses on medieval (especially monastic) history, archaeology, and ethnobotany — along with more than 100 exposed tombs under the floors of the abbey church.

Excavations at Pompeii in Italy have allowed the reconstruction and osteological analysis of a family unit rather than a monastic population, a supposition that will be confirmed through DNA testing and multivariate analysis. Thirteen skeletons found in several rooms of the house of C Iulius Polybius are the remains of victims of the eruption of Mount Vesuvius in 79 A.D. The excavation was carried out between 1966 and 1978 and the recovered skeletal material boxed for later analysis, which has only just been undertaken. The commingled bones — mainly large skull fragments, mandibles, and long and short bones — were first sorted into individual skeletons by laying them out in anatomical order, estimating the age and sex of each individual, and comparing coloration and the characteristics of the adhering matrix. About 10 percent of the material remained unassigned. Each skeleton was cleaned, labeled, and placed in a new box. They were found to include three adult males, three adult females, four boys, a girl, a child of unknown sex, and a nine-month fetus. The bones were analyzed craniometrically, odontometrically, and osteometrically. Samples of DNA were successfully extracted from the cortical bone of each skeleton and are being analyzed. The sample, though small, was determined to reflect the age structure of an ancient population, consisting of 50 percent adults (Henneberg, Henneberg, and Ciarallo 1996). Because all of the individuals died at the same time, the age structure is believed to mirror the living population of Pompeii (Henneberg and Henneberg 1999a).

The bones have revealed the morphology of Pompeii's inhabitants, being used to estimate average stature and body weight for males and females (Henneberg and Henneberg 1999a). They have also been used in studies of health and pathology. Pompeiians were found to suffer from arthritis, dental caries, childhood diseases, blood-borne infections, and injuries including bone fractures (Henneberg and Henneberg 1999a). Analysis of spina bifida occulta was carried out on a sample of 124 adult sacra of individuals to determine that percentages in Pompeii fall within the ranges of similar populations (Henneberg and Henneberg 1999b). Because they were well-preserved in hardened ash above the water table, the skeletal remains are ideally suited to osteological and DNA examinations. But what brings the Pompeiians back to life even more so than DNA analysis and other sophisticated studies is the facial reconstruction that has been carried out on four of the skulls.

The Isola Sacra Project, Italy

Another excavated assemblage being exhaustively studied consists of the remains of approximately 2,000 individuals from an Imperial Roman necropolis located along an ancient road connecting Ostia and Portus. The "Isola Sacra Project" is being conducted by the Anthropology Section of the National Prehistoric Ethnographic "L. Pigorini" Museum of Rome, in collaboration with other Italian and international institutions. The main research topics include morphological variation, paleodemography, paleoepidemiology, paleonutrition, and taphonomy. The results of the studies have been published on CD-ROM as part of the Digital Archives of Human Paleobiology (DAHP), which has been developed since 1996 to share scientific research and interpretation and offer the "virtual export" of single specimens and entire anthropological collectons from museums and laboratories. The DAHP, promoted and funded by the Italian National Research Council, offers introductory and explanatory texts, methodological protocols, images (including radiographs, CT-scans, 3D reconstructions, and microscopic images), analytical databases, figures, tables, graphs, and extensive bibliographies.

The bones excavated from the Isola Sacra cemetery, which is located about 23 km west of Rome, constitute probably the most complete collection from the Classical period in Italy. The cemetery was exposed between 1925 and 1940 by G. Calza, but was not completely excavated. When the zone in which it was located was designated for land reclamation in the 1970s, an archaeological research project was proposed by the Archaeological Superintendency of Ostia. Systematic excavations began in 1973 and were conducted by the Superintendency, the University of Rome "La Sapienza," and the University Institute of Oriental Studies of Naples. The first phase of the study, lasting until 1982, involved the recovery of skeletal remains of about 1,000 individuals previously discovered by Calza, which had been left haphazardly scattered on the floors of the tombs. A number of skeletal elements (mainly crania) representing 64 individuals were selected from the subsample based on their degree of preservation, and were used for preliminary morphological analyses by the Department of Animal and Human biology at "La Sapienza." The second phase of excavation, from 1988 to 1989, yielded significant numbers of skeletons from undisturbed single and multiple burials, all in an excellent state of preservation and completeness. Funerary and burial practices were complex and diverse and ranged from simple interments in sand to cremations to monumental multiple tombs. Burial receptacles included wooden coffins, terra cotta sarcophagi, and amphora.

In 1992, the Superintendency and the University of Rome entrusted the organization, restoration, documentation, and systematic study of the entire sample to the Anthropology Section of the National Prehistoric Ethnographic "L. Pigorini" Museum of Rome. This became the Isola Sacra Project. The skeletal series now includes approximately 2,000 individuals of both sexes and all age groups, making it quantitatively and qualitatively one of the most significant skeletal collections from Mediterranean Europe for the Classical period. The objectives of the Isola Sacra Project are to organize, catalog, and conserve the collection; to tentatively reconstruct the individual skeletons originally excavated by Calza; to study the diagenetic process of bone and dental tissues by macro- and microscopic study; to determine odontoskeletal biological characteristics, patterns of variation, and models of growth; and to assess health, nutrition, and other characteristics of the population. The researchers also intend to apply high-tech investigative methods, develop original analytical protocols; create elaborate reference models; publish the data and images in CD-ROM format; and create multimedia products for teaching purposes. Preliminary results have been published in several areas, including paleodemography, paleonutrition, paleopathology, cranial and dental size variation, age-related bone changes, bone and dental histology, and molecular biology. The project is a model of skeletal research and of the dissemination of the results to other researchers.

The Greenland Norse

In 1998, Niels Lynnerup published the results of a survey of all of the Greenland Norse skeletal material available at the Laboratory of Biological Anthropology in Denmark. The study also included Norse material located outside the lab, including material stored at the Danish National Museum and the Zoological Museum. Most of the material available for study was collected in cemetery excavations done by professional archaeologists and excavators, but poor preservation in many cases left some of it irrecoverable. Shallow burials subjected many of the remains to root damage and rain caused the calcium to leach from skeletons buried in coffins, making them brittle. Many of the bones that have been curated were subject to the application of a lacquer or preservative that has loosened the outermost surface of the bones, making them subject to crumbling at the slightest touch. Some crania may have expanded due to humidity.

The Norse from Iceland had colonized the southwestern part of Greenland 1,000 years ago and maintained two major settlements for 500 years. Assuming an overall churchyard population of some 25,000 individuals over a 450 year period, Lynnerup calculated an average of about 55 deaths per year, and some two to four burials per church per year. Excavations — not all of which yielded extant remains — included the following examples:

- Benedictine Convent (Narsarsuaq): Excavations by C.L. Vebaek in the 1940s revealed interments below the church walls and several layers of burials in the church-yard. Preservation of the twenty graves was poor and no skeletal material could be secured. Eleven skulls were brought back for study. Four samples were radiocarbon dated.

• Gardar (Igaliko): Seven crania and six skeletons found by J. Mathieson in 1830 were not recovered and a skeleton determined to be Bishop Jon Smyrill (d. 1209) was reinterred. Poul Nørlund and Aage Rousell recovered 13 skeletons in 1926 and dated the cathedral to 1150–1250 A.D. Samples from three skeletons were radiocarbon dated and a probable case of acromegaly was identified.

• Herjolfsnes (Ikigait): O. Kielsen excavated this site in 1831, having found a cranium the year before. In 1900, Gustav Meldorf removed bones that had eroded out of a small cliff, including several crania and a complete skull that was brought to Denmark. Major excavations by Poul Nørlund in 1921 yielded remnants of 110–120 burials, but only 20 skeletons could be removed because of their poor condition. Three skeletons were radiocarbon dated to 1400–1450 A.D. and two cases of cribra orbitalia (porotic hyperostosis) were found.

• Sandnes (Kilaarsarfik): First excavated in 1765, digging at this site continued in the nineteenth and early twentieth centuries. In 1903, Daniel Bruun recovered five human crania and several other bones. Bruun's excavation site was analyzed by Nørlund and Roussell in 1930, who uncovered 42 individual interments and several disturbed burials. One grave contained a family apparently struck down by an infectious disease.

• Thjodhilde's Church, Brattahlid (Qassiarsuk): Among the bones found in 1961 was a cranium identified as Norse, leading to the theory that this was the first Christian church in Greenland. Radiocarbon dating confirmed that the cemetery was in use for about 30 years beginning in 1000 A.D. All 155 interments were laid out along a west-east access and only a few were in coffins. A mass grave contained the disarticulated bones of 13 individuals, five of which exhibited cut and stab wounds, probably indicative of feuding. Although this churchyard is the only one to have been fully excavated, it has not yet been determined how representative it is.

Six specimens had been found outside known churchyards and several skeletons were found extending below the actual church foundations, rendering date testing of the building useless in dating the remains themselves. The relationship of the remains to the places of worship, however, are of great importance: "The combination of skeletal material and archaeological evidence is one of the few available resources for studying how closely the Norsemen conformed to the laws of the church in their everyday life" (Lynnerup 1998). Almost all burials found in Norse churchyards have an east-west orientation. The position of the arms varied over time and is helpful in dating burials. Bodies were buried in shrouds or in wooden coffins. Secondary burials of bundled and disarticulated bones were found to have been deposited in the churchyards, but "bone heaps" appear to be the remnants of disturbed graves.

Of the existing Norse specimens in Danish collections, all 457 were studied by Lynnerup (1998). Although 94 of the analyzed specimens represented only a single skeletal element, the minimum number of individuals was calculated to total 378. Postcranial remains were underrepresented, illustrating past practices of securing only the crania. The sex distribution was about 50/50, but 200 specimens, including 56 subadults, could not be sexed. Subadults accounted for 16 percent of the material.

The crania and most of the pathological specimens were x-rayed. Thirty-eight cases of osteoarthritis were documented, mostly afflicting the cervical vertebrae, but the levels of this and other degenerative diseases were found to be consistent with other medieval populations. Trauma observed include healed and unhealed cut wounds, a single long bone fracture, and wounds possibly caused by slingshots and crossbows.

The Battle of Little Bighorn at Crow Agency, Montana

> Besides the physical details reflected in the bones, their contexts — on the field of battle, buried in the Custer National Cemetery, set on museum shelves, and even stashed in personal collections — all tell us something about how our society's view of proper treatment of the dead has evolved and how battlefields have changed in meaning. — Douglas D. Scott, P. Willey, and Melissa A. Connor (1998)

The Battle of Little Bighorn, more commonly known as "Custer's Last Stand," cost the U.S. Army more than one percent of its strength, having resulted in 268 casualties. The story, documented historically, has been confirmed osteologically. George Custer, a graduate of West Point, was only 26 when he was appointed lieutenant colonel of the newly formed Seventh Cavalry in July 1866. The Seventh Cavalry was composed of 12 companies made up of a total of 43 officers, 125 noncommissioned officers, 652 enlisted personnel, a band, surgeons, and a veterinarian. After a court-martial and a one-year suspension, Custer returned to duty in 1868 and led his troops against a Cheyenne village, killing more than 100 Indians and capturing 53, while losing 20 of his own men. In 1876, Custer and the Seventh Cavalry rode out as part of a three-pronged offensive against the Sioux and Northern Cheyenne led by General Alfred Terry and Colonel John Gibbon from the east and General George Crook

from the south. Crook's forces, 1,000 strong, depleted their ammunition supply and were forced to retire. Uninformed of this, Terry and Gibbon continued the offensive. Custer's regiment separated from the rest of Terry's forces and on the morning of June 25th entered the valley of the Little Bighorn, where Custer divided them into three elements. Captain Thomas McDougall's men guarded the pack train, Captain Frederick Benteen's men scouted to the south and cut off any potential escape routes, and Custer and the rest of the men headed toward the Indian encampment. Before attacking, Custer assigned three companies to Major Marcus Reno and ordered him to follow the west side of the river and attack from the south. Custer followed the east side of the river with the remaining five companies, with the apparent purpose of crossing and attacking at the north end of the village (Scott, Willey, and Connor 1998).

Reno's men encountered heavy opposition and retreated across the river, taking up a defensive position up on the bluffs. Custer sent a message to Benteen asking him to bring ammunition packs. Benteen reached Reno, and McDougall's company joined them a short time later. They assumed that Custer and his men were pinned down somewhere to the north and attempted to head in that direction, but were driven back by Indian fire. They maintained their position that night and the next day, with sharpshooters defending the enlisted volunteers who went to the river to get water for the wounded and to retrieve the body of Lieutenant Benjamin Hodgson. By the morning of June 27, the Indians had abandoned the village and a scouting party brought back news that Custer and at least 197 of his men lay dead on a ridge above the river. Later that day, as many as 214 dead were counted and it was determined that there were no survivors. "Officers spent most of the day examining evidence of trails across the field, the positions of bodies and companies, and other signs that might offer a glimpse into the course of events" (Scott, Willey, and Connor 1998).

Reno's men were detailed to bury the dead quickly on June 28th and were assisted by men from other units. It was a difficult task because the regiment had only the spoons and cups from the mess kits to dig the rock-hard soil with, so most of the bodies on the ridge and in the valley merely had earth heaped up over them where they were found. In addition, the casualties were difficult to identify due to severe mutilation and the action of the heat, which left them swollen and discolored and caused the limbs in some cases to become detached when the bodies were moved. "Viewed in the context of the history of warfare, the hasty burial of the dead at the Little Bighorn was not uncommon" (Scott, Willey, and Connor 1998).

The dead included five members of the Custer family: Lieutenant Colonel George Custer, his nephew Harry "Autie" Armstrong Reed, his brother-in-law Lieutenant James Calhoun, and his brothers Captain Tom Custer and civilian guide Boston Custer (Scott, Willey, and Connor 1998). Also killed was Bismarck *Tribune* reporter Mark Kellogg, who had accompanied the Seventh Cavalry to report on the expedition. Only 56 of the 210 dead on the Custer battlefield are recorded as having been recognized at the time of burial, one by the name on his sock, another by his shattered glass eye, and a third by the initials tattooed on his arm. More than three quarters of Custer's officers were identified, compared to only 15 percent of the privates. Captain Henry Nowlan staked the officers' graves and sketched a map of their locations. The soldiers at Reno's position were also buried, many of them in rifle pits. Of the 52 men who died at this location, 47 were identified, most likely because the burial detail consisted of survivors from the same company and battle as the dead (Scott, Willey, and Connor 1998).

The surviving members of the Seventh Cavalry returned by steamer to Fort Abraham Lincoln in North Dakota. While several of the survivors were later killed in action during the Nez Percé War of 1877 and in the massacre at Wounded Knee in 1890, one of them — Private Frank Braun — died a few months later from the gunshot wound he had sustained at Little Bighorn. Post surgeon Dr. J.M. Middleton excised part of Braun's wounded femur and hip and sent them to the Army Medical Museum (now the National Museum of Health and Medicine), where they remain today. The rest of Braun's body was buried in the fort cemetery, later being reinterred at Custer National Cemetery (Scott, Willey, and Connor 1998).

In 1877, General P.H. Sheridan ordered his brother and aide Colonel Michael Sheridan to properly inter the remains of the fallen officers at Little Bighorn. The expedition left Fort Abraham Lincoln in May 1877 escorted by Company I of the Seventh Cavalry and quartermaster Captain Henry Nowlan, who had marked the graves of the officers during their initial burial. The bones of the identified officers were exhumed on July 3, placed in pine boxes, and transported for shipment downstream. The exposed remains of some of the other men, and — at the request of his father — the remains of Lieutenant Crittenden, were reinterred on the field where they had fallen, some by heaping earth over them and others by being buried in a hole dug for the purpose. According to a contemporary newspaper account, all traces of flesh had disappeared from the bones, write Scott, Willey, and Connor (1998), who also point out that "In short, the idea that Little Bighorn was the only battlefield where skeletons lay exposed is untrue. This is conveyed as a consistent theme on other Indian War battlefields ... the recovery of all bones of a body was not as important in the cultural context of the nineteenth century as it is in today's world. Failing in total recovery was not an indication of a lack of respect but of a different perception of what was important. The detailed recovery of a body's bones became important only with the rise of forensic skills necessary to conduct identifications from bones. Otherwise the bones themselves were merely symbolic of the person, and a symbolic representation was all that was necessary."

One set of remains was assumed to be Custer's, but it is believed that not all of the skeleton was recovered at that time (Willey and Scott 1999). Some of the officers were buried in national cemeteries and some in private or municipal cemeteries. Custer's remains were transported to Poughkeepsie, New York, and stored in the vault of a friend for the summer. In October 1877, the coffin was carried by steamship up the Hudson River to the U.S. Military Academy at West Point. After a funeral ceremony, the remains were reinterred in the U.S. Military Academy Post Cemetery, as his widow had requested. The grave was later marked by a large granite obelisk (Willey and Scott 1999).

Before and after the official exhumations, skeletal remains from the battlefield were collected for various reasons. In April 1877, assistant Surgeon Robert W. Shufeldt recovered a human skull, mandible, and two vertebrae as medical specimens and sent them to the Army Medical Museum in July 1881. In July 1877, P.W. Norris, the newly appointed superintendent of Yellowstone National Park, made an unauthorized journey to the battlefield to exhume the remains of his friend Charley Reynolds. He was accompanied by photographer James Fouch, who took the earliest known photos of the battlefield. Norris located Reynolds' remains by using Nowlan's sketch map and kept them with him for more than a year until he was able to bury them at his home. In 1878 or 1879, Lieutenant George S. Young of the Seventh Infantry took a trip to

the battlefield and came away with several souvenirs, including a human thoracic vertebra transfixed by an iron arrowhead. The bone and other items were retained by Young's family for many years and were finally donated to the Smithsonian Institution in 1967. The skull of an unburied skeleton located in a ravine was collected by a party of five men who passed by the battlefield in August 1884. The teeth, which had exceptionally fine gold dental work, were examined by Dr. C.S. Whitney, but the disposition of the skull is unknown. And in April 1886, a skull cap was discovered by Hospital Steward James Carroll of Fort Custer and donated to the Army Medical Museum three years later. In addition, more than a dozen other documented discoveries of human bone since 1877 have been attributed to actions other than formal archaeological investigations (Scott, Willey, and Connor 1998).

Not long after the burial expedition returned, General Sheridan conducted an inspection tour. He found the skeletons already eroding out of their newly constructed graves, partly as a result of a severe thunderstorm, and ordered a cleanup of the field, a task that took 60 troopers four hours. Over the next two years, the bones became exposed again as a result of natural erosion, animal scavenging, and human vandalism. In April 1879, Captain George Sanderson of the Eleventh Infantry at Fort Custer was ordered with his men to again rebury the battlefield remains. He reported finding very few exposed bones (the remains of four or five bodies in his estimation) and buried them on Last Stand Hill. He topped the grave with a cordwood mound. In addition, he had the horse bones — which he believed had led to stories of poorly buried bodies — gathered and placed in a mound. That same year, the site was designated the Custer Battlefield National Cemetery (Scott, Willey, and Connor 1998).

In 1881, a detail of soldiers commanded

Horse bones at the Custer Battlefield in 1879 that led to claims that the dead soldiers were not properly buried. Photo courtesy of the Little Bighorn Battlefield National Monument.

being split between the Custer field, the Reno-Benteen field, and the site of the valley fight, which explains why there are more markers on the Custer battlefield than men who fell in that location (Scott, Willey, and Connor 1998).

Yet more remains later turned up during improvements to the park or were turned in by tourists. In 1958, archaeologist Robert Bray found a human skeleton at the Reno-Benteen defense site during preparations to build walking paths. When a visitor brought an adult human tooth to the park staff after a cigarette fire had burned away the grass and brush of the battlefield in 1983, archaeologist Richard A. Fox, Jr. surveyed the ground and submitted a report to the National Park Service's Midwest Archaeological Center. A dig sponsored in part by the Custer Battlefield Historical and Museum Association was commissioned and headed by Douglas D. Scott, P. Willey, and Melissa A. Connor. In 1984, Scott, Willey, Connor, Fox, and 63 volunteers swept the battlefield visually and with metal detectors. When human remains were found, osteologist Clyde Snow joined the team. During the following two years, with the addition of geoarchaeologist Dr. C. Vance Haynes, they excavated about 37 of the 252 grave markers (Scott, Willey, and Connor 1998). Some of the finds are described below:

by Lieutenant Charles Roe of the Second Cavalry was sent to disinter the remaining soldiers' bones, rebury them, and top the new grave with a granite monument brought to the site on sledges. The monument was placed at the site of the existing cordwood marker and a mass grave ten feet wide was dug next to it to contain the disinterred remains. In 1890, 14 years after the battle, Captain Owen Jay Sweet led the party that erected the marble markers that still commemorate the locations where the soldiers fell. He reported finding the bleaching skeletons of 29 men that had remained unburied and marked them also. The markers were all placed on the main battlefield instead of

• Marker 7: This area was excavated in 1984 and again in 1989 because human remains were eroding out of the adjacent trail. About 20 skull fragments, teeth, several vertebrae, a fragment of a sternum, and several unidentified fragments were recovered. The remains are those of an individual 20–36 years old. The skull was apparently crushed by a blunt instrument around the time of death and a missing cervical vertebra may indicate decapitation in a single blow with a sharp instrument.

- Markers 9 and 10: Excavation at these paired markers revealed skull fragments, ribs, vertebrae, scapula, sternum, hand and foot bones, a right and left humerus, a left radius and ulna, and some smaller bones. Several skull fragments and both arms were in correct anatomical position and suggest that the soldier was buried face down. The sternum and an arm bone have cut marks. Bullets were found in the thorax and skull. The remains are consistent with an individual 30–40 years of age and 5'10" tall. From a list of 13 possible identities, researchers narrowed the candidates down to 11.

- Markers 33 and 34: Human bone had been eroding from this area in 1983 and it was excavated the following year. Fragments of a skull, teeth, cervical vertebra, wrist and hand bones, and a coccyx were found. The remains indicated an individual 35–45 years old. The face indicates racially mixed (white and Native American) parentage and the teeth suggest a pipe smoker. Photographic superimposition was used successfully to compare the remains with the only soldier to fit the description, scout Mitch Boyer.

- Marker 105: Excavation revealed a complete left lower arm and hand along with bones of the right hand, back, and foot. The remains are those of an adult male 30–40 years old and about 5'3" tall. The foot had a healed fracture and the vertebra a wound from a knife or arrowhead.

Although the spot is historically identified with Lieutenant Algernon Smith, researchers have excluded him as too tall and have listed nine possible identities.

- Marker 128: The burial contained the skeleton of a white male 19–22 years old and roughly 5'7" tall. One leg was still encased in its boot, indicating that is had probably not been moved since the original burial, but the other bones had been disturbed. Differential weathering indicated that the left side had been exposed for several months. There were gunshot wounds to two ribs and a bullet fragment was found in the left lower arm. There were cut marks on both femora and the clavicle. The skull was missing but remaining fragments indicate a forceful blow to the head. Several of the nine soldiers whose age and height met the criteria were ruled out as having been historically identified elsewhere on the battlefield, but specific identification was not possible.

In addition to excavating the markers at the battlefield, the team reinvestigated earlier finds. At the Reno-Benteen defense site, where Bray had discovered a skeleton in 1958, they found a skull, mandible, and many post-cranial bones believed to have been partially disturbed and reburied. The skull was elongated due to a congenital defect and the teeth showed evidence of poor dental health and some growth interruption during youth. Age of the individual was estimated at 21 years and height at 5'7¾" and artifacts suggest that his body was wrapped in a piece of tent at the time of interment. In an area known as the "L-Entrenchment," where human bones had been brought to the surface in the 1950s by rodent burrowing, two burials were excavated and age and height estimated (Scott, Willey, and Connor 1998).

The team also analyzed the partial remains in the park's museum collection.

They were measured, examined, photographed, chemically analyzed, x-rayed, and — in the case of bones with unique characteristics — molded and cast. Some were found to be animal bones and others had been misidentified anatomically. After the mistakes were rectified, the collection totaled 37 human bones and a tooth and represented the remains of 16 individuals. The specimens included four hand bones and a left tibia discovered in 1941, a right radius and ulna found in 1942, a wrist bone found in 1954, bones of the foot, fingertip, and wrist found in 1956, a left parietal skull fragment found in 1957, a tooth found in 1959, a weathered adult left first metatarsal found in 1988, an adult left mandibular fragment found in 1993, an adult left wrist bone found in 1995, and a number of other bones and fragments whose discovery date and location were not recorded (Scott, Willey, and Connor 1998). Most of the skeletal material held by or repatriated to the Little Bighorn Battlefield National Monument has been reburied in the Custer National Cemetery in marked graves, with the most recent reburial conducted in 1994. Bones and fragments that had not been analyzed by that time, or have been found since then, will be reinterred later, possibly marking the 125th anniversary of the battle, explains Willey (personal communication, June 24, 1999).

Processing of the battlefield remains from the Reno-Benteen site included casting of the complete skulls, facial reproduction, and photographic superimposition, activities that led to the probable identification of Sergeant Miles O'Hara. Another possible identification was made of a skull, left humerus, and right clavicle discovered in 1989 eroding from a river bank. The skull indicated an adult white male between ages 30 and 40 who had been ill with fever at some point during his life. The bones suggested a height of 5'8". The teeth were in good shape, some having been lost after death. Broken teeth and a horizontal fracture across the face below the nose are indicative of blunt force trauma. The possible identities were narrowed down to six, but the lack of photographs precluded superimposition. A facial reconstruction, however, led descendants of the Botzer family to notice a family resemblance. No DNA could be extracted from the bones to test the relationship, but a photograph turned up and lent support that the remains are those of Sergeant Edward Botzer (Scott, Willey, and Connor 1998).

Remains from the other battle sites had been transferred to the Custer Battlefield National Cemetery in 1903, 1928, and sometime before 1941. The cemetery also received remains discovered during road construction, including those of Lieutenant John Crittenden, who was reburied with full military honors. In 1992, the skeletal remains that had been reburied in Section A of the Custer National Cemetery were exhumed for osteological examination and possible identification. After examination, the bones from the Custer National Cemetery were reinterred in August 1994, but the analyses were revealing:

• Grave 453: This grave contained bones from at least three individuals, some of which had been gnawed by animals. One of the skeletons was missing only some ribs, vertebrae, and smaller bones of the wrists, hands, ankles, and feet. The remains showed no indication of gunshot wounds or mutilation. The individual was a gracile white male at least 30 years old, standing at 5'5⅓". The skull had evidence of a well-healed fracture above the right eye and the bones showed numerous degenerative changes. The soldier had good oral health, but may have ground his teeth. The remains are thought to be those of Corporal George Lell, a conclusion that will be verified when a DNA sample is obtained from a living member of the Lell family for comparison with

DNA extracted from one of the skeleton's teeth by the Armed Forces Institute of Pathology.

- Grave 455: This grave contained the skeleton of a robust white male age 25 to 35 and standing 5'10⅔". He had a healed fracture of the radius and possibly of a metatarsal. In addition, he suffered from degenerative disks and osteoarthritis, poor oral health, and a gunshot wound in the right ilium. Of the five possible identities, the remains are most likely those of Farrier Vincent Charley, and the headstone has been changed to reflect this. His gunshot wound is consistent with the historical record and his healed injuries and robusticity are in keeping with his profession. Although no photographs exist for comparison, a facial reconstruction was prepared.

- Grave 456: The remains in this grave were poorly preserved due to the proximity of a sprinkler head. However, most of the larger bones were present. There are cuts on the bone, probably from both mutilation and exhumation. A cut on the cranial vault may indicate scalping and three cuts near the femoral head may indicate dismemberment of the thigh. The proximal end of the humerus contained metal fragments, suggesting a gunshot wound. The remains were those of an adult white male between 20 and 30 and standing 5'9½" tall. There were signs of a low-grade bodywide infection and numerous indications of growth interruptions, but good dental health. Of the nine possible identities, the skeleton was tentatively identified as that of Private William Meyer.

- Grave 458: This well-preserved skeleton was missing only the smaller bones of the hands and feet. Parts of the right tibia and fibula were sun-bleached and weather-checked, indicating that they had been exposed. A cut on the left side of the skull may be the result of scalping, cuts near the right shoulder indicate dismemberment of the arm, and cuts in the pelvic area and thigh may represent slashing mutilations. The remains are those of a white male age 20 to 25, standing about 5'8½" tall, with poor dental health. Indications are that he drank coffee and had degenerative joint disease. Possible identities were narrowed down to five, but none was certain.

- Grave 942: This grave contained two interments, one of which was of a Native American woman between the ages of 45 and 60 and standing 5'3" tall. A few ribs, vertebrae, and most of the bones of the hands and feet were missing. Parturition pits indicate that she had borne at least one child. The skeleton showed signs of several episodes of delayed growth and pathological modifications that may have been caused by tuberculosis, metastatic carcinoma, or early Padget's disease. Although the cranial features were consistent with Plains Indian groups, it is believed that she was not contemporaneous with the battle. The remains were compared with bones found nearby by Jason Pitsch in 1993 and many elements matched. The bones were reunited almost 70 years after death and buried with appropriate ceremony on the Crow Reservation in May 1994.

- Grave 517A: One of the skeletons in this grave was estimated to be a male between 30 and 45, standing 5'11¼". Indications of trauma and degenerative changes included two healed rib fractures, joint disease in the radius, moderate osteoarthritis and osteophytosis in the vertebrae, and severe disk deterioration. Dental health was poor and the teeth were stained and grooved from smoking a pipe. Of four possible identities, the most intriguing was that of George Custer himself, who meets the age and stature requirements and whose wound was consistent, but who was said to have abstained from tobacco. If the remains are those of Custer, it would indicate that the 1877 exhumation was incomplete: "If this evidence is correct, then his West Point grave could contain Custer, part of Custer, or someone else altogether" (Willey and Scott 1999). Further doubt is cast upon the nineteenth-century recovery of Custer's remains by Clyde Snow, who points out that Custer's grave did not contain remnants of the blankets and canvas tent sheets he was buried with, nor did it include the remains of his brother Tom, who was said to have been interred by his side (Joyce 1991). Because the Custer family objects to exhumation of the remains at West Point, researchers hope to analyze DNA extracted from tooth samples that could then be matched to that of a descendant or to extant samples of Custer's hair, writes Willey (personal communication, June 24, 1999). Unfortunately, Willey reports (personal communication, May 30, 2000) that the tooth samples analyzed by the Armed Forces Institute of Pathology did not produce DNA.

During the excavations, a number of specimens — some of questionable authenticity — that were said to have been collected on the battlefield were returned to the museum. These included a tooth and the top of a cranial vault, found in the artifact collection of a deceased Pennsylvania man, that were mailed to the Little Bighorn National Monument in 1992. In 1994, the Sioux City Public Museum in Iowa returned four specimens that were noted to have been found in July 1900, but from which little could be concluded. The same year, the culmination of a lengthy and successful law enforcement investigation led to the return of a bone that had been found near Marker 174 in the early 1980s (Scott,

Willey, and Connor 1998). Remains from Little Bighorn that are curated at other institutions were also examined. In 1988, Douglas Owsley examined the remains that had been donated to the Army Medical Museum by Dr. Shufeldt one hundred years earlier. Shufeldt had described his discovery in 1910. Accompanied by upwards of a dozen Sioux scouts, some of whom had participated in the battle, "I pushed on ahead of the command and so became the first white man that had been over some parts of the field since the massacre took place.... I found the skeletons of the unburied dead, just where they had fallen..." he writes (Shufeldt 1910). He dismounted to examine the skeleton of a soldier in the Reno area, retrieving the skull and the arrow-points that had killed him. The skull was determined to be that of a white male with gracile features, between 27 and 35, with dental problems. The skull exhibits blunt instrument trauma to the left frontal and temporal areas and possible damage to the left cheek from a heavy sharp instrument. Facial reconstruction was carried out, but no similarities with photographs of the possible soldiers were noted (Scott, Willey, and Connor 1998).

None of the remains examined by the team were those of the estimated 30 to 300 (50 being the most widely accepted figure) Sioux and Cheyenne combatants, whose skeletons may still be in the valley, and whose deaths have not been commemorated. And they do not include the bones of hands and feet that had been severed from the soldiers' bodies and taken to the village, where they were displayed on poles. Neither did they examine a necklace in the Plains Indian Museum at Cody, Wyoming, made of 14 fingers said to be the trigger fingers of the troopers (Scott, Willey, and Connor 1998).

If all the elements from all of the soldiers on the field were recovered, there would be a total of 55,544 bones. Those actually recovered and studied amount to 2.4 percent of this total. Easily observable skeletal manifestations were the trauma of horseback riding, dental health and disease, and the use of tobacco. Although a few of the skeletons show signs of decapitation and dismemberment, wounds from gunshots, arrows, and scalping left few indications on the skeletons. Using their age estimations and army records, the researchers found that a sixth of the soldiers in the Seventh Cavalry were under the minimum enlistment age of 21 years at the time of the battle. They determined that 21 percent of Custer's regiment had served less than one year, but that raw recruits were not a significant factor in the outcome of the battle. "It is obvious that the skeletal analyses cannot replace the historic documents. The skeletons are, however, the material evidence of the lives and deaths of Seventh Cavalry troopers, helping to clarify, amplify, and correct the historic record. It is equally apparent from this study that neither history nor archeology has the entire story. Both are needed to build a more complete picture of the past" (Scott, Willey, and Connor 1998). That picture continues to get more detailed as additional bones turn up in in the park and in museum collections across the country.

Harewood Cemetery in Charles Town, West Virginia

Like the researchers at the Custer Battlefield, James Starrs of George Washington University is attempting to flesh out the often sketchy historical record through the analysis of excavated skeletal remains. He initiated a project to locate the unmarked gravesite of Samuel Washington, the younger brother of George Washington. If successful, the descendants of Samuel Washington (the "Uncle of our Country," as Starrs affectionately calls him) will be given the opportunity to memorialize his grave. Starrs explained (personal communication, July 17,

1999) that the grave may have been deliberately left unmarked to discourage graverobbers, but that it is more likely that a temporary marker was erected without ever having been replaced by a permanent marker and has since disappeared. Harewood — a working farm — is now owned by Walter Washington of Austin, Texas, who gave his approval to the project (Starrs 1999).

Samuel Washington died on September 26, 1781, at age 47 and was presumably buried at his Harewood estate three miles west of Charles Town, West Virginia. Records indicate that some ten people were buried in the family graveyard prior to 1800 and two more in the early 1800s, none of whose graves are marked. In addition to Samuel Washington, they include his son Thornton, who died in 1787 at age 29, his fourth wife, Anne Steptoe Washington, who died in 1777 at age 39, and his nephew Charles Lewis, who is said to have died at age 14 while visiting Harewood. Starrs hoped to identify Samuel Washington's remains by determining age and sex from anatomical and anthropological markers, examining the ribs and vertebral column for lesions symptomatic of the tuberculosis that may have caused his death, and comparing DNA from the bones with living relatives and occupants of the other graves (Starrs 1999).

The discovery of the remains proved difficult, despite the use of modern technologies. The site was first mapped and a grid created. A preliminary site survey was conducted by geologist George C. Stephens in September 1998, revealing that the acidity and drainage of the soil is very suitable for the preservation of human remains. In November, James Mellett of Subsurface Consulting Ltd. used ground-penetrating radar outside and within the walled graveyard to detect about 13 subsurface anomalies that were believed to represent the disturbed soil of individual grave sites. "It is these sites marked as most probably burial sites which

James Starrs at the site of the Harewood cemetery excavation in West Virginia.

Soil from one of the burial excavations being sifted at the Harewood site.

One of the burial excavations at the Harewood site in which human remains were found.

will be the primary focus of the exhumations," wrote Starrs (1999) in his application to the State Historic Preservation Office. After a meeting with Starrs in April 1999, an ad hoc burial committee issued a two-year excavation permit with the understanding that all human remains would be reburied at the end of the field investigations (Starrs 1999).

The first phase of the excavation lasted from May 1 through May 9, 1999, with the area canopied to protect any exposed human remains and secured at all times by a team member. The excavation team included (among others) Anthony Falsetti, Michael Warren, and John Schultz of the C.A. Pound Human Identification Laboratory; Todd Fenton of Michigan State University; and James Frost, Deputy Chief Medical Examiner of West Virginia. The dig was initiated with a specially equipped backhoe and the topsoil was analyzed by magne-

tometer and metal detector. When the burial surface was reached, as indicated by depth readings and changes in soil coloration, digging proceeded with the use of shovels and hand tools. The unmarked graves of four individuals were found to extend outside the cemetery wall, built in the 1920s.

Disturbed soil from the burials was screened for artifacts and smaller bones. Skeletal remains and artifacts (helpful in dating the burials) were collected, documented, photographed, bagged, and assigned an identifying number and letter designation. Care was taken not to contaminate any of the specimens slated for genetic testing. Each bone underwent on-site anthropological analysis, radiography, toxicology screen, and microscopic analysis of hairs and fibers. Off-site analysis of nuclear or mitochondrial DNA extracted from small samples of skeletal material was to be performed at the Armed Forces Institute of

Pathology laboratory in Rockville, Maryland, after which the residue will be returned for reburial (Starrs 1999).

The second phase of the excavation was conducted from July 16 to July 20, 1999. The soil within the walls of the graveyard was removed down to undisturbed levels without revealing any burials, despite the earlier indications from ground-penetrating radar. Excavation then concentrated on an area outside the wall, where an underground anomaly had beeen detected in May but was thought to have been accounted for by a large boulder. Digging with the backhoe uncovered a decorated shard of glass at a depth of 2½ feet. Excavation with hand tools and brushes commenced, revealing a fragment of coffin wood. Coffin nails, a coffin hinge, and a long segment of coffin wood 20 to 29 inches long were discovered at a depth of 48 inches. Beneath that, the scanned and screened soil revealed several finger bones, some toe bones, a heel bone, and a patella. A total of 18 bones were recovered and the grave was excavated completely to a depth of 5½ feet. The size of the finger bones suggested that the individual was male. Because only small bones were found, the grave may represent one of the three removals documented in the historical record, since a disinterment would have left the coffin and typically several of the smaller bones in place.

While the excavation did reveal evidence of burials, Starrs was puzzled that more unmarked graves were not found inside the cemetery wall. The idea that it was meant to leave room for future burials was unsupported, since the last burial had occurred in 1846. After further unsuccessful explorations were made outside the wall south of the grave that had been located, the burial pit was filled in and the excavated area inside the wall was refilled manually and by backhoe. The entire area of activity was graded, raked, and later seeded. Footstones were placed on the four previously unmarked graves that had been discovered within the wall, but the grave beyond it was left unmarked at the request of the Washington family. "[I]t was evident that any further excavations at this time would be recklessly random in nature and without a sound scientific or factual basis," wrote Starrs in the "Second Interim Report on the Harewood Property Excavations" he submitted to the West Virginia Division of Culture and History. When analysis has been completed, a final report will be submitted to the state and will include the results of the full DNA profiling. All artifacts will be turned over to Walter Washington for curation and all human remains will be reburied in the cemetery in caskets donated by a local funeral home.

African-American Cemeteries

Excavations of nineteenth-century African-American cemeteries, two in Philadelphia and one in New York, illustrate the interest that minorities have in their past and the concern they feel toward their ancestors — sentiments mirrored by the physical anthropologists as they extracted information from the bones before they were reinterred. Philadelphia's First African Baptist Church (FABC) community developed a partnership with scientists during a project to excavate associated cemeteries at two locations. The FABC Cemetery at 8th & Vine Streets was excavated in 1983 and 1984, revealing just under 150 individuals, whose remains were reinterred in 1987. The FABC Cemetery two blocks away at 10th & Vine Streets was excavated in 1990, revealing the remains of 85 inviduals, whose remains were reinterred in 1995.

The Philadelphia digs began by obtaining the proper paperwork: "Because of the sensitive nature of the archaeological and osteological remains at the First African Baptist Church Cemetery, archaeologists decided early on that the best course of action for handling the human burials at the site would be to reinter them after excavation and analyses. A petition was presented to the Philadelphia Court of Common Pleas, Orphans Court Division, to 'grant leave' to remove human remains from the First African Baptist Church Cemetery and reinter them in Eden Cemetery in Delaware County, Pennsylvania, after suitable analyses had been performed" (Parrington 1984). The petition required a three-week public notice of the hearing that was held on June 8, 1983, during which the court granted permission for the excavation. Despite the necessary formalities, the dig was made accessible to the public. During the 1983 and 1984 field seasons, the Afro-American Historical and Cultural Museum, located three blocks away, advertised and conducted approximately a dozen site tours, attended by an estimated 500 people. A wooden platform was constructed at the site so that the public would have a safe and unobstructed view. Casual visitors were also welcomed and given detailed handouts and occasionally an impromptu lecture by field personnel. It is believed that well over 3,000 people visited the site off the street during the excavations (Parrington 1984).

The FABC cemetery excavations offered a remarkable chance to learn about lifestyles and mortality of one of Philadelphia's nineteenth-century minority groups. They afforded an opportunity to study health conditions, disease patterns, bone traumas, and nutrition. Examination of the skeletal remains was carried out by J. Lawrence Angel and his staff at the Smithsonian Institution, who diagnosed several diseases from which the population suffered, including rickets, arthritis, and caries. The analyses turned up some interesting facts. One of many bone traumas observed was a fractured femur that had knitted together with a six-centimeter override, indicating a probable lack of medical attention at the time of the injury. The skull of another in-

dividual exhibited a large group of benign tumors on the frontal bone and showed signs of an autopsy that may have been performed to determine the cause of resultant behavioral changes. Age and stature of each individual was estimated and gender was determined. It was also hoped that specialized analysis would reveal family relationships of individuals deposited in the same graves, either as multiple or successive burials (Parrington 1984).

In contrast to the positive community involvement in Philadelphia was the political controversy stirred up by the discovery of African-American remains in New York City. It began in 1991 when archaeologists from Historic Conservation and Interpretation, an archaeological salvage and consulting firm, examined maps of the site for a proposed federal office building near Water Street in Manhattan. The map indicated that a "Negros Burial Ground" occupied a five- or six-acre area on the lot. The space was large enough to have contained the burials of as many as 20,000 Africans and poor whites, but it was assumed that the cemetery had been abandoned and that most of the graves would have been destroyed during the excavation of basements in the nineteenth century. To the surprise of the building planners, test excavations conducted six weeks before construction was due to begin revealed 420 skeletons in only a small portion of the site. This made it the largest and earliest collection of African-American remains and possibly the largest and earliest collection of American Colonial remains of any ethnic group (Fagan 1995).

The discovery of the cemetery was an opportunity for researchers, but a setback for the General Services Administration, the federal agency charged with constructing and managing government buildings. GSA regional director William Diamond admitted that the agency would never have bought the land if it had known it would have to remove hundreds of skeletons before sinking the office tower foundation (Fagan 1995). Their frustration was interpreted as lack of concern by the African-American community, whose anger was aroused by several slights. The site had been referred to as a "potter's field," which seemed to diminish its importance. Environmental impact statements had been distributed by the GSA to more than 200 federal, state, and city agencies and local community groups, but did not alert civic groups in predominantly black neighborhoods. An oversight committee formed by Senator David Patterson recommended on-site study by African-American specialists, but the GSA chose physical anthropologists from the city's Metropolitan Forensic Anthropology Team to conduct the field analyses. The decision left the community feeling that they had no control of their own heritage, with the fate of the burial ground being decided by white bureaucrats (Fagan 1995).

Under great pressure to finish the task, the archaeologists removed the skeletons and transferred them to Lehman College in the Bronx to undergo conservation, after which they were to be studied at Howard University — a traditionally African-American institution located in Washington, D.C. — under the direction of anthropologist Michael L. Blakey. However, Blakey toured the Lehman facility and found inadequate environmental controls and careless storage of fragile bones. Heightened sensitivity led to numerous misconceptions, including rumors that the bones would not undergo any archaeological study at all. When several burials were accidentally destroyed by a backhoe operator digging the tower's foundation, outrage ensued. In April 1991, black activists concerned about the lack of African-American involvement in the scientific aspects of the excavation staged a one-day blockade of the site to stop construction.

The protest was successful. During a meeting of the House Subcommittee on Public Buildings and Grounds held in New York, it was revealed that the GSA had been aware that the land it intended to develop had once held a historic burial ground and that they had made no contingency plans in the event that human remains were found. Excavation on the pavilion site was halted and President George Bush signed Public Law 102-393 ordering the GSA to cease construction of the pavilion portion of the project and approving $3 million for the construction of a museum honoring the contribution of African-Americans to Colonial New York City. The firm of Historic Conservation and Interpretation was replaced with John Milner Associates (JMA), the West Chester, Pennsylvania, contractor that had completed the successful excavation of the FABC cemeteries in Philadelphia. JMA removed the last of the exposed burials, bringing the total number of skeletons recovered to 427 (Pearson 1999). Blakey was commissioned to develop a research design in consultation with JMA and a number of black scholars. He was also appointed as scientific director of a five-year research program on the remains to take place at Howard University. New York's black community, whose ancestors had been forced to bury their dead outside existing city limits, were included in the planning of the reburial of the remains, an African Burial Ground memorial, a burial ground exhibition in the office tower, and a museum of African and African-American History in New York.

CONTEMPORARY SITES

Contemporary excavation sites fall into two categories. Those that are of medicolegal significance, such as the recovery of the remains of a murder victim, must follow certain protocols. Those that are not of interest in the legal sense must abide by the law, but need only follow standard archaeological procedures. In both instances, the objective is to learn as much about each individual through the analysis of the skeletal remains. The relatively new field of forensic anthropology has been applied in non-criminal cases or those beyond the statute of limitations in order to maximize the results of the investigation. Scientists like William Maples (d. 1997) and James Starrs have built up impressive lists of historic and contemporary skeletons they have studied. Others like Clyde Snow uncover dozens or hundreds of fairly recent skeletons that they wish, for the sake of the victims and their families, were not available for study — not because they could not be found, but because the genocide they represent had not occurred.

William Maples, during his tenure as director of the C.A. Pound Human Identification Laboratory at the University of Florida, investigated the deaths of President Zachary Taylor (d. 1850), conquistador Francisco Pizzaro (d. 1541), the family of Czar Nicholas II (d. 1918), and civil rights advocate Medgar Evers (d. 1963). In addition, Maples examined the remains of Joseph Merrick (the "Elephant Man") to better understand Merrick's disfiguring disease. Clyde Snow confirmed the identity of the remains of Auschwitz experimenter Dr. Josef Mengele (d. 1979). James Starrs has excavated the remains of outlaw Jesse James (d. 1882), assassin Carl Weiss, and the victims of cannibal Alferd Packer, and almost had the opportunity to exhume the remains of Lizzie Borden (d. 1927). The sensational cases, even if the deaths occurred long ago, grab the headlines. And their reanalysis using modern techniques is certainly challenging to researchers. But even these studies are undertaken with great consideration for the use of this valuable science. "We shouldn't try to attack trivial questions," explains Clyde Snow (Stone 1995). "We should have a legitimate historical question

that needs to be answered." Usually, the questions that need answering are less historical and more immediate, such as the restoration of identity to a newly discovered but anonymous set of bones. Having examined human bones of all kinds, the forensic anthropologist is uniquely trained to do just that:

> The forensic anthropologist brings to such work a vast experience with the analysis of dried bone. Most have trained by analyzing hundreds of prehistoric burials, historic burials, and contemporary remains, and have thus seen, through a unique window of time, the effects of long-term, intermediate, and short interment of bone. They have also seen the effects of differing soil types, soil pressures and staining, and disturbance. They know the osteological impact of carnivores and rodents, and the results of inexpert recovery techniques. They have seen the trajectory of the skeleton through its growth, maturity, and decline. Though pathologists, radiologists, orthopedists, and others deal with bone in their own more limited contexts, anthropologists alone deal with the full range of dried bone specimens, from the fossil hominids of 4 million years ago to the John Doe whose badly decomposed body was discovered yesterday [Rhine 1998].

Even though the techniques of today are an improvement over those of yesterday, extracting the maximum amount of information from a skeletal excavation requires both archaeological training and knowledge of osteology and skeletal biology. Even professional archaeologists may lack familiarity with the human skeleton, and police officers and others lacking in both archaeological and anatomical training are strongly cautioned by forensic anthropologists against attempting excavation or recovery of remains themselves. "The average forensic anthropologist will have studied several dozen skeletons as an undergraduate — and hundreds, perhaps thousands, more since," notes Stanley Rhine (1998). Forensic anthropologists are therefore rightly called upon when a skeleton is found or when disaster strikes. For instance, a team led by Maples was called upon to assist the Metro-Dade Office of the Medical Examiner in the identification of victims from the crash of ValuJet Flight 592 in 1996 and staff from the Armed Forces Institute of Pathology assisted in the investigation of the Oklahoma City bombing and the crash of TWA Flight 800.

Forensic anthropology frequently requires field work. It also requires careful documentation, since the findings may be called into question during legal proceedings. Clyde Snow takes on both challenges in a humanitarian effort that has taken him around the world: Guatemala, Bolivia, Chile, Columbia, the Philippines, Rwanda, Sri Lanka, Bosnia, Croatia, and the Congo. Snow has a number of tools at his disposal to help with the identification of human skeletal remains. The computer he carries allows him to perform discriminant function analysis, a statistical method of assessing eight skull measurements to deduce sex (with approximately 95 percent accuracy) and race (approximately 80 percent accurate). "The information and programs it contains represent a distillation of data gathered by dozens of scientists from the bones of thousands of men, women and children who have lived from prehistoric times up to the present" (Browne 1991). He also has access to a large collection of skulls — many mutilated by bullets, axes, or bludgeons — at the Oklahoma State Chief Medical Examiner's office.

Snow may be best known for his work in Argentina, where he has identified many of the *desaparecidos* ("disappeared ones"), victims of government-sanctioned massacres that occurred in the 1970s. His work at Avellaneda Cemetery in Buenos Aires is recounted in *Witnesses from the Grave* (Joyce and Stover 1991). At least two hundred enemies of the state had been dumped in the 600-acre cemetery. The mass grave had been discovered accidentally during Snow's 1996 search for a victim of Ramón J. Camps, who was being prosecuted by the city's federal court. Instead, a gravedigger uncovered 11 skeletons stacked on top of one another. Some of the skulls contained bullet holes and the remains were identified as those of a woman and her family who had disappeared in 1977. Snow asked the court for permission to continue the excavation, but the court declined. The excavation resumed in June 1987, when he was asked by a judge in the city of La Plata to look for the body of a woman shot to death in 1976. Again the team found something other than what they were looking for:

> The bones they found in the undergrowth didn't belong to *desaparecidos*, but rather to unfortunates whose families had failed to keep up with the annual payment of a grave tax to the cemetery. Once in arrears, these graves are repossessed. Gravediggers remove the bones and cart them to one of the *osarios*, shafts dug into the earth and topped with cast-iron plates like manhole covers. Into these the bones are ignominiously cast. The *equipo* [Equipo Argentino de Antropología Forense] figured that bones scattered on the surface ... had fallen off wheelbarrows destined for the *osarios* and that cemetery workers had flipped them over the wall into the courtyard, the one place where they would never be seen [Joyce and Stover 1991].

The cemetery workers may be faulted for laziness, but they made reliable witnesses to the genocide Snow was attempting to uncover. One of them described the repeated arrival of military vans carrying bodies that were stacked in the trenches the workers were forced to dig: "A trench four feet deep and a dozen yards wide stretched the length of the west side, against the brick wall. Cemetery workers had built a wooden roof over the trench, casting parts of it in contrasting shadow and bright sunlight. Inside the trench stood eight earthen mounds.

Scores of skeletons, some fully exposed, some with an arm or leg bone poking out of the dry brown earth, lay in small mesas carved out of the ground. In some places, bones were jumbled together in heaps like a game of pickup sticks. Shreds of clothing, shoes, sandals, a raincoat, belt buckles, nylon stockings, and a scarf adorned some of the bones. Many of the skulls showed single gunshot wounds to the head. In the shadows of the trench, an army of red ants crawled from bone to bone" (Joyce and Stover 1991).

To process the remains, Snow's team cleaned up the derelict morgue in the cemetery to use as a laboratory. To gather information, one of the team members interviewed the relatives of those missing and tracked down medical records and personal histories. That same team member was saddled with the duty of informing the families of positive identifications. Snow's endeavors in Argentina were rewarded by a number of convictions. In fact, Snow is one of the fathers of forensic anthropology. His experience includes two decades of accident investigation for the Federal Aviation Administration. His recent efforts as a freelance consultant have been commissioned by medical examiner's offices across the United States, the F.B.I., Physicians for Human Rights, Americas Watch, Amnesty International, and the United Nations (Brown 1991). Even if Snow's findings do not always bring perpetrators to justice, they at least refute revisionists who claim that the massacres never happened. "It is hard to argue with a skull," he remarked during a television appearance. He has now investigated more than 3,000 cases and the list continues to grow.

3

Collections

Great collectors have given rise to great collections. The directed attempt to obtain skeletons for study by Carl August Hamann and T. Wingate Todd at Western Reserve University in Cleveland resulted in one of the premier osteological collections in the world. During his 40–year career at Washington University Medical School in St. Louis, Robert J. Terry secured more than one thousand skeletons from student dissections, a number that continued to grow after his retirement. These collections are notable for their numbers (more than 3,500 in the Hamann-Todd Collection), but also for the care and foresight with which they were collected. By preserving vital statistics and medical histories for each individual, his or her skeleton can play a statistical role in studies based on average measurements and demographics.

The value — and the practice — of collecting human bones was passed on from one generation to the next, leaving a lasting and usually growing legacy. Robert Terry had studied under George Huntington (also a mentor to T. Wingate Todd), who amassed more than 3,800 cataloged skeletons that are still the basis of studies. Terry had also been a student of Sir William Turner (d. 1916), the leading British anatomist of his day, who built up a collection of human skeletons at Edinburgh University that had been exhumed from old churchyards (Tobias 1991). Terry was suc-

ceeded by skeletal biologist Mildred Trotter, who added hundreds of remains to the collection that still bears his name. W. Montague Cobb, after assisting Todd in his harvest of skeletal remains, was inspired to assemble the largest documented collection of African-American remains for biological study. Terry also influenced Raymond Arthur Dart (d. 1988), who worked for him in 1921 and was then appointed to the Chair of Anatomy at the University of the Witwatersrand in Johannesburg, South Africa. Dart began a collection there that was doubled by his successor, Phillip V. Tobias.

Some inspiration was less well-intentioned. Large numbers of skulls were assembled by craniologists to support their foregone conclusions about the superiority of the white race, ideas later taken up by Nazis and others. The collections have since been put to more scientifically sound use, but their history has its place in the growth of many disciplines. Another wrong turn taken in the nineteenth century was the assumption that the bumps on the head had an exact correlation to the thought processes of the brain inside. While the tenets of phrenology were discredited, its practitioners — Franz Gall, Joseph Hyrtl, and Samuel George Morton among them — left notable and sizable collections of skulls that are still curated. Phrenological collections, often with a famous skull as their centerpiece,

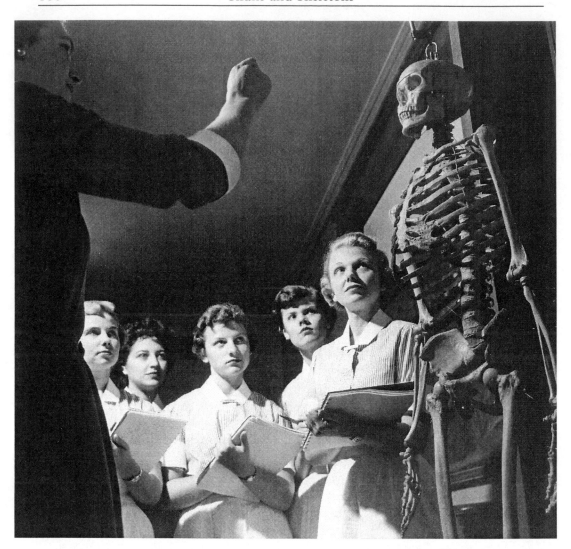

A teaching specimen of a skeleton being used at the School of Nursing at Wesley Memorial Hospital in Chicago, ca. 1951. Photo reprinted with permission of the Northwestern Memorial Hospital Archives.

became the core of several institutional collections in the United States and Europe.

Museums, including those maintained by the Royal College of Surgeons of England, amassed specimens of medical interest, from the representative to the anomalous, many of them donated by their members. Surgeon John Hunter, like the phrenologists, often went to great lengths to obtain unique specimens, and although the ends may not justify the means, the results are an unparalleled collection that is still of great use to students and researchers. Other institutions were repositories for excavated ancient remains and their collections increased as digs worldwide continued. Skeletal remains recovered by Ales Hrdlička form part of the collections at the Smithsonian Institution, the San Diego Museum of Man, and other museums here and abroad. While some assemblages of archaeologically-recovered remains are subject to repatriation, the documented skeletal collections — obtained from unclaimed bodies or by consent — are not in jeopardy. Whether curation will continue, and especially if it may not, skeletal collections are being studied thoroughly, meticulously, and gratefully.

COLLECTORS AND COLLECTING

> *Documented skeletons are a particularly valuable research asset.... The accumulation of documented skeletal specimens from different geographical regions is therefore a most laudable goal, even if building a collection is also a slow and difficult process.*
> — *Stanley Rhine (1998)*

Many scientific disciplines are advanced through the analysis of human skeletal remains. As collections grow, so do opportunities, as Douglas Ubelaker (1982) points out about one such field:

> Paleopathology has evolved from a sporadic interest in the ancient, medically unusual specimen to a complex discipline that encompasses many fields. Growth has been augmented tremendously by the acquisition of numerous, large, documented samples of human skeletons and technological advances in radiography, histology, the chemistry of bone and mummified soft tissue, and trace-element analysis. Although advances have been numerous, many of the present needs are the same as in the past. Still relevant is [Earnest A.] Hooton's plea in 1930, "We shall never be able to acquire any satisfactory basis for study of palaeopathology until clinical pathologists and anatomists cooperate in the preservation of skeletal material of known clinical history.

It was the directed collection of skeletons by anatomists like Robert Terry and T. Wingate Todd that marked the intersection of anatomy and physical anthropology. In fact, Todd felt so strongly that the two should remain a single discipline that he fought the formation of the American Association of Physical Anthropologists, though he later became its president.

The father of American physical anthropology is, by consensus, Ales Hrdlička (d. 1943), who was born in the Czech Republic and came to the United States as a teenager. Hrdlička was the first curator in physical anthropology at the Smithsonian's Bureau of American Ethnology and a field anthropologist at the American Museum of Natural History. His measurement and cataloging of thousands of skulls (including those collected by George Huntington) made him the most knowledgeable human craniologist in the U.S. (Schwartz 1998). In 1918, he founded the *American Journal of Physical Anthropology*. He received his training in Paris, where surgeon and anthropologist Paul Broca (d. 1880) had founded the Société d'Anthropologie de Paris in 1859, the Laboratoire d'Anthropologie de l'École d'Medicine in 1867, and the École d'Anthropologie in 1875, known collectively and informally as "Broca's Institute." Broca had calculated average cranial capacities from large Parisian cemetery populations from the twelfth, eighteenth, and nineteenth centuries, but the results did not conform to his ideas that those of higher class should have a higher capacity and that brain size should increase over time (Gould 1996). Broca also had other ethnocentric preconceptions that he passed along to his students, as C. Loring Brace notes (1982): "To exorcise the demons of our past, the first thing we must do is to realize that the race concept that we inherited was partially the result of Hrdlička's failure to confront the racism in the ethos of the French anthropology that he admired so uncritically."

Hrdlička and Earnest Hooton (d. 1954) represented the mainstream evolutionary approach (emphasizing racial comparison, biological determinism, and the racial "inferiority" of African-Americans) as opposed to the "Boasian school" named after Franz Boas (d. 1942) of Columbia University, who stressed the developmental plasticity of body and mind, environmental effects, and racial equality (Rankin-Hill 1994). Boas began acquiring Indian skeletons from the American Northwest in 1888 and selling them for $5 per skull or $20 per complete skeleton. In addition to his own finds, Boas purchased from collectors William and James Sutton and soon had 200 crania and half as many skeletons. Stored at the American Museum of Natural History, the museum declined to purchase the remains, so Boas moved them with him to Clark University in Worcester, Massachusetts, where he had accepted a teaching position. Boas used the remains in his expanding collection and the growing skull collections at the Field Museum, of which he was temporary curator, to demonstrate through empirical research that blacks, whites, and other races were biologically equal (Thomas 2000). "Franz Boas ... made short work of the fabled cranial index by showing that it varied widely both among adults of a single group and within the life of an individual," writes Stephen Jay Gould (1996). Hooton, on the other hand, spent years classifying a select sample of the 2,000 skulls excavated by Alfred V. Kidder from Pecos Pueblo near Santa Fe, New Mexico (and repatriated to the Pecos and Jemez Pueblo in 1999), into eight morphological types (Thomas 2000). Hrdlička's studies — though close-minded in hindsight — led him around the world in search of specimens and earned him the nickname "Skull Doctor" among Native Americans. He noted that Eskimos were more inclined than other Aboriginal groups to permit him to study the skeletons of their dead. Of a looted site near Barrow, Alaska, he writes, "There were remnants of hundreds of skulls and skeletons ... and we brought back four sacks full of specimens, the Eskimo carrying his with utmost good nature" (*Anthropological Survey* 1930). Hrdlička's largest excavation in Alaska yielded a quantity of skeletons that accounted for 5 percent of the human remains curated at the Smith-

sonian at the time and now repatriated to Alaska, where they are available to researchers at the Alutiiq Museum (Thomas 2000).

Hrdlička was of course not the first to measure and classify human skulls. Johann Friedrich Blumenbach (d.1840) had recorded anthropometric and morphologic descriptions of human crania in the late eighteenth century, although his thesis on modern human diversity was based on the examination of only 82 skulls (Walker In press). Other analyses followed, many of them using only a subset of the skulls they examined to prove their points. In the 1950s, G.K. Neumann developed a model to explain the peopling of the New World in which he placed all Amerindian populations within a "Mongoloid subspecies." He classified them into eight races based on their geography, cultural association, and morphological similarity. Neumann's classification of North American crania was based on study of over 10,000 skulls, but he actually utilized only a small number of the total in the formulation of his classification, with two types based on less than 20 specimens each (Armelagos, Carlson, and Van Gerven 1982).

Craniometry had ardent supporters long after it had fallen out of favor with many scientists. People were grouped into categories based on the shapes of their heads and the ratios of skull measurements after the publication of Darwin's theory of natural selection and well into the middle of the twentieth century in the work of Hrdlička, Hooton, and other influential skeletal biologists. The idea that human variation can be adequately accommodated by a few, fundamentally different racial types coincided conveniently with beliefs in racial inferiority and superiority and helped to justify slavery and racial inequality. In addition, the idea of a straightforward relationship between the shape of a person's skull and their genetic makeup meant that cranial differences could be used as a powerful tool to reconstruct population movements and historical relationships, one of the principal goals of anthropology. And lastly, the typological approach solved the practical computational problem of being unable to statistically compare quantitative observations made on skeletal collections of any meaningful size (Walker In press). At the same time, phrenology — which went from science to fad over the years — promised the initiated the ability to assess a person's character from the shape of his or her head. So both scientists and laypersons enthusiastically collected skulls from which to distinguish racial characteristics and diagnose personality traits. Polygenists, who ranked the races hierarchically, looked for skeletal signs of racial primitiveness to back up their beliefs. Phrenologists sought out the skulls of the famous to look for indications of their talent in the contours of their crania.

Phrenologists founded societies and outfitted them with libraries and the indispensable collection of skulls, casts, and drawings. When the Central Phrenological Society was formed in Philadelphia in 1828, its members procured a large collection of skulls and casts from Edinburgh. A society in Boston with 144 members purchased an extensive collection of casts, later preserved at the Harvard Medical School, and exhibited a group of more than 100 "racial" skulls (Davies 1971), also acquiring the willed skull of Spurzheim (Colbert 1997). In addition to offering casts of the skulls of John Quincy Adams, Voltaire, Sir Walter Scott, Thomas Hart Benton, Aaron Burr, Napoleon, and Henry Clay, Orson Squire Fowler and his brother Lorenzo sold real human skulls "imported from ancient battlefields" for five to ten dollars, with those of "rare races" available for 30 dollars and up (Davies 1971). The centerpiece of a society's or an individual's collection was usually the skull of a renowned or depraved individual. If they

did not own such a skull, they borrowed one around which to plan an exhibit. A phrenological society formed in Washington, D.C., in 1824 was offered the opportunity to examine the skull of executed murderer Alexander Tardy, which had been procured by their secretary — and surgeon-general of the U.S. — Alexander Brereton (Davies 1971). When the remains of Daniel Boone (d. 1820) were moved from Missouri to Kentucky in 1845, his skull was passed around among the prominent citizens who had been invited to the capitol and a plaster cast was made so that local phrenologists could study it at their leisure (Murphy 1995). A group of phrenologists meeting in Dublin in 1835 had the lucky opportunity to handle the skull of Jonathan Swift (d. 1745) when his grave in St. Patrick Cathedral was opened to check for water damage (Weil 1992).

The quest for skulls was competitive and the demand was insatiable, as Henschen (1965) describes:

> Phrenology gave rise to the enthusiastic collection of skulls and casts of skulls. Not only those of famous men but also those of lunatics and criminals were in demand, for obvious reasons. Both serious doctors and charlatan adventurers were eager to possess skulls and skull-casts to display in their waiting-rooms and surgeries…. By the beginning of the nineteenth century the whole situation had degenerated into a positive scramble for skulls; churchwardens, undertakers and gravediggers being the main source of supply.

Two of the more notorious acquisitions were the skulls of Franz Josef Haydn (d. 1809) and Emanuel Swedenborg (d. 1772). Haydn's head was procured from his grave in a churchyard near Vienna by amateur phrenologist Johan Peter. Peter prepared and examined the skull, adding it to the collection of the crania of executed prisoners that he had obtained as a prison superintendent. By the time the theft was discovered during the reinterment of Haydn's remains on the estate of his patron, the skull was in possession of Joseph Rosenbaum. Not wanting to part with it, Rosenbaum offered another skull in its place, returning the authentic skull to Johan Peter on his deathbed years later. A tug-of-war in Vienna after Peter's death was finally resolved in 1954, when the skull was reunited with the rest of Haydn's remains at Eisenstadt. Swedenborg's skull was also replaced with a substitute so that it could join the many others in the collection of John Didrik Holm, a Swedish sea captain and phrenologist. Ironically, the substitute itself was displayed in a phrenological museum from 1819 to 1823, when it was replaced in the casket. Though the whereabouts of Holm's large collection are unknown, two skulls purported to be Swedenborg's vied for authenticity — one recovered from the casket and the other tracked down in a London antique shop (Henschen 1965). In 1978, a skull purported to be that of Swedenborg was offered at auction by Sotheby's and fetched $3,200 from a Swedish bidder (Murphy 1995).

The history of skull collecting has also been peppered with people who desired them not to practice their hobby but to add them to their "cabinets of curiosity." Robert Ripley, prodigious collector of oddities, is among this group. A contemporary example is Bill Jamieson of Golden Chariot Productions, although Jamieson points out that the material he collects must have a meaning, a provenance, a history (personal correspondence, January 20, 1999). In addition to mummies and shrunken heads, his collection of tribal art includes dozens of skulls, many of them from Borneo and New Guinea, and implements made from human femurs. One of Jamieson's nineteenth-century counterparts, R.W. Shufeldt, had more opportunities to obtain skulls firsthand and less consideration for the cultures from which they came. He initiated his collection with the skull of an executed bank rob-

ber who he had dissected in college and followed that up by procuring skulls for himself and his acquaintances. His attempts were sometimes thwarted, for instance when he was prevented from removing the remains of an Indian from a burial scaffold by his native guides. He did, however, confess to surreptitiously pocketing the jawbone that he found on the ground some distance away: "It is now, thirty-two years afterwards, an excellent pen-rack on the table where I am writing this article in my study" (Shufeldt 1910). Indians also prevented his looting a Zuni graveyard and rattlesnakes came between him and a skeleton in the southwestern U.S. In Arizona, Shufeldt had been told by a ranchman of an Indian burial site containing more than 60 skulls. "This lot I intended to obtain, if possible, at one haul," he later related (Shufeldt 1910). He and two others set out in a mule-drawn ambulance, entered the canyon, and located the cache, only to find that it was guarded by three or four armed Navajo sentries. Shufeldt considered himself lucky to get away with his life and later came into possession of a Navajo skull by other means: making off with the head of his recently killed native washerwoman.

Such stories do not reflect well on their subjects, particularly when they considered themselves men of science. But it has been the assiduous study of human skeletal remains — some of them admittedly collected under unethical circumstances — that has allowed the science of physical anthropology to move beyond racial stereotyping and in fact to refute and replace it with better principles and practice. Contemporary physical anthropologists and those of related disciplines acknowledge the history that precedes their work, but no longer gather human skeletal specimens to grace the mantel. Although they do sometimes seek out the heads of the famous, it is not to feel phrenologically for Mozart's "bump of music," but to reassess his life and death using modern methods and thereby enrich history. The procurement of human skeletons remains as important as — many would argue more important than — in the past, with large, unbiased, well-documented collections the goal of today's collector.

Franz Joseph Gall

Of Dr. Gall and his skulls
who has not heard.
— Edinburgh Review, 1803

Austrian physician Franz Joseph Gall (d. 1828) pioneered the theory of cerebral localization and named it "phrenology," the study of the mind, although Colbert (1997) claims that he preferred the term "craniology." Not only did Gall's theory propose that certain areas of the brain were responsible for certain mental faculties, but that the strengths of these areas were reflected in the external form of the cranium and could be diagnosed by doing an analysis of the skull. Phrenology spawned the sister sciences of craniology, anthropometry, and psychognomy, all of which were based on quantitative analysis of the head. "Although it must be acknowledged that Gall had hit upon what was in principle a correct line of reasoning, he soon allowed himself to be misled into the realms of pure speculation. He began to teach that these different 'organs' of the brain were so strictly delimited and so prominent on the surface of the brain that they could cause protuberances in the outer contours of the cranium, where they stood out so boldly that they were both visible and tangible...." (Henschen 1965). Well-developed areas left bumps on the skull and poorly developed areas left hollows.

Gall's theory, which could not be proven scientifically, began to be attacked. When his protegé Johann Caspar Spurzheim (d. 1832) carried his speculations even further, the theory was ridiculed and degenerated into a fashionable pastime for the idle.

Specimens in Dr. Gall's Skull Collection at the Städtische Sammlungen Archiv-Rollettmuseum. Photo courtesy of the Rollettmuseum, Baden, Austria.

Gall was expelled from Austria after the emperor prohibited the teaching of phrenology in 1802. He attempted to apply his "science" to the rehabilitation of criminals and met some success in a few prisons in Germany and the Netherlands, but his ideas were found to be socially unacceptable. He encountered severe criticism from medical circles in Germany, but he and Spurzheim attracted support in France, Great Britain, Sweden, and North America (Henschen 1965). Gall lectured to explain and attract attention to his theory, sometimes marking skulls for members of the audience.

Gall amassed a huge collection of skulls that he was unable to take with him when he left the country. He was such an assiduous collector that the Viennese used to specify in their wills that their crania should be protected from his researches (Davies 1971). Gall did acquire many of his specimens in Vienna: the remains of suicides, executed criminals, and the insane. Dr. Gall's Skull Collection is housed in Baden, Austria, at the Städtische Sammlungen Archiv-Rollettmuseum. Founder Anton Franz Rollett (d. 1842) had an interest in natural history and incorporated Dr. Gall's skull collection into his museum and library. The museum was open to the public, but privately owned by Rollett and his heirs until 1867, when it was bestowed on the city of Baden. The museum changed locations several times over the years and was reorganized and united with the city archives by Rollett's son Hermann (d. 1904) in 1876. The museum closed for an extended period during World War I and World War II, with another interruption between 1955 and 1957, during which the collections were cleaned and organized. Volunteer curator Hildegard Hnatek reports that the museum is being accessed by an increasing number of scientists, some of whom are presumably there to examine Dr. Gall's *Schädelsammlung*.

Samuel George Morton

Samuel George Morton (d. 1851) was a physician and anatomy professor practicing in Philadelphia. He had been influenced by theories of polygenism and the hereditarian views of phrenologists during his studies at the University of Edinburgh. To put the theories to the test, he began to amass a large collection of human crania from all over the world in the 1820s. Using cranial measurements to compare them, he derived a hierarchy of racial types with blacks at the bottom, American Indians intermediate, and whites at the top. The rankings were based on brain size as measured by the cranial capacity of the skull, and Morton used them to defend the idea that the races were separate species (Gould 1996). Morton's craniometric approach to understanding human variation set the stage for much of the osteological research done by physical anthropologists during the rest of the nineteenth century and beyond (Walker In press). His published description of the Indian skulls in his collection, *Crania Americana*, was a pioneer work in the field of American anthropology.

To his discredit, Morton manipulated data, as Stephen Jay Gould (1996) discovered upon reexamination. Morton measured the capacity of 144 Indian skulls and calculated a mean of 82 cubic inches, a full 5 cubic inches below the Caucasian norm. As it turns out, Morton's sample is strongly biased by a major overrepresentation of an extreme group — the small-brained Inca Peruvians. Thus, Morton included a large subsample of small-brained people to pull down the Indian average, but excluded just as many small Caucasian skulls (Hindus) to raise the mean of his own group. He must not have deemed this improper because he did not hide it. "All I can discern is an a priori conviction about racial ranking so powerful that it directed his tabulations along preestablished lines," writes Gould (1996).

To his "cranial library" Morton added American Indian skulls recovered from archaeological sites and contemporary native skulls purchased after smallpox and other epidemics swept across Indian country (Thomas 2000). In addition to the skulls in his own collection, Morton had the opportunity to examine more than 100 skulls sent by his friend George Gliddon, who was U.S. consul for the city of Cairo. The skulls were from the tombs of ancient Egypt and became the subject of Morton's *Crania Aegyptiaca* of 1844. After showing that whites surpassed Indians in mental endowment, he would now demonstrate that the discrepancy between whites and blacks was even greater and had been for more than 3,000 years (Gould 1996). This work, too, shows skewed results. All of Morton's minor numerical errors favor his prejudices. The differences in brain size reflect differences in stature based on sex, and the single pure Negro skull in the sample was female (Gould 1996).

Because it provided a foundation for their theories about race, Morton's work was well-respected by his contemporaries. His collection, which numbered more than 1,000 skulls at the time of his death, drew fame and visitors. Louis Agassiz (d. 1873) recounted his 1846 visit in a letter to his mother: "Imagine a series of 600 skulls, most of Indians from all tribes who inhabit or once inhabited all of America. Nothing like it exists anywhere else. This collection, by itself, is worth a trip to America" (Gould 1996). The collection now resides at the University of Pennsylvania Museum of Archaeology and Anthropology.

Joseph Hyrtl

Prominent Viennese anatomist and phrenologist Joseph Hyrtl (d. 1894) had an enormous collection of skulls and casts from around the world. Hyrtl's renown brought the skulls of some famous individuals to him. Upon the death of his brother Jacob in 1868, Hyrtl inherited a skull believed to be that of Wolfgang Amadeus Mozart (d. 1791) to add to his casts of the skulls of Beethoven and Schubert. Mozart's skull had reportedly been taken from its grave some ten years after death by gravedigger Joseph Rothmayer, from whom it passed to Joseph Radschopf, and then to Jacob Hyrtl in 1842. The skull, missing the jawbone, was bequeathed to the Mozarteum in Salzberg by Joseph Hyrtl's widow upon her death in 1901. The Mozarteum directors put the skull on exhibit the following year, but removed it from display in the 1950s because they thought the exhibition in poor taste and because there was no conclusive evidence that the skull was in fact Mozart's. Attempts to authenticate the skull in the early twentieth century failed, but in the 1980s a team of French anthropologists led by Pierre-François Puech claimed to have positively identified the skull through portraits, descriptions, medical history, and facial reconstruction (Bahn 1991). A few years later, six scientists at the Vienna Museum of Natural History also reconstructed the head, resulting in a completely different likeness. The Mozarteum will continue its efforts to determine whether the skull belonged to Mozart and lend it to medical researchers attempting to establish cause of death (Murphy 1995).

In 1874, a committee representing the Mütter Museum of the College of Physicians of Philadelphia completed their negotiations with Joseph Hyrtl to buy 139 skulls from Central and Eastern Europe for their own collections. The idea may have been conceived by patron George McClellan, who had studied under Hyrtl in 1872. The purchase gave legitimacy to the museum, marking its change from a personal collection to a full-fledged medical museum. The entire collection remains on display at the Mütter Museum to this day. The skulls date from 1868 to 1914. Dates, places, and causes of death are indicated for each, along with any pathologies to be noted, and the individuals' names and occupations when known. Two typical examples follow:

Romania
Vasili Draganu, Age 23
Eastern Orthodox soldier
Died of typhus in Bucharest

Saxon, from Transylvania
Male, Age 36
Day laborer
Died of delirium tremens
Keeled cranial vault (tapers to a point
  in the middle)

The Hyrtl Skull Collection includes examples from Austria, Crete, Croatia, Egypt, Galicia, Greece, Hong Kong, Hungary, Italy, Moldavia, Persia, Russia, Switzerland, Thailand, and the Ukraine. One skull is noted to be from the catacomb of St. Stephen and many are noted to belong to gypsies. A few of the craniums have been sawed, but most of the skulls are uncut and include the mandible. Several causes of death are represented: natural, suicide, war casualty, execution, and murder (including by stabbing and gunshot). The ages range from 13 up, but most seemed to have died in their early 20s. One of the skulls — Geysa Fekete de Galantha, a Hungarian deserter — is featured in a photograph by Joel-Peter Witkin included in the 2000 edition of the calendar that the Mütter Museum publishes.

George S. Huntington

Dr. George Sumner Huntington (d. 1927) was anatomy professor at the College of Physicians and Surgeons in New York from 1886 to 1924. Rather than dispose of the skeletons of the cadavers dissected at the medical school, he preserved them for skeletal biological research. The bodies consisted primarily of European immigrants and residents of New York. Unclaimed, they had become the property of the state and were obtained by the college from sanitariums, poorhouses, and morgues in all boroughs of the city. The skeletons bear the marks of dissection. Many are incomplete, with the cranium frequently missing or cut, ribs and sternae sometimes absent, and only one side of the body represented in some cases. They are, however, well-preserved and well-documented. And they have been put to good use.

Dr. Huntington influenced and mentored Robert Terry, T. Wingate Todd, and Ales Hrdlička. It was the latter who brought the collection to the Smithsonian Institution:

> Huntington and his collection had numerous long-term effects on Hrdlička's budding anthropological career. On a basic level, the data he gathered from Huntington's ever-increasing collection inspired some of Hrdlička's earliest anthropological publications and provided the standard of comparison for all of his later studies on the Smithsonian's vast stores of skeletons. Through trades of materials with Huntington, Hrdlička later acquired about 1,200 of these skeletons for his own use at the Smithsonian Institution. His exposure to the Huntington collection also influenced his Smithsonian career by its organization, or more specifically, its lack thereof. Before beginning research on this material, Hrdlička first had to organize and catalogue the material; and convinced Huntington himself to adjust his accession procedure to facilitate and enhance record-keeping (Jones-Kern 1997).

The more than 3,800 skeletons in the Huntington Collection are curated at the Smithsonian's National Museum of Natural History in Washington, D.C. All cataloged individuals have known names, sex, age, ethnic origin (and usually nationality), cause of death, and — in some cases — height and place of collection. The specimens include examples of trauma, infections, tumors, and congenital diseases. Approximately 2,800 (75 percent) of the specimens are male. About 10 percent of the collection consists of U.S. blacks, with the majority consisting of immigrants from Germany, Italy, Ireland, and — to a lesser degree — Sweden, Scotland, and France. For 60 years, the collection was organized by element, with hands, feet, and crania stored together. Recently, the collection was fully re-inventoried and reorganized into individual skeletons. Some errors were found, including multiple individuals given the same museum catalog number, but will be rectified. "...[A]s long as the researcher is aware of these problems, this invaluable collection is now available for study," writes collections manager David R. Hunt (unpublished draft, April 1998).

Robert J. Terry

Robert J. Terry (d. 1966) headed the Anatomy Department at Washington University Medical School in St. Louis from 1899 until his retirement in 1941. His interest in human anatomy was focused on normal and pathological variants in the skeleton. Aware that there was a lack of research material in the areas of skeletal biology, anatomy, and pathology, Terry began to collect the skeletons of cadavers used in the Medical School's anatomy classes. Beginning the collection in 1910, Terry had, by the early 1920s, established a uniform protocol for collecting, cataloging, macerating, and storing the skeletons. Cadavers earmarked for the osteological collection were used only for the dissection of soft tissue so that the bones could be preserved in their whole state. In some cases, the calvarium was cut for brain dissection. Post-cranially, only the ribs and sometimes the sternum were cut for access to the internal organs. In a few cases, vertebral bodies were sampled for histological examination. After dissec-

tion, the bones were macerated in hot water for 72 hours, brushed and scrubbed to remove the flesh, dried at room temperature, and then degreased by exposure to benzene vapors. This would remove some of the fats, but Dr. Terry was adamant that the bones not be completely void of fats, which would leave them brittle and susceptible to damage. He felt the bone would preserve better with some fats still present and "the long-term preservation of this heavily studied collection shows that Dr. Terry's foresight was correct," writes David Hunt (unpublished draft, September 1998).

Upon Terry's retirement in 1941, skeletal biologist Mildred Trotter (d. 1991) took over his position and continued to collect skeletons until her retirement in 1967. In addition, she tried to balance the demography of the collection, focusing on younger individuals — especially the underrepresented white females. The majority of these willed their bodies and some wrote personal and medical histories, although only a few of these histories still survive. Under the guidance of Terry and subsequently Trotter, some 2,000 documented skeletons had been processed. In the 1950s and 1960s, however, retirements, renovations, and changing research focus at the Anatomy Department at Washington University resulted in decreased interest in continuing support of the Terry Collection and plans to bury it were initiated. Looking ahead to her retirement, Trotter approached her friend T. Dale Stewart at the Smithsonian Institution about transferring the collection for permanent curation. In July 1967, this transfer to the Department of Anthropology at the National Museum of Natural History was completed. Receipt of transfer, copies of the death certificates, other records, and the correspondence of Terry and Trotter are housed at Washington University Medical School.

The documentation that accompanies each skeleton consists of morgue records with the name (which is not released to the public), sex, age, ethnic identity, cause of death, date of death, morgue or institution of origin, permit number, and various dates and records related to autopsy, embalming, and medical history. Families sometimes provided nationality and occupation. A bone inventory completed after the maceration process indicated damaged or missing bones and sometimes included biological age estimates. The inventory list recorded pathological and normal osteological variants observed during the autopsy and charted dentition. Some 60 to 65 percent of the collection includes anthropometric measurements and photographs of the cadaver and plaster death masks were prepared for nearly half of the specimens. Curated with the collection are also 1,078 hair samples. The skin samples that had been collected and preserved in paraffin were incinerated in the 1960s when renovations to the Anatomy Department building in St. Louis required demolition of the Cold Room where these tissue samples were stored.

Today, the Terry Collection consists of the skeletal remains of 1,728 individuals: 461 white males, 546 black males, 323 white females, 392 black females, five Asiatic males, and one of unknown origin. Dates of birth range from 1822 to 1943. Age at death ranges from 16 to 102 years, with the majority of individuals 45 or older. There is a deficiency in young white females under 27 years, but there are representative numbers of younger age ranges. The Terry Collection has now been used for decades as a source of comparative standards and for investigation of bone changes correlated with age, sex, and race. Since the 1940s, most landmark studies based on anatomical collections have utilized the collection for research or to test results. In 1970, Trotter developed equations to estimate stature that are still very much in use based on the bones of approximately 850 males and females in the Terry Collection and about 4,100 males

killed during World War II and the Korean War (Ubelaker 1989).

The cadavers from which the Terry Collection skeletons were harvested had been obtained from local hospital and institutional morgues, with a small portion collected from other institutions in the State of Missouri. They had become the property of the state when they went unclaimed or were signed over by relatives. After the Willed Body Law of Missouri was passed in 1955–1956, requiring a signed release from individuals or their immediate family members to use the body for scientific purposes, the cadavers were predominantly those of middle and upper incomes rather than those of lower income that the collection had been primarily composed of up to that time. A study by M.F. Ericksen (1982) asks whether data derived from dissecting room populations can be safely applied to present-day clinical and forensic problems, the assumption being that people who will their bodies are likely to represent a more privileged group than those who arrive in the dissecting room from the city morgue. The study suggested that the Terry collection may present a false picture, which could be resolved with more data.

The collection is in use daily, with studies ranging from anthropological to clinical. Researchers often bring their own osteometric boards, especially if they are making comparisons with other collections, to avoid introducing any errors into their results. The museum, however, has all the standard equipment for bone measurement, electron microscopy, three-dimensional imaging, photography, radiography, CT-scanning, and bone histology. Specimens from the collection are rarely allowed off the premises, but may be accessed by physical anthropologists or other researchers on-site, with between 150 and 200 researchers taking advantage of the opportunity annually. In the past 20 years or so, only three or four loans have been allowed and for only one or two days to use equipment not available at the Smithsonian. Any requests for destructive sampling by outside researchers and museum staff must undergo a rigorous review by a sampling committee, the collection management staff, and museum conservators.

The Terry Collection includes an example of achondroplasia (dwarfism), the results of various tumors, and specimens of healed trauma. Trauma was the cause of death in many cases, with tuberculosis causing or contributing to death in many others. The collection also includes a famous example of multiple myeloma. None of the skeletons were x-rayed before maceration, but several specific bones have been since, including some of the crania and about half of the tibias. None of the bones has undergone DNA testing, mainly because of the expense. The bones have remained in good condition, although the storage facility could be modernized. Hunt would like to see the bones curated in shallower drawers to prevent their wear and tear during handling. Hunt does not systematically survey the skeletal materials to assess their condition, but sees 35 to 40 percent of the collection each year in the process of showing it to researchers. Robert Terry has provided an invaluable research asset, but the number of specimens in the collection will remain stable. Hunt explains that no active search for new skeletal materials is underway and that the Smithsonian Institution does not have the facilities to process bodies offered by the medical examiner's office.

Carl August Hamann and T. Wingate Todd

Carl August Hamann (d. 1930) and Thomas Wingate Todd (d. 1938) were both remarkable for having achieved so much during their careers and for having begun those careers at such young ages. Hamann, who had distinguished himself in Philadel-phia as a surgeon and anatomy demonstrator, was hired by Western Reserve Medical School in 1893. At age 26 he was the youngest full professor in the institution's first 100 years and by 1911 he was Cleveland's leading surgeon (Jones-Kern 1997). Todd had found himself, at age 23, in sole charge of the Anatomical Department at the University of Manchester until the appointment of Dr. (later Sir) Grafton Elliot Smith in 1909. In addition to his responsibilities as a faculty member, Hamann wanted to build an anatomical teaching museum. He began to collect and mount animal and human specimens. By 1912, the Hamann Comparative Anatomy Collection included more than 100 human skeletons, in addition to mammal skeletons. When Hamann was appointed dean of the medical school in 1912 (a post he held until his retirement in 1928), his position as chair of anatomy was offered to Todd, who was recommended by Arthur Keith and by Smith, whose skeletal specimens from Nubia Todd had cataloged in England.

"He [Todd] straightway began the most complete documentation possible of each of the unclaimed deceased whose remains came to the anatomical laboratory," reports W. Montague Cobb (1959). The skeletons were harvested from unclaimed bodies obtained from Cleveland's Cuyahoga County Morgue or city hospitals. To fully make use of this resource, Hamann was instrumental in having the Anatomical Laws of the State of Ohio revised so that Todd would be notified by the city hospitals, the workhouse, and local mortuaries when they had unclaimed bodies in their possession. The bodies were delivered to the medical school where they were measured, weighed, photographed (full-face and profile), documented, embalmed, dissected, and macerated (Jones-Kern 1997). Maceration was accomplished by the use of dermestid beetles (Gottlieb 1982). The cleaned bones were numbered and stored in pine boxes.

The skeletal collection of the Hamann Museum of Comparative Anthropology and Anatomy as it was stored in pine boxes on the campus of Western Reserve University. Photo courtesy of the Cleveland Museum of Natural History.

During Todd's tenure, the collection increased to include well over 3,000 human skeletons. Even so, it is not the quantity of skeletons that makes this collection so important, it is the quality of the data that accompany them: "The tremendous scientific significance of this collection is not so much in its size, but in its accompanying set of personal information. Each individual entombed in the collection also has a file that contains the anthropometric and demographic data taken from that person at death. These data include name, age, sex, ethnicity, cause of death, cranial capacity, and more than seventy anthropometric measurements listed on a standardized form. In addition, stereoscopic pictures and x-rays made of the individual at the time of his or her curation are included in the file, along with the results of any autopsies or dissections performed" (Jones-Kern 1997). Todd was appointed director of the newly named Hamann Museum of Comparative Anthro-

pology and Anatomy in 1920. When a new building was constructed to house the medical school in 1924, the first floor became home to the museum.

Sadly, the collection fell into disarray after Todd's premature death at age 53 in 1938. The museum was scaled back and eventually closed. The skin and hair samples were lost. The thousands of skeletons were stored in their original wooden boxes in closets, basements, attics, and even coal bins on campus. After deciding it could no longer maintain the collection, the medical school at Case Western Reserve University considered burying the bones or transferring the collection to the Field Museum in Chicago. Instead, it was offered on permanent loan in 1951 to the Cleveland Museum of Natural History, to which it was transferred over the next twenty years. The Hamann-Todd Osteological Collection is now housed in the museum's Laboratory of Physical Anthropology. After the acquisition of the collection, the museum received foundation grants and private donations that allowed it to purchase an automated compact storage system in the safe, environmentally-controlled facility. By 1976, the post-cranial remains were placed in plastic drawers with protective foam padding and the skulls were housed in boxes. The collection was completely inventoried and relabeled. The radiographs were converted to microfiche. By the early 1990s, the records attached to each specimen were computerized. The original records were transferred to acid-free files. Under the direction of collections manager Lyman Jellema, and with financial support from the National Science Foundation, the bones were cleaned of more than a ton and a half of grease. One half of the ribs were not degreased, but were instead bagged with each skeleton in the event that future studies require its presence. The collection is now internationally recognized as a model of museum curation techniques (Jones-Kern and Latimer 1996).

The collection has been studied intensively by Todd and many others. From it Todd discerned a pattern of changes in the skeleton from which the approximate age of an individual could be determined, thereby providing a tool still used by forensic anthropologists in identifying unknown skeletalized remains (Jones-Kern 1997). He and his staff published a series of papers on epiphyseal union, cranial suture closure, vertebral morphology and pathology, facial growth, cadaver anthropometry and demography, cranial capacity, and osseous anomalies and pathology (Cobb

The **Hamann-Todd Osteological Collection as it is currently curated in the Department of Physical Anthropology at the Clevelend Museum of Natural History. Photo courtesy of the Clevelend Museum of Natural History.**

1959). Todd's work shows an unusual freedom from bias. The standard practice before his time was to collect facts that fit one's preconceived ideas, usually regarding race and ethnicity. Instead, Todd based his scientific principles on great quantities of data, from which he drew conservative and incontrovertible conclusions that sometimes caused him to abandon his earlier assumptions. "Todd was nearly alone among his peers in the extent to which he allowed the data to shape his beliefs" (Jones-Kern 1997). Today the collection and associated records are used to conduct research in anatomy, anthropology, dentistry, evolutionary biology, history, medicine, primatology, and other fields. Because the individuals are named, early telephone books can be consulted and the addresses located on a map to pinpoint local outbreaks of tuberculosis. Studies have been conducted on the effects of TB, syphilis, and periostitis on the human skeleton. Scientists have also used the collection to assess the medical care of early twentieth-century Cleveland, including thoracoplasty (removal of ribs of advanced TB patients) and fracture patterns. Recent projects have examined the evolution of human walking, relationship of age and sex to long bone fractures, and an analysis of bone mineral density (Jones-Kern and Latimer 1996). The collection forms the basis of many important studies in human evolution because it includes, in addition to the human bones, the largest collection of chimpanzee skulls in the Western Hemisphere and an irreplaceable one-eighth of all the gorilla skeletal material now in existence (Gottlieb 1982). Curator Bruce Latimer has used it to explain, among other things, why our uniquely bipedal species is prone to back problems, and previous curator Donald Johanson used it to assess the height of the incomplete fossil skeleton of Lucy.

Research on the 3,592 remains in the Hamann-Todd collection has not slowed. "More researchers currently visit the collection annually than all other museum collections combined. Since 1990 alone, more than 140 scholarly publications (roughly one every two weeks) have been based on research conducted at the museum using the Hamann-Todd skeletons—an impressive testament to the collection's scientific significance" (Jones-Kern and Latimer 1996). Although underrepresentative of children (containing only about 25 or 30 skeletons aged 16 or under) and biased toward blacks (half of the specimens are African-American), the collection is a unique source of information about living conditions at the turn of the century, particularly for the lower economic classes. The causes of death represented by the remains include diabetes, anemia, syphilis, pneumonia, typhoid fever, meningitis, tuberculosis, apoplexy, alcoholism, exposure, suicidal drowning, and homicidal knife and gunshot wounds (Gottlieb 1982). Pathologies include osteomyelitis, periostitis, dental problems, and "cranking fractures" in which the upper humerus is broken when turning a car crank. The pathology specimens include a teaching collection begun by Hamann and continued by Todd. Each of the skulls in the collection is sectioned, since the brains were removed during dissection, and in fact the skulls outnumber complete skeletons by more than 400. The specimens include the remains of the victims of Cleveland's "Torso Killer," who murdered and dismembered prostitutes in 1938 (Gottlieb 1982). One skeleton belonged to Mary O'Brien (d. 1924), an Irish immigrant who lived, worked, and fought in the Irish Free State Army as a man. Two skeletons stored side by side are those of men who killed each other—one by gunshot and the other by the cutting of his throat by his dying victim (Drexler 1986). The curator does not allow loans of material from the Hamann-Todd Osteological Collection, but the Department of Physical Anthropology's casting laboratory—which produced the study casts of the Lucy skeleton—offers urethane and plaster reproductions of the human and non-human specimens. Invasive testing is only allowed in special circumstances. Another foundation grant will allow the department to digitize all of the photos and x-rays associated with the collection, which will then be added to the Museum's website for access by researchers. The acceptance of donated and unclaimed bodies ended with Todd's death, but great care has been taken to preserve his legacy.

W. Montague Cobb

> *When our present system of collecting skeletal material was instituted, local mores were such that the ground had to be carefully prepared in respect to the value of such a collection and the care which must be observed in its conservation if it is to find the greatest use.*
> —*W. Montague Cobb [1936]*

William Montague Cobb (d. 1990) began harvesting cadaver skeletons to combat racism. An African-American and an activist in the black community, Cobb realized the value that empirical data on human variation has as an antidote to racism (Walker In press). When Cobb entered graduate school, the craniometric studies of the nineteenth century used to legitimize slavery had been succeeded by craniology, which continued to justify racial inequalities. Cobb's lifework became dedicated to exposing and destroying racism by replacing it with a corrected understanding of human biology (Rankin-Hill and Blakey 1994). After receiving his M.D. at Howard University Medical School, Cobb was sent to Western Reserve University where he helped T. Wingate Todd assemble what is now known as the Hamann-Todd Osteological Collection. Cobb's Ph.D. dissertation was a massive and much-needed survey of human anthropological materials and methods of documentation, processing, and preservation (Rankin-Hill and Blakey 1994). He determined that only 5 percent of the skeletal material in America's great museums was of African-American origin (Cobb 1936).

Cobb returned to Howard with his doctorate in 1932 and established a Laboratory of Anatomy and Physical Anthropology. The dissecting lab was outfitted with eighteen cruciform dissecting tables, eleven museum cases, and large sinks at each end of the room. The exhibits in the display cases, illustrated with skeletal specimens, are enumerated by Cobb (1936): (1) The organization and work of the laboratory, including the demographics of the cadaver population and the preparation of human remains, (2) Human development, (3) Variations by sex and race, (4) The skull, (5) Pathologies, and (6) Skeletal development. The facilities provided for an optimum 72 students, four to each cadaver. The macerating room was equipped with a specially-ventilated macerating chamber, racks to hold up to 700 boxed skeletons, a cabinet of 96 bone drawers, a band saw, and other necessary furniture and tools. The embalming room contained photographic equipment and adjoined the morgue, which had a cooler to accommodate 18 cadavers and immersion vats with a total capacity of 104 cadavers (Cobb 1936).

Now outfitted and equipped for the task, Cobb began to systematically collect and prepare the skeletons of cadavers from the dissecting room, along with detailed anatomical, demographic, and medical records. When bodies were delivered to the embalming room by the city morgue, the information on their death certificates was transcribed onto admission forms that were also used to record the dates of dissection, maceration, and skeletal preparation. The forms were kept in cross-referenced files that also contained clinical histories when available, drawings and descriptions, photographs, x-rays, and the results of later skeletal examinations, such as age estimations. The cadavers were measured, photographed, and disinfected if necessary. They were then embalmed by injection and immersed in a 2 percent phenol solution until needed, at which time they were washed and dissected. During the course of dissection, the skulls were disarticulated from the spine and sawn in a way that allowed optimum results for their salvage. Maceration followed and any remaining flesh was cleaned from the bones under a stream of water with rotary wire brushes. Each of the cleaned bones was numbered and filed in a correspondingly numbered box and the skull was assembled with pins (Cobb 1936).

Cobb's objectives in the teaching of osteology were to impart established conservation techniques, the use of proper methodology, and a respect for the human remains they were using. Cobb (1936) explains, "In these documented skeletons the student studies not merely a set of bones, but the remains of a human being.... An attitude of physician to patient is cultivated between student and cadaver and skeleton, rather than the indifference reflected in the frequent use of souvenir calvaria for ash trays in physicians' sancta." During the dissection, bones from the collection of the region being studied were laid out on the table next to the cadaver. In addition to Cobb's carefully harvested skeletal collection, a collection of miscellaneous, commingled bones of approximately 70 individuals existed, about half having been salvaged over the previous two years in anticipation of Cobb's plan. The lab also inherited a number of teaching specimens, including two complete and two partial skeletons; a mounted vertebral column; mounted osteological preparations to show articulations and ligaments of the pelvis, knee, foot, and shoulder; two mounted fetal skeletons; one disarticulated fetal skeleton; and miscellaneous young bones showing separate epiphyses (Cobb 1936). The miscellaneous collection included only skull fragments, so Cobb was careful with the newly available complete crania: "Last year, for the first time in the history of our medical school it was possible for each student in the class to have in his hands a complete skull when this part was being studied collectively. Despite sincere effort on the part of students to avoid damage to these skulls there is an inevitable toll of injury to this material, so only the first sixty of the skulls in our collection are used for teaching purposes" (Cobb 1936). Once the collection had reached a certain size, each student was assigned a skeleton for study on the premises.

Cobb returned to Western Reserve University for a portion of each summer for six years under appointments as a Fellow or Associate in Anatomy. In this way, he continued his research on human craniofacial union (suture closure) using the Hamann-Todd collection. Cobb then went to St. Louis to study the 1,500 skulls assembled at Washington University by Robert Terry (Rankin-Hill and Blakey 1994). By 1936, Cobb's own collection had grown to include 182 skeletons (Cobb 1936). Today, the W. Montague Cobb Human Skeletal Collection is comparable to both the Terry and Hamann-Todd collections in the quality of data that can be derived from it. The collection includes anatomical records on 987 individuals and the preservation of more than 700 documented skeletons. It is unique as a sample of the eastern urban population of the United States. The collection provides an irreplaceable biological record of the development and pathology of the poorest Washingtonians, from the years of the Great Depression until 1969 (Rankin-Hill 1994).

Ironically, in 1969 Cobb was prompted to take leave from Howard in the wake of protest in which students targeted him as a symbol of the university establishment and boycotted his classes, forcing him from the chairmanship of the Department of Anatomy, a post he had held since 1947. Faculty members petitioned for his reinstatement and by the end of the year a new university president appointed him the first Distinguished Professor of Anatomy. He was named Distinguished Professor Emeritus in 1973. At the time of his death, Cobb had authored 1,100 publications and taught over 6,000 anatomy students. Cobb's legacy is being preserved and utilized. In 1992, with the assistance of the National Science Foundation, new quarters to house the Cobb Collection and a working physical anthropology laboratory were established in the College of Arts and Sciences at Howard University (Rankin-Hill and Blakey 1994). The collection is now stored in a seven-room, climate-controlled research and curatorial facility formally designated the W. Montague Cobb Biological Anthropology Laboratory, explains curator Michael Blakey (personal correspondence, May 26, 2000).

Robert Ripley

Robert Ripley (d. 1949), who created his first *Believe It or Not!* illustration in 1918 and opened his first exhibit in 1933, is the father of a worldwide entertainment enterprise that draws some 9 million visitors a year. A constant traveler and collector of oddities, Ripley collected numerous human skulls and bone artifacts that are now on display in three dozen "Odditoriums" around the world or stored in an Orlando, Florida, warehouse. His finds have been augmented by hundreds of new acquisitions over the years. Today, the Ripley Collection boasts more than 250 human skeletal exhibits in its collection of more than 20,000 items, relays vice president Edward Meyer (personal communication, January 18, 1999). The human skeletal artifacts include Tibetan skull bowls, flutes, rosaries, and nearly a dozen *rugens*, costumes consisting of armlets, a hat, a chest plate, and an apron made completely of human bone and worn by shamans. "Every inch of these outfits is carved human bone. They are the most spectacular of all of our bone artifacts," stresses Meyer (personal communication, January 20, 1999). In an article in *USA Today* (Buckley 1999), president of Ripley Entertainment Robert E. Masterson is pictured with one of the Tibetan skulls, worked with silver and ivory, having a hinged cap — and containing his business cards. The skull bowls include traditional examples that are capped with silver and have an ornamented base and more modern examples that have features highlighted in silver and semi-precious jewels and stand on silver pegs inserted in the underside of the jaw.

The Ripley collection includes necklaces, buttons, pipes, and flutes made from human bone, Tibetan drums made from human skulls covered with snake skin, and Tibetan altar bowls made from the skulls of holy men. It also includes a rare skull from the Asmat tribe of Dutch New Guinea, with decorations of beadwork, fruit seeds, feathers, and engraved symbols on the forehead (Cooperthwaite 1978). An itemized list of major human skeletal exhibits in the Ripley's collection (those on display and in storage) includes the following:

- 63 Tibetan bowls made from human skulls
- 34 Tibetan flutes made from human femurs
- 31 Tibetan drums made from human skulls
- 25 tribal ancestor skulls from New Guinea, New Caledonia and the New Hebrides decorated with clay, paint, and shells
- 19 human bone daggers from various South Seas tribes and Tibet
- 16 Tibetan rosaries made from human bones
- 16 Tibetan necklaces made of human bone carved into skull-shaped beads
- seven etched tribal ancestor skulls from Borneo and the Philippines
- seven trophy skulls from Borneo, New

Guinea, and various South Sea islands, decorated with shells, beads, and feathers

- four trephined skulls from Peru, Egypt, and Europe

- four bone scoops from prehistoric Europe

- three canes made of human bone by eighteenth-century Hawaiians and nineteenth-century American prisoners

- two skulls mounted on fiber to be worn by grieving widows of the Dyak tribe of Borneo

- two teaching skeletons from European medical schools

Other skeletal material includes a skull with a North American Indian arrowhead embedded in it, the skull of an Englishman who had horns surgically implanted in his head, a European skull with pointed teeth, a skeleton dressed in armor that was used in nineteenth-century initiation ceremonies, a skull crafted into a coffee urn, a mask made from a cranial vault; and various human bones and skulls used in rituals and for divination.

At any given time approximately half of the collection is in storage, where each specimen is cataloged and photographed before being sent to one of the growing number of Ripley's Believe It or Not! museums, most of which are franchised. The warehouse, which is the size of a football field, is purposely kept nondescript to avoid a repeat of past fires and break-ins. "Some of the 70-odd shrunken heads accumulated by Ripley and his disciples over the years are stashed in a big, blue metal cabinet surrounded by racks of bare skulls, some on stocks, some festooned with feathers, some stacked like grapefruit," reports Buckley (1999). Objects including human skeletal artifacts continue to be accessioned by staff members and freelance agents from private collectors, auctions, and flea markets. Most of the ethnographic material has been ac-

quired from a dealer in Melbourne, Australia. "We are still actively buying bone artifacts and are always interested in purchasing them," says Meyer (personal communication, January 20, 1999).

THE INSTITUTIONS

Collection of human remains at many institutions is still an active process. A documented skeletal collection is being acquired at the University of Tennessee as a byproduct of experiments in taphonomy, as discussed in a later chapter. An anthropological archive of skeletons of known age, sex, occupation, places of birth and death, and cause of death is being assembled at the Wiener Laboratory in Athens, Greece. Researchers today strive for balanced skeletal assemblages that reflect the norm, but even when a skeletal sample is biased, for instance, consisting only of battle casualties, plague or starvation victims, immigrants, slaves, or members of an isolated religious group (Brothwell 1981), much can be learned.

Yesterday's scientists, however, sought the unusual. When Irish giant Cornelius MacGrath returned to Dublin in the mid-eighteenth century after a European tour showcasing his height of 7'8", his poor health led to his death. His death led to theft of his body by students at Trinity College and the preservation of his skeleton at the school (Thompson 1968). When Joseph Merrick (the "Elephant Man") died in 1890, his skeleton was preserved and added to the anatomy museum at the Royal London Hospital Medical School. The Warren Anatomical Medical Museum at Harvard University curates the skull of Phineas Gage (d. 1861), who survived for 3 years after a tamping iron was blown through his head from behind his left eye through his brain and out the top of his skull. Five years after Gage's death, his skull and the tamping iron were sent to his physician Dr. John Harlow and from there made their way — along with a plaster bust taken during life — into the museum's collections. Modern scientists make good use of what were previously only curiosities, diagnosing Merrick's condition and pinpointing the damage to Gage's brain to explain how it affected his subsequent behavior.

The American Museum of Natural History in New York curates several collections of human skeletal remains that are little-known except to physical anthropologists and even then sometimes only by accident: "While on a fellowship a few years ago at the American Museum of Natural History," writes Jeffrey H. Schwartz (1998), "I came across hundreds of examples of cranial deformation as I rummaged through thousands of skull-size boxes in search of specimens to use in the project I was pursuing." According to a survey conducted by Mahmoud Y. El-Najjar in 1974, the American Museum of Natural History curated a quantity of skeletal collections at that time that numbered in the hundreds: 1,084 from Austria, 962 from Hungary, 866 from Bolivia, 696 from New Mexico, 643 from Mexico, 637 from Egypt, 549 from North Africa, 435 from Germany, 414 from Peru, 346 from Greece, 346 from British Columbia, 318 from Melanesia, 252 from Arizona, 247 from Polynesia, 199 from West Africa, 182 from Czechoslovakia, 174 from Florida, 173 from Oregon, 170 from New York, 154 from Turkey, 110 from Point Barrow, and 100 from India (El-Najjar 1977). The museum's holdings include the von Luschan Collection of some 277 African Black skulls (Krogman and Iscan 1986), a morphology collection harvested from dissected cadavers, and a large sample of ancient western and eastern Inuits' skeletons (Schwartz 1998). The latter collection brought the museum a great amount of negative publicity at the turn of the twentieth century. Some of the bones were those of

Greenland Eskimos brought to New York by explorer Robert Peary (d. 1920). Dying within months of their arrival, their bodies were dissected, their brains examined and preserved, and their skeletons harvested for the museum's collection. One of the survivors, a young man named Minik (d. 1918), was outraged when he saw the exhibit of his father's skeleton in the museum. Realizing that the funeral and burial of his father's remains had been a farce held only for his benefit, Minik repeatedly requested their return, but was denied (Harper 1986). The remains of Minik's father and three other Inuits were only recently reburied in Qaanaaq (Thomas 2000).

The specimens — typical and unusual — at many museums and institutions have been carefully cataloged over the centuries. The process of cataloging continues as collections grow or are reorganized. Rosine Orban, physical anthropologist and head of the Laboratory of Anthropology at the Belgian Natural History Museum, relates that she is in the process of creating a detailed list of their skeletal collections, which include the Koksijde series (1,000 individuals from a medieval Cistercian monastery, including the complete skeleton of an achondroplastic dwarf), the Schoten series (50 nineteenth-century northern Belgium skeletons of known age and sex), three twentieth-century Aboriginal skeletons from the Belgian Congo, and a large number of prehistoric bones: 300 Neolithic individuals from the Meuse Valley, two nearly complete Neandertal skeletons from Spy, the Neandertal mandible of La Naulette, and the Neandertal femur from Fond-de-Forêt (personal correspondence, January 19, 1999). Occasionally, provenance of material in museum collections is lacking. A group of 87 skulls at the Museu Municipal Darder d'Història Natural in Banyoles, Spain, includes examples of cultural deformations, disease and aging processes, and supernumerary bones, but little is known about the collection except its accession date of 1916. In other instances, collections have been partially dispersed. The Museum of Anthropology at Naples University still retains 2,000 of the human skulls collected by Giustiniano Nicolucci (d. 1904), but the nineteenth-century anthropologist sold many others to American and British museums.

Even when a collection is not growing, it does not remain static. Janet Monge, keeper of the Physical Anthropology Collections at the University of Pennsylvania Museum of Archaeology and Anthropology, notes that the museum has not accessioned any skeletal remains within the last 20 years. But the thousands of skeletons that they do curate, occasionally supplemented by loans of skeletal material from other institutions, still provide a rich basis for study even decades later, as Monge explains (personal correspondence, September 16, 1999): "As technology changes and the questions of anthropological and archaeological context are refined and enlarged, the usefulness of the collection changes. This is true now as well as in the past. As with all scientific explorations, the knowledge is cumulative and dynamic. For example (in the abstract) the use of imaging techniques has vastly changed the way we view the collections. Until a few years ago, we exclusively used x-ray technology for analyses, now of course we have moved to include MRI and CT analysis. As a consequence the research questions have increased in level of sophistication. Thus, there is no 'end' to research on collections that actually have been curated in many museums around the world for over 100 years."

Many of the large public natural history museums were established in the mid-nineteenth century for the purposes of popular education and scholarly research. "These museums provided an institutional framework within which the large skeletal collections could be consolidated from the smaller private collections of physicians and wealthy amateur archaeologists. These new museums had the resources necessary to maintain staffs of professional research scientists and to augment their osteological collections through purchases from private collectors and the sponsorship of archaeological expeditions throughout the world" (Walker In press). In the U.S., the most important natural history museums from the perspective of collections of human skeletal remains are the Smithsonian Institution (established in 1846), the Peabody Museum of Archaeology and Ethnology at Harvard (est. 1866), the American Museum of Natural History (est. 1869), the Field Museum in Chicago (est. 1893 as the Columbian Museum), the Phoebe Hearst Museum (est. 1901 as the Lowie Museum of Anthropology), and the San Diego Museum of Man (est. 1915). During the twentieth century, the number of museums with significant holdings of human skeletal remains rapidly increased and by 1998, about 700 federal and private institutions in the United States possessed skeletal remains from an estimated 110,000 individuals (Walker In press).

Substantial collections can also be found in Europe. The Landesmuseum für Vorgeschichte in Halle, Austria, was founded as the Provinzialmuseum in 1884. Since then, it has accumulated a collection of 12,000 human skeletal remains from archaeological sites in the region of Sachsen-Anhalt. Most of the bones in the museum, which is currently closed for renovations, date from mesolithic to modern times. The Archaeological Monument Preservation Agency in Rottenburg am Neckar curates one of the largest skeletal collections in Germany, with excavated specimens from hundreds of sites in the state of Baden-Württemberg. Since 1989, the Agency has made a concerted effort to maintain the remains as a central osteological archive, employing osteologists to organize the remains and prepare them for scientific analysis. The material fills up about 6,000 storage containers and dates from 8,000 B.P. until recently. About 2,000 of the 3,000 boxes currently in the archive have been organized, with an additional 3,000 or more expected from branch offices. The work involves cross-referencing the information, including field notes, that accompanies the bones. This data, currently stored on cards (each of which is kept with its respective specimen), includes a reference number, the exact geographical location of the excavation, a description of the site, the description and measurements of the skeletal elements, and an approximate dating of the bones. The skeletal remains at the agency are in storage rather than on display, but the storage area is nearing capacity, due mainly to salvage archaeology during building construction in cities like Cologne.

Many museums have developed as repositories of medical specimens. The Musée Dupuytren was founded in 1835 in connection with the Medical School of Paris. Professor Dupuytren (d. 1835) had suggested founding a Chair of the Pathology and Anatomy Institution, but his legacy was insufficient to underwrite the post. Instead, Dupuytren was encouraged to use his fortune to create a museum of pathological anatomy. The museum was set up the year of his death in a gothic building at the school. Some of the oldest and most spectacular exhibits in the museum were anatomical wax models, but the bulk of the collections were skeletal. Several thousand bone specimens had been acquired and ranged from skulls to joint sections to entire skeletons. These included the skeleton of an individual with osteomalacia that had been presented to the Academy of Surgery in 1752 and the skeleton of a young native of the Ivory Coast who had died of yaws and whose remains were obtained in 1926 by Dr. Colonel Bothereau-Roussel. A highlight of the collection was the skeleton of the nineteenth-century performer Pipine, who

had phocomelia, and other deformities represented by fetal skeletons. Numbers of additional skeletal specimens exhibited signs of tuberculosis, osteomyelitis, periostitis, rickets, scoliosis, and tumors. Over time, despite attention to specimens such as the skeleton of Odilon Marc Lannelongue (d. 1911), the museum began to fall into ruin and maintenance of the collections became an increasing problem. While many of the specimens were kept on display, some were transferred to the Cochin Hospital. Since 1967, the collections have been installed in a pavilion within the former clinical school. They are now curated by Paul P. Saint-Maur and still include many of the old favorites.

The University of Leeds in the United Kingdom curates a pathology and anatomy collection of about 3,500 specimens that includes some 200 or 300 bones, either dry or in formalin. The collection is being recataloged by Patrick J.R. Harkin of the Division of Clinical Sciences in the School of Medicine, who has made the inventory available online (www.hci.leeds.ac.uk/museum). in this way made remotely accessible to students and researchers. The specimens include, a giant cell tumor of the tibia (No. 3139) in a 30-year-old woman, which was treated by amputation, and an example of chronic osteoarthritis (No. 1315) resulting in flexion and extension deformity (a "claw hand"). Other specimens have more detailed stories attached to them. An ulna with a false joint (No. 1037) belonged to a 40-year-old male who received a blow on the arm in 1864. Though wrapped for months in a starch bandage and appearing to have healed, the fracture failed to unite and the specimen was procured after the man's death in Wakefield Gaol. A bisected left knee and leg (No. 1095) illustrates the medical history of an unfortunate nine-year-old who suffered multiple tuberculous lesions including a tuberculous cavity in the diaphysis of the tibia. The leg, which also reveals ankylosis of the femur and tibia, was amputated, as was his left elbow. Another child, age ten, also suffered from tuberculosis since infancy. The specimen (No. 1204) is that of his mandible, which exhibits osteitis and necrosis, although his knee, elbow, tarsus, and phalanges were also involved.

When researchers attempt an inclusive survey, they must gather their information from widely dispersed collections, unless the museum they are consulting has been designated a national repository. Judyta Gladykowska-Rzeczycka (1991), for instance, based a study on the paleopathology of tumors on groups of thousands of remains excavated from dozens of cemeteries (2,584 skeletons from Czechoslovakia, 2,653 from Poland, and 2,763 from the Baltic Coast). Often, institutions curate skeletal assemblages unique to their country's cultures. In addition to a number of prehistoric human remains dating to as early as 6,000 B.P., the Museum of Natural History in Shanghai, People's Republic of China, houses the skeletons of more than 100 individuals (from which they are now extracting and studying DNA) that were excavated in 1986 in Hami Xingjiang autonomous prefecture, relates department chair Yongqing Xu (personal correspondence, February 8, 1999). In addition to the Jomon skeletal series (272 individual skeletons from eight prehistoric sites), the museum in the Department of Physical Anthropology at the University of Tokyo curates the Edo late medieval/early modern skeletal series of 923 skulls, 308 femora, and 253 tibiae and the Koganei Collection of Ainu skeletons collected in Hokkaido (Suzuki 1991). A skeletal series at the Xinjiang Medical College comprises more than 115 contemporary Chinese individuals and the Department of Anatomy at Sapporo Medical College curates a series of 113 Meiji Japanese skeletons ranging in age between 20 and eight and having death dates between 1927 and 1944.

The skeletal collections at the University of Coimbra in Portugal total more than 2,000 remains obtained from within the country. The Medical School Collection comprises 585 skulls obtained from the Schools of Medicine in Lisbon and Porto and from the University of Coimbra's Anatomical Theater by faculty member Bernardino Luís de Machado Guimarães (d. 1944) between 1896 and 1903. The International Exchange collection includes 1,075 skulls collected by Eusébio Barbosa Tamagnini de Matos Encarnação (d. 1972) from the Cemitério Municipal da Conchada in Coimbra. The Coimbra Identified Skeletal Collection of 505 individuals was recovered from the same cemetery, probably between 1915 and 1942, but has associated records documenting name, parents' names, birthplace, sex, death date, age at death, place of death, cause of death, occupation, marital status, and exhumation. The records — computerized since the mid–1990s — have facilitated dozens of research projects. The remains are curated by the Anthropological Museum from the University of Coimbra's Faculty of Sciences and Technology. They are stored in wooden boxes labeled with the individual's catalog number and color-coded according to gender (Santos 2000). The Anthropologische Rudolf-Virchow-Sammlung in Berlin, Germany, was established in 1956 and is now attached to the school of medicine at Humboldt University. Their collection includes the remains of approximately 7,000 individuals excavated locally from the churches of Nicolai and Petri; cemeteries that held the remains of monks, soldiers, and the poor; and an ossuary near Leipzig representing the inhabitants of a village over a 300–year period. Also curated are about 8,000 crania from around the world (including South America, Central Africa, Egypt, and Melanesia) that had been collected during the 1800s by geographers, travelers, doctors, and military officers. "The collections are open only for scientific purposes and not to the public," writes curator Dr. Creutz (personal correspondence, March 2, 1999).

The bulk of institutional collections of human remains is rarely visible to the public, despite the fact that displays of human remains are among the most effective tools for luring people into museums (Walker In press). The University of Pennsylvania Museum exhibits only some of its Egyptian mummies and none of its skeletons from around the world. Unlike many other institutions, the Natural History Museum in London has much of its skeletal material on display to illustrate burial practices or show the context in which it was found. Many of the human skeletons were acquired by Sir Hans Sloane (d. 1753), personal physician to King George II. Exhibits in the Department of Prehistoric and Romano-British Antiquities include reconstruction of a later prehistoric European burial (the Barnack burial), an Iron Age British cranium (the Deal skull) shown wearing its crown, and an infant skeleton from Stonea, Cambridgeshire, displayed in a medical context to illustrate the frequency of infant mortality in Roman Britain. The Department of Western Asiatic Antiquities displays a plaster-molded skull and a tomb group of seven skeletons from Jericho and two skulls from Ur, one wearing a helmet and the other a headdress. The specimens are used in anthropological research, as is the skeletal material in the Department of Egyptian Antiquities, only some of which is on display. Remains from ancient Egypt are used in research on funerary practices and paleopathology. Larger groups of material from recent excavations in the Sudan dating from Neolithic to Early Christian are in storage and are being studied by a physical anthropologist doing work on stature, pathology, and DNA research, writes Julia Walton (personal correspondence, March 3, 1999).

Unfortunately for researchers, many American institutions are in the process of dismantling their skeletal collections in order to comply with NAGPRA, which is discussed in a later chapter, or to accede to the prevailing wishes of the community. Prehistoric Native American material recovered in the twentieth century during excavation by the Work Projects Administration and the Tennessee Valley Authority is being inventoried and deaccessioned by the Frank H. McClung Museum at the University of Tennessee. Some of the remains in the Human Osteology Collections at the University of Wyoming have been reinterred, including a sample of 31 pioneers whose graves were accidentally discovered and some of which have been reinterred. Two other pioneer samples loaned to the university for osteological analysis and since reburied include remains from the earliest Mormon Cemetery in Salt Lake Valley, Utah, dating from the late 1840s to the early 1850s, and 13 excavated burials from two West Texas boothills, dating from the 1870s (Gill 1994).

Much larger collections have also been reburied. One of the few archaeologists concerned with recovering and curating human skeletal remains prior to the late 1950s, W.H. Over was director of the museum at the University of South Dakota in Vermillion from 1912 to 1949. Over studied many of South Dakota's most important sites and did field research at more than 200 sites in 43 countries, recovering human skeletal remains at about 15 percent of them. Typical of his time, Over gave preference to the best specimens — those of crania and of adults. "He did not keep all the skeletal remains he uncovered, only the better preserved or 'more interesting' ones" (Owsley and Jantz 1994). Soon the W.H. Over Museum collection consisted of more than 500 skeletons from 37 Plains Woodland, Middle Missouri, and Coalescent tradition sites in South Dakota dating from 800 to 1900 A.D. Some assemblages had been excavated under federal salvage programs in conjunction with other institutions. Two cemeteries

(Four Bear and Swan Creek, from which some 90 individuals were recovered) were excavated by W.R. Hurt. Four large cemeteries (Larson, Leavenworth, Mobridge, and Sully, which yielded a total of nearly 2,000 individuals) were excavated under the direction of William Bass, who in 1977 arranged for the Over collection to be transferred temporarily to the University of Tennessee for osteological analysis (Owsley and Jantz 1994). The Over collection has been used to supply evidence for the argument that treponemal infections (yaws, endemic syphilis, venereal syphilis, and pinta) were endemic in the New World before European contact (Schermer, Fisher, and Hodges 1994). Despite its potential and the need to reexamine what has been learned from the skeletons, the Over Museum human skeletal collection was recalled by the South Dakota Office of the State Archaeologist in 1985 for reinterment, which took place the following year.

In some European museums, the skeletal collections are not at risk of being lost, but in danger of not being fully utilized. Other skeletons, teaching specimens, have been used by generations of students. Skeletons are necessary tools in the teaching of several sciences. This has only become more apparent over the centuries, during which time osteological collections have been accumulated and acquired by institutions internationally. "Such collections exist in museums, university laboratories, and medical schools on every continent in the world and are indispensable to the teaching of anatomy and human variation and to learning about medical and biological aspects of human history" (Ubelaker and Grant 1989). As important as quality is quantity, since reliable statistical analyses of post–Paleolithic human remains require a series of at least 40 or 50 skeletons of the same gender (Brothwell 1981). Opportunity and resources will perhaps allow today's and tomorrow's researchers to fully document collections that are to be repatriated, study series that have not received sufficient attention, and reanalyze collections that will remain above ground as part of our collective cultural heritage.

National Museum of Natural History, Smithsonian Institution, Washington, D.C.

"America's attic," as the Smithsonian has affectionately been called, should perhaps be known as "America's closet," since it contains so many skeletons. Most of them are curated in the Department of Physical Anthropology. "We're not in the least like Mother Hubbard," said curator Lucile St. Hoyme, "As a matter of fact, we've got so many craniums in our cupboards that our colleagues sometimes jokingly refer to our section of the museum as 'the skullery'!" (Carmichael 1971). A survey conducted in 1974 by Mahmoud Y. El-Najjar (1977) revealed that at that time the Smithsonian Institution was the custodian of the following skeletal collections with numbers of one hundred or more: 14,326 from Northern Mexico, 4,666 U.S. whites, 3,531 from Peru, 1,109 from New Mexico, 998 from Virginia, 822 from California, 820 from Connecticut, 749 from Maryland, 749 Aleuts, 655 from Arizona, 548 from Illinois, 517 U.S. blacks, 347 from Arkansas, 285 from Tennessee, 235 from Missouri, 211 from Hawaii, 196 from Russia, 184 from Louisiana, 175 from Florida, 169 from Mongolia, 160 Eskimos, 152 from Kentucky, 151 from Palestine, 144 from the District of Columbia, 120 from Mississippi, 123 from Alaska, 112 from China, and 108 from Washington. Collections manager David Hunt explains (personal communication, March 19, 1999) that until the 1960s, the Smithsonian Institution was the primary clearinghouse (and usually storehouse) for skeletal materials recovered during excavations, particularly those that were federally funded.

About 46 percent of the human remains in the collections are from North America, a large percentage is from South America, and the rest are from Europe and Africa. The collections continue to grow, but not as quickly as in the past. Within the United States, excavated materials are more often curated at local institutions or universities. Internationally, human remains are covered under the Antiquities Act which limits their removal, and they are now accessioned only with permission from international governments. If this permission — in the form of a donor letter — has not been or cannot be obtained, the materials remain uncataloged and unaccessioned. The Smithsonian has many such "orphaned" collections, but none at this time that include human remains. So the numbers of skeletons at the National Museum of Natural History are most likely to increase when other institutions decide to divest themselves and offer their collections to the Smithsonian. As described, this was how the Smithsonian acquired two of its larger series, the Terry Collection and the Huntington Collection.

Rather than acquiring new specimens, the Smithsonian has been in the business of deaccessioning many of its human remains, said to have numbered some 35,000 prior to NAGPRA, of which approximately 18,000 were Native American (Preston 1997). The institution has maintained a Repatriation Office since the mid–1980s to conduct research within the collections and negotiate with Native American tribes. Skeletal materials are measured and photographed before they are repatriated, but museum policy — and often Native American request — dictates that no samples be retained and no x-rays be taken. Future researchers will have to rely on the data that has already been collected from remains that will no longer be available for analysis. Research on the Terry series and other collections that have a permanent place within the Smithsonian's walls continues daily.

National Museum of Health and Medicine, Armed Forces Institute of Pathology, Washington, D.C.

By order of Surgeon General William A. Hammond in a circular issued in May of 1862, U.S. Army medical officers were directed to collect "all specimens of morbid anatomy, surgical or medical, which may be regarded as valuable; together with projectiles and foreign bodies removed, and such other matters as may prove of interest in the study of military medicine or surgery." Thus began the collections of the Army Medical Museum, known since 1988 as the National Museum of Health and Medicine (NMHM).

The collection process was a rather messy one, as collections manager Lenore Barbian explains (personal correspondence, November 6, 1998). The bones were procured after amputation or at autopsy, with skulls collected from the trenches by surgeons on special duty to the museum. The gross tissue was removed and the specimens were wrapped in cloth, tagged with a number and the name of the sender, and preserved in diluted alcohol. After a barrel or casket was filled with specimens, it was sealed and shipped (with a separately mailed inventory) to the surgeon general's office, which soon had to designate a special floor and hire German consultants Frederic Schafhirt and sons Adolph and Ernst to process the material. Brigade Surgeon John Hill Brinton, who was authorized to collect and arrange the specimens for the museum, made a practice of visiting the battlefields both to promote cooperation among the surgeons and to collect material himself. Brinton also requested specimens from the doctors attending survivors, for instance the jaw fragment lost to a shell by Private W.H. Knaup of New Jersey (Henry 1964). Hammond's order requested that the objects be accompanied by short explanatory notes. The information attached to and derived from the specimens was compiled in several volumes. *The Medical and Surgical History of the War of Rebellion* was published in 1879 and catalogs, in most cases, the soldier's name, his company, the battle in which he was injured, the type of injury, and the name of his surgeon. The museum was the first in the world to keep such detailed and well-documented medical records during wartime and the feat has never been replicated, notes Barbian.

The museum includes some specimens donated by the soldiers themselves. After the Battle of Gettysburg in 1863, a leg arrived compliments of Major-General Daniel E. Sickles. The limb had been amputated above the knee after being irreparably damaged by a 12-pound cannonball. The case (number 446) is described in Volume IX of *The Medical and Surgical History*. Major-General Sickles of the U.S. Volunteers had been in command of the Third Corps when he was wounded on July 2, 1863, and treated in the field. The bones of his leg and the ball that had crushed them were prepared and placed on display at the museum, where they were visited by Sickles until his death in 1914. The shattered bones, cannonball, and a newspaper clipping showing Sickles visiting his leg are currently included in an exhibit entitled "To Bind the Nation's Wounds: Medicine During the Civil War" that also includes examples of an infected amputation stump, a gunshot wound to the skull, a shell wound of the wrist, and an accidental shot to the left foot.

Research on the records and remains of military casualties during the Civil War was necessary as surgeons devised standardized treatments for injuries. After the war, army doctors shifted the focus of their collecting activities to the Indian Wars in the western U.S. and the treatment of arrow wounds (Walker In press). With the help of medical officers, the museum began to amass a collection of crania, mostly of American Indians, from which craniometric data was culled. Some ethnographic material that had been collected with the skulls was exchanged with the Smithsonian Institution for anatomical materials including 376 of the nearly 1,000 skulls in the collection at that time. The skulls were later returned to the Smithsonian: "After some 30 years of medically unfruitful measurement of the cubic capacity, the length and breadth, the facial angle, and other characteristics of skulls, it was decided that such determinations pertained more properly to anthropology than to medical study. On 8 May 1898, therefore, the Museum's collection of crania, by then numbering 2,206 specimens, was transferred to the Museum of Natural History" (Henry 1964). This would have included the skeletal remains of hundreds of Cheyenne villagers killed at Sand Creek by Colorado troops in 1864 and dozens of skeletons forwarded by post surgeon B.E. Fryer between 1868 and 1872 (Thomas 2000).

The medical collection continued to grow and by 1892 numbered 29,486 specimens (Henry 1964). They included damaged vertebrae from President James Garfield, who had been shot in 1881 and autopsied by museum pathologist Daniel Smith Lamb (d. 1928). Contributions surged during the Spanish-American War after the surgeon general's office issued revised instructions for the delivery of specimens. More appeals were made to camp pathologists after the turn of the century, resulting in a total of 47,313 specimens by 1916, a number that doubled by the end of World War I and reached one million by the 1960s. The museum had begun to store a large part of its collections prior to World War II, withdrawing items from exhibit and placing them in warehouses on Maine Avenue, Columbia Pike, and the southwest Washington waterfront. But by 1949, it offered more than 300 displays.

The museum outgrew several locations

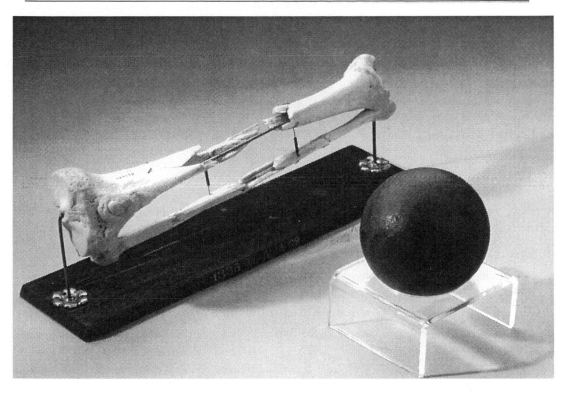

The leg bones of Maj.-Gen. Daniel E. Sickles and the cannonball that shattered them. Photo courtesy of the National Museum of Health and Medicine, Armed Forces Institute of Pathology.

in Washington, D.C. From a series of 3,500 specimens on shelves in the surgeon general's office on Pennsylvania Avenue, N.W., where the first collections catalog was issued, the museum was moved during the Civil War to a building on H Street, N.W., leased from W.W. Corcoran. After the war, at which time the museum owned 7,630 specimens and was receiving an annual appropriation of $5,000, the collections were housed in Ford's Theatre on 10th Street, N.W. The theatre had closed after the assassination of President Abraham Lincoln, from whom skull fragments and other items had been preserved and presented to the museum. In 1888, the museum was moved to the "Old Red Brick" building that had been constructed next to the Smithsonian "castle" on Independence Avenue, S.E. In 1946, material was moved across the street to Chase Hall. In 1955, when the AFIP moved to a new building at the Walter Reed

Army Medical Center, the museum remained on the National Mall and shared its building with the Army Surgeon General's Library. This became the National Library of Medicine and moved in 1962, allowing the museum to expand its exhibit area and better organize its holdings. That same year, the "Old Red Brick" was designated a National Historic Landmark, but in an unprecedented act, the historic landmark status was transferred from the building — soon torn down to make way for the Hirshhorn Museum and Sculpture Garden — to the collections themselves.

The collections have undergone several reorganizations over the last 150 years. In the nineteenth century, the Civil War collections were separated from the general anatomical and pathological material. In 1919 a restricted-access professional museum (the Cornell Museum) was created. In 1933, the exhibits were rearranged in new display cases that had been purchased with a bequest from Dr. William F. Edgar (d. 1897). At about that same time, curator Capt. Hugh Richmond Gilmore, Jr., complained that insufficient staffing was causing the museum to become a storehouse of poorly arranged and poorly exhibited pathological specimens and that record keeping was falling behind (Henry 1964). In 1946, the Army Medical Museum began to function as a component of the Army Institute of Pathology (later the Armed Forces Institute of Pathology), whose director reported that "the initial post-war stage of chaos with hundreds of boxes of items of unknown type, number, location or condition has given way to a stage of concentrated storage of items of generally known type, condition and location" (Henry 1964). By 1948, more than 126,000 museum items had been transported, cleaned, repaired, sorted, cataloged, cross-referenced, indexed, filed, accessioned, wrapped, packed, and stored, with damaged items salvaged or discarded (Henry 1964). When the "Old Red Brick" was demolished in 1968, the museum's collections were placed in cardboard boxes to await the construction of a new facility attached to its parent institution at Walter Reed. The museum reopened in 1971, but closed again for several years. In 1976, Congress designated the Armed Forces Institute of Pathology as the national medical repository, of which the museum collections represent a subset. Ten years later, research pathologist Marc Micozzi was appointed director and took on the challenge of bringing the collections up to modern management standards and practices. The specimens were inventoried, organized, physically arranged, and provided with security and controlled environments to the extent that the present location allows.

Today the National Museum of Health and Medicine on the Walter Reed campus curates more than 3,000 dry bone specimens. They are organized first by the collections listed below, and secondarily by body part, a typical storage technique:

- Civil War Skeletal Collection, 1862–1865 (2,000 specimens)

- Indian Wars Collection, 1866–1900 (150 specimens)

- Anatomical Preparations, ca. 1850–1920 (300 specimens)

- Gibson Collection, ca. 1868 (200 specimens)

- Prehistoric Native American Collection, ca. 4000 B.P.–1850 A.D. (150 specimens)

- Historic Native American Collection, 1862–1899 (35 specimens)

- Nineteenth Century Collection, ca. 1862–1899 (150 specimens)

- Twentieth Century Collection, ca. 1900–1930 (150 specimens)

- Fetal and Subadult Collection, ca. 1880–1920 (75 specimens)

- Smithsonian Collection, 1870–1899 (25 specimens)

- Forensic Anthropology Collection, 1960–1995 (40 specimens)

Some of the specimens — including those salvaged from the battlefields of the Civil War — were actively acquired, and other specimens were donated or purchased. The museum bought some of its fetal skeletons from Ward's biological supply house at the turn of the century. Others were donated by doctors in private practice. The collection also includes a number of trophy skulls from the Vietnam War, which are not on public display.

On permanent exhibit at the museum are a series of skeletons showing human development and ranging from a fetus of four months' gestation to a five-year-old child; the articulated skeleton of a 25-year-old man of average height (although that height is exaggerated by the spaces left between the bones so that they can be fully visualized); a revolving skeleton with red and blue markings indicating the location of the major muscles; and a skull prepared using the method developed by Beauchene, a French doctor who prepared bones so that they could be seen in true anatomical relation to one another. Interactive exhibits demonstrate the various types of bone (long, short, irregular) and bone tissue (cancellous, compact). Also on display are examples of bone fractures and remodeling, joints and ligament attachments, bone abnormalities including dwarfism, and the facial reconstruction of a skull excavated in Connecticut in 1990. Perhaps the most striking exhibit is the seated skeleton of a 47-year-old soldier who had served in the Spanish-American War in 1898 and willed his remains to the Army Medical Museum. At the time of his death, this man had been unable to move, bone having formed across all of his joints. A disputed diagnosis of chronic rheumatoid arthritis to explain the ossification is currently being resolved by further study.

The museum's exhibits have been popular since its inception. In 1867, it was visited by more than 6,000 people, an average of more than two dozen a day. More than 81,000 were admitted in 1935 and attendance reached 100,000 three years later. In the 1940s, more than 200,000 visitors a year toured the museum, with 363,000 visiting in 1959 and a record-breaking 587,000 in 1960. By the mid–1960s, the public exhibits drew almost 1 million visitors annually (Henry 1964). Research on the skeletal materials is conducted by museum staff and individuals in the areas of bioarchaeology, Civil War medical history, forensic anthropology, forensic pathology, human biology, orthopedic injury, pathology, paleopathology, and physical anthropology. Several studies of specimens in the NMHM collections focus on the skeletal effects of healing. The staff also offers lectures, organizes an annual course in forensic anthropology, provides teaching specimens to local medical schools, and supports federal consultation activities in forensic anthropology.

Mütter Museum, College of Physicians of Philadelphia

The Mütter Museum in Philadelphia was established by its namesake, Thomas Dent Mütter, who wanted to showcase the medical rarities he had collected. The College of Physicians of Philadelphia had already begun a museum of pathological anatomy at the suggestion of Dr. Isaac Parrish (d. 1852) and had so far acquired 92 specimens. In 1856, Dr. Mütter — facing retirement because of ill health — offered the College of Physicians the substantial teaching collection of anatomical and pathological specimens that he had amassed as professor of surgery at Jefferson Medical College. The offer came with an endowment of $30,000 to pay for a curator, a lecturer, and the construction and care of a new fire-proof building to house the 1,700 specimens. The agreement was signed in 1859 and Dr. Mütter died two months later at age 48.

The Mütter collection was installed at 13th and Locust Streets in Philadelphia and served as a complement to the College's library, which had begun in 1788. The skeletal specimens in the original collection included numerous examples of anchylosis, caries, deformities, fractures, wounds, exostosis, necrosis, and osteosarcoma. One of the original exhibits — still on display — is the skeleton of a woman whose rib cage was compressed by the tight lacing of a corset. In addition to upkeep, the endowment funds were used to purchase additional collections from Europe, including the Hyrtl Skull Collection already described. Surgical and autopsy specimens were also contributed by fellows of the College, who acquired them from their hospitals and private practices. Some Civil War specimens were sent from

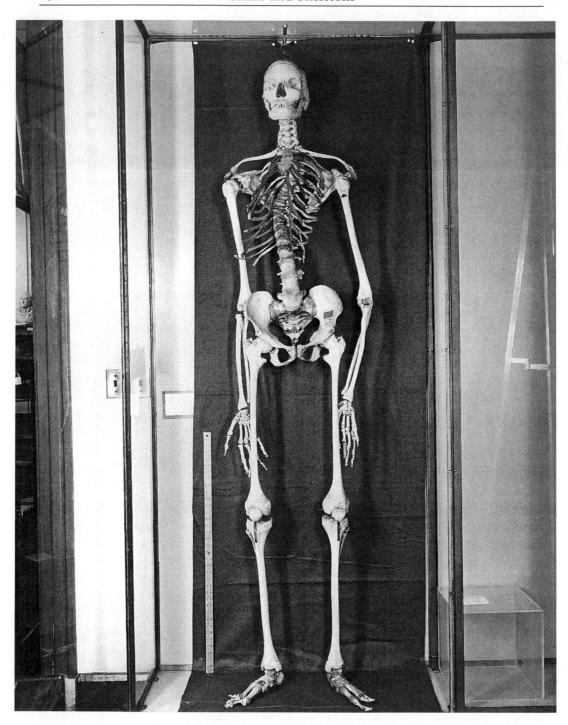

Pages 130–134: Skeletal specimens on display at the Mütter Museum. Page 130, giant; page 131 left, achondroplastic dwarf; page 131 right, hydrocephalic child; page 132, woman whose rib cage was compressed by the tight lacing of a corset; page 133, Harry Eastlack, Jr., who suffered from myositis ossificans progressiva in which the connective tissue turns to bone; and page 134, the skeleton of Harry Eastlack, Jr., from the rear. Photos courtesy of the Mütter Museum, College of Physicians of Philadelphia.

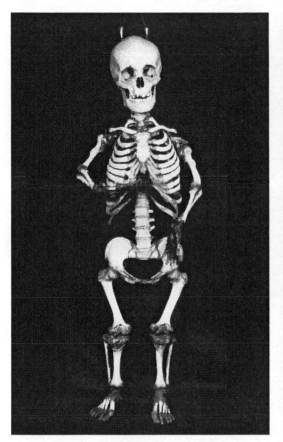 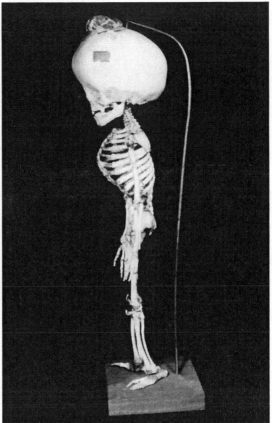

the Army Medical Museum (now the National Museum of Health and Medicine) in exchange for duplicate teaching specimens.

As the collections grew, so did the need for space. In 1908, a new building on 22nd Street between Chestnut and Market Street was constructed to house the College and its museum. Still, the exhibits were crowded and eight-foot-tall redwood display cases were packed with as many specimens as possible. Quantity was valued over selectivity, requiring a large amount of shelf space. As the website (www.collphyphil.org/muttpg1.shtml) describes, "The museum as it was first installed in the new space was in marked contrast to the elegant materials and furnishings of the rest of the building. It retained in its appearance a strong connection to the utilitarian medical museums typical of nineteenth-century hospitals and medical schools.... [T]he museum's purpose lay not

in the decorative display of selected artifacts, but in the organized assemblage of teaching materials which were to be available to the student or researcher as were books on a library shelf."

More than 75 years later, the exhibit areas underwent major renovation. The galleries were painted, carpeted, and air-conditioned. The exhibits were reinstalled in the original display cases that had been refinished, fitted with track lighting, and shelved with glass rather than the original redwood. The cases surround the balconies main gallery of the two-story museum and contain hundreds of specimens, though only about 10 percent of the museum's holdings are exhibited. The Mütter Museum now houses more than 20,000 items, including some 900 fluid-preserved anatomical and pathological preparations, 10,000 medical instruments, 400 anatomical and

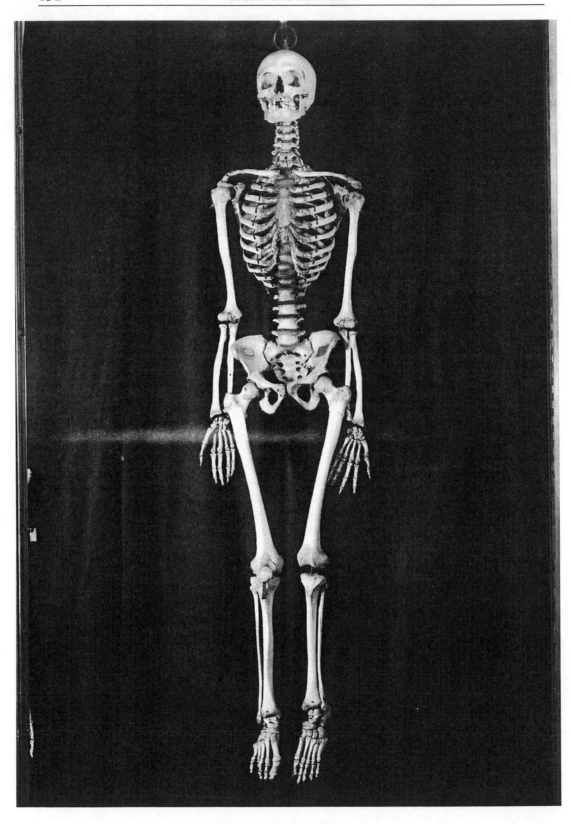

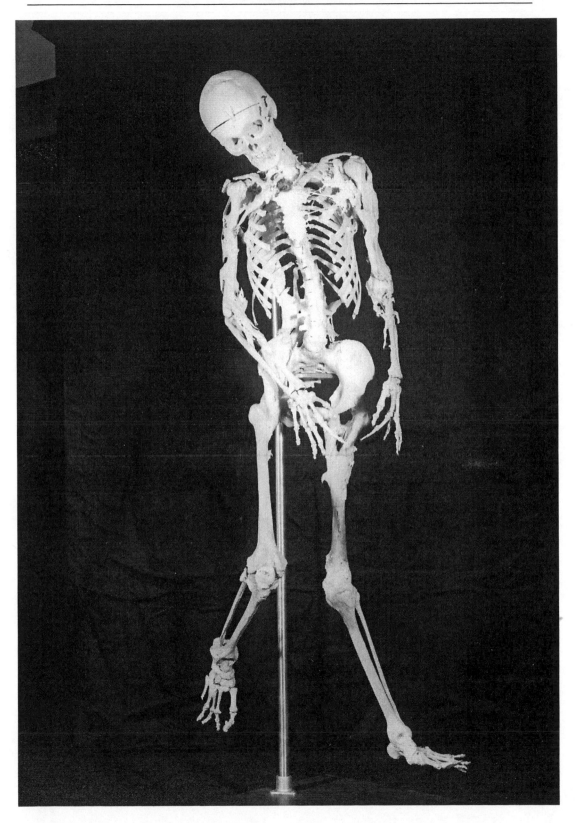

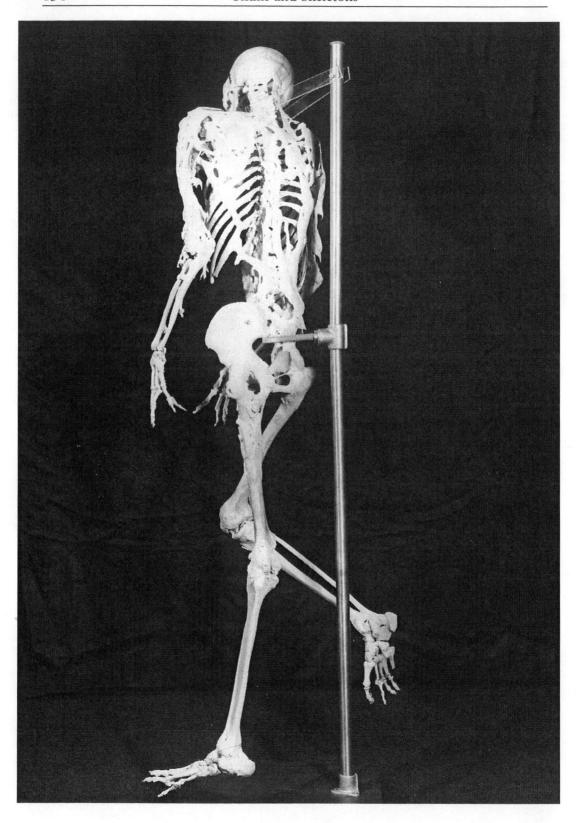

pathological models, and 1,500 medical illustrations. Many specimens on display are skeletons, and only a few of them (including that of Lucas Puskarczyk, age 32, for comparison) are what would be considered normal, in keeping with Mütter's original intent:

• Giant skeleton: The remains of a 7'6" man from Kentucky estimated to be between the ages of 22 and 24 that were purchased in 1877 for $50 from Professor A.E. Foote, a purveyor of anatomical preparations. The terms of sale precluded any inquiry into the man's identity. The skeleton — the second tallest on display in the world — was cleaned and mounted after its accession by the museum's preparator, Mr. R.H. Nash, who was criticized for making it more symmetrical than it would have been in life. Suffering from what was later diagnosed as kyphoscoliosis, the young man would have been stooped and may have been bedridden.

• Dwarf skeleton: The skeleton of a 3'6" female achondroplastic dwarf that was procured after her death in a house of prostitution in Norfolk, Virginia. She had become pregnant in 1856, but was unable to deliver the child due to her pelvic deformity. The doctor attempted a craniotomy on the fetus to save her life, but this was unsuccessful. A Caesarean section was performed to remove the dead baby, but the mother died of peritonitis three days later. The damaged fetal skull is on display next to her skeleton.

• Conjoined twins: A fetal skeleton of cephalothoracopagus twins fused at the head and chest, donated by Dr. Warrington.

• The effects of syphilis: Skulls exhibiting syphilitic changes.

• The effects of rickets: Pelves showing deformities caused by vitamin D deficiency.

• Pathologies of the teeth and jaws: Skulls exhibiting dental anomalies and jaw fractures.

• Club foot: A fetal skeleton with talipes varus, donated by George McClellan.

• Hydrocephaly: Skeleton of Thomas Jeff, a six-year-old male with extreme hydrocephalic rupture of the skull, which was 27¾" in circumference. Also on display are two hydrocephalic fetal skulls and the hydrocephalic skeleton of a fetus aborted at eight months.

• Scoliosis: The vertebral column and pelvis of a woman showing lateral and antero-posterior curvature.

• Ossification: The skeleton of a 39-year-old male with myositis ossificans progressiva, a disease with no known cause or cure in which the connective tissue turns to bone. The man, Harry R. Eastlack, Jr., died in 1973 and bequeathed his skeleton to Dr. Howard H. Steel, who presented it to the Museum in 1979.

In addition to the pathological specimens, a number of exhibits demonstrate skeletal development before and after birth. A series of jaws in which the teeth have been exposed show their growth from fetus to adult. A purchased series of disarticulated fetal skeletons ranges from the fourth month of gestation to birth. And a series of eight fetal skeletons, prepared in Vienna and purchased in 1881, shows development from the second month of gestation to postpartum.

In the late 1970s, the specimens on exhibit were culled and many that had been on display for years were placed in storage. The drawered storage cabinets include a collection of skull sections prepared by Matthew Crier in the nineteenth century, skeletal materials used as teaching specimens by Dr. John H. Brinton. Many of the specimens no longer on display are accompanied by the case history, the source (whether donated or purchased), and bibliographic references that discuss the case. Unfortunately, most of these stored specimens are in need of a cleaning, since Philadelphia's industrial pollution covered them with a dark layer of soot before the advent of air conditioning. In another storage area known as the "bone room" there are shelves holding additional skeletal collections, all of the specimens draped with a thick layer of plastic to protect them. A rack in the room holds seven or eight skeletons, although the museum's published calendar for the year 2000 notes that a total of 23 are curated for use as a study collection. Other specimens include a skull with several gold teeth, affectionately known as "Old Bony," on which dental students in Norristown, Pennsylvania, practiced. One shelf contains the skulls of British and Canadian soldiers from World War I that were brought back for the Mütter Museum by a doctor. Although all of the skulls are identified by name, there was not as much effort at that time to return the remains to the families.

The Mütter Museum collection includes a small number of Aboriginal American remains. Although the 19 Peruvian skulls on display to illustrate trephination are casts, the 48 Native American skulls in the storage area are authentic crania from Midwestern mounds. Director of the museum Gretchen Worden notes that almost all of them are unaffiliated with a tribe, but that she has complied with the provisions of NAGPRA (personal correspondence, September 25, 1999). The Mütter collections and exhibit areas will soon be enlarged with funds set aside from nearly $2 million in federal grants received by the College of Physicians. Executive director of the College Marc Micozzi explains that the museum should be a resource, not merely a repository (Uhlman 2000).

Staatliches Museum für Völkerkunde, Dresden, Germany

The State Museum for Anthropology in Dresden houses the collections of Carl Gustav Carus (d. 1869), a follower of craniologist J.F. Blumenbach who had acquired plaster masks of celebrities and criminals. Carus disagreed with the principles of Franz Gall, but the museum also curates several specimens from Gall's phrenological collection. Though little known today — and subscribing to the ethnocentric racial classifications of his times — Carus was considered a genius by his contemporaries. In 1875, an anthropological society was founded in Dresden by Dr. Adolf Bernhard Meyer (d. 1911). The society was sponsored by the Royal Collections for Arts and Sciences, which were housed in the Medical Academy until 1864 and then transferred to the Museum of Natural History. The collections included the Carus Collection of several hundred plaster masks. Like Carus, Meyer was looking for correlations between the body and the mind, but he now had the science of anthropometry to assist him (although its principles, too, were flawed). Having taken many measurements during his travels in New Guinea, Meyer concentrated his attention on acquiring specimens from Australia and the Pacific and Indonesian islands. In 1876, Meyer accessioned 135 skulls from Papua New Guinea. He also built up a network of researchers with whom he exchanged ethnographic and anthropological specimens that today — with the advent of genetic testing — hold great promise for researchers. Over the next 30 years, Meyer received from his colleagues skulls and hair collected in Indonesia, plaster masks and hair from Polynesia and Micronesia, plaster masks from Malaysia, and skulls from the Philippines, New Guinea, and the island of New Ireland in the Pacific. About 400 of the 4,094 specimens in the museum collection had been donated by

Arthur Baessler (d. 1907), with others added by successive museum directors. But by the early twentieth century, specimens were hard to come by, since even remote parts of the world were tapped by dealers in antiquities.

During World War I, the museum lost many of its international contacts and most of its funding. A scientist named Struck began excavations of medieval remains in central Europe in hopes of adding some human skeletons to the collections. When the State of Saxonia (of which Dresden is the capital) unified with federal Germany, the museum was renamed and the branches of zoology and anthropology divided. The events of World War II posed new problems. The museum was renamed the "State Museum for Zoology, Race Science, and Anthropology." The racial classifications that had been derived from anthropometry were used to support Nazi ideology and to help determine Jewish ancestry, which gave the field of anthropology a bad name. Damage repair — both physical and political — was coordinated by Dr. Klaus Günther beginning in 1942. Boxes of specimens that had been removed to Weesenstein castle, Schafenstein castle and Königstein fortress during the war for safekeeping were returned to the Museum for Anthropology.

Directorship of the museum was taken up in 1946 by Dr. Rose Hempel, who checked the collections for damage and found that all of the wet specimens had been lost in the bombing of Dresden. Most of the specimens were still in storage until the 1960s, when ethnographic research on the collections was begun by Frank Tiesler. Among other studies, Tiesler conducted a comparison of the medieval bones from Wolkenstein in the collection with skeletal material being recovered during mass exhumations in the Annaberg graveyard. An anthropologist from the University of Berlin was employed by the museum beginning in 1976. The collections were completely unpacked and reorganized (with the exception of the skeletal remains collected in Wolkenstein and Annaberg, which remain carefully boxed), and the exhibits were reworked. The museum officially reopened in 1979. The collections today include a number of ancestor skulls and modified crania. Skulls from the Parari Delta in New Guinea have been colored with soil- or plant-based paints. Skulls from Borneo and the Fly River in New Guinea have intricate carvings on their surfaces. The eyes of skulls from New Hebrides and the Solomon Islands are inset. Skulls prepared by the Mundurucú people of South America are covered with mummified skin, feathers, and artificial eyes. They had also been bound with string to modify the shape of the head as it grew.

Museo di Antropologia ed Etnologia, Florence, Italy

The collections at the National Anthropology Museum in Florence have been growing since the institution was founded by Paolo Mantegazza in 1869. A large part of the collection is made up of human bones, carefully conserved and meticulously cataloged. Mantegazza initiated the collection with two crania and a mandible that he had obtained during a visit to the Canary Islands. In addition to contributing his own acquisitions, he sought specimens from other scientists to improve the museum's collections. Mantegazza issued requests to his colleagues and those of other professions by publishing announcements in journals. In 1871, he suggested that Italian doctors supply him with modern Italian skulls, which Mantegazza would then be able to exchange for skulls of other races or time periods. In 1874, he asked that diplomats, doctors, and businessmen living in the European colonies mail human crania, bones, and cultural artifacts to the museum, objects which would then be preserved in their memory. Among the resulting accessions were a series of human bones from Florence's medical school that includes the skeleton of a famous giant known as the "Child of Castello." Mantegazza's efforts were rewarded when Angelo Bargoni, the public instruction minister, decided to make the National Anthropology Museum a central repository of anthropological materials from universities and museums throughout Italy. During the year following this decision, some 500 human skulls and bones were transferred to Florence for curation. The collections continued to grow through donations, purchases, exchanges, and archaeological expeditions worldwide.

As he acquired new specimens for the museum, Mantegazza cataloged them chronologically according to their arrival at the institution, but without noting the dates of their discovery. This omission has led to some confusion regarding the museum's history. By 1887, however, there were 3,667 specimens in the collection — not all of them human remains — and 4,416 by the turn of the century. By 1909, 40 years after it was founded, the museum had cataloged 3,460 skulls and 171 complete skeletons, some 69 percent of today's totals. In addition to a room of their own in the museum, the skeletal remains shared part of a large gallery with the ethnologic material. A separate room was set aside for the anatomical specimens. To accompany the catalog, a card index was prepared indicating the geographic origins of the specimens. When the museum moved to its present location in the Palazzo Nonfinito in the 1920s, the bones were organized into two groups, one consisting of the crania and the other of prehistoric and postcranial remains. After World War II, the museum acquired casts of the skulls of the Medici family and the Hokkaido collection of Japanese Ainu remains, collected and donated by Fosco Maraini. In 1952, Edmea De Filippi donated several items that had been collected by her husband in Western Tibet in 1913

and 1914, including a bone apron. "The bone seems to lose, at least in part, its actual anatomic identity, in that it is worked and manipulated so that it becomes an integral part of an object thus acquiring a symbolic meaning which goes beyond its bodily essence," reads the English guide book. Today, only a small portion of the skeletal material is on public display and is arranged in exhibits devoted to particular cultures, to human evolution, and to the field of physical anthropology. Only in 1990 was the human bone collection officially designated a national treasure.

In 1986, the Tuscany Region developed and sponsored a project to computerize the catalog based on the paper records. The project has been modified to incorporate new technological developments. Still organized geographically, the specimens are listed in a database that includes the catalog number and a description of the specimen; the sex, age, date, and other information obtained from it; the discoverer and date of discovery; the current condition of the remains; the accession date; the location in the museum; a description of associated materials, such as photographs; and the economic value of the specimen. The program allows catalogers to add special notes and offers various filtering devices to organize the data. Complete through 1997, the catalog includes 5,726 numbered specimens.

Museums of the Royal College of Surgeons of England, London

The Museums of the Royal College of Surgeons of England include the Hunterian Museum, the Odontological Museum, and the Wellcome Museums of Anatomy and Pathology. The most well-known of these is undoubtedly the Hunterian Museum because of its association with surgeon and anatomist John Hunter (d. 1793). In fact, although some of the specimens have continued value as scientific artifacts (such as examples of the osteological effects of tertiary syphilis and bone necrosis), the collection as a whole is displayed as a historical entity which reflects Hunter's perception of the relationship between structure and function in living organisms. The human skeletal remains in the Hunterian Museum show fetal development and the effects on bone of trauma, disease, and the healing process. The Odontological Museum is laid out as a natural history collection and has approximately 150 human skeletal specimens on display, although the entire collections include some 260 human crania and approximately 3,000 preparations (including casts) of human jaws and teeth (Spencer 1997). The exhibits demonstrate the eruption and development of the dentitions and the pathology and normal anatomy of human teeth, and include a section of human mandible showing the relationship of the teeth to the supporting bone. The Wellcome Museums, which are not open to the public, exhibit a small number of complete skeletons as well as individually mounted preparations, including an example of leontiasis ossea in which the bones of the face are deformed by tumor-like masses. The collections include a large number of human skeletons of known age, particularly of children, mostly assembled during the term of William Henry Flower (d. 1899) as conservator (Spencer 1997).

John Hunter spent a lifetime and a fortune (very roughly estimated at £100,000) building up his collection. During his final years, he had employed more than 50 servants and preparators. The work was done at home, which apparently did not bother Mrs. Hunter:

> As the wife of the world's most indefatigable anatomical collector and experimenter, Anne had a lot to put up with, and she put up with it cheerfully. No complaint escaped her as the house overflowed with mummified exotics, with pickled double-headed babies, with fossils, skeletons and cadavers, while students, draughtsmen and dissectors scurried from room to room, reeking of dye and decay, their arms bloodied to the elbows. The yard was a Golgotha of bones, animal and human ... [Kobler 1999].

In 1760, Hunter had leased a plot of land in Earl's Court in Kensington, purchasing adjacent land and adding a sunken cloister to the existing main house. Access to the cloister was through a tunnel entered from a ramp in the rear. The copper boiler in which he reduced cadavers filled a corner of the chamber, and he installed a chimney and tight-fitting doors so that no effluvia would escape. Hunter acquired two adjacent houses in Leicester Square in 1783 to use as his laboratory and living quarters. He installed his anatomical collection in the upper floor of the addition he had constructed to join them together. Hunter amassed 963 preparations of human and comparative osteology and 583 dental preparations. At the same time, Hunter gave lectures, although he didn't enjoy it and they were sometimes poorly attended. In an example of his good humor, upon drawing only a single audience member he dragged a skeleton into the room, seated it, and with a grin began, "Gentlemen ..." (Kobler 1999).

John Hunter's prize acquisition was the skeleton of Irish giant Charles Byrne (d. 1783), who had died at the age of 22. Byrne was aware that his height of nearly eight feet made him a target of anatomists, particularly since he made his living drawing attention to himself. He was later proven right when they surrounded the house in which he lay dying "as harpooners would an enormous whale," according to contemporary newspaper accounts (Thompson 1968). In an attempt to prevent his body from being dissected after death, he left instructions for his corpse to be guarded constantly until it could be placed in a lead coffin and sunk in the Thames estuary. His plans were thwarted by Hunter, who sent a spy to the deathbed to learn where the hired guards drank. After difficult negotiations, Hunter paid them the enormous sum of £500 to divert the body to his carriage. "Upon arrival at Earl's Court he wheeled the body through a subterranean passage into a chamber containing a big copper caldron. He filled the caldron with water, lit a fire under it, and cutting the body into manageable segments, popped them in to boil away the flesh. The hasty process turned the bones of the Irish giant brown, but in all other respects they formed, when fitted together again, a splendid skeleton" (Kobler 1999). Hunter kept his prize a secret for two years, placing it on display two years after that. Frank Buckland measured the skeleton during a visit to the museum and recounted Byrne's story in his *Curiosities of Natural History* (1873), adding the footnote, "Mr. Cliff told me how this skeleton was procured, or rather purloined, but the story might not please some of my readers." Hunter might have enhanced his reputation further by being the first to determine the cause of giantism if only he had removed the top of Byrne's skull and seen evidence of a pituitary tumor diagnosed in 1909 by Conservator Sir Arthur Keith and Harvey Cushing (Wilkins 1991, Bondeson 1997).

Byrne's 7'7" skeleton was among the 13,500 preparations purchased by the Crown from the estate of John Hunter six years after his death and presented to the Royal College of Surgeons, where it has remained on display ever since. Hunter's will had suggested that the collection be offered to the government, but Parliament took its time in making a decision. Hunter's assistant William Clift (d. 1849) stayed on to maintain the specimens during the hiatus and was deservedly named conservator by the newly created Board of Curators in 1800. The Hunterian collection became the nucleus of the museum that opened in Lincoln's Inn Fields in 1813. The total of 113 human osteological specimens soon increased, largely through donations from private collectors, colonial administrators, and explorers. But Clift was also instrumental in the growth of the museum, acquiring numerous specimens — including the remains of executed murderers whose dissection the Royal College of Surgeons was obligated to undertake — and preparing a catalog of the collections in the 1830s (Kobler 1999).

A proud acquisition of John Hunter's brother-in-law, Sir Everard Home (d. 1832), was the skeleton of "Sicilian dwarf" Caroline Crachami (d. 1824), who stood less than 20 inches tall. Home had seen Caroline several times in London, where she was exhibited by a Dr. Gilligan. Gilligan, with whom Home became friendly, stated that the child had been born in Palermo in 1815 weighing only a pound. After being presented at the court of King George IV, Caroline became extremely popular and received more than 200 visitors before her early death in 1824 of what was later confirmed to be tuberculosis. A week after Caroline's death, her father turned up from Dublin to claim her body, explaining that he had allowed Gilligan to exhibit her in order to meet his expenses and had read about her death in the newspaper. Mr. Crachami learned that Gilligan had bragged that he could earn as much money on Caroline *after* her death, having been offered £500 from several anatomists for her remains. Further investigation brought the father to Home's house, where he learned that Home had indeed purchased the body on behalf of the Royal College of Surgeons. Home paid Crachami £10 and honored his request to have a last look at the child by bringing him to her dissection, which was well underway. Crachami embraced the dismembered corpse and the tragic scandal was written up in the newspaper. Crachami left for Dublin and Gilligan was rumored to have fled to France. Despite Home's promise to the father that the dissection would not continue, he ordered that Caroline's skeleton be prepared and mounted. Standing for years next to the Irish Giant in the Hunterian Museum, Crachami's skeleton was recently relocated to the Odontological Museum, reflecting renewed interest in the study of tooth and bone development to establish age at death.

Sir Everard Home also acquired the notable skull of the "Two-Headed Boy of Bengal," which is still on display. The child had been born in India in 1783, and was lucky to have survived at all. The midwife who delivered him was so frightened by his appearance that she threw him into the fire, leaving him badly burned. The boy had the remnants of a conjoined twin in the form of a second head upside down on his own. The two heads were of the same size and covered with black hair at their junction. The upper head ended in a necklike stump and showed reflexive movements, absent corneal reflexes, weak reaction to light, malformed ears, and a small tongue. The lower jaw was small, but capable of motion, and the secretion of tears and saliva was plentiful. The two joined heads had independent eye movements. The parents exhibited the child in Calcutta for money, covering him up between shows, until he was fatally bitten by a cobra at age four. His body was buried despite several offers for it, but the grave was predictably plundered. The graverobber, Mr. Dent of the East India Company, dissected the body (noting that the brains were separate and distinct) and kept the skull, which he presented to Captain Buchanan of the same outfit. The captain presented it to Home upon his return to England. Home regretted that no men of science had been able to examine the boy while alive, and while he did see that the two halves of the skull were not separated by a septum of bone, he failed to conclude that the child was an example of conjoined twins of the craniopagus type (Bondeson 1997).

In addition to its most famous specimens, the museums also acquired the following skeletons: Charles Freeman, the "American giant" (d. 1854) whose 6'8½" skeleton was purchased at death for £2 and articulated by Mr. Willmost for twice that amount; John Thurtell, a criminal hanged in 1824 and dissected at St. Bartholomew's Hospital; and William Cordes, a murderer executed in 1828.

The college's collections were also augmented by several large skeletal series, some donated and others purchased:

- Davis Collection: A series of nearly 1,800 human crania and a small number of skeletons purchased in 1879 for £1,000 from craniologist Joseph Barnard Davis (d. 1881). The skulls, recovered from around the world, were inventoried in a well-illustrated catalog.

- Nicolucci Collection: A total of 166 crania and skeletons, including both ancient and modern specimens from Italy and Greece, purchased in 1870.

- Hutchinson Collection: 100 crania recovered from Peruvian burial grounds and presented to the museum by the Royal Anthropological Institute in 1873.

- African slaves: The skulls of 20 Africans who died of cholera while awaiting transportation presented to the Royal Geographical Society in 1859 by explorers Richard Francis Burton (d. 1890) and John Hanning Speke (d. 1864).

- Egyptian skulls: 100 skulls recovered near Giza by Richard Burton and presented to the museum in 1879.

- Egyptian skeletons: 14 skeletons and 12 crania recovered from Fourth Dynasty tombs by Egyptologist William Flinders Petrie (d. 1942).

- Bones from India: A large collection of skeletal material from the Andaman Islands in the Bay of Bengal received in the mid-nineteenth century.

The skeletal material in the museums has been put to good use, beginning early on. In the mid-nineteenth century, surgeon James Paget (d. 1899) spent several years cataloging the pathology collections and identifying among Hunter's specimens those showing a thickening and deformation of the bone, which he called osteitis deformans, now termed Paget's Disease.

During a German bombing raid on May 11, 1941, the Museums of the Royal College of Surgeons (then a single entity) were gutted, destroying at least 60 percent of the Hunterian collection, including many of Hunter's original preparations. The skeletons of Byrne and Crachami survived, having been evacuated to a place of safety, and the specimens that were saved were put in storage until the museum reopened (Bondeson 1997). Some 5,000 skeletal specimens survived the bombing and were transferred to London's Natural History Museum. These include a human cranium determined to be of Neandertal origin that was found on the cliffs of Gibraltar in 1848, presented to the museum by surgeon George Busk (d. 1886) in 1868, and moved to the Natural History Museum in 1948. They also include Middle Paleolithic skeletons excavated from the Mount Carmel Caves in Palestine by Doroth Garrod (d. 1968) and Theodore D. McCown (d. 1969) in the 1930s. The remains were extracted from one-ton blocks of breccia at the museum, documented and examined at the college's research station in Kent, and later divided between the Natural History Museum in London and the Rockefeller Museum in Jerusalem. The Natural History Museum also curates an Egyptian skeletal collection acquired in the Aswan region by Grafton Elliot Smith (d. 1937) and presented to the college in 1907. Transferred from the Natural History Museum to the Royal College of Surgeons were 16 crania excavated by Charles Leonard Woolley (d. 1960) at the fourth millennium site of Al Ubeid in Mesopotamia, supplemented in 1931 by finds from Woolley's excavations at the Royal Cemetery of Ur.

After World War II, the surviving specimens were subdivided into today's four institutions, with a pathological museum and an anatomical museum opening first, followed by the Odontological Museum in 1959. The Hunterian Museum reopened in 1963 and contains approximately 3,500 original specimens augmented by 2,500 non–Hunterian specimens added since 1813 and arranged in the same manner as John Hunter's original museum (Spencer 1997).

Museums of the Royal College of Surgeons of Edinburgh

The Royal College of Surgeons of Edinburgh maintains three museums, one of which — Playfair Hall — houses one of the largest and most historic collections of surgical pathological material in the U.K. Playfair Hall is only open to registered postgraduate students and fellows of the college, although members of the public age 15 or older may arrange for a guided tour. The establishment of an anatomical museum had been suggested by the Guild of Barber Surgeons of Edinburgh in 1699. The suggestion soon brought donations, among the earliest of which were a skeleton with mummified muscles attached, mounted in a mahogany case and bearing the inscription, "Gifted by Archibald Pitcairne Doctor of Medicine Fellow of the Royal College of Physicians 1702," and another skeleton mounted in a similar case and inscribed, "These anatomical preparations were gifted to the Incorporation of Chirurgian Apothecaries of Ed. by Alexr. Monro 1718" (Tansey 1982). These and subsequent preparations were exhibited in the original Surgeons' Hall.

A significant number of early specimens were donated by Professor John Thomson and his assistant James Wardrop, probably from their private collections. The college also received the comparative anatomy collection of anatomist John Barclay (d. 1826), who had built it up over a period of 21 years and offered it as a gift in 1821 with certain conditions, including the appointment for life of Robert Knox as conservator and the completion of a suitable hall to house the collection. The inventory of the collection recorded 1,168 items, but a large part no longer exists. The same year that Barclay offered his collection, the curators negotiated with the family of Dr. Meckel of Halle in Germany to acquire his collection, but the family would not accept their offer of £5,000 and withdrew it from consideration. In 1822, the college gave William Cullen (d. 1829) a salary of £300 per year and a budget of £500 per year to acquire specimens for the museum in Paris, but he returned with only 23 specimens (Tansey 1982). A more successful venture was the acquisition of the Bell Collection in the late 1820s. The more than 3,000 anatomical and pathological specimens collected by James Wilson and Charles Bell at the Great Windmill Street School of Anatomy and Medicine in London were purchased for £3,000. One consequence of acquiring the Bell Collection was the need for additional exhibit space, remedied by the purchase of a nearby house until the construction of a new "Surgeon's Hall," which was ready for occupation in 1832. The new building included a maceration room in the basement and had three rooms for the preparation and repair of specimens. Later renovations in one of these rooms turned up a human rib cage wrapped in straw and a newspaper bearing an 1855 date (Tansey 1982).

Administration of the museum had been formalized in 1804, when the college appointed curators in the form of a management committee. Curator James Russell (d. 1836), a former president of the college, played an important part in negotiations for the acquisition of established collections. The actual care of the collection and the preparation of specimens remained the responsibility of Professor John Thomson until the appointment of a series of keepers. In the 1820s, the position of keeper was replaced by that of a salaried conservator charged with keeping the specimens in a proper state of preservation and being available to explain the exhibits to museum visitors. The post was applied for by Dr. Robert Knox (d. 1862), who wrote in 1824, "Engaged now for a long period solely in the study of Comparative Anatomy and Physiology, I have felt more than most anatomists the great want of a proper museum, and of an osteological collection, without which, researches into comparative and human Physiology, cannot be carried out" (Tansey 1982). Knox offered to create such a museum, the costs to be borne by the Royal College of Surgeons. Knox's help was accepted and he collaborated with the keepers from 1824 to 1826, during which time he was not paid, but was reimbursed £100 for expenses. Knox's relationship with the curators changed in 1828, probably due to his involvement in the Burke and Hare scandal and the appointment in 1829 of his rival James Syme as one of the curators. Knox finally tendered his resignation in 1831. To curb the liberty and authority that Knox had enjoyed, the college imposed restrictions that prevented later conservators from maintaining museums of their own or assisting in the formation of others.

During his tenure as curator (1841 to 1843), John Goodsir donated a number of specimens demonstrating comparative anatomy. When his younger brother Harry took over his post between 1843 and 1845, it was decided for economic reasons to exclude the public from the pathology galleries and to abstain from accepting new specimens. The curation of the existing specimens was managed poorly by Harry Goodsir's successor, Hamlin Lee, whose preparations were not identifiable, in bad condition, and out of arrangement, according to the minutes of a curators' meeting held in 1852, during which it was presumably decided to relinquish Mr. Lee of his duties. Later Conservator Charles Walker Cathcart (who served from 1887 to 1900) accessioned more than 1,300 specimens, many of them personal donations, and suggested publishing a new catalog, which was later done. A brief term by Theodore Shennan was followed by the 17-year conservatorship of Henry Wade, during whose tenure (1903 to 1920) it was proposed that the college dispose of the Barclay Collection. Instead, a hall that had contained research laboratories was renovated and a gallery created to house the specimens. The new gallery was soon expanded to the building next door, where larger specimens were exhibited on free stands and smaller specimens were displayed in cabinets (Tansey 1982).

In 1921, the conservatorship of the museum was taken up by David Middleton Greig, who had donated his pathological collection the previous year. Greig's specimens illustrated diseases of bone and abnormalities of the skull and included some 300 skulls, a small number of which are still on display. The collection did not include the remains of Greig's assistant James Jack, an achondroplasic dwarf, who bragged about having outlived him. Acquisitions did include the Obstetrician Collection of J. Haig Ferguson; the Otorhinolaryngology Collection of J.S. Fraser and A. Logan Turner; and the Dental Collection of J.H. Gibbs. The museum's policy at that time was to display all specimens in the collection, which resulted in marked overcrowding. During World War II, the specimens were safeguarded by storing them in the basement of the college and repaired as necessary by a single staff member. The collection was rehabilitated, clinically documented, and photographed by Conservator James Norman Jackson Hartley after the war. In 1955 it was finally decided to display the specimens selectively. The material had by then been augmented by collections donated by dentist and dental historian J. Menzies Campbell (displayed in the Dental Museum) and pathologist E.K. Dawson. Duplicate specimens were placed in reserve. The collection was renumbered and the general catalog revised and cross-referenced for easy access to the items on display and in storage.

Museum of Man, San Diego, California

The San Diego Museum of Man owes its existence to the Panama-California Exposition hosted by the city in January 1915 to celebrate the opening of the Panama Canal. The exposition had as its theme "The Story of Man Through the Ages" and featured an exhibit coordinated by Aleš Hrdlička, curator of the Division of Physical Anthropology at the Smithsonian's National Museum of Natural History. Hrdlička sent expeditions to Africa, Alaska, the Philippines, and Siberia. In addition, he personally collected skeletal material, including four historic crania from Mongolia and pathological bones from 30 sites in Peru. Hrdlička's Peruvian digs did not require much digging, since the 500- to 1,000-year-old skulls he collected in 1910 and 1913 were recovered from the surface of looted sites. Spencer L. Rogers explains (Merbs 1980), "Dr. Hrdlička traveled to Peru and found that no excavation was needed as most of the ancient cemeteries had been despoiled by artifact hunters. Skulls and bones littered the surface of the sites. Because of this, he was able to examine an immense number of specimens and to make a selective collection in a relatively short time. The disadvantage to this was the lack of cultural association and disassociation of the bones."

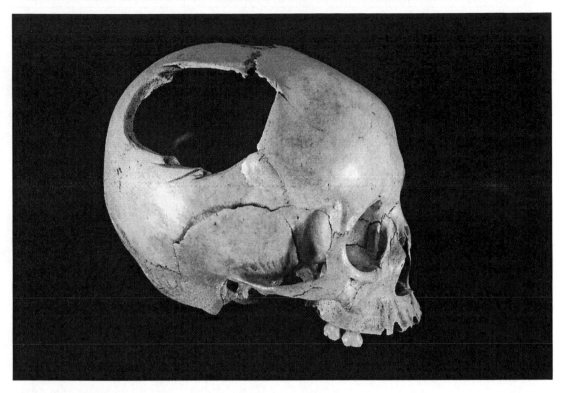

Cranium of prehistoric adolescent female from Cinco Cerros, Peru, exhibiting massive trephination with no signs of healing. Specimen #1915-2-257 from the Hrdlička Collection. Photo courtesy of the Museum of Man, San Diego.

The skeletal remains showed, among other things, that the New World diet of corn, may have led to iron deficiency anemia. Other skeletal material excavated for the exposition included four crania and numerous post-cranial bones recovered from St. Lawrence Island, Alaska, by Riley D. Moore in 1913. The bones show possible syphilitic changes and include an example of a fused vertebral column. The material was assembled to illustrate the skeletal biology of pre–Columbian American Indians. Trephined skulls were included as examples of Aboriginal surgery (Merbs 1980). The exhibited material was to become the property of the corporation conducting the exposition, with any surplus to be given to the Smithsonian. As the exposition drew to a close in November 1915, George Marston and a group of fellow citizens formed the San Diego Museum Association with the mission of retaining the collection of over 5,000 items and establishing a museum of anthropology. Edgar L. Hewett, director of Santa Fe's School of American Research and one of the organizers of the exposition, was chosen to head the museum.

During World War II, the museum was given its current name, but the exhibits were dismantled and the collections stored. The museum space was converted to a hospital by the U.S. Navy, after which they paid reparation costs for damages to the building, but many of the specimens had deteriorated and broken, and records had been lost. Prior to the war, the focus of the museum had been on collection and research. After Clark Evernham took up directorship in 1951, the museum focused on public support and involvement. His successor, Lowell E. English, strengthened the museum's financial base and began a Collector's Club

with 37 founding members. Under his directorship (1972 to 1981), the Harkelroad
Collection of Southern California archaeological material was accessioned. Douglas
Sharon became director in 1981 and oversaw
large-scale capital improvements, enhanced
exhibits, and the addition of important collections including the Stanford-Meyer Osteopathology Collection, bringing the total
number of items in the museum's research
collections to 67,000.

A walk through the Museum of Man
is an osteological adventure. In addition to
part of the Chaffey Collection of skulls assembled by Dr. Eugene Boring, exhibits in
September 1998 included the following:

• Zapotec skull rack: A 2,000-year-old
  skull rack from Oaxaca, Mexico, the presence of lower jaws indicating that the
  heads were still fleshed when placed on
  the rack.

• Aztec skulls: The incised ceremonial skulls
  of enemies.

• Hallstatt skulls: Decorated skulls of family members displayed in the chapel at
  Hallstatt, Austria.

• Melanesian skulls: Skulls from New Hebrides modeled with clay and fiber.

• Tibetan skullcaps: Crania called *tod-pa*
  or *kapala* when bejeweled that were used
  as drinking bowls by monks.

But an even greater number of specimens
reside behind the scenes as elements of two
important research collections.

The Stanford-Meyer Osteopathology
Collection was acquired from Stanford University in 1981. The assemblage consists of
3,500 single specimens of bone representing
1,500 individuals, of whom some 400 are
documented (with age at death, cause of
death, and occupation). The specimens
show disease and trauma and were collected
at autopsy by Arthur M. Meyer between

1920 and 1940. Retained for research and
teaching purposes, they were stored in the
school's anatomy department. The bulk of
the collection, now housed at the Museum
of Man, is being actively studied after lan-
guishing for years. About 500 of the specimens were transported to the University of
California at San Diego by Donald Resnick
to be x-rayed and the radiographs used in
the second edition of his book, *Diagnosis of
Bone and Joint Disorders*. The remaining
skeletons in the Stanford collection, consisting of nearly 1,000 individuals, were acquired in 1998 by the University of Iowa.

The Hrdlička paleopathology collection is also extensively documented. Storage
improvements, catalog description, and conservation of the more than 1,000 specimens
in the Hrdlička collection were sponsored in
part by a National Science Foundation grant
in 1978. The osteological descriptions and
pathological diagnoses were rewritten by
Charles F. Merbs — incorporating information from Hrdlička's original catalog, his
field notes obtained from the National Anthropological Archives, and records from
the Smithsonian — and published by the
museum. The collection includes examples
of the following pathologies: fresh and
healed fractures; ossification of ligament;
tuberculosis; eburnation; mineral loss;
ankylosis; spondylolisthesis; dislocation of
humeral head, radial head, and femoral
head; possible surgical amputation; tooth
wear, tooth loss, and alveolar resorption;
abscess; caries; enamel hypoplasia; osteoporosis; porotic hyperostosis (cribra
orbitalia and cribra crania); osteoma;
osteomyelitis; osteophytosis; osteitis; periostitis; lytic lesion; possible carcinoma;
auditory exostoses; temporo-mandibular
osteoarthritis; macrocephaly, bony spurs,
ossicles, and tubercles; and perforating lesions. The specimens in the catalog are photographed and arranged anatomically, with
bones from the same individual cross-referenced. Except for 24 cases with multiple

bones from one individual, the majority of specimens in the collection are single bones (Merbs 1980). Some of the specimens, including an example of fusion recovered in San Xavier, Patagonia, were collected by Hrdlička in 1910 during an expedition sponsored by the Smithsonian Institution. Others — skull fragments, vertebrae, and long bones — were collected in Arkansas, Louisiana, and Mississippi by Clarence B. Moore in 1909.

Hrdlička's Peruvian material includes skulls and skull fragments of prehistoric children and adults. One of the skulls still wears a headdress and bears some hair. Some specimens in the Hrdlička collection exhibit artificial cranial deformation in the form of lambdoidal, frontal, occipital, vertical, and frontal-occipital flattening. Six crania from Sica Sica, Bolivia, one of which belonged to a prehistoric adolescent, show cranial deformation by binding the head. Also collected by Hrdlička were examples of trephination by abrasion, scraping, straight and curvilinear cutting, and drilling. Some of the perforations are partial, some are complete, and some are healed. The Hrdlička collection also includes examples of prehistoric trauma, for instance an adult cuneiform with a projectile point embedded in it and a metacarpal showing a healed fracture, which were collected in Arizona in 1887. In addition to material collected by and for Hrdlička, the collection that bears his name includes three skulls and a mandible from Twelfth-Dynasty Egypt, collected in Lisht in 1908 during an exploration by the Metropolitan Museum of Art in New York. It also includes bones that had been intended for the Army Medical Museum, including skulls of a historic adult male and female from Richmond, Virginia, and a cranium from a Mexican battlefield (Merbs 1980). Curator Rose Tyson makes available to researchers an annotated slide set of the Hrdlička collection, which includes 42 examples of trephination and 65 examples of pathologies and anomalies. Also available is the museum publication *Human Paleopathology and Related Subjects: An International Bibliography* (1997), with upgrades released on disk.

The skeletal material curated by the Museum of Man is numbered by year and cataloged on cards, explains Tyson (personal correspondence, September 3, 1998). When deciding on which skulls to exhibit, Tyson chooses examples that have a full face, that are not delicate, and that are not rare in case they are needed for research. The bones and the documentation about them are accessible to researchers at the museum's laboratory. The Stanford-Meyer and Hrdlička collections will remain available, and studies based on them continue. Also curated are a group of 5,000-year-old specimens from La Jolla, California, and a number of infant skulls collected in New Mexico by Edgar L. Hewett between 1935 and 1937. Electron microscopy has been carried out on the latter collection. The museum does not sponsor expeditions, so new additions to the collections are acquired by donation.

Anthropologische Staatssammlung, München, Germany

The Anthropolocal Collection in the State Collections for Natural Sciences of Bavaria was founded by Johannes Ranke (d. 1916) of the University of Munich, who became the first German professor of anthropology in 1886 and directed the museum until his death. Ranke had a huge private collection of original and restored prehistoric specimens, most of them from Bavaria, which he donated to the state in 1885. The collection remained intact and was exhibited separately, but was initially part of the Paleontological Museum. By 1902, the size of the collection had grown and it was renamed "Anthropological-Prehistorical Collection of the State." By 1927, the prehistoric and anthropological collections had been separated.

Unfortunately, World War II hit the museum very hard. Literally so on April 25, 1944, when most of the collection was destroyed. Surviving specimens included the skulls from the Ofnet cave, skeletons from the town of Neuessing, and the first skeleton to be found at the Olduvai site in Tanzania. The reduced collection was exhibited in the School of Art and was without a director until 1949. With no funding, the museum was rebuilt very slowly but now curates approximately 30,000 complete skeletons dating from the early Paleolithic to modern times. Some of the material was recovered from medieval graves in the Bavarian towns of Altenerdings and Straubing. The collection, headed by Gisela Grupe, is located at Karolinenplatz and is the only one of its kind in Germany that is not affiliated with a university. The museum employs two researchers and two preparators and is host to visiting scientists from around the world. The focus of the collection is prehistoric life and researchers study skeletal variation and osteological clues to illness, diet, and other population characteristics. Teeth have been cross-sectioned to study age at death and age-related degeneration of bone tissue. But in general, histology, x-rays, DNA typing, and other methods are used to avoid excessive damage to the specimens. Genetic testing of the Ofnet skulls, which include those of adults and children, will help scientists determine family relationships. Signs on the skulls of blunt force trauma point to violent deaths, but the reason for the killing and for the caching of the skulls remains elusive.

Peabody Museum at Harvard University, Cambridge, Massachusetts

On November 9, 1866, an exhibit opened in Boylston Hall at Harvard University. The display included crania and bones of North American Indians, a few casts of crania of other races, and several other artifacts. Altogether they consisted of some 50 specimens, half of which were contributed by the curator of the newly established Peabody Museum and the other half transferred from Harvard College. The collection grew quickly, with the local public responding to an appeal by making 36 donations in the museum's first year. These included a group of 75 crania from Peru presented by E. George Squier and a series of 21 skulls obtained by Sanford Dole on the Island of Kauai in what were then the Sandwich Islands (Brew 1966b). Surplus and duplicate specimens were offered by the Boston Athanaeum, the Massachusetts Historical Society, the Peabody Academy of Science in Salem, the American Antiquarian Society in Worcester, the American Medical Museum, the Museum of Comparative Zoology, the Warren Anatomical Museum at the Harvard Medical School, the Smithsonian Institution, the Carnegie Institution of Washington, the Boston Museum of Natural History, and the Pilgrim Society in Plymouth. The president of Harvard University at the time hoped that the museum would also provide a home for Aboriginal remains scattered in private collections. But the endowment of the museum by philanthropist George Peabody provided for the firsthand collection of specimens. In his letter of gift to the trustees, Peabody directed that "in view of the gradual obliteration or destruction of the works and remains of the ancient races of this continent, the labor of exploration and collection be commenced at as early a day as practicable; and also that, in the event of the discovery in America of human remains or implements of an earlier geological period than the present, especial attention be given to their study, and their comparison with those found in other countries" (Brew 1966b). Peabody conveyed $150,000 to the museum, $45,000 of which was to be devoted to acquiring and preserving objects and books, $45,000 to establish a professorship in American Archaeology and Ethnology, and $60,000 to use as a building fund.

By the time a museum building was erected in 1877, it was barely adequate to house the existing collections. Two additions were eventually added. The museum's first director and curator was Jeffries Wyman, a natural scientist with a deep interest in the prehistoric American Indian. In 1882, physical anthropologist Cordelia A. Studley was added to the staff. Three years later, Frederic Ward Putnam (d. 1915) was appointed to the chair that Peabody had endowed, thereby founding the oldest continuously operating department of physical anthropology in the country. In 1886, the pathological material in the museum was surveyed by W.F. Whitney, who noted (ahead of his time) "the necessity of preserving the bones of the skeleton as well as the skull" (Ubelaker 1982). In 1896, the first doctorate in physical anthropology was awarded to Frank Russell, who stayed on to conduct research and teach until his death in 1905. And in 1913, Earnest A. Hooton joined the staff, accepting between one and three graduate students a year beginning in the mid–1920s.

The first specimen to have been cataloged at the Peabody was a Native American cranium discovered in Chelsea, Massachusetts. It was followed by skeletal material recovered from a series of excavations. Burial mounds near Aledo, Florida, were excavated by Henry Gillman in 1878. A large burial mound and associated sites in Marion County, Kansas, were excavated by Edwin Curtiss in 1879. Between 1881 and 1897, the Madisonville and Turner mounds in Little Miami Valley, Ohio, were excavated by Putnam and C.L. Metz. In the 1920s, Alfred V. Kidder excavated more than 2,000 Pecos, Comanche, and Apache skeletons (since repatriated to the Pecos National Historical Park for reburial) that became one of the largest single-source collections of historic remains. The assemblage was also one of the first to be systematically studied, and offered clues to nutrition, trauma, disease, cranial variations, and work-related stresses of farming. With its history of sponsoring excavations, the Peabody Museum's importance lies less in single specimens than in the unique assemblages it has acquired. The museum curates bones from around the world, in addition to Native American remains. According to a survey conducted in 1974, the museum curates 3,122 skeletons from northern Mexico and 525 from Egypt. As the director in 1966, J.O. Brew, noted: "When it is realized ... that as many as 175 accessions have been recorded in one year, the impossibility of a truly representative listing becomes apparent. This is particularly true of physical anthropology. Skeletons have a tendency to appear singly, and often far from complete at that. Sometimes it is only one bone" (Brew 1966a).

Phoebe Hearst Museum of Anthropology, University of California, Berkeley

The collection at the Phoebe Hearst Museum has been curated on the Berkeley campus since 1931. Some 8,000 human osteological specimens are numbered among its estimated 3.8 million items. The skeletal remains include primarily individuals from North America, South America, and Egypt. The descriptive catalog is available to researchers by appointment, but has not yet been entered into a computer database. This has so far not hindered interested scholars, as assistant director Kathleen L. Butler points out (personal communication, June 17, 1999): "Research on the collection is conducted by Native Americans, university students and faculty, and government researchers. Results have been published in journals and government reports."

The museum was founded in 1901. Most of the specimens were acquired in the first half of the twentieth century by private individuals and university archaeologists. The first director of the museum was Frederick Ward Putnam, who simultaneously directed the Peabody Museum at Harvard and the American Museum of Natural History. In 1959, Kroeber Hall was built to house the museum and anthropology department. The museum was named in honor of faculty member Robert H. Lowie, but the name was changed in 1991 to honor the museum's founder, Phoebe Apperson Hearst (d. 1919). Hearst had become the first female member of the University's Board of Regents in 1897 and had proposed establishing the museum — the first west of Chicago — and the department of anthropology. She had become interested in anthropology while living in the East and continued to make important contributions to the museum, which she supported completely during its first seven years, until her death. Among the acquisitions that Hearst's support made possible are four important collections with the following themes: classical Greece and Rome (collected by Alfred Emerson), archaeology of ancient Egypt (collected by George Reisner), ancient Peru (collected by Max Uhle), and the living cultures and prehistory of the California Indians (collected by Alfred Kroeber). Today, the Californian collections are the largest and most comprehensive in the world, and the Egyptian and Peruvian holdings are among the top three or four of their kind, according to a summary of the museum's history written by Ira Jacknis.

Maxwell Museum of Anthropology, University of New Mexico, Albuquerque

The Maxwell Museum of Anthropology curates archaeological and forensic human skeletal remains. The archaeological material comprises one of the largest human skeletal collections in the American Southwest and consists of over 3,000 individual skeletons whose dates range from 2000 B.P. to recent. The forensic material includes a collection of documented skeletons that have been donated since 1973 and the remains of individuals who are part of active and inactive cases for the New Mexico Office of the Medical Investigator (OMI). Among the documented skeletons is that of Hans Zopf, whose suicide several years earlier was not reported by his wife until 1977. After the investigation of the death, the widow donated the remains to the museum, but insisted on "visiting rights" and came to see the skeleton several times. "With those visits it became clear to me that unlimited visiting rights to skeletal remains are not the best idea since sliced bread," writes Stanley Rhine (1998). Another specimen is the skeleton of a man nicknamed "Dead-Eye" because of an attack with a weapon like a meat cleaver or axe that destroyed his right eye and cut into the cheekbone beneath it. The skull wounds show healing, since the victim survived for several years, and are the best evidence of the assault, as Rhine (1998) explains: "Museum records include no documentation of his attack, injury, and treatment, but his bones tell us a good deal of the story."

The bones were once prepared in the lab by maceration and boiling, but odors and increased volume prompted the administration to object. The operation was moved to the Office of the Medical Investigator, which had been newly equipped with two fume hoods (Rhine 1998). The curator Joseph F. Powell and the staff of the museum work as forensic anthropology consultants to the OMI. "We also work closely with state and federal agencies on issues related to the inadvertent discovery of human remains, and on assessments of cultural and/or biological affiliation of these remains," explains Powell (personal correspondence, August 17, 1999). In fact, they have had to do the latter on the Native American remains in their own collection in order to comply with federal law. While conducting their NAGPRA inventory, they took the opportunity the compile standardized data from the bones. The museum recently collaborated with the Jemez Pueblo tribe and Harvard's Peabody Museum to complete an analysis of the Pecos collection spurred by descendants. Other research involving the prehistoric collections is first reviewed by a curators' committee in consultation with Native American tribes.

In addition to the prehistoric remains and documented skeletons, the Maxwell Museum houses about 1,500 skeletons for the Museum of New Mexico's Laboratory of Anthropology. The collections at the Maxwell Museum are intended entirely for research and none of the human remains are on display. They actively solicit donations through a body donor program and through their work for the OMI, so the documented skeletal collection continues to expand. The collections at the museum are used in a variety of research projects, from the functional morphology of Neandertal hands to the identification of carnivore damage patterns on ancient and modern bone. In addition to students and faculty of the Department of Anthropology, the collections have been studied by researchers from 74 institutions since 1995, resulting in dozens of scientific publications.

Musée de l'Homme, Paris

A thorough exhibit of prehistoric remains at the Musée de l'Homme in Paris includes skulls and casts representing many species. *Homo erectus* is represented by a mandible from the Canary Islands; a skull from Bodo, Ethiopia; a skull from Kenya; a skull from Olduvai in Tanzania; the skeleton of "Turkana Boy" from Kenya; a skull from Syria; a skull from India; and several male and female skulls from the Zhoukoudian site and other locations in China. Examples of *Australopithecus* include the skull of "Miss

Ples" from Sterkfontein, South Africa; a skull from the Transvaal; skulls from Koobi Fora, Kenya; skeletal remains from Olduvai; and the skull of the Taung child from South Africa. *Homo habilis* specimens include two skulls from Koobi Fora and some post-cranial remains from Olduvai. Pre-Neandertal skulls include one from Petralona, Greece, and another from Steinheim, Germany. *Cro-Magnons* are represented by a skull from Dordogne. The display also includes several crania and a femur from Java.

But perhaps the most eye-catching specimen in the collection is not prehistoric, but historic: the skull of René Descartes (d. 1650). The philosopher and mathematician had been buried in Stockholm, but his remains were returned to his native France 16 years after his death. Unfortunately, the repatriated remains did not include Descartes' head, an omission that was discovered when the casket was transferred to the Panthéon in 1819. The Swedish press reported that the skull had been sold during an auction of the effects of a professor named Sparrman. Swedish chemist Jöns Jacob Berzelius tracked down the cranium, which carried the names of several possible owners: Ol. Celsius, J. Haegerflycht, Anders Anton von Stierneman, 1751, and J. Ågren, 1797. Written on the forehead were the words, "The skull of Cartesius, taken by Israel Planström in 1666 when the corpse was to be transported to France" (Henschen 1965). The cranium was returned to France in 1821, but has not remained united with the skeleton. The Musée de l'Homme collections also include the lab specimens of Paul Broca and the skeleton of Nicolas Ferry (d. 1764), better known as Bébé, the court dwarf of King Stanislaus Leczinski of Poland from the age of four until his death at age 21 (Bondeson 1997).

University of Helsinki, Finland

A large skeletal collection at the University of Helsinki is currently being cata-

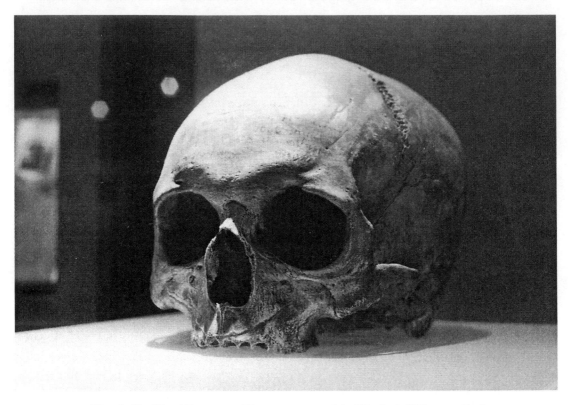

The skull of René Descartes. Photo courtesy of the Musée de l'Homme, Paris.

loged and reorganized by Niklas Söderholm. Previously curated in the Department of Anatomy, the collection is now housed in the Department of Forensic Medicine and will later be transferred to the Finnish Museum of Natural History. Guidelines for the future use of the collection for teaching and research have been formulated by an ethics committee, which recommended repatriation of a small number of the remains, some of which lacked provenance and were in poor condition anyway, having been damaged by bombs in World War II. The collection is roughly divided into two major parts. The first part consists of approximately 1,500 skulls, all but about 200 of them Finnish. The second part consists of skulls and post-cranial remains and includes the following assemblages:

• The A Series: A documented collection of 200 skeletons of individuals for whom age, sex, stature, identity, and cause of death are known. The specimens were acquired from 1910 to the 1930s and population consists mostly of prisoners and poorhouse residents.

• Boulevard Bones: An archaeological assemblage named for the street in which the bones were found during twentieth-century construction of house foundations. Boulevard Street is located next to a cemetery that was used from the seventeenth to the early nineteenth centuries. The specimens consist of some 500 skulls (curated in the larger skull collection) and the postcranial remains of approximately 100 individuals.

• Bonefinds: Specimens recovered from excavations and expeditions made by Helsinki's National Board of Antiquities, which supervises archaeological research in Finland. The dates of the bones range from Neolithic to recent historical material.

• Investigated Crimes: A collection of animal and human bones that have been sent by the police to the Department of Anatomy for analysis.

• The Sámi Collection: An assemblage of about 150 skulls and bones from 70 individuals. Although the bones will be repatriated to the Sámi museum in Inari, Finland, the specimens will remain available for future research.

• Miscellaneous Bones: Bones used as reference material and teaching specimens.

Söderholm has created a database and is using it to conduct a complete inventory of the collection. Included in the database is as much of the following information about each specimen as possible: a description of the remains and their condition; estimated sex, age, and stature; where the individual was from; where and by whom the bones were collected; and the original reason for their collection. The skulls and post-cranial remains are stored in boxes and protected by foam and archival paper.

The Helsinki collection was founded by professor Evert Julius Bonsdorff in the mid-nineteenth century. Bonsdorff had been inspired by the skeletal collection of his teacher Anders Retzius in Stockholm, Sweden. Bonsdorff collected anatomical and zoological specimens, from which the human osteological specimens were later divided. The size of the collection increased rapidly between 1870 and 1890 with many of the skulls collected by medical students during their travels. Other specimens from around the world were donated by Finnish scientists and explorers. By the twentieth century, the collection included about 200 skulls, some of which had been exchanged with specimens from scholars around the world. In this way, 60 Hungarian skulls were obtained in exchange for the same number of Finnish skulls. The collection was used frequently by researchers from 1900 until the end of World War II, after which studies dropped off and the specimens were relegated to the basement. The most popular specimens for study were the skulls, upon which some ten doctoral dissertations and 20 articles in professional journals were based. Data collected from the specimens allowed Antti Telkkä to develop a method of predicting human stature from the long bones that is still quoted in international osteological literature 50 years later.

University of Missouri, Columbia

As the largest institution of higher education in Missouri, the University of Missouri at Columbia curates more archaeological collections than all other institutions and museums in the state combined. The skeletal remains have accumulated during a long history of excavations in Missouri and elsewhere conducted by university personnel since the mid–1930s. Other material has been donated by individuals and institutions. In addition, the university is a recognized federal repository for bones recovered by the Corps of Engineers and the Missouri Department of Transportation. Altogether, the collections at the Museum of Anthropology include the remains of approximately 2,700 individuals, primarily from the prehistoric period. The age of the material spans from about 5000 B.P. to 1500 A.D.

The University of Missouri is in compliance with the provisions of NAGPRA, although the museum's director, Michael J. O'Brien, is personally and professionally opposed to the legislation. "I don't hold out too much hope that prehistoric skeletal collections will be available for much longer," he writes (personal correspondence January 14, 1999). One of the problems O'Brien had to confront early on was that the vast majority of material was prehistoric in origin and difficult to assign to any single cultural group. Museum staff continue to meet with tribes and their affiliates and plan to honor two claims by the Sac and Fox and by the Iowa Tribe of Oklahoma. During the NAGPRA inventory, non-destructive analysis of the skeletal remains proceeded and the collections continue to be used constantly by professional and post-graduate researchers. Due to the sensitivities about human remains (although no specific objections had been raised), none of the skeletons has been on display in the museum since the 1980s. They continue to be available to scholars and no requests to conduct research on them have been turned down.

4

Decoration

A chandelier assembled from four-teenth-century bones. A 30-year-old Vietnamese skull modified to hold a candle. Saints of all ages encased in gold, jewel-encrusted reliquaries. And generations of skulls inscribed with the names and dates of their former occupants. These are examples of the use of human skeletal remains as decorative items. The utilization or modification of the bones may be the intent, such as the painting of modern trophy skulls. Or it may be merely a consequence of venerating or identifying the remains, as with holy relics or the painted skulls of Hallstatt, Austria. Much of the decoration of and with human bones would doubtlessly not have been performed without an abundance of raw material to work with. Rather than stack the accumulated bones of their brothers, the Capuchins in Rome and Palermo arranged them in motifs on the walls and ceilings of chapels. A patron in the Czech Republic paid an artist to make visually appealing use of piles of bones removed from the overcrowded cemetery, a commission the artist thanked him for by crafting the patron's coat of arms from those same bones. In some cases, the patterning of bones and decoration of skulls is a tradition carried on over many years. In other cases, an element of Aboriginal culture such as headhunting is mirrored in modern society, for instance in the collection and coloration of the skulls of enemies during war. The graffiti laughingly applied to a trophy skull is in direct contrast to the name respectfully painted on an ancestor skull. But no matter the reasons, the actions have resulted in collections distinct from other large accumulations because of the visible marking or arrangement of the mortal remains of those who have gone before and who the artists will of course follow — or have already.

MODIFIED BONES

Skulls and bones have been decorated and modified in many cultures, in some cases to venerate the dead and in other cases to celebrate their conquest. The skulls found in excavations in Jericho had been plastered and painted to restore their features. Elsewhere in the world, skulls have been gilded, etched, painted, and covered with shells or feathers. Various objects have been placed in the eye sockets and ribbons or cords have been used to hold the jaw in place and to allow the skull to be displayed by hanging it on the wall or from the ceiling. Among the 20,000 remains curated by Mexico City's National Museum of Anthropology and History are long bones that were notched to create musical instruments, skulls with deliberately enlarged foramina so they could be stuck on poles, and skulls with holes made in both sides indicating that they were strung together. Worked bones, including altered long bones and modified skulls and skull fragments, have been found during excavations at seven sites in British Columbia that date between 1000 B.P. and 500 A.D. "The skull seems to have been a prized part of the human skeleton, with the maxilla and mandible being only somewhat less so," write Owsley, Mann, and Baugh (1994). Other modifications to skulls have been even more utilitarian. The shape of the cranium lends itself to transformation into a drinking vessel. Although most often associated with the Tibetans, skulls in which the base has been removed to form a bowl have been found in Spain, France, Mexico, Moravia, Peru, and Scandinavia. The ancient Celts and many of the nomadic tribes of central Asia made utensils including cups and lamps out of human skulls.

Decorated or manipulated skeletal remains become relics meaningful to an individual, a family, or an entire culture, and usually change hands after those individuals or cultures have died off. But the collection of a certain type of worked bone — the holy relics of Christian saints and martyrs — crosses cultures and offers a form of solidarity among Roman Catholics worldwide. The broad symbolism these relics carry as a whole belies their curious history, both individually and collectively, and the lengths to which the faithful have gone to obtain the skull of a saint or the finger bone of a martyr. Modification in the case of these relics may consist of dividing the bones so that they may be parceled out to churches. The relics thus obtained are enshrined in precious metals, installed on the altar, and venerated by those who believe in their power and authenticity, and who are not put off by the morbid aspect of this means of worship. In fact, the ghoulishness attached to collecting the bony remains of our fellow humans — holy or not — is often muted by making our mark on them.

Hopewellian Culturally-Modified Bones

Native Americans of the Hopewell culture modified the bones of the dead while they were still fresh. The reason for working the bone, a task that would have been quite unpleasant, is unknown, but some clues are being unraveled by Cheryl Johnston, who has made it the subject of her doctoral dissertation (personal correspondence, January 11, 1999). Among the specimens she has examined are maxillae, mandibles, and sometimes whole crania that have been modified by drilling holes, grinding down surfaces, and incising designs on them. The bones were recovered from burial mounds dating from roughly 1,500 to 2,000 years B.P. Johnston is addressing whether the individuals represented by the modified bone were related to the rest of the burial population; whether they represent a single sex or fall within a certain age range; and how they are distributed spacially within mounds and within regions. Stephen Nawrocki (1997) writes that cut and polished mandibles have been found at nearly 60 sites in eastern North America, with some discovered in large caches. Hopewell sites have also yielded rattles, a whistle carved from a radius, perforated cranial vault fragments, copper-covered femora, painted and clay-masked non-trophy skulls, and carved bones including cranial vault fragments, femora, ulnae, and radii. Trophy skulls, some of which were painted with red ocher, exhibit defleshing cutmarks, drilled perforations, grinding, and polishing from repeated handling. A cache of 16 was found in Ohio at Turner Mound 3, the largest group located in a single feature in a Hopewell site. The skulls may be the bones of relatives preserved through devotion or custom, the remains of slain enemies retained through pride or revenge, the remains of individuals with desirable qualities or spiritual power the owner hoped to possess, or bones used for magical purposes (Nawrocki 1997).

The preservation and treatment of trophy skulls continued to be practiced in Late Woodland Hopewell culture, and worked animal bone artifacts date from Archaic to Mississippian times, but other modified human remains are not found after the Middle Woodland period and are most common to Midwestern sites. That a majority of the specimens are from male skeletons may indicate the raw material was harvested during times of warfare (Johnston et al. 1997).

Johnston, Nawrocki, and two other researchers pooled their knowledge about Hopewellian culturally-modified human remains to analyze 26 specimens from four Ohio sites including the Hopewell Mound Group, Harness, Seip Mound 1, and Raymond Ater Mound. Their examination revealed that the artifacts were non-utilitarian and made most often from the maxilla, mandible, or other part of the skull, but occasionally from post-cranial elements. None of the Ohio jaws had been split, but all of those from Indiana and Illinois Middle Woodland sites had. The Indiana and Illinois specimens were also found to be more heavily worked than those from Ohio. The 22 or more modified hemi-mandibles found in a cache at the Mount Vernon Mound in Indiana, a collection that has since been reburied, show signs of having been scraped and abraded, possibly while cleaning the bone surfaces. They were then heavily ground along the inferior border. The rami were also ground and the symphyses were broken and smoothed, a process that obliterated sexually dimorphic features. In such cases, the researchers assigned sex on the basis of dental metrics and found that all of the Hopewell material they had examined had come from the skeletons of young to middle adult males and females, with no subadults represented (Johnston et al. 1997).

Painted Skulls in Hallstatt, Austria

The *totenkapelle* (death chapel) of St. Michael's cathedral in Hallstatt, Austria, contains the painted skulls and stacked bones of about 1,200 individuals exhumed from the village cemetery since the eighteenth century. The chapel has become a tourist attraction and an admission fee is charged. While the painting of skulls is commonly associated with Hallstatt, the custom is not unique to that village and was traditional in certain areas of the Alps. Painted skulls can be found in many German-speaking areas and the custom is believed to have begun with and been maintained by Bavarians. The painting typically includes the name of the deceased and the years of birth and death. Sometimes the social status is given and flowers and wreaths are added to accompany the text. The cleaning, bleaching, and painting of the skulls was usually carried out by the gravedigger, the local teacher, a family member, or a traveling artist. The painting of names was intended to identify the dead and thereby assist descendants in praying to the right soul for spiritual guidance, although there was no guarantee that the skulls had not been mixed up when removed from the graves. Symbolism was also used in the decorations, with crosses drawn for luck, snakes representing the transitory nature of life, and green wreaths indicating the remains of unmarried men and women. Other elements were merely decorative and styles varied with the region. In Bavaria, a few of the skulls were decorated with red roses and green leaves, a practice more common in Austria, where gold and silver colors were also used. In the Braunau area of Austria, some skulls were completely covered with blue, green, and rose paint — and later with silver or gold leaf. In German-speaking parts of Switzerland, painted ribbons and coats of arms were added. In at least one case, the text written on a skull documents

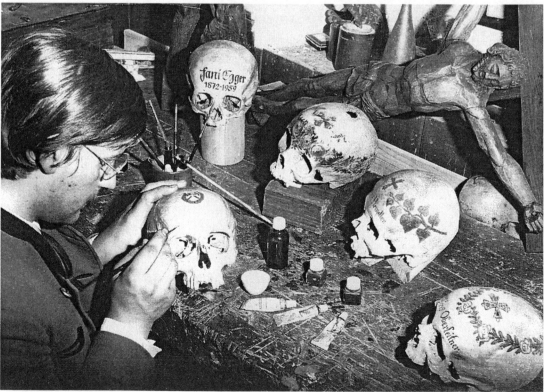

Top and bottom: **Painted skulls at Hallstatt, Austria. Photos courtesy of the Museum of Sepulchral Culture, Kassel, Germany.**

Skulls being decorated by Karl Trausner in Hallstatt. Reprinted with permission of Thames & Hudson from *The Human Skull: A Cultural History,* by Folke Henschen (New York: Frederick A. Praeger, 1965).

murder: "From the hands of holdup men/ died Ignatz Winkler/ farmer at the Winkler estate/ at Holz, the 21st of February 1849" (Werner and Werner 1985).

Aside from Hallstatt, many of the decorated skulls and the chapels that housed them have disappeared over time and are documented only in the historical literature. In 1805, a small chamber next to the Chapel of St. Anna in Viechtach was said to contain an abundance of painted and decorated skulls. Despite an "unhealthy odor," the chamber was visited regularly by the locals. Another bone house in Eggelsberg in upper Austria contained more than 100 skulls painted with golden wreaths. The eye sockets were painted dark green with a golden rim and each of the skulls was mounted on a wooden stick, rather than being piled up. Several collections of painted skulls were visited by author Marie Andree-Eysn. She

toured the Hallstatt cathedral in 1897 and counted 4,000 skulls, of which about 200 were painted (most with a wreath of red roses around the name). During the course of her research, Andree-Eysn also observed 8,000 skulls in a church in Keyserberg, between 6,000 and 8,000 in the crypt of a church in Zabern, and a vast amount of skeletal material (estimated at 104 cubic meters) in a bone house in Schorbach (Werner and Werner 1985).

The documentation that has been painted on the foreheads of the skulls in Hallstatt has been helpful not only to descendants of the dead, but to researchers. In 1993, T. Sjøvold of the University of Stockholm published a study based on the assemblage. Sjøvold located church records to confirm the identities and dates of 500 of the individuals, most of whom died between 1780 and 1890, and found that at about

1850, the individuals represented by the skull sample amounted to about 20 percent of the living population. Analysis of the skulls, supported by the Swedish Natural Science Research Council, is intended to test certain biological assumptions including heredity of cranial measurements and nonmetric traits, secular trends in skull size and shape, and the dependence of cranial metrics and nonmetrics on the age of death. Sjøvold is also determining the frequencies of population-specific nonmetric traits. The results of his research take into effect possible incorrect identifications.

Many words exist in German to describe the areas in which bones were stored, among them *beinhäus* (bone house), *Beingruft* (bone grave), *beinkammer* (bone chamber), *beinkeller* (bone cellar), *beinraum* (bone room), *schenkelhaus* (thigh house), and *seelkammer* (soul chamber). According to seventeenth-century church regulations, bone houses were to be closed with a gate and locked to prevent unauthorized access (Werner and Werner 1985). Bone storage buildings proliferated in the Alps region. They were typically circular in shape and had a cellar in which the bones were stockpiled and a ground floor chapel for conducting funeral masses. In the Kärnten and Steiermark areas of Austria, it was the custom to pile the bones around a central pillar, leaving only a narrow passageway between them and the walls. The long bones in Hallstatt are stored on wooden racks in a fifteenth-century vault, a democratic arrangement that has given rise to the local saying "*So ist's recht, da liegt der Meister bei seinem Knecht,*" which translates as "That's all right, here lies the master next to his slave" (Lorz 1986). In some areas, each skull is stored in a wooden box, often black and sometimes including detailed information that may be used to confirm fading or missing writing on the skull itself. This is typical of Berchtesgaden and Salzburg in Austria (Werner and Werner 1985).

It is thought that the custom of painting exhumed skulls arose from the rapid reuse of graves, and secondary burial is documented from the twelfth century, but it is questioned whether the cities grew so quickly in the fourteenth and fifteenth centuries as to fill up cemeteries designed to hold great numbers of plague victims (Werner and Werner 1985). In the Hallstatt area, the exhumations are attributed to the steep and stony terrain, which limits the number of graves and necessitates their reuse. Folke Henschen (1965) writes (possibly mistakenly) that the exhumations in Hallstatt were done en masse on a regular basis. Paul Barber (1988) theorizes that the custom of disinterring the dead, which was practiced by the Celts, did not originate with a need to save space but with a desire to ensure that the body had finished decomposing and that the soul had therefore escaped to the beyond.

The tradition of skull painting began to wane by the mid-eighteenth century. By that time, secondary burial was strongly discouraged and many of the bone houses were used for other purposes, for instance the one associated with the Church of St. Stephanus in Munich, which has been used as a regular mortuary since 1791. In some areas, though, painting continued well into the twentieth century. A bone chamber in Margarethenburg contains 55 skulls, the most recent of which is dated 1916, but painting is believed to have continued until 1930 (Werner and Werner 1985). Paul Barber (1988) documents secondary burial in the area into the 1960s. Kurt Lorz (1986) indicates that as recently as 1986, the tradition was being carried on by Valentin Idam, a woodcutter and gravedigger who lived in a house at the Hallstatt cemetery, which suggests that it may continue to this day.

Trophy Skulls

The direct acquisition of trophy skulls requires participating in the ancient activity of headhunting. The gruesome activity of taking heads, scalps, and other body parts during warfare can nearly be considered a cultural universal, according to Phillip L. Walker (In press), and — although suppressed — has continued to the present day. Historically, headhunting has been associated mainly with Melanesians and other Pacific Islanders. It is sometimes connected to the practice of cannibalism, but has been carried out for a number of reasons. In her memoir *My Life with the Headhunters*, Wyn Sargent (1976) explains that the Dyaks of Central Borneo believed that burying an enemy's head near the body of a deceased parent provided a servant in the afterlife and consequently, "Sometimes the heads numbered in the hundreds." Indirect acquisition of such skulls is not such a bloodthirsty task, but has in the past been challenged by demand for such specimens. "Heads collected by the New Zealand Maori tribes were prized by early nineteenth-century European collectors," write Sledzik and Ousley (1991). The Smithsonian Institution curates two Indonesian trophy skulls.

Trophy skulls acquired during modern warfare may be collected directly or indirectly. Sledzik and Ousley (1991) define a trophy as a memento of achievement or victory, including the opportunistic or passive collection of human remains and the deliberate perimortem collection of skeletal material. In other words, a head removed at the time of death or a skeletonized skull recovered later. At the National Museum of Health and Medicine, Sledzik curates a series of trophy specimens consisting of five complete human crania, one partial skull, five metacarpals, and a tooth. The authenticity of the specimens as trophies is fully documented. The skulls were confiscated under U.S. Army Regulation 688-4 (War Trophies) when U.S. servicemen attempted to bring them home from Vietnam in the early 1970s. Nearly all of the specimens were modified or decorated postmortem — usu-

ally with paint, marker, or crayon — and are described below:

• Skulls No. 1987.3017.02 and 1987.3017.03: These specimens surfaced at the Da Nang field office in 1971 when two American servicemen asked customs inspectors about the procedures for shipping a skull to the U.S. The crania were confiscated and transported to the AFIP for identification. The first skull is estimated to be a Mongoloid male between the ages of 15 and 20. The graffiti on the first skull include names, peace signs, and drawings (a marijuana pipe, flowers, a bearded man). "Chu Lai Trip Skull" is written above the orbits. Other markings read, "Today's pigs are tomorrow's bacon," "My prayer deck," and "This is what happens to you if you drop too much, just a matter of time!!" The second skull, also male and aged between 22 and 25 years, bears the inscription "Little Al" across the forehead. Black paint has been applied to create eyebrows and a mustache. Both orbits are filled with red candle wax and carbon discoloration is visible on the posterior region of the palate.

• Skull No. 1987.3017.05: This Mongoloid cranium, the sex of which has not been conclusively determined, was confiscated from a U.S. serviceman in 1972 when he was apprehended for possession of heroin and marijuana. The graffiti read, "Jimi Denver Colorado," "El Reuben Chicano," "Castro," "Things Go Better with Castro Coke," and "Stay High Stay Alive." "Jimi Vivar, 70 71, que loco!" is written in the orbits.

• Skull No. 1987.3017.09: This partial specimen was seized by customs agents checking U.S.-bound shipments at the Da Nang field office. An American soldier had packaged the skull and attempted to mail it to his wife. The skull is that of a 30- to 40-year-old Mongoloid male. Its

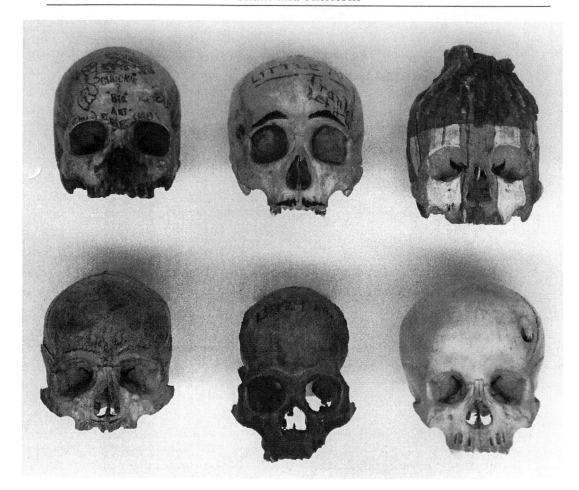

Trophy skulls confiscated from U.S. servicemen who had served in Vietnam. Photo courtesy of the National Museum of Health and Medicine, Armed Forces Institute of Pathology.

dark color and the presence of soil on the internal surface of the frontal bone may indicate burial. The palate and existing teeth have been painted black, but the skull bears no graffiti. Candle wax drippings and carbon deposits are present in the nasal areas.

• Skull No. 1987.3017.23: This skull was obtained from a U.S. serviceman at Pleiku during the summer of 1972. The specimen is that of a 25- to 35-year-old male and the postmortem cultural modification is substantial, including application of blue paint; decoration with Day-Glo reddish pink, yellow, and orange

paint; melting of candle wax over nearly the entire calvarium; drilling of a hole (possibly to suspend the skull); and the removal of the nasal conchae, the ethmoid, and parts of the orbits.

Most of the trophy skulls in the NMHM collection exhibit a patina from frequent handling, loss of fragile parts, and missing anterior teeth. Their "clean" appearance suggests above-ground decomposition (Sledzik and Ousley 1991).

The collecting of war trophies by American soldiers was not all that unusual. When the remains of Japanese soldiers from the Mariana Islands were repatriated in

1984, as many as 60 percent of them were missing the skull. Military forensic pathologists at the Armed Forces Institute of Pathology see one or two cases each year of trophy remains from the Pacific theatre of World War II and Vietnam (Sledzik and Ousley 1991). Skulls from World War II were actually easier to bring home, since the bags of returning U.S. military personnel were not searched like they were after Vietnam. Sometimes souvenir skulls turn up when the houses of former G.I.s are legally searched for other reasons and other times are found at the local dump, having been disposed of during a move. First suspected to be the remains of murder victims, the skulls are turned over to a forensic laboratory for identification. Even when murder is ruled out, possession of the skulls usually violates various state laws.

Forensic anthropologist William Bass identified a trophy skull while investigating a case in eastern Tennessee in 1973. The police were looking for the skull of a decayed body that had been found in a river. A newspaper story resulted in two skulls being turned over to authorities. One of them was a cranial vault that was ruled out because it was of a younger age. The skull had been found in a paint can inside a junked car by the car dealer who purchased it. Indications that it was a trophy skull included the adherence of house dust, the presence of paint specks, and the enlargement of the foramen magnum. It was revealed that the man who owned the property on which the car had been parked was in the Pacific theater during World War II. Bass (1983) explains, "While securing one of the islands in the Pacific, he had come across a Japanese fighter plane that had crashed. In the cockpit was the skeleton of the pilot. He reached in, picked up the skull, and brought it back to Morgan County." The veteran admitted to breaking away much of the occipital bone so that he could insert a light bulb and use the skull as a Halloween decoration.

Skulls brought home to the United States as war trophies continue to turn up and more are expected to surface as veterans of World War II die and their families discover and dispose of the souvenirs (Bass 1983, McCarthy 1994). A cranium found on the shores of Lake Springfield in Springfield, Illinois, turned out to be a trophy skull. The skull, missing its teeth and lower jaw, was found in February 2000, having been exposed by the lowest water levels the lake has seen since 1977. The skull was examined by Sangamon County Coroner Susan Boone, who noted it to be very worn and calcified. After news of the discovery broke, an 18-year-old came forward and identified it as a World War II souvenir that had been in his family for generations. When he became superstitious about it, he threw it in the lake not far from where it was found. His identification of the skull was confirmed by a splotch of gold paint and other details that he described. The police department and the coroner's office planned to work together to properly dispose of the remains.

Even more disturbing than skeletal souvenirs from war are those from murder. And when the collector is a serial killer, the souvenirs mount. When police searched the Milwaukee apartment of Jeffrey Dahmer (d. 1994) they found seven skulls: two on the top shelf of a closet, two more in a computer box, and three others in the top drawer of a filing cabinet that also contained an assortment of bones in the bottom drawer. The remains had been stockpiled from the individuals Dahmer had strangled in 1990 and 1991, after which he dissolved their flesh by immersion in acid and cleaned the skulls by boiling them in a kettle on the stove. The keeping of trophies by murderers reminds them of the conquest and assists them in reliving the crimes. Dahmer explained that the skulls kept him company in his solitude. He painted some of them, including that of Ernest Miller, a 23-year-old he killed in 1990. The identities of the skulls were confirmed through dental records and the crimes were of course devastating to surviving family members. "It's hard for us," Miller's uncle is quoted as saying, "When we last saw Ernest, he was full of life, a very caring and loving person. And when we went to the coroner's office, there was nothing but a skeleton" (Dvorchak and Holewa 1991).

Holy Relics

The relics of saints and martyrs had great symbolic value from the beginnings of Christianity. Followers of Christ so firm in their beliefs that they were willing to die for them inspired others to trust their own faith and join the religion. Masses were said over the tombs of Christian martyrs. As Christianity grew, so did the cult of relics, in which the bodily fragments of deceased saints were not only revered, but believed to have many of the qualities and powers that the saints had while alive. Among the first whose bones were venerated were St. Ignatius of Antioch (d. 107 A.D.) and St. Polycarp (d. 167 A.D.). Phillip L. Walker (In press) writes that the belief among Christians that proximity to the bones and other body parts of saints could bring miracles was common as early as the fourth century. In many ways, relics were believed to control their own fate by influencing living humans to locate them when lost, move them from one church to another, and punish those who have humiliated them. Conversely, the relics were punished if they failed to protect the community (Geary 1978).

Those who were buried in close proximity to holy relics were believed to be raised up with the saints on the Day of Judgment. Some relics even performed miracles on themselves, exuding an oil or liquid — most often colorless and odorless — variously called manna, unction, myrrh, medicinal liquor, balm, or distilled bone oil.

The oil was given off by the bones of St. Nicholas (d. 324) for more than 1,600 years with only four interruptions. The substance was found by scientists at the Institute of Hygiene of the University of Bari in Italy to be a biologically pure combination of hydrogen and oxygen. Sea water, rainwater, filtered water, and spring water were ruled out as sources, so its formation remained a mystery. When the reliquary was examined in the presence of a pontifical commission in 1953, the bones were found to be immersed in a clear liquid two centimeters deep, despite the fact that the container was water-tight and secure. The relics of St. Walburga (d. 779) also exude manna, but only between October 12th (the day the remains were transferred to their present location) and February 25th (the anniversary of the saint's death) of each year. The manna given off by the relics of St. Elizabeth of Hungary (d. 1231) is imbued with a delicate perfume. Manna is typically collected in ampules which then become relics themselves (Cruz 1997).

With so much power in a single bone, no wonder St. Gregory of Nyssa remarked in the fourth century that the dust from the martyred body of St. Theodore had been carried away as if it were gold (Bentley 1985). To the symbolic value of relics was added a monetary value and with commerce came greed and fraud. Soon relics were being divided up, bought and sold, fought over, lost and found, and stolen (Bentley 1985). St. Augustine complained about the relic trade in the early fifth century after the Catholic church had attempted unsuccessfully in the fourth to prevent abuses by forbidding transference of bodies and interference with the bodies of martyrs (Stevenson 1978). But Geary (1978) points out that it was in the pope's best interest, at least politically, to allow the trade in relics (especially those removed from the catacombs) to reinforce the importance of Rome as the center of Christianity.

Holy Relics. Reprinted from *Relics: The Forgotten Sacramental* with permission of Saints Alive! and ICHRusa.

Translation of the head of St. Simon Stock. Reprinted from *Relics: The Forgotten Sacramental* with permission of Saints Alive! and ICHRusa.

Middlemen quickly took up the challenge of fulfilling the desire for relics. The most infamous of these was a Roman deacon of the early ninth century named Deusdona. With his brothers Lunisius and Theodorus, he made a lucrative living supplying relics from the catacombs of Rome, through which he guided not only tourists, but clients. Those who could not come to Rome were paid a sales call by Deusdona, who carried with him sample specimens and a list of what was available (Stevenson 1978), or visited with him when he made the rounds of monastic fairs (Geary 1978). Customer taste varied over time and by region. The relics of Roman and Italian martyrs were the fashion in the ninth century. "The Roman martyrs were immensely popular and regardless of which other saints and martyrs reposed in one's own crypt, abbots considered the acquiring of some famous body from Rome a necessity," writes Geary (1978). Anglo-Saxon kings were interested in continental saints from Brittany and Normandy. By the eleventh and twelfth centuries, the French were in the market for relics of Frankish or Gallic saints (Geary 1978). Eventually, the demand outgrew the supply — since Moslem Spain was the only area where martyrs were still being produced — and the relics sold by Deusdona and others were no longer genuine.

The clientele of the relic dealers consisted mainly of important abbots, bishops, and kings. The trade flourished between the ninth and eleventh centuries, when it was the practice of aristocrats to build personal relic collections. Eager collectors of relics with the means to pay for them didn't ask too many questions about how they were obtained, so the merchants catered to them (Geary 1978). In fact, when one of Deusdona's competitors, a Frankish cleric named Felix, stole the remains of a saint from a monastery in Ravenna, he was provided with a horse on which to escape by the archbishop who purchased the relics (Geary

1978). As they ran low on merchandise, the relic dealers often sold the body of a saint several times over — and not only by dividing it up. "The multiplicity of bodies or identical relics of saints was a constant phenomenon that only occasionally caused serious disputes or disagreements" (Geary 1978).

The treatment of human remains as objects of religious veneration gradually resulted in the accumulation of substantial skeletal collections (Walker In press). Churches and other religious institutions sought to enhance their power and prestige by acquiring a large collection of holy relics. Relics drew visitors, who made pilgrimages to pay them homage, and inspired generosity among those hoping to obtain the saint's favor. In the ninth century, the monastery at Fulda in Germany purchased relics of saints Alexander, Emerentineus, Fabian, Felicissimus, Felicity, Sebastian, and Urban from Deusdona and relics of saints Agapitus, Calistus, Cecilia, Columbana, Cornelius, Degna, Emerta, Eugenia, Georgius, Mans, and Vincent from his rival Felix (Geary 1978). Hundreds of saints are represented in the more than 1,000 reliquaries in the Encarnación Monastery in Madrid, described by Lawson and Rufus (1999): "Skulls, bones, powdered blood and bits of desiccated flesh comprise a holy motel, all the relics fastidiously labeled with the saints' names. The reliquaries are shiny boxes shaped like churches, houses, hearts, hands, heads, pill-boxes, columns and crosses. Peek through crystal windows to see the remains, though the boxes' cumulative golden sheen will make you squint."

Rivaling many church altars were the private collections of a few individuals of both means and determination. In the tenth century, England's King Athelstan (d. 940) capitalized on numerous marriage alliances and diplomatic negotiations to garner a vast array of relics and augmented those received as gifts with others purchased from France

(Geary 1978). In the sixteenth century, his acquisitiveness was matched by two men. Philip II (d. 1598) of Spain was a zealous Catholic determined to collect the remains of as many saints and martyrs as he could. He commissioned an envoy who procured 11 complete skeletons, thousands of skulls and long bones, and numerous other skeletal elements that he housed in the Escorial, his residence outside Madrid (Walker In press). But even Philip could not match the success of Martin Luther's patron Elector Frederick III (d. 1525) of Saxony, who amassed 19,013 holy relics by 1520. The collection, kept at the castle of "Frederick the Wise" (not "Frederick the Great," as has sometimes been reported) in Wittenberg, Germany, was cataloged in 1509 by Lucas Cranach (d. 1553) when it comprised only 5,000 items (Bentley 1985).

The excitement of those eager to acquire and venerate relics was matched by the passion of those who attacked the cult (Bentley 1985). During the persecution of Diocletian (d. 313), many martyrs were buried anonymously and in collective graves, leading to later estimates that the number of saints represented by extant relics was only a fraction of the total (Hertling and Kirschbaum 1956). Ironically, the more Christians were persecuted, the more relics were available as symbols of the faith (Bentley 1985). Many existing relics were lost during the Norman invasion of the eleventh century, the Protestant Reformation of the sixteenth century, and the French Revolution of the late eighteenth century. The relics of St. Martin of Tours, for instance, were moved from place to place to safeguard them from the Normans, then dispersed by the Protestants, and finally lost during the French Revolution. Certain ironies did result. When French troops ransacked Rome in 1799, they stole the bejeweled reliquaries, but left the skulls behind as valueless. During the sacking of other cities, soldiers pocketed relics to sell back to the Catholics

later. And when the Protestants mixed and buried the bones of the patron saint of Oxford, St. Frideswide, with those of a nun who had renounced her vows, their attempt to demoralize resulted in the saint's relics being preserved to this day (Bentley 1985).

Not only did churches have to safeguard their relics against persecution, they had to guard them against theft. Nearly 100 accounts exist of relic thefts dating from the reign of Charles the Great to the age of the crusades (Geary 1978). Relics were burgled by individuals hoping to make a profit from them, but they were also stolen by other churches or monasteries. The reasons for such thefts are listed by Geary (1978): to establish new religious foundations, to give focus to existing devotion to a saint in a particular location, to provide protection during periods of political turmoil, to outdo rival churches, to channel popular devotion, and to compensate for loss of revenue. Acquisition of a "new patron" reinforced a church's hold on lay devotion and the charity necessary to fund church construction and other needs. The practice was so common during the Middle Ages that the Latin term *furta sacra* arose to describe it. And it was not limited to England and western Europe, as Geary (1978) points out: "Italian envy of the East's great store of saints resulted in a number of thefts culminating in the sack of Constantinople in 1204 when the Venetians carried off the city's choicest relics." Ironically, a story of theft attached to a relic actually increased its value. Theft has also been excused when it resulted in the preservation of a relic that would otherwise have been lost.

The installation of relics in Roman Catholic churches had been reinforced early on by church canons instructing that each newly built church include the relic of a saint or martyr in the altar. This notion paid homage to the building of the first churches over the tombs of saints. By the ninth century, church architecture featured impressive crypts in which to bury the dead of the parish, but also to showcase the relics. Churches with the relics of the Apostles were considered superior and in this regard, Italy dominated with Apostolic relics in Rome, Milan, and especially Ravenna (Geary 1978). During the twelfth century, the relics were moved upstairs to the altars. To stock the crypts and altars, the Roman catacombs and other repositories were mined. The body of St. Sebastian was removed and placed in a chapel in St. Peter's cathedral by Pope Gregory IV. Victor of Rouen brought the relics of 23 martyrs from Rome to France (Geary 1978). Pope Paul I, whose reign followed the relaxation of Roman laws forbidding burial within the city, moved more than 100 relics inside Rome's walls (Bentley 1985). He was outdone by Boniface IV, who moved a reported 28 wagon-loads of relics to the Pantheon, and Paschal I, who had the remains of 2,300 martyrs transferred to the church of S. Prassede (Stevenson 1978).

Some churches are known especially for their collections of holy remains. The number of virgins martyred with St. Ursula is believed to be exaggerated, but their relics fill an entire room in a church in Cologne, Germany. "Here is a riot of relics," writes James Bentley (1985). "On all four sides busts bearing bones are ranged on shelves, all looking happy, even prim in death. Many have the tops of their heads sliced through, so that you can lift off the corona and look down on the skull. In between the rows of shelves rise glass cupboards containing more saintly skulls, wrapped in red embroidered cloths.... And above the shelves, on all four walls, thousands and thousands more bones are arranged in brilliantly inventive patterns, protected by wire-netting. This, however, is no macabre art; this is a holy cult. And on the altar itself, in a glass container, is the little skull of Queen Ursula." According to her legend, St. Ursula traveled from England to Rome in either the third or fifth

century with 11,000 virgins, all of whom were murdered by pagans during a stop in Cologne. The women were canonized and assigned a single collective feast day. Sculptures of their heads and torsos containing their bones line the walls of the *Goldene Kammer* (Golden Chamber), a chapel dating to the seventeenth century that is attached to the Basilica of St. Ursula. The loose bones thickly texture the upper walls — "A veritable tsunami of ribs, shoulder blades and femurs is arranged in zigzags and swirls and even in the shapes of Latin words" (Lawson and Rufus 1999) — and the torso-shaped reliquaries alternate with gilded skulls. Through rosette-shaped windows over their hearts, the bones inside can be seen. On the altar reside four reliquaries containing arm bones. Whether these are truly the remains of Ursula and her followers or bones recovered from a graveyard to illustrate the legend and therefore lure pilgrims to Cologne, the bones are both visited and venerated.

Holy relics (or to be fair, the saints represented by them) have as many admirers today as they did in the Middle Ages. Sometimes instead of having to make a pilgrimage, admirers have the relics brought to them. The bones of St. Thérèse of Lisieux toured the United States from October 5, 1999, until January 28, 2000. including a brief stop at Georgetown University. The reliquary was brought to St. Peter's Basilica in Rome on October 19, 1997, at which time Pope John Paul II proclaimed the saint a Doctor of the Church. The relics afterwards traveled to France, Belgium, Luxembourg, Germany, Italy, Switzerland, Austria, Slovenia, Brazil, Holland, Russia, Kazakhstan, and Argentina. The tour was sponsored by the Carmelites with permission of the National Conference of Catholic Bishops and the itinerary was posted on the Internet (www.thereserelicsusa.org/). Many saints, however, must still be visited in more than one location because of traditions that continue to exist today: "An enterprising member of a local holy order possessed by a sense of order would induce the St. Paul monastery to trade its leg of St. Gregory Theologos with Koutloumousio to be combined there with the saint's left hand so that gradually, after further such exchanges, the Athos monks might reassemble nearly complete skeletons of departed holy men for display and veneration. As things are now, if you want St. Gregory in all his glory you have to make the rounds of various monasteries and assemble him piecemeal in your mind, a definite challenge to people who are scatter-brained" (Weil 1992).

Exceptions to the general rule, some saintly skeletons have remained intact. The Sisters of St. Joseph of Carondelet in south St. Louis, Missouri, house the complete remains of several early saints in their motherhouse. The collection of relics constitutes one of the rarest in the U.S. Although St. Anthony's Chapel in Pittsburgh claims to have the largest collection in this country with 4,000 relics, and the Maria Stein Chapel outside Cincinnati boasts approximately 600, the relics in St. Louis consist of entire bodies rather than just fragments. The skeletons of St. Aurelia, St. Discolius and St. Nerusia Euticia are wrapped in gauze and dressed in brocade tunics, with wax applied to their faces. The relics of St. Berenice, St. Berisimus, St. Vincent, and St. Aurelius are enshrined within or near the altar. In addition, the motherhouse has single bones from 70 other saints, which are displayed in five glass niches along the front of the altar. But it is the relics in their entirety that are the focal point. "It's the first thing that people go to when they enter the chapel," says archivist Sister Charlene Sullivan (Little 1998).

Accompanying their continued display and veneration, the trade in relics continues. Requests for relics of saints and martyrs are now fulfilled by the Vatican, although church officials tend to deemphasize the importance of relics today. The Vicariate in Rome supplies relics for public veneration to priests and to churches, although new Catholic churches have not been required to have a saint's relic in their altars since the 1960s. Requests from individuals may need to be supported by a letter from a bishop, since relics are no longer distributed by the Vatican for private veneration. It is sometimes possible to obtain them for private veneration directly from religious orders, though, for instance the relics of St. Elizabeth Ann Seton distributed by the Mother Seton Shrine in Baltimore. Relics distributed by the Vatican and other sanctioned sources are not sold, but donations to the church are encouraged. The recipient is usually asked to reimburse for the cost of the container and other expenses, an amount that typically totals 15 dollars. The Vatican also authenticates relics, relying not only on traditional methods (documentation of miracles associated with them), but on modern scientific methods. In 1215, the church officially prohibited the public veneration of new relics until their authenticity had been vouched for by the Pope (Serafin 1998). Today the church only approves the veneration of saints and those blessed by its authority, although it extends this approval to servants of God and venerables for whom an official process of beatification is underway. But authenticity is not all-important, since as Joan Carroll Cruz (1984) advises, "It should be noted that if a relic is false, the saint would still be honored since we pray not to a bit of bone, but to the saint to whom it is supposed to belong."

One of the most prodigious contemporary guardians of holy relics is Chevalier Thomas J. Serafin, V.V., who has accumulated more than 1,200 in his collection. Through a group he founded called the International Crusade for Holy Relics (ICHRusa) and his "Saints Alive!" website, Serafin is actively reeducating Roman

Catholics about the importance of venerating and preserving relics. The ICHRusa does not condone the selling of relics and strongly urges all Catholics to comply with the Code of Canon Law regarding their veneration (Serafin 1998). The website warns of a new twist on an old problem — not the sale of fraudulent relics, but the illicit sale of authentic relics at enormous profit and without regard for their sacred character. Serafin points out that even if a dealer touts the authenticity of a relic by offering the associated documentation, he or she is breaking the contract written on that document — albeit in Latin — that expressly forbids the relic's sale. These sales take place in antique shops, at flea markets, at auctions, and on the Internet. In addition, the age-old problems of fakery and thievery persist and the salesmen are just as greedy and persuasive as they have been in the past. On his website, Serafin warns, "Dealers try to maximise their profit by saying that a relic is rare or unique or that this may be your only chance to obtain this highly sought after relic, etc. This is just rubbish. Relics were, and are, distributed in tens of thousands from religious orders and from the relic office in Rome. Remember that the items being sold were obtained from these sources originally without any difficulty, and probably for about a twentieth of the price that you are being asked to pay. Don't be taken in!" It is permissible to purchase relics, explains Serafin, in order to save them from desecration, keeping in mind two considerations: that the money may be better spent devoted to other charitable causes and that rescuing relics may encourage their market.

ARRANGED BONES

The ceiling of this chapel of death, built in 1776, is thickly blanketed with hundreds of human skulls, each positioned above two crossed leg bones. Though the bones don't really move, they look like a swarm of hideous monsters descending upon you as you enter the room. The 3,000 additional skulls and dismembered skeletons lining all the walls don't offer much reassurance. Not enough bones for you? Then ask the attendant to open the door to the crypt, where 21,000 more skulls await.
— Kristan Lawson and Anneli Rufus describing the Kaplica Czaszek (Chapel of Skulls) in Czermna, Poland [1999]

A small number of examples survive of human remains being organized into decorative designs on the walls and ceilings of churches and chapels, although this was not an uncommon practice in past times. At least as early as the fifteenth century and into the eighteenth century, the French began organizing what Philippe Ariès (1982) calls "this enormous mass of bones that was perpetually being heaved up by the earth." Bones were displayed artistically over the galleries of the charnels, on the porches of the churches, or in small chapels made for the purpose. In the nineteenth century, when such transfer of bones was outlawed, it was tolerated in western Brittany and persisted there until World War I. Examples may still be seen in the ossuaries (called *garnals*) of the area. These lesser-known instances are, however, overshadowed by a few especially renowned bone churches in Europe.

One famously decorated church is that of São Francisco in Evora, Portugal. A chapel's walls have been formed by long bones, its six pillars have been decorated with ribs and arm bones, and its ceiling lined with skulls (Weil 1992). This *Capela dos Ossos* (Chapel of Bones) contains the skeletal remains of 5,000 Franciscan monks and a sign among them reminds visitors, "We bones who are here await your bones." Travelers Kristan Lawson and Anneli Rufus (1999) describe the sight: "Created 300 years ago, the chapel is neatly paneled with ribs, ulnas, femurs and all your favorites. Exuding a good solid sense of mortality, meticulous patterns of bones completely cover the walls and pillars." Also in Portugal, a chapel of bones behind the Church of Carmo in Faro contains the remains of monks removed from the churchyard when it reached capacity at the turn of the nineteenth century. "Completed in 1816, the chamber's walls and steeply domed ceiling are thoroughly 'tiled' in skulls and thousands of yellowed bones, industriously arranged with geometric symmetry. Hollow eye sockets stare out at you from every angle so sepulchrally that the crucifix standing in a niche looks whimsical by comparison" (Lawson and Rufus 1999). The sometimes mummified and sometimes skeletonized remains of more than 8,000 monks line the walls of the catacombs in Palermo and the Capuchins continued to add more until the late 1800s.

Some arrangements of bones — in these cases temporary — are towers of skeletal remains raised out of respect. When a paupers' cemetery in Bangkok was threatened by construction of a freeway in 1997, the unidentified or unclaimed remains of 21,347 individuals were removed and carefully stacked in displays that were further embellished by the application of gold leaf to some of the skulls. That and the sprinkling of fragrant water on the bones is believed to curry religious favor. The five-day funeral ceremony culminated in one of the largest cremations ever performed. Other bone constructions that no longer exist were erected as warnings. The Turks of the Ottoman empire often constructed skull towers to terrorize their enemies. One well-known example, which stood from the sixteenth until the middle of the nineteenth century, was a pyramid at Houmt Souk (capital of the Tunisian island of Djerba), which was built with the crania of the victims massacred at the Spanish garrison of Philip II (d. 1598) (Weil 1992).

Many existing European bone churches did not result from an attempt to frighten the viewers, but from overcrowded cemeteries or the provision of alternate interment. A chamber in the Santa Maria dell'Orazione e Morte (St. Mary of the Oration and Death) in Rome was used to give a Christian burial to the bodies of the unknown dead. Established in 1551 for this purpose, the religious confraternity stood skeletons in niches, created skull and crossbone motifs on the walls, and designed a cross, two candelabra, and three chandeliers from human bones. Lining the length of the room are two glass cases holding an additional 140 skulls, many inscribed with the individual's name and date of death (Weil 1992). The Church of S. Maria Della Grazia in Comiso, Sicily, contains 107 skulls resting in horizontal niches. Built and consecrated by Capuchin friars in 1616, the church was supplemented by a "Chapel of the Dead" in the eighteenth century. The skulls of the friars are on the right wall and laypersons are on the left. The skulls (and the mummified remains in the chapel) have been examined by physical anthropologists and determined to be mostly male. The skulls were analyzed, described, and photographed in their original positions, and further studies have been planned. Similar chapels dating to as early as the thirteenth century are located in the Basilica of S. Domenico Maggiore in Naples, the Church of S. Bartolomeno in Navelli, the Church of S. Stefano in Ferentillo, the Church of the Dead in Urbania, and the Cathedral of Venzone (Fornaciari and Gamba 1993).

Church of Santa Maria della Concezione in Rome

The Capuchin church and adjoining friary on the Via Vittoria Veneto in Rome were first occupied in 1631. Some years later, papal architect Michael of Bergamo began arranging the 300 cartloads of monks' bones that the Capuchins arrived with, a task that outlasted him. The arrangement of the

A crypt in the Church of Santa Maria della Concezione in Rome.

bones began at the end of the seventeenth century and ended with the entrance of the Italian Army into Rome in 1870 (Zeiger 1999). The several galleries that the bones fill are referred to as the Capuchin catacombs or the Capuchin cemetery. In the words of Lisa Zeiger, Jason H. Byrd, and Phoebe R. Stubblefield (1999), "Capuchin choreography is no shuffling danse macabre...." The dominant motif is floral and the effect is characterized as blossoming growth rather than grim decay. Each of the chapels and galleries has its own unique human bone creations:

• The Crypt of the Skeletons: A skeletal grim reaper on the vaulted ceiling grasps a sickle in one hand and a scale in the other. The sickle is made from a scapula and three fibulae and the scale consists of an ulna and a fibula with baskets made of what are most likely innominate bones

linked by metatarsals. The reaper is encircled by four rings of bones — cervical vertebrae, calcanei, thoracic vertebrae, and lumbar vertebrae (Zeiger 1999). Toward the back of this gallery, which contains mostly the bones of children, is a clock created from vertebrae, foot bones, and finger bones (Emerson 1998).

• The Crypt of the Resurrection: Two arches on the side walls are formed by skulls and long bones and frame two robed, reclining skeletons (Emerson 1998). Bones have been applied like ceiling molding and consist of nine types in geometric arrangement. In the central section, two rings of ten sacra each, interspersed with vertebrae, form rosettes that terminate in ten lumbar-vertebrae points. The rosettes are centered in frames of thoracic and lumbar vertebrae. Quatrefoils of four sacra complete the center row

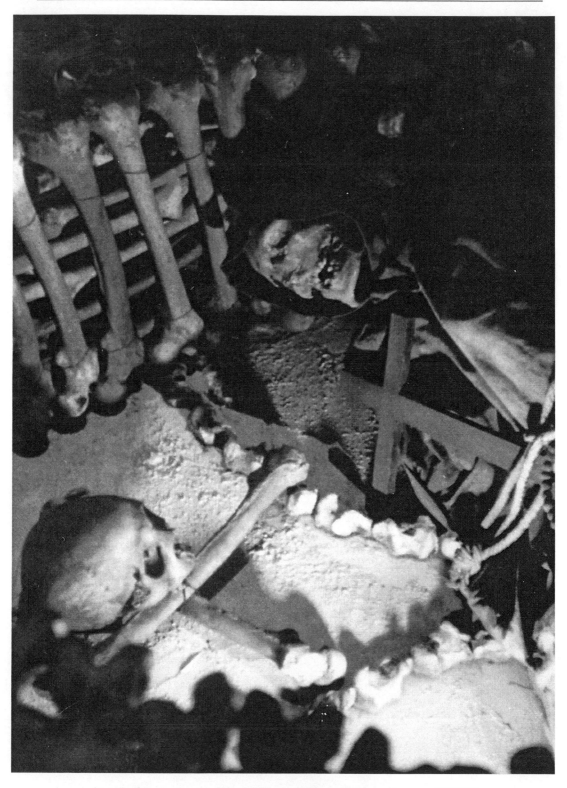

Detail of the crypt. Reprinted with permission of Kristan Lawson (© 1999).

of decoration. The outer bands of scrolling motifs are composed of flowers of cervical vertebrae with ribs for stems. At certain points paired metatarsal and metacarpal bones interrupt the repeat. The borders are composed of vertebrae with interior bands of fibula. The doorway arch is ornamented with crania on distal ends of femora covered by scapulae (Zeiger 1999) and a lamp hanging in the corridor is surrounded by four more flowers made of sacral bones (Emerson 1998).

- The Crypt of the Leg Bones and Thigh Bones: Two wide strips of vertebrae and a row of leg bones on the ceiling frame a ribbon of shoulder blades. Five-petaled roses anchor the corners, and a central oval of pelvic and sacral bones encloses jawbones studded with vertebrae, with a nosegay of shoulder blades on either side. Some of the bones — which in this crypt are believed to date to the 1860s — have been used to form the coat of arms of the Franciscan Order. Above the shield, the crown has a base of vertebrae with overlapping rings of tali above. Its cross is constructed of a vertical humerus and a horizontal radius and is surrounded by thoracic vertebrae. On each side of the crown, a horizontal border of more overlapping circles of tali is edged with calcanei below and clavicles above. Two crania sit on the altar and another cranium flanked by femora rests on the step below, forming a triangular arrangement (Zeiger 1999).

- The Crypt of the Pelvises: A large baldacchino made entirely of pelvises and fringed with dangling vertebrae towers over this central niche (Zeiger 1999). It also includes two reclining skeletons in arched niches with a background of foot bones and kneecaps. The rear wall is lined with pelvic bones. The central rosette is made up of four shoulder blades surrounded by vertebrae. Jawbones are prominent in the frieze and a winged skull watches from the hallway (Emerson 1998).

- The Crypt of the Skulls: Two skeletons rest in curved niches formed by long bones supporting a cornice of skulls. On the back wall, dozens of skulls face another skull, flanked by painted wings, on the opposite wall of the corridor (Emerson 1998).

The Capuchin catacombs have had a number of notable visitors over the centuries. The Marquis de Sade toured the galleries in 1775 and found the trip well worth the travel. Nathaniel Hawthorne (d. 1864) found it a bit more grotesque, but described it in his novel *The Marble Faun*:

> The arrangement of the unearthed skeletons is what makes the special interest of the cemetery. The arched and vaulted walls of the burial recesses are supported by massive pillars and pilasters made of thigh-bones and skulls; the whole material of the structure appears to be of a similar kind; and the knobs and embossed ornaments of this strange architecture are represented by the joints of the spine, and the more delicate tracery by the smaller bones of the human frame. The summits of the arches are adorned with entire skeletons, looking as if they were wrought most skilfully [sic] in bas-relief. There is no possibility of describing how ugly and grotesque is the effect, combined with a certain artistic merit, nor how much perverted ingenuity has been shown in this queer way, nor what a multitude of dead monks, through how many hundred years, must have contributed their bony framework to build up these great arches of mortality. On some of the skulls there are inscriptions, purporting that such a monk, who formerly made use of that particular headpiece, died on such a day and year; but vastly the greater number are piled up indistinguishably into the architectural design, like the many deaths that make up the one glory of a victory [Hawthorne 1889].

New York, St. Louis, Liverpool, Toronto, Sydney.   JAMES M. DAVIS.

Copyright 1897, by B. W. Kilburn.

13124. Mummies and Skulls in the Catacombs, Rome.

A wall of skulls depicted in an 1897 stereoscopic viewing card. The legend indicates the photograph was taken in the catacombs of Rome, but the image appears to be from Rome's Church of Santa Maria della Concezione.

For Hawthorne, the catacombs were an extensive memento mori. Mark Twain (d. 1910) found the galleries more artistic than unnerving, joking that the old masters had been at work. In his 1869 novel *The Innocents Abroad*, Twain wonders what is going through the mind of his guide:

> The reflection that he must someday be taken apart like an engine or a clock or like a house whose owner is gone, and worked up into arches and pyramids and hideous frescoes, did not distress this monk in the least. I thought he even looked as if he were thinking, with complacent vanity, that his own skull would look well on top of the heap and his own ribs add a charm to the frescoes which possibly they lacked at present.

The Capuchins are still closely involved with the skulls of their brothers, giving tours and dusting the galleries weekly.

Authors of the twentieth century have also weighed in with descriptions. In his book *Famous Caves and Catacombs*, William H. Adams (1972) calls the Capuchin catacombs "most impressive ... a kind of mosaic composed of fragments of bones." Robert

Wilkins (1991) goes further to suggest it may be the most awesome display of bones, though not to everyone's taste. He compares the arrangements to armorial displays in military museums and comments that although most of the individuals are anonymous, the composite effect of their remains is indeed memorable. Philippe Ariès notes that each bone is used according to its shape, with pelvic bones arranged in rosettes, skulls stacked in columns, long bones used to support the arches, and vertebrae threaded to form garlands or serve as candlesticks. Ariès (1982) writes that "the walls and ceilings are covered with a decorative ossuary in which bones replaced pebbles or shells.... Here the charnel is no longer merely a repository; it is a stage set in which the human bone lends itself to all the convulsions of baroque or rococo art. The skeleton is exhibited as a theatrical prop and itself becomes a spectacle. Of course, it does not have the vegetative life that seems to persist in the mummy; it has lost its individuality. It is a collective life that animates this décor through the grinning mouths of hundreds of heads, the gestures of thousands of limbs." Tom Weil (1992) provides his own poetic description of the crypts: "Tibiae, vertebrae and other skeleton components decorate the walls and ceiling in elaborate designs and fantasies, including wreaths formed by skulls, arabesques of arm and leg bones, arches, angular patterns, a hand and foot bone chandelier above a rib cage altar, while in bone-built alcoves nestle skeletal figures clothed in baggy brown monks robes."

Folke Henschen (1965) calls the semi-subterranean vaults "macabre" and "bizarrely decorated," but adds some additional background information, explaining that the bones of more than 4,000 monks have been preserved in the catacombs. The bodies were first buried in earth specially brought from Palestine and deposited on the floor of two of the chapels. After the remains had skeletonized, they were exhumed and disarticulated. A final description comes from Kristan Lawson and Anneli Rufus (1999), who visited the catacombs more recently: "The scrambled remains of several thousand Capuchin monks adorn this complex, with one room dedicated to skulls, another thoroughly done in pelvises. Covering walls and ceilings, the bones are arranged in floral patterns and other shapes, including an ominous hourglass and a mock angel made of a skull with scapulae for wings. Dressed in the trademark brown capuchin habit that gave cappuccino its name, several mummified monks recline leisurely amid their brothers' bones, while others stand around." The bones remain static as generations of travelers make their way to Rome to have a look.

Sedlec Ossuary near Kutná Hora, Czech Republic

I wondered how the raw materials had been arranged for Rint to work from: a pile of ribs, a pile of long bones? Or did the woodcarver paw through the jumble of skeletons until — aha! — he found just the decorative object he needed? How familiar had he been with human anatomy before he began? Did he recognize what all he was working with or didn't he spare it a thought, reducing the bones to sizes and shapes?
— Loren Rhoads [1999]

In a rather remote location is a famous and spectacular bone church. The *kostnice* or ossuary at Sedlec is situated near the town of Kutná Hora, about 44 miles (70 km) east of Prague in the Czech Republic. When silver mining in the area caused the population in Sedlec to boom, the church associated with the town's Cistercian monastery (founded in 1142) was renovated and expanded. After some soil from the Holy Land was spread on it by an abbot in 1278, the churchyard became a popular burying ground among locals and some people as far away as Poland, Belgium, and southern Germany (Merbs 1995). One hundred years later, and due in large part to the spread of the bubonic plague, more than 30,000 bodies had been buried in the cemetery. To these burials were added the casualties during the Hussite wars of the fifteenth century. In 1511, one of the monks was charged with removing the bones from the overcrowded cemetery and depositing them in the gothic-style All Saint's chapel that had been built in 1400. This monk, who was according to legend half-blind, arranged the bones into six huge, flat-topped pyramids nearly 20 feet wide and 20 feet tall. During the eighteenth century, the chapel was remodeled by a well-known Czech architect. In 1860, local woodcarver Frantisek Rint was commissioned with using these stored bones — the remains of some 40,000 people — to decorate the chapel, a task for which he was paid 12,000 guilders and which took him ten years. Rint was obviously proud of his final achievement, having signed and dated it — "1870 F. Rint of Ceská Skalice" — in his familiar medium of human bones. The work was supported by the Prince of Schwartzenberg, whose family had

Pages 178–181: Skeletal decorations at the Sedlec Ossuary, including a chandelier incorporating every bone in the human body and the Schwartzenberg family crest. Photos courtesy of George Higham.

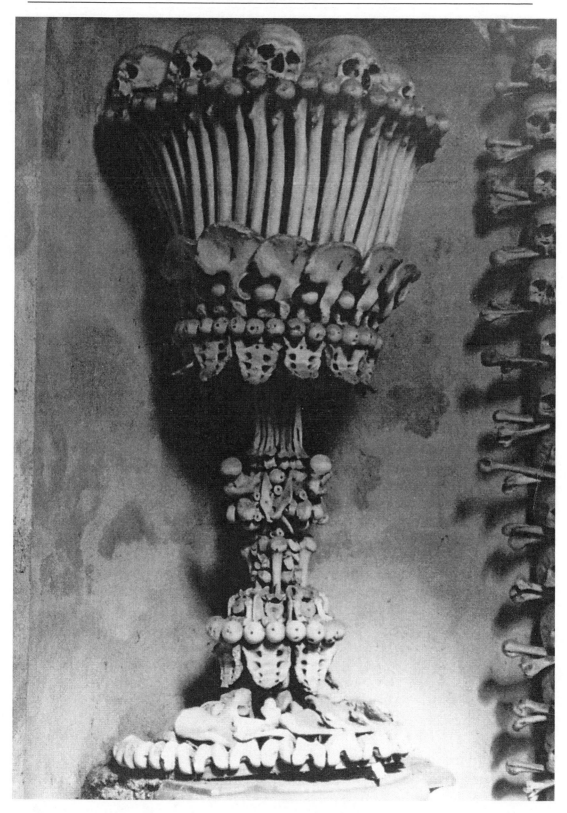

purchased the monastery in 1784 when its operations were terminated by Emperor Joseph II (d. 1790). Although it has a long history, the Sedlec ossuary has kept up with the times and offers that history — with accompanying photographs — on its website (www.kostnice.cz) through which it accepts e-mail inquiries.

One of the most striking creations is a chandelier that contains every bone in the human body. The chandelier hangs about seven feet above visitors' heads. Though it is kept clean of wax, the candles in it have been lit on All Souls' Day (November 2) for requiem masses (Rhoads 1999). The kostnice's website also points out the two monstrances beside the main altar. Another eye-catching creation is the Schwartzenberg crest attached to the framework in front of one of the remaining bone pyramids and topped by a crown composed of skulls, pelvic bones, scapulae, femoral heads, and ribs. On the lower right of the crest, a bird made of bones can be seen plucking at the empty eye socket of a skull (Merbs 1995).

The Sedlec ossuary has not been the subject of scientific study, but has been observed by physical anthropologist Charles Merbs. Merbs points out that the wing of the bird in the crest consists of the hand and wrist of an individual who had suffered from such severe arthritis that the bones had fused into a single mass. He also reports, "The bones used to decorate the kostnice were undoubtedly selected for their appearance and uniformity, with the remainder from the two dismantled pyramids, said to consist of another 40 cubic meters of bone, buried under a large iron cross in the cemetery. The bones on display do not exhibit the expected shades of yellow, brown, or black, reflecting the natural color of bone or pigments absorbed from the soil in which they had been buried, but are uniformly white, the result of their being disinfected in chlorinated lime by Rint. The overall effect of this kostnice on its visitors is usu-

ally one of awe, with at least some appreciation of the art created from human bones" (Merbs 1995).

The Sedlec ossuary was featured in a short film by Czech animator Jan Svankmaier in 1970. The 1970 film entitled "Ossuary" is black and white, runs 11 minutes, and is accompanied by a female vocalist singing the lyrics of a poem by Jacques Prevert called "How to Make the Likeness of a Bird." In the opening scene, a snail is crawling slowly in the eye socket of a skull. The camera then enters the ossuary and shows various structures and ornaments built of bones. The film may be watched by downloading it from the Svankmajer home page on the Internet (www.awn.com/heaven_ and_hell/SVANK/svank1.htm). The haunting moving images and voice are worth downloading. The ossuary has also been featured on popular television shows, including the August 29, 1999, episode of NBC's "You Asked for It," in which historian Dan Levine calls Rint the "Michelangelo of bone art." And the ossuary has been included in the 1998 book *Memento Mori* containing text by Bohdan Chlibec and Mojmir Horyna and photographs by Václav Jirásek, Robert V. Novak, and Ivan Pinkava. Loren Rhoads describes that "The photographers slipped behind the iron grates fencing off the pyramids to reveal the cant of disintegrating geometry as the skulls rolled out of place. They climbed over the rail into the sacred alcove to shoot the monstrance lens to eye socket. They documented cobwebs and shattered skulls and the crumbling plaster of the walls, revealing the sadness and decay behind the breathtaking chandelier and chalice." In the explanatory text, the authors suggest that the modern pilgrim cannot appreciate the ossuary in the intended manner and express regret that it is now a tourist attraction. They claim that access abolishes all secrets and leads to superficiality and banality. Rhoads finds the attitude insulting and notes that tourist dollars fund renovations of the ossuary, which would otherwise crumble to dust (Rhoads 1999).

Rhoads visited the Sedlec ossuary herself and described it in her journal, *Morbid Curiosity*:

> The chapel was cool as the inside of a refrigerator and relatively dark. It didn't smell of death, or rot, or even of mold. There wasn't a hint of corruption in the crypt. Despite the stained and crumbling plaster on the walls, the scent was curiously neutral.... Each corner of the crypt held a huge pyramid of bones. I suffered a momentary flicker of disappointment. With 40,000 skeletons, each with an excess of 200 bones, I had expected to see many objects arranged from bones. But this was not a catacomb in the Parisian sense, not a labyrinth of tunnels full of bones stretching away underground. This was only a room. A small room. You could twirl around in the center of it and see the bones of all 40,000 people, most of them stacked in these four huge pyramids (Rhoads 1999).

Rhoads goes on to describe jawbones strung end to end that formed loops like chain links and gentle slats of shoulder blades that fanned out to form platters which supported skulls. She found the kostnice peaceful and not at all sacrilegious. Particularly struck by the chandelier, she writes, "It was beautiful in a way I knew was changing me forever even as I stood there trying to make sense of it" (Rhoads 1999).

The church is open daily from 9 A.M. to noon and 2 to 4 P.M. from April through November and welcomes visitors, who must first walk a mile from the nearest bus stop and then purchase tickets (for 60 crowns, about $2.00) from an office a half block from the ossuary. An additional fee is asked for a photo pass. Postcards, viewbooks, and a guide in English are offered for sale. Once inside the chapel, guests are instructed not to touch the bones, but some of the skulls located farthest from the guard show evidence of having been tagged by graffiti artists (Rhoads 1999). The Sedlec Kostnice is managed by Karel Koubskytel, who also maintains the website. Most of the cemetery land from which the bones in the ossuary were disinterred was sold to support the monastery during hard times and now consists of only a tiny plot filled with mostly modern marble monuments (Rhoads 1999). The lure to visitors, other than those who come to pay their respects at the graves, is of course inside the chapel.

The Preparations of Frederik Ruysch

Anatomist Frederik Ruysch (d. 1731) used skeletal remains and other human tissues as the medium for his unique creations. Unfortunately, not a single tableau survives, but many have been described and illustrated in the historical literature and a large number of the anatomical specimens that he acquired and preserved are still extant. Ruysch was born in the Netherlands, became a pharmacist, studied medicine at Leyden, and took his doctor's degree in 1664. He became interested in anatomical dissection while caring for victims of the plague. Teaching in Amsterdam, he chaired the department of anatomy beginning in 1665, and later chaired midwifery and forensic science. In the latter capacity, he was appointed "doctor to the court," which gave him access to the bodies of executed criminals and babies found in the harbor (Luyendijk-Elshout 1970).

Ruysch kept a museum of specimens which soon became well-stocked and by 1690 filled ten cases with human anatomical material alone. In one of the cases, the transience of life was illustrated by 25 fetal and infant skeletons, with mayflies, strings of pearls, small candles, a wreath of flowers, or star-shaped melon seeds — all symbols of brevity — in or hanging from their skeletal hands. The proverbs accompanying this display included "Man's life is but a game,"

Anatomical tableau by Frederik Ruysch. Reprinted from *Thesaurus Anatomicus* (Amsterdam: J. Wolters, 1703) with permission of the Wellcome Institute Library, London.

"What is life? A transient smoke and a fragile bubble," and "Time flies and cannot be recalled" (Luyendijk-Elshout 1970). Ruysch opened his museum, which occupied five rooms of his house, to the public twice a week. Ruysch's tableaux incorporated plants, shells, skeletons, dismembered limbs, and other curiosities, but most of the material was derived from the human body. What looked like rocks were gallstones and what appeared to be trees were sections of the vascular system. The arrangements were labeled with inscriptions, among which were the following: "Why should I long for the things of this world," "Death spares no man, not even the defenceless infant," and "Man that is born of woman is of few days, and full of trouble." These sayings accompanied two fetal skeletons, one holding a miniature sickle and the other weeping into a mesentery handkerchief. This tableau and several others were engraved by C. H. Huijberts, which is fortunate since the originals have been lost. In a second tableau, two skeletons (one sobbing with the inscription, "We, robbed of this sweet life and torn from the breast, are carried off by horrid Death and laid in the dark grave," and the other laughing, with the inscription, "After undergoing so many misfortunes in this life, set free at last by death I triumph silently") are arranged between the dried tracheas and bronchial tubes of humans and calves. In a third tableau, the central skeleton laments, "Ah fate, ah bitter fate," while playing a violin with a dried artery for a bow. Another tiny skeleton conducts the music with a baton, a third skeleton grasps a spear made from the vas deferens, and a fourth is depicted with a feather on its skull (Luyendijk-Elshout 1970). In addition to the moral connotations of Ruysch's tableaux, they were appreciated by his contemporaries for their scientific value (Roberts and Tomlinson 1992).

Ruysch put his original collection up for sale in 1715. It was purchased for 30,000 gold guilders by Russian Czar Peter the Great two years later and moved to St. Petersburg. Rumors surfaced that many specimens had spoiled when the sailors on the transport ships siphoned off and consumed the alcohol. More misinformation about the destruction of the specimens was spread during World War II, but they had been protected during the siege of Leningrad by storing them in the basement of the museum. In any case, more than 900 specimens remain in the Kunstkammer of Peter the Great in the Leningrad Academy of Science. A catalog prepared in 1947 listed 935 specimens, including the skeletons of children and a giant (Mann 1964). In his eighties, Ruysch began a second anatomical collection that was sold at his death to the King of Poland, John Sobieski (Roberts and Tomlinson 1992), and was later acquired by the University of Wittenberg (Talbot 1970). An auction scattered many of his other preparations, and with the exception of a few recovered by Amsterdam anatomist Andreas Bonn, none of the specimens prepared by Ruysch are curated in the Netherlands (Luyendijk-Elshout 1970). Ruysch's motto was "Come and see." Although we can no longer do that with his unique tableaux, we can — if willing to travel to Russia — have a look at his other anatomical preparations.

5

Curation

Procuring human bones for study is not an easy task. Where they have accumulated in large numbers — catacombs, ossuaries — they are unlikely to be released for analysis. Attempting to dig them up from the ground offers no guarantee of success and those that are uncovered accidentally are often available to scientists for only a brief time before being reinterred. One alternative is buying bones from retail establishments, which has become increasingly expensive as international sources for skeletal remains dry up. Another option is to acquire human skeletons directly through an active body donation program. The bones may be harvested after the body has been put to other good uses, for instance medical dissection or forensic anthropological research. Each means of procurement has its drawbacks, as William Bass (1987) explains: "Human skeletal materials used in physical anthropology laboratories generally are obtained from medical supply houses, dissecting rooms, or archaeological sites. Skeletal remains purchased from medical supply houses are expensive, those obtained from dissecting rooms may include parts that have been sectioned, and those from archaeological sites may be incomplete or poorly preserved."

Once bones have been obtained, they will in many cases require cleaning. If flesh adheres, it may be removed by soaking, boiling, or exposing them to a special variety of beetle. The bones will then require degreasing. If brittle, bones may require the application of a preservative. Depending on their intended use, dismantled skeletons may be articulated and skulls may be reconstructed. Measurements of the bones may assist in solving a crime, if the remains lack identity. Or the measurements may be added to a database that assists in identification indirectly by offering estimates and averages of stature and other characteristics. As important as preserving the specimens is preserving the information that is gained from them. If the bones deteriorate or the collection is dismantled, documentation according to contemporary osteological standards remains as a paper and electronic shadow of the actual physical remains. The record may be augmented by casts, photographs, and the results of any testing performed. But ideally, except in active forensic cases in which a curated skeleton usually means an unsolved murder, bones will remain in organized collections accessible to researchers today and tomorrow.

PROCUREMENT

In past decades, India and Bangladesh were the foremost suppliers of human skeletons. Those countries then prohibited their export as an affront to national dignity (Maples 1994), though India has since

Michael Charney of the Forensic Science Laboratory, Fort Collins, Colorado. Reprinted with permission of Charlie Fellenbaum.

resumed. Retail and mail order establishments have turned to other areas of Asia to replenish their stock. Although the prices have risen, skeletons may still be purchased in whole or in part from companies including Skulls Unlimited in Oklahoma City and the Bone Room in Berkeley, California, or through catalogs such as the Catalog of Carnage from Tempe, Arizona. The Catalog of Carnage offers first class natural bone human skeletons with cut calvaria, hinged jaws, removable arms and legs, artificial teeth, tripod stands, zippered dust covers, and an accompanying chart for $3,499. Human skulls range from $399 for a fourth-class specimen with few teeth and possible staining or damage to $995 for a first-class specimen with between 28 and 32 real teeth. Fetal skulls are available for $450. Other skeletal elements are priced accordingly and are sold as subsets (hands or feet for $174, atlas/axis for $139.95, ossicle set for $49.95) or as single bones (femurs for $159.95, scapulae for $89.95, tibias for $99.95, fibulae for $64.95, humeri or radii for $59.95, and ulnae for $39.95). Ribs are sold individually at $14.95 each. The Catalog of Carnage states, "All sales final on natural bone items" and — in keeping with the unpredictable market — "Price and availability subject to change without notice." The Bone Room offers complete skeletons (articulated or disarticulated) for $2,000 to $2,500, vertebral columns for $275 to $375, articulated hands and feet for $150 and $125 respectively, pelvis for $175, and individual skeletal elements ranging from ribs and vertebra for $8 each to a femur for $60. Skulls range from $250 to $700, depending on the age and condition. The Bone Room also sells casts and leases natural bones by the week.

Dealers in skeletal remains can never be certain of their supply, but neither can they preclude the possibility of being offered something out of the ordinary. In March 1998, Henry Galiano, owner of Maxilla and Mandible in Manhattan, bought a human cranium from a middleman representing a collector of curios. After cleaning, the skull appeared to be that of an early hominid and was complete except for the jaws. The skull was examined by Eric Delson, a paleoanthropologist at the City University of New York, who assessed it as belonging to a male, probably in his 20s, falling within the range of *Homo erectus*, but with a much smaller brain capacity than *Homo sapiens*. Galiano decided not to turn a profit on the specimen, which might have been sold for up to half a million dollars at auction, when he learned of its history. The skull had been unearthed in 1997 by a farmer in central Java in the Solo River Valley near the discovery of the first *Homo erectus* fossils by Eugène Dubois in 1891. It was examined and described in Jakarta by physical anthropologist Doedhi Hartono, after which it was sold to a dealer, who in turn sold it to some American tourists. Instead of adding it to his display case, Galiano returned the cranium to Indonesia for study ("Missing Link" 1999).

Skulls Unlimited in Oklahoma City

> *Skulls Unlimited International provides the finest museum quality articulated and disarticulated specimens available. Each specimen is cleaned and whitened to exceed educational standards.... We take pride in our complete product line, and we are sure that you will soon see that skulls can be an invaluable teaching aid, or just an addition to your home or office.*
> *— from the 2000 catalog*

Skulls Unlimited, which was established in 1986, has become the world's leading supplier of osteological specimens. These include human remains, which are priced based on availability and quality. Three classes of skulls are offered at prices ranging from $249 to $599, based on their condition and intended usage: first or museum quality are anatomically complete (including all the teeth) and in perfect condition, second or teaching and handling quality may have minor imperfections or damage, and third or arts and crafts quality may have extensive damage or missing parts (such as the teeth or mandible). First-quality fetal skulls are priced at $450. There are additional charges for cut calvaria and spring-held jaws. Complete skeletons are also offered, ranging from $1,995 to $2,895, with an additional $100 for the stand. Do-it-yourselfers may choose to order disarticulated skeletons at prices ranging from $1,395 to $1,895. Hands and feet are sold articulated or disarticulated and range from $125 to $175. Vertebrae are also sold as sets, with cervical, thoracic, or lumbar available for $20 and an atlas/axis set for $50. Long bones range from $39 for a radius or ulna to $99 for a femur. Ribs are $8 each. The prices do not include shipping, but RUSH orders are accepted. While most of the bones are standard specimens, they have handled pathological specimens, including a syphilitic skull peppered with holes and a skeleton with rickets.

Skulls Unlimited maintains stock of anywhere from 600 to 1,000 pieces, including approximately 50 skulls and a dozen skeletons on hand at any one time. President Jay Villemarette relates (personal correspondence, October 23, 1998) that most of their business is done by mail order and through their website (www.skullsunlimited.com), although they do operate a retail store in Oklahoma City. Although they occasionally sell specimens wholesale to their colleagues, most of their sales are to institutions and they direct their marketing efforts to the educational community, explains Villemarette. Sales of human skeletal remains account for about 10 percent of overall sales. A typical order consists of between one and five skulls or half a dozen ribs, with their largest order for human bones totaling more than $10,000. Less than one percent of their sales of human bones are to individuals, most of them medical students. They get repeat customers on a regular basis and do not share their mailing list.

Skulls Unlimited sells gift certificates, accepts payment by check, money order, or credit card, and offers a ten-day return guarantee, but puts the legal onus on the purchaser. The catalog warns, "Please note, if you order any item(s) from us that you cannot possess according to the laws of your state or country, Skulls Unlimited accepts no responsibility for this act and will hold you responsible for any penalties and legal fees incurred by Skulls Unlimited. Please be aware of your local laws before purchasing specimens that you may be in doubt of." Villemarette has not experienced any backlash from heightened sensitivity about human remains and has received more inquiries about the source of their supply of animal bones (personal correspondence, October 23, 1998). The mail order catalog states that all specimens are legally and ethically obtained from suppliers around the world, from whom they obtain skulls that would otherwise be discarded or destroyed. In addition to natural bone specimens, they offer human skeletal components molded from the natural item by hand in unbreakable plastic. Standard skull reproductions start at $89, and complete skeletons at $349. They also sell models of the skulls of early humans, including Neandertal, *Homo habilis*, and Cro-Magnon. In addition to its inventory, the company offers its services to prepare specimens acquired by local and out-of-state universities. Most of the skeletons they procure for resale arrive clean, but they maintain a colony of dermestid beetles to deflesh the skeletons that they prepare for

others about six times a year. One of their most interesting custom cleaning orders was to prepare the skeleton from one of the worst untreated cases of scoliosis, a specimen proudly depicted in the catalog.

Forensic Anthropology Center at the University of Tennessee, Knoxville

Imagine a fenced-off area of a college campus strewn with corpses in various situations and states of decay. Such a place exists and was the brainchild of forensic anthropologist William Bass, who arrived at the University of Tennessee in 1971. Bass established the Forensic Anthropology Center in 1987 to observe and document the results of decay on the human body. The "body farm," as it is familiarly known, serves as an outdoor laboratory. The anthropology department's website explains that the focus of the program in forensic anthropology is the application of skeletal biological principles and techniques to the identification of decomposing and skeletal remains. The results of the ongoing research furnish law enforcement agencies with details about taphonomy that assist in the identification of bodies discovered days, weeks, months, or years after death. In fact, the staff of the Department of Anthropology has provided human identification services through the State Medical Examiner System for the District Attorney General's Office, arson investigations, and various state and local law enforcement agencies and county medical examiners for more than 25 years. They receive about fifty requests a year to recover bodies from the field or consult about them in the morgue. The department collaborates with the Departments of Pathology and General Dentistry at the University of Tennessee Medical Center to enhance their expertise in medicolegal investigations.

Once the bodies have given up their secrets by decaying in a wide range of settings, their bones are turned over to the anthropology students for further study. The skeletons join others that are stored in boxes on floor-to-ceiling shelves in the Anthropology Department. Some 2,000 remains are curated, of which the individuals from the research facility total more than 100 — and counting. These documented skeletons serve to test students' grasp of what they have been taught and they are typically given a set of bones and asked to determine its gender, age, and other information. Part of their training also occurs when they recover the skeletonized remains from the body farm, a task that foreshadows later recovery of murder victims from the field. The remains are inventoried and transported to a processing lab on campus. Because the cleaning of skeletons is a very specialized task, no equipment industry has grown up to serve it. Bass has borrowed from the culinary sciences for what he calls a "Crock-Pot approach to cleaning a body" (Montgomery 1999). Skeletons are simmered in a giant soup kettle and skulls in a smaller electric pot. Biz laundry detergent is added to the water and meat tenderizer is sometimes used to help remove the flesh. The bones are allowed to dry, numbered, and stored in hinged cardboard boxes that measure three feet long. The boxes are stacked on shelves in two rooms in the anthropology department along a curved corridor.

Bass brought a sizable collection of prehistoric human skeletal remains with him when he came to the University of Tennessee. He had excavated them from the northern Plains area of the U.S. during dam building on the Missouri River by the Corps of Engineers. Approximately 5,000 skeletons were recovered by Bass and his archaeologists during his work for the Smithsonian Institution (1956 to 1960) and during excavations funded by the National Geographic Society and the National Science Foundation (1961 to 1970). The prehistoric

bones have been the basis for many masters' theses, doctoral dissertations, and research articles. The human populations of the Plains region are now some of the most thoroughly researched subjects of skeletal biology. As Native Americans began attempting to recover skeletal remains for reburial in the early 1980s, Bass confides (personal correspondence, June 24, 1999) that he envisioned trying to teach without a skeletal collection. For this reason he began to build a new one from modern populations. The university was already curating the state forensic collection received from the medical examiner's office, which offered excellent teaching specimens of gunshot wounds and other trauma. Bass began what he refers to as the donated collection. Skeletons are added to this collection in three ways: the receipt of unclaimed bodies through the medical examiner's system (which saves the State of Tennessee $700 per body in burial fees), the donation of bodies by next-of-kin, and the bequest of bodies made prior to death. The center has received only a few willed bodies so far, but about 75 people have completed body donation forms. After his own death (and observed decay), Bass's skeleton will be among those in the donated collection. "Why should I stop helping students when I retire or when I die?" he asks. "There's material here that other people can use" (Montgomery 1999). When that time comes, leadership of the center will be taken up by Bass's former student Murray Marks, now an associate professor in the department.

Dr. Bass and his students are grateful to the body donors for their generosity. An annual memorial service is held to honor them and convenes around a representative skeleton from the collection. A recent memorial service was attended by James McSween, whose wife's body was donated to the facility at her request, and their son. Mrs. McSween's bones show evidence of her open-heart surgery. When they were shown to her family, her husband noted that she had been a teacher when alive and continued to teach in death. McSween and his son were told that they were welcome to visit any time (Smith 1999). Ironically, Bass admits (Montgomery 1999) that he has not had the courage to examine the remains of a friend and colleague from the History Department whose body bequest was carried out upon his death a few years ago.

HANDLING, STORAGE, AND TRANSPORT

The physical integrity of bones that have reached the laboratory depends on a number of factors affecting them prior to their arrival. These include the acidity of the soil in which they were buried, the length of time the bones were exposed to the environment, and the medical condition of the individual. Another factor is the care with which they were handled en route. Bones should be wrapped individually and isolated from each other using newspaper, styrofoam, or other packing material, but avoiding cotton because it will adhere to the specimens (Rhine 1998). If they are being transported by private vehicle, bones may be placed in cardboard boxes, but if they are being sent by rail or on board a ship, they should be packed in strong wooden boxes (Brothwell 1981). To avoid damage to the bones after they reach the lab, they should not be handled by untrained people without supervision and extreme care should be used when they are measured or photographed. Breakage will inevitably occur during the course of handling osteological material, but the temptation to test the mechanical properties of dry bone by probing, twisting, poking, stabbing, and scraping should always be resisted (White 1991). Skulls should be picked up with both hands, providing support from underneath (Skinner and Lazenby 1983). They should never be lifted by the eye orbits and should not be placed directly on the table, but instead rested on a bean-bag or donut ring (Bass 1987). Care should be taken during washing to prevent the facial area of the skull from breaking or collapsing (Brothwell 1981).

The bones in a newly recovered assemblage should be sorted and sided, removing any non-human material and organizing according to element. Great care should be shown when handling bones from existing assemblages, as Tim D. White (1991) suggests: "Respect any system of organization in which you find skeletal material. Never mix bones and teeth of different individuals, even for a short time or with the best of intentions. Remember that mixing of bones results in a loss of contextual information — an action that is potentially even more devastating then physical breakage of an element.... Bones reshelved in the wrong place are almost impossible to retrieve." For long-term storage, acid-free cartons and inert polyfoam should be used and the use of polyethylene bags closed by cotton twine or nylon rather than metal twist ties, adhesive tape, or staples is recommended (Buikstra and Ubelaker 1994).

Broken bones should be repaired with quick-drying cement. Small pieces should be glued together first, then larger pieces should be fitted together, taking color and texture into consideration when matching broken edges (Bass 1987). Application of varnishes or other protective coatings should be avoided for several reasons: they may not aid in preservation, they may inhibit observation, and they may preclude later chemical and microscopic analysis. Rhine (1998) cautions that treatment of the bones should always be reversible and preservatives removable if necessary. Don R. Brothwell (1981) advises the use of preservatives only when the bone is liable to disintegrate, and discourages the use of hot paraffin wax (which may cause cracking to worsen) and shellac (which may peel).

Synthetic resins may be used, but should only be applied in the laboratory after the bones have been washed and dried. With the proper equipment, polyvinyl acetate may be applied in the field to strengthen brittle bones. Rhine (1998) encourages the use of a preservative if bones are to be maintained in a permanent research collection, since it will strengthen them and render them less susceptible to expansion and contraction with changes in humidity and temperature. Human skeletal remains should be kept in a protected environment, but do not necessarily require conditions that are environmentally controlled. They may still develop problems, however. Salt in bones recovered from a marine environment will crystallize, causing cracking. Excavated remains placed in a dry environment, such as bones in a charnel house, can develop traces of algal or fungal growth (Schultz 1997). Although researchers are more likely to hurt the bones than vice versa, there is a risk of acquiring disease from human remains that decreases rapidly with time and loss of soft tissue. This includes exposure to tuberculosis and, in historic skeletons, arsenic. The greatest risk is common infection from cuts or scratches, which can be prevented by using gloves (Ubelaker 1995).

CLEANING AND DEGREASING

Skeletal remains that have been recovered from the field or are to be harvested from a cadaver require cleaning and degreasing. The first step is the careful removal of as much soft tissue as possible without damaging the bones. "This is slow, delicate, messy work that nobody really cares to talk about very much," admits Stanley Rhine (1998). If only a limited amount of desiccated tissue adheres, it can be dislodged using small instruments (Ubelaker 1989). Bones that are already skeletonized may be rinsed over a screen with water that is not too hot and brushed to remove any dirt (Brothwell 1981, Bass 1987). "A gently pulsating stream of water is useful for flushing dirt out of foramina and various fissures and impressions, and soft toothbrushes work for most other surfaces. The water washes the dirt away and a screen over the drain will ensure that nothing small like a tooth or bone fragment gets lost" (Rhine 1998). There is a danger of washing away potential evidence in a forensic case, however, so bones under investigation should not be unnecessarily cleaned (Skinner and Lazenby 1983).

One way to remove flesh from a skeleton is to take advantage of the natural appetite of *Dermestes lardarius*, the "carrion" beetle. This method has its pluses and minuses. The advantages to using dermestid beetles are that they do a neat and thorough job (Rhine 1998). They do not cause warping of the bones or loosening of the teeth in the skull (Krogman and Iscan 1986). Left in the dark to do their dirty work, dermestid beetles will skeletonize the body in four to six weeks. The disadvantages, as listed by Stanley Rhine, are that they require closely controlled temperature (84°F or 30°C) and humidity, are eager to escape any enclosure, and cause a pervasive, unpleasant odor. "For these reasons, most forensic anthropologists, while admiring the end result and envying the luxury of just sitting back and letting the beetles do all the work, do not use them" (Rhine 1998).

Another way to rid the bones of the soft tissue is to macerate them. This procedure involves submerging the remains in a container of water, which is decanted every few days. Decomposing flesh will be carried away each time the water is changed, but the method may take weeks. Chemical solutions may be added to the water to speed up the process or it may be brought to a finish by simmering the bones to remove any remaining tissue. The advantage of maceration is that it protects the surface of the bones against any alteration caused by scrubbing (Rhine 1998). Instead of macerating in water, the bones may be soaked in household bleach (sodium hypochlorite) and sodium hydroxide, followed by defatting with acetone. Alternatively, they may be "gently simmered" in a 10 percent solution of enzymatic cleaner (commonly found in certain brands of laundry detergent including Biz, Borax, and Oxydol) and water, which will leave them both bleached and degreased (Krogman and Iscan 1986). The Terry method is another variation that involves immersing the bones in hot water (96° to 98°C) for up to 72 hours, after which the remaining soft parts are removed with a hard bristle brush or a soft wire rotating brush. The bones are then placed on a tilted drain board and allowed to dry at room temperature. When dry, they are degreased with benzol over approximately 17 hours and allowed to stand for a day. The bones are then dipped in a very thin solution of glue and carbolic acid and lastly dipped in 10 percent formalin (Krogman and Iscan 1986). Other techniques have been devised to accelerate the preparation of skeletal material. A method published by R. G. Snyder, A. Burdi, and G. Gaul recommends cutting away excess tissue, placing the remains in a bath of 1 part antiformin (a mix of sodium carbonate, bleaching powder, water, and hydroxide solution) to 8 to 10 parts water, boiling gently, and then degreasing in benzol for one or two hours (Krogman and Iscan 1986).

DOCUMENTATION

It is important when documenting human skeletal remains to be consistent, both within an assemblage and in general so that assemblages can be compared and electronic databases will be accurate. It is also imperative that provenance be preserved. Each bone in an assemblage should be clearly labeled with the museum catalog number, site number, burial number, or other designation using permanent waterproof ink and writing in a place that does not obscure anatomical landmarks or pathological lesions (Ubelaker 1989, Bass 1987). A drop of hardener may be applied to softer bones to provide a surface for numbering (White 1991). Analysis of the cleaned and numbered remains should be systematic. Guidelines for standardized data collection from human bones have been published by Buikstra and Ubelaker (1994). The standards are based on a report prepared by a volunteer committee and published by the Paleopathology Association in 1991 and a workshop conducted the same year by the Field Museum of Natural History. The measurements and observations cover the following topics: bone pathology; nonmetric variation; inventory and osteometric analysis; dental inventory, pathology, and cultural modifications; computer imagery and illustration; bone histology and chemistry; dental metrics and morphology; taphonomy; cranial deformation; subadult development; and adult aging and sexing. Of primary importance is creating an inventory of the remains to serve as a description and as a basis for comparative statistical analyses. The completeness of the remains should be indicated, since most archaeologically recovered skeletons will be missing some bones due to cultural activities, natural processes, incomplete recovery, or substandard curation procedures. The effects of natural processes and cultural modifications should be reported on a recording form detailing postmortem changes.

Physical anthropologists at the University of Tennessee in Knoxville have taken advantage of modern technology to both offer a useful research tool to their colleagues and to guard against the loss of data represented by the burial of undocumented remains. The Forensic Data Bank compiles information on human skeletal remains and encourages participation among those in the field of forensic anthropology. The database was begun in the early 1980s and has incorporated large amounts of data from the Smithsonian Institution, the Human Identification Laboratory at the University of Arizona in Tucson, and the Forensic Anthropology Center at the University of Tennessee in Knoxville. The reasons for creating the Forensic Data Bank are explained by its creators, Peer Moore-Jansen, Stephen D. Ousley, and Richard L. Jantz (1994):

> The skeletal biology of Americans is changing due to secular changes, migrations, and gene flow. In the absence of large modern collections, a data bank is necessary to keep pace with the changing U.S. population. A data bank does naturally impose certain limits on research, since all possible data cannot be collected. But it does preserve data that would otherwise be lost when buried, and has the added possibility of including individuals from around the country and around the world.

The systematic collection of information from forensic cases, an idea that had been talked about for years, provides a more adequate basis for deriving standards, primarily for race, stature, sex and age determination, than the anatomical collections upon which many of the current standards rest. As of 1994, data from more than 1,200 cases, of which 900 are of known race and gender, had been gathered. Much of the data collected is general information about the individual and the case: age, sex, race, stature, weight, handedness, date of birth, place of birth, occupation, blood type, number of pregnancies and births (for female subjects), date reported missing, date of discovery, date of death, time since death, manner of death, whether the body was found buried or exposed, estimated period of decay, nature of the remains, place of discovery, medical history, congenital malformations, den-

tal records, bone lesions, and perimortem injuries. In addition, the bones are inventoried and measured with particular attention to the skull, from which 24 measurements are gathered. Also recorded are observations that assist in aging a skeleton, including cranial suture closure, epiphyseal closure, and changes to the pelvis and rib ends. A modestly-priced software program called "FORDISC" uses the accumulated data to generate custom discriminant functions based on available cranial measurements and has assisted in the identification of remains from Operation Desert Storm and the Branch Davidian compound in Waco, Texas. New versions of the software are released to provide new estimates based on the latest information (Moore-Jansen, Ousley, and Jantz 1994).

Holland's Ministry of Culture has taken steps to see that the important medical collections in that country are inventoried. A grant of 12 million guilders was awarded in 1997 to reexamine the collections at five Dutch universities: Lieden, Amsterdam, Groningen, Utrecht, and Delft. The project began at Lieden, where the collections were inventoried, duplicates deaccessioned, and a computerized database created. The database, which is made available to participating universities and museums, includes the name of the institution at which the specimens are curated, the type of collection (for instance, pathological), a description of the specimens, the size of the collection, the condition of the remains, and the use of the specimens in teaching and research. The information can be sorted by any of these variables. Assessment of each collection was carried out at the same time and — based on its pedigree, completeness, use, and potential for future research and exhibition — it was designated as nationally important and serving as a standard or regionally important and expendable. The inventory process revealed totals of 35,000 to 40,000 wet and dry preparations at the major universities. The collections at these "old" universities date back to at least the early nineteenth century, when each was prescribed by law to maintain a cabinet of medical and comparative anatomy specimens. Before that time, professors used their own collections for teaching. The collections of Albinus and Ruysch were housed at Lieden, that of Petrus Camper in Groningen, and that of Jan Bleuland in Utrecht. Amsterdam acquired the nineteenth-century Vrolik collection, which includes specimens of anthropology, comparative anatomy, pathology, and teratology. The Utrecht University Museum curates a pathological skeletal collection of some 500 specimens — including examples of rickets, cancer, fractures, tuberculosis, and syphilis — amassed by Albert Narath (d. 1924), professor of surgery. As the medical field developed and universities merged with local academic hospitals, some of the Dutch collections were split up. The remains of approximately 30,000 individuals recovered during cemetery excavations were stored in the Department of Physical Anthropology at Utrecht. When the department was closed in the early 1980s, most of the bones were transferred to Rijksdienst voor het Oudheidkundig Bodemonderzoek, with a smaller amount going to the appropriate regional archaeological depot, provided it had special permission to keep human skeletal remains. Improvements for more selective collection, better conservation, and prudent deaccessioning were recommended as part of the project. In keeping with one of the aims of the European Associations of Museums of the History of Medical Sciences, which is to conduct a census and create an index of public and private collections, the inventory will incorporate the major holdings of other institutions, including the Free University in Amsterdam, Nijmegen, Maastricht, and Rotterdam. The database will be posted on the Internet.

Whether documenting bones electronically or by other means, the information should offer accessibility and comparability to other scholars. When drawing or photographing the human skull, it should be positioned with reference to the Frankfurt plane, a standard orientation that allows valid comparisons and approximates the position of the head during life. Both isolated and commingled bones in an assemblage should be photographed and radiographed (Buikstra and Ubelaker 1994). When photographed in the lab, bones should be placed on a black velvet background to improve color accuracy and eliminate shadows (White 1991). The photographs, radiographs, CT-scans, data collection sheets and other paper records should be curated along with the specimens themselves, preferably under environmentally controlled conditions (Buikstra and Ubelaker 1994). If the bones comprise a forensic case, the chain of evidence must be preserved. Stanley Rhine (1998) suggests placing the specimens in paper bags labeled with the case or control number and location information and stapled shut. The boxes in which the bags are placed should also be labeled and taped shut.

RECONSTRUCTION AND REPRODUCTION

There are many reasons to reconstruct the skeleton from the loose bones and even more important reasons to reproduce the likeness of an individual from his or her skull. There are equally valid reasons to make copies of bones by casting them. During analysis of human skeletal remains, the bones are typically laid out on a table in correct anatomical order. But if a skeleton is to be used for teaching, reference, or display, the bones have to be articulated. A metal rod is generally used to string the vertebrae together, but connecting the rest of the bones is a more difficult task. Eric

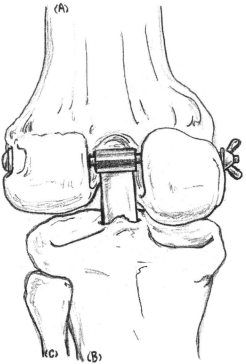

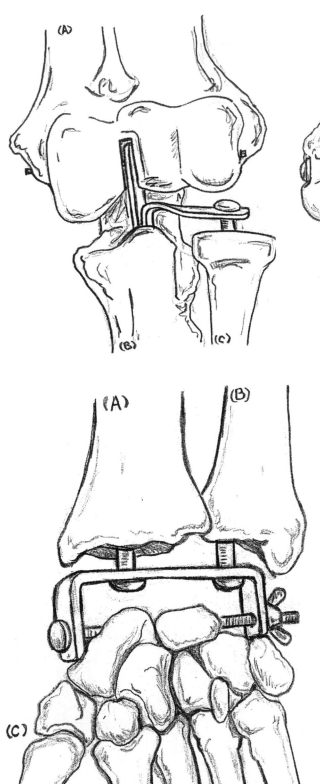

Top left: **Articulation of the humerus (A), ulna (B), and radius (C).** ***Top right:*** **Articulation of the femur (A), tibia (B), and fibula (C).** ***Bottom left:*** **Articulation of the radius (A), ulna (B), and hand (C). Sketches by Eric Humphries, reprinted courtesy of Skulls Unlimited, Oklahoma City.**

Humphries articulates human skeletons for Skulls Unlimited and explains that they manufacture their own hardware for the purpose from stripped stainless steel. An L-shaped piece allows the radius and ulna to rotate as they do in life. Special spring-hung hardware was devised to articulate the skeleton of the scoliosis patient that they prepared.

Casting bones serves several purposes. Casting by companies such as Medical Plastics Laboratory, Inc., and Kronen Osteo (manufacturers of Bone Clones®) became popular 20 years ago when export of natural skeletons was banned in some countries. Excavated prehistoric remains are molded and the

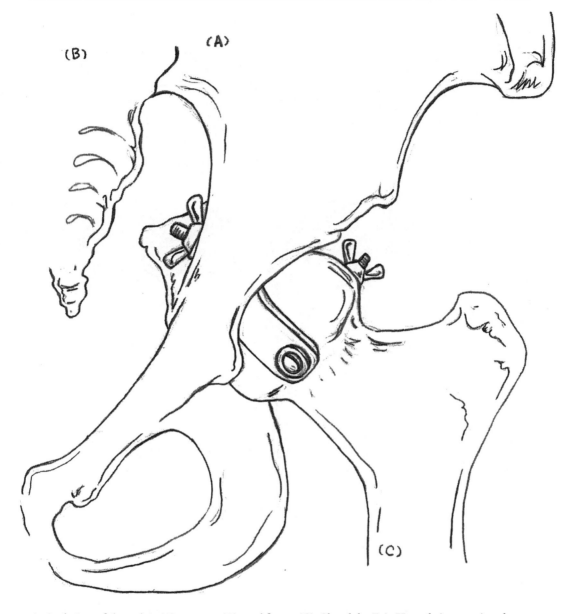

Articulation of the pelvis (A), sacrum (B), and femur (C). Sketch by Eric Humphries, reprinted courtesy of Skulls Unlimited, Oklahoma City.

first casts produced are identified as record casts and secured in case the original fossils are ever lost or destroyed (White 1991). It was to visualize the faces of Neandertals and Cro-Magnons that methods of facial reproduction were developed (Krogman and Iscan 1986). It is now possible to perform this three-dimensional build-up of physiognomy on a computer image of the skull rather than the skull itself, but most practitioners use the actual specimen or a cast of it. The technique based on average thickness of facial tissues has been used since the late nineteenth century. A new technique that reconstructed facial muscles and other tissues rather than using average tissue depth was developed by Gladys P. Curry, who self-published a textbook on facial

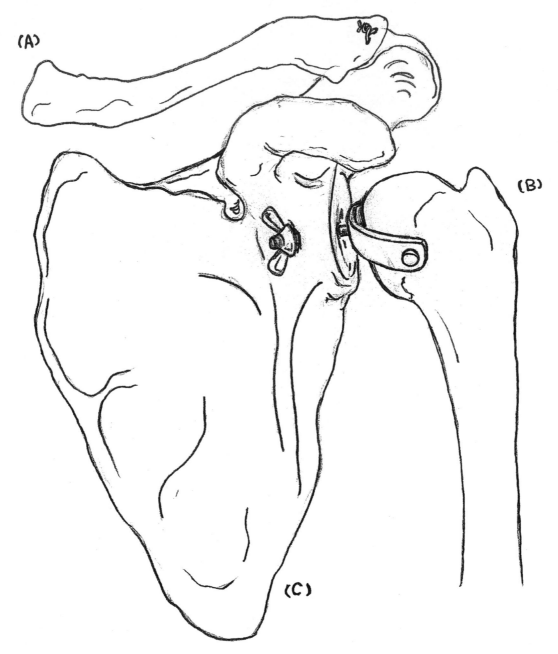

Articulation of the clavicle (A), humerus (B), and scapula (C). Sketch by Eric Humphries, reprinted courtesy of Skulls Unlimited, Oklahoma City.

reconstruction in 1947. A similar method was introduced by M. M. Gerasimov in 1971 (Rhine 1998). While bringing to life the faces of prehistoric individuals and historic figures, the most useful application of facial reconstruction is to identify the dead from their anonymous bones. The resulting likeness is not proof, as Rhine (1998) points out: "An identification is never made on the basis of the clay face itself. The face only provides a spur to dislodge records that could not otherwise be found, which in turn

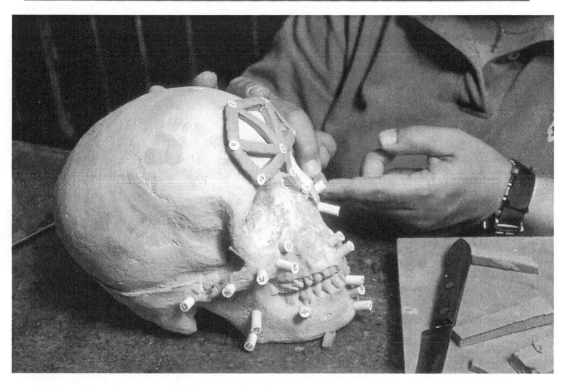

A step in the process of facial reconstruction. Reprinted with permission of Charlie Fellenbaum.

allows the identification to be made in the usual accepted way." One of the foremost practitioners of this combination of art and science is Betty Pat Gatliff, who — during more than 30 years in her Skullpture Lab in Oklahoma — has reproduced the faces of the victims of John Wayne Gacy, among many others. Her work on forensic cases does not allow the time to make molds and cast the skulls, she explains (personal correspondence June 4, 1999), so the work is performed on the original specimen within ten days of receipt. Gatliff shares her skills during classes at the F.B.I. Academy in Quantico, Virginia, twice a year and workshops around the country, including one at the Cleveland Institute of Art, where she uses model skulls from the Hamann-Todd Collection.

Facial reproductions at the University of Manchester in England follow prescribed policies. The skull is first rendered dry and sterile by a conservator and then molded and cast to preserve the original for further examination (in forensic cases) or to avoid damage to fragile ancient or modern specimens. If a skull is incomplete, it is first rebuilt from the fragments and any missing areas filled in. Casting a skull is difficult due to the numerous holes, undercuts, arches, thin and delicate areas, and fine surface detail, and sometimes the mandible is cast separately. Ancient skulls require support from the inside and all skulls are protected from moisture during the process by wrapping them with aluminum foil. Alginate is then applied using a split mold technique and coated, when set, with a supporting plaster jacket or "mother mold." Usually only a single cast can be made from a mold, which becomes damaged and distorted. The cast is made with plaster and, if it is a faithful replica of the original, is then mounted for facial reconstruction (Prag 1997).

IDENTIFICATION

*It is not generally appreciated how
indelibly and in what detail the record
of an individual's life may be inscribed
in the structure of his skeleton.*
— Sir Sydney A. Smith [1939]

Facial reconstruction (or reproduction) in an attempt to attach a name to unidentified human remains requires the presence of the skull. Continued refinement of other techniques used in forensic identification relies on continued availability of documented skeletal materials (Rathbun and Buikstra 1984). Substantial collections are sometimes curated by coroners and medical examiners. The skeletons of more than 859 individuals have been collected from autopsies at the Department of the Chief Medical Examiner-Coroner in Los Angeles and include individuals under the age of 18, Mongoloids, and women, all underrepresented in some of the other documented collections, including the Hamann-Todd Collection (Suchey et al. 1984). From this and other osteological collections, many techniques have been developed to narrow down the search for an individual's identity. Bone may be examined microscopically to estimate age by counting osteons and osteon fragments which increase over time (Kerley 1984). Interorbital features of the skull offer additional means to differentiate between races (Gill 1984). Discriminant function analysis is a sophisticated mathematical approach to sexing skeletons. A set of specific measurements are taken from the skeleton and each is multiplied by its respective weight in the formula, after which the products are summed. The sexes are separated by a numerical value, below which the remains are most likely female and above which they are most likely male. Different formulae weights are used for skeletons of different racial groups (Rathbun and Buikstra 1984). Using these and other techniques, experienced investigators may be able to determine sex, age, race, stature, occupation, pathologies, malformation, healed fractures, perimortem injuries, cause of death, and other details (Rhine 1984).

Sometimes circumstances make identification much harder than the standard textbook case, however. Skinner and Lazenby (1983) also point out that traditional autopsy procedures on skeletonized remains, such as the sawing of the skull, are "positively inimical to the methods of the forensic anthropologist." In the wake of warfare follow other difficulties. After the Vietnam War, a cottage industry sprung up in Southeast Asia that left few remains undisturbed and many deliberately modified. In the hope of selling or bartering the bones of American casualties, dealers removed the incisors and, in one case, lengthened the femurs, of native remains to pass them off as Caucasian (Holland, Anderson, and Mann 1997). The U.S. Army maintains a Central Identification Laboratory in Hawaii for the processing of remains that may belong to the more than 2,000 individuals missing from the Vietnam War, 8,000 from the Korean War, and some 80,000 from World War II and the Cold War. The task is often made more difficult by the cultural practices of foreign governments curating the skeletal remains of U.S. service personnel. For instance, North Vietnamese Army protocol called for interment near the place of death, followed later by disinterment, cleaning, disinfecting, boxing, and warehousing of the bones, which were periodically removed from the boxes and dried over a charcoal fire to check the growth of mold. The use of insect repellent and the commingling that resulted from this practice have limited the success of DNA extraction and sequencing (Holland, Anderson, and Mann 1997).

While genetic fingerprinting offers great potential, the morphological uniqueness of each skeleton is often a factor in identification. The existence of a pathology or anomaly in a bone or bone fragment may be enough to exclude possible individuals when determining identity (Rathbun and Buikstra 1984). Pathology may have resulted from a disease, several of which leave permanent effects in the form and structure of the skeleton. The resulting peculiarities of a skeleton may be matched up with records of an individual made while alive. Like facial reconstruction, photographic superimposition may suggest an identity, but is not conclusive. Comparative radiography, on the other hand, may allow positive identification from skeletonized human remains. In radiographic comparison, x-rays must be taken at the same angle and distance, features are likely to be more clearly defined in the x-rays of skeletonized remains, and some artificial difference may appear due to postmortem trauma to the skull or alterations made during life produced by trauma, surgery, infection, or disease processes (Ubelaker 1984). Nevertheless, frontal sinus patterns on record can be matched to those of a victim just as dental records can be used to identify a skeletonized body from the remaining teeth. Not only are forensic anthropologists of enormous help during the recovery of human bones, they are able to confirm that the remains are human, segregate the commingled remains of multiple individuals, and make estimations — based on a wealth of accumulated knowledge — about characteristics likely to assist in identifying those who might otherwise remain John and Jane Does.

C.A. Pound Human Identification Laboratory, University of Florida, Gainesville

Here lie bones burned and boiled, drowned and desiccated; bones that once lay buried, long forgotten, are now summoned back suddenly into the light of day; bones of martyred innocents, and bones of double-dyed murderers, all lying side by side, equal and silent beneath the impartial eye of science. We have few living visitors, and those who are admitted must show they have good reason to enter. But the dead are welcomed, and we show them every courtesy.
—*William R. Maples and Michael Browning [1994].*

William Maples called the laboratory he founded a "fleshless village of the dead." He describes, "Bones creamy white, butterscotch yellow, dirty gray, sooty black, tangled and tumbled, boxed and loose, articulated and arrayed: a whole community of skeletons is kept here under lock and key, entrusted by chance and the state of Florida to my care" (Maples and Browning 1994). Most of the skeletons are out of sight, stored in boxes that line the shelves of the back wall. The bones in the boxes represent hundreds of active cases — unknowns or homicide victims — dating back to 1974. "'Active' is a relative term," says current director Anthony Falsetti (personal correspondence, January 28, 1999). "But, I curate them all, because someday…. Everybody deserves a name." Dr. Maples began accepting forensic cases in 1972, when he was the curator of the Florida Museum of Natural History. With an increasing caseload, a generous endowment from friend and University of Florida graduate C. Addison Pound, Jr., and matching funds from the State of Florida, Maples established the C.A. Pound Human Identification Laboratory in 1991. The laboratory, on the campus of the University of Florida in Gainesville, functions as a subunit within the Department of Anthropology. Dr. Maples designed the lab himself and equipped it with two ventilation systems, three odor hoods, a safety shower, and a security system to protect the chain of custody of evidence. Dr. Falsetti came to the lab in 1996 from the National Museum of Health and Medicine and worked with William Maples for about six months until Maples' death in 1997.

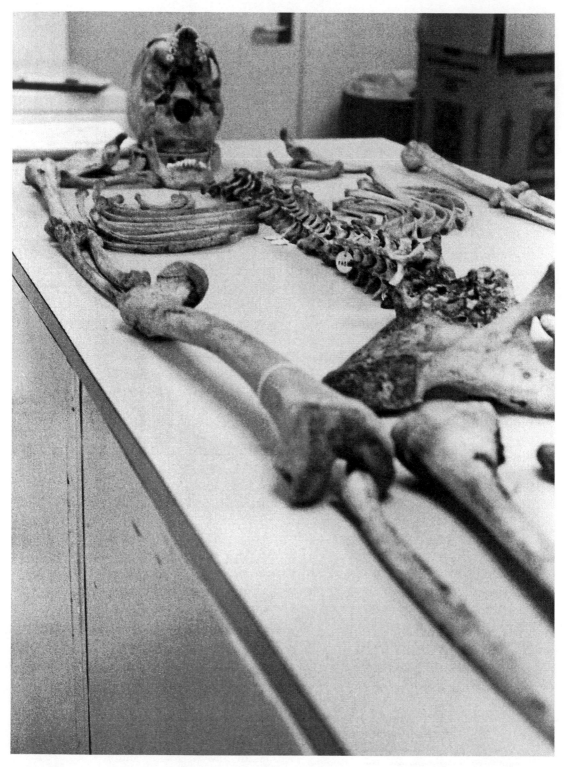

The bones of a skeleton placed in anatomically correct position for analysis. Photo courtesy of the C.A. Pound Human Identification Laboratory, University of Florida, Gainesville.

Handling between 100 and 120 cases annually, the Pound Lab is now one of the busiest forensic anthropology laboratories in the country. Although it doesn't have a formal mission statement, the lab's purpose is to identify human remains and analyze skeletal trauma and pathology. This purpose is carried out by its director, a secretary, a part-time lab manager, a half dozen graduate students, visiting fellows, and fourth-year medical students from the university. The work is done mainly for Florida law enforcement agencies and the state's 24 medical examiners, but extends outside the state to include a number of cases of national and international interest. While they sometimes receive cases from the military and from civilians requesting consultation, they are under contract with the New York State Police, the Suffolk County Police in Onandaga, New York, and the Dallas Police Department. Falsetti is frequently required to testify in court and he and his staff are often called on to recover remains from the scene. When remains are received in the lab, they are fumigated, if necessary, to rid them of any insects. Adhering soft tissue is removed by maceration. Chemicals are not used during the cleaning process in the event that recovery of DNA from the bones is warranted. DNA testing is done at an outside facility and only at the request of the agency with which they are working. Any bullet fragments discovered among the remains are turned over to the appropriate law enforcement agency unless they are embedded in the bone. Each bone is numbered in India ink with an assigned case number. The bones are inventoried, reconstructed if necessary, photographed, and x-rayed. Sex and race are determined when possible, and epiphyseal unions are examined to estimate age. As many as 78 measurements are recorded. A detailed dental record is completed and dental radiographs are sometimes made to assist in identification.

The laboratory is a training ground for graduate students in forensic anthropology and forensic pathology. Unlike other academic units, research on the skeletal remains is not published because of their status as active forensic cases. Unlike the proverbial dissecting room, where bodies are the butts of jokes and the subjects of student pranks, the C.A. Pound Lab has maintained a respectful attitude under its previous and current director. "I do not allow my students to dress up a skeleton, to put hats on skeletons, or to put cigarettes in their mouths. I do not allow them to give the skeletons humorous names, like Roscoe or Alphonse or anything of that nature," wrote Maples. "[I]t is my belief that every set of remains deserves a certain minimum of respect. We owe them that" (Maples and Browning (1994). Falsetti, who studied under William Bass at the University of Tennessee, always treats the human remains with respect. The work at the lab is serious business and the staff is earnest about carrying it out. Having seen their share of bludgeoned skulls, they are building a collection of tools — some of them donated by the manufacturers — to match the marks they see on bones with tool mark comparisons they make on soft wood. Evidence such as the number of blows a set of marks represents is crucial, since striking more than once indicates intent. With a closed-cabinet x-ray machine and the capability of processing black and white film on site, the lab has also carried out photographic and radiographic superimpositions. When remains are successfully identified, they are returned to the medical examiner, who completes a death certificate and releases them to the family, or — with the medical examiner's permission — to the funeral home chosen by the family.

In addition to the skeletal material that is associated with active cases, the laboratory has received five donated skeletons and has purchased two adult teaching skeletons and a fetal skeleton. The specimens they have examined over the years include individuals of all ages, including the remains of a teenager they are currently trying to identify. They have handled two trophy skulls and they curate the remains of two Native Americans, one of which came from an autopsy collection. As a consequence of Florida's Buried Body Law, which makes any remains more than 75 years old the property of the State Archaeologist, the lab has received several sets of bones that are 100 years old or more and that are — as the property of a government agency — subject to NAGPRA. Although Falsetti states (personal correspondence, May 20, 1999) that he is not actively collecting skeletal remains for the purpose of building a teaching collection, the number of remains at the lab grows as they continue to store unidentified remains at the request of various medical examiners who lack the space to do so.

6

Repatriation

Until recently, the issue of reburial has been polarized into two major camps — those advocating universal reburial and those advocating permanent preservation in repositories. With the parties firmly entrenched at these extremes, there has been little or no opportunity to compromise. It has become increasingly clear that there is too much at stake to allow such a confrontation to persist.
— Douglas H. Ubelaker and Lauryn Guttenplan Grant [1989]

It is difficult to compromise when there seems to be no middle ground. Most Native American groups are opposed to any analysis of Indian remains and call for repatriation and reburial. The majority of physical anthropologists believe that the bones of prehistoric American Indians should not only be examined and tested, but should remain available so that the results of those tests can be confirmed and future technologies can be used to draw even more information from them. With the passage of the Native American Graves Protection and Repatriation Act (NAGPRA) in 1990, the United States government gave the advantage to the Native Americans, putting the burden on museums and other institutions that receive federal funds to accommodate them. The legislation attempts to right past wrongs and recognizes the spiritual attachment that Native Americans feel toward their ancestors. But the law has been faulted for several reasons, not least of which is the vague definition and determination of that ancestry. To whom do the bones belong? To those who claim direct descendence or those who consider them part of our collective human heritage? Who should be given precedence? Those whose respect for the remains demands their burial or those whose respect is characterized by careful curation and study? Are the firmly held beliefs of these two groups mutually exclusive?

In general, Native Americans view their treatment and the treatment of the remains of their ancestors by anthropologists as ethnocentric and arrogant. In their opinion, the nineteenth-century view of Indians as specimens has been carried into the twenty-first century as their bones are begrudgingly returned for burial. They feel that scientists have belittled their beliefs and have excluded them from participating in the research of their own history (Thomas 2000). But even these generalities are oversimplified. There is no universal mindset among Native Americans regarding the repatriation issue, although many tribes have certain beliefs in common and they have joined forces in various combinations to reclaim their dead. Native Americans are almost unanimous in their belief that the exhumation and study of human remains is a spiritual violation. Most are also strongly opposed to any testing techniques that deface the skeleton and find the public display of skeletal remains and publication of

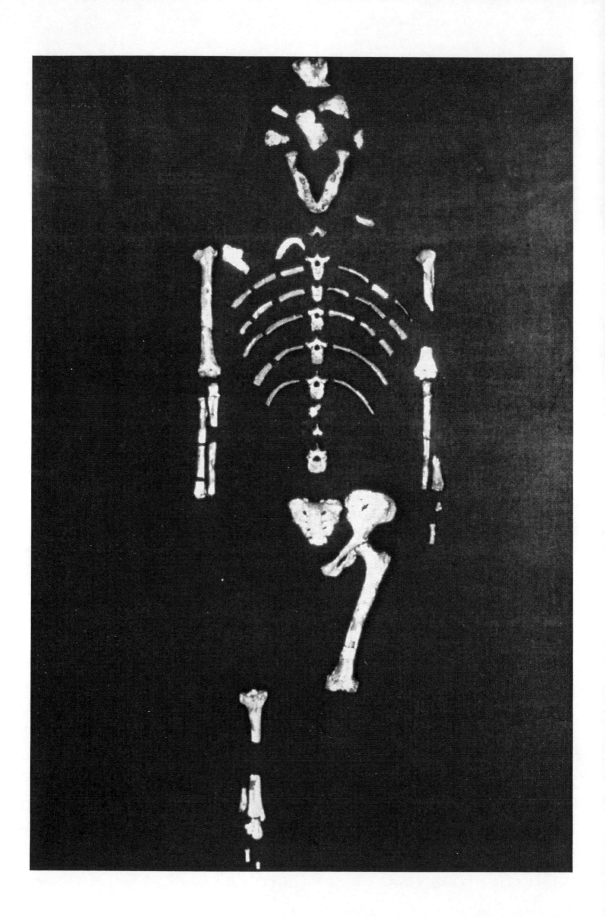

photographs of them particularly offensive. They often feel that curated bones are "imprisoned" and that excavation, analysis, and storage prevent the normal passage of the soul and cause spiritual ailments among the living (Ubelaker and Grant 1989). "Most Native Americans believe that respect for the dead is more important than any knowledge of the past that might be gained by digging up graves," they explain (Echo-Hawk and Echo-Hawk 1994). Some Native Hawaiians believe that even the publication of information about skeletal collections harms the spirits of the dead (Walker, In press).

Some Native American groups, including American Indians Against Desecration (AID), are more militant than others, insisting that any activity inconsistent with reburial is an act of desecration and disrespect and that their oral history does not need to be supplemented by data derived from human remains (Ubelaker and Grant 1989). Phillip L. Walker (In press) points out that because scientific research aimed at documenting the past may conflict with traditional beliefs, it has the potential to undermine the authority of tribal leaders and may thus be seen as subversive. But not all Native American tribes object to the scientific investigation of their past. Tribes including the Zuni, Navajo, Makah, and Pequot operate their own archaeological research programs (McManamon 1995). While the Navajo employ a non–Indian archaeologist to deal with human remains, since for them it is taboo even to speak about the dead, the Chumash Indians of southern California have traditionally had a member whose familiarity with the human skeleton allowed this "custodian of the algebra," as he was called, to arrange the bones in anatomical order and to determine whether they had

belonged to a man or woman, skills that were useful during the frequent relocations of their cemeteries (Walker In press). Those tribes willing to consider alternatives to reburial — for instance, storing the remains on Indian land and allowing access to scholars at their discretion — may find museums more receptive to repatriation requests (Ubelaker and Grant 1989). Some tribes may, however, disagree with the conclusions drawn by non–Indian researchers. The Hopi, for instance, suggest explanations other than cannibalism for the indicative signs Arizona State University researcher Christy Turner has found on the skeletal remains of their ancestors, the Anasazi.

Native Americans work hard not to lose any of the ground they have gained. Many tribal leaders believe that compromise will be misconstrued as a sign of weakness (Thomas 2000). In many cases, the skeletons become much more than the sum of their parts. As Walker (In press) states, "[I]t is easy for the control of bones and burial sites to become enmeshed in larger battles over unrelated economic and social issues concerning the control of land and natural resources, environmental preservation, and so on." Insensitivity toward Native American remains, including the ways in which they are stored by researchers, is seen as a symptom of the disrespect that their modern counterparts feel from the scientific community. This perceived disrespect has a long, unflattering history that the scientists acknowledge. The double standard in which white graves were protected and Indian graves excavated was exemplified by the characterization in the 1906 Antiquities Act of native remains as archaeological resources to be permanently curated in public museums. Museums amassed staggering numbers of Indian remains and artifacts to preserve this "dying culture"

Opposite: **The skeleton of "Lucy," discovered in Hadar, Ethiopia, in 1974 by Donald C. Johanson and Tom Gray. Reprinted with permission of the Institute of Human Origins.**

before they realized Native Americans were not going to vanish (Echo-Hawk and Echo-Hawk 1994). Anthropologists do not defend the fathers of their fields, who collected their raw material from fresh graves and looted sites, except to say that they were unrestricted by the sense of ethical responsibility that now guides the physical sciences. They do defend their right to conduct research on existing collections of human remains, even though those remains may have been unethically procured, unless a direct biological relationship can be established between the bones and their claimants. They do not feel that curation is disrespectful and make this assertion collectively. Ethical guidelines adopted by many professional associations and governmental agencies dictate treating human remains with dignity and respect, allowing descendants to control the disposition of the remains of their relatives, and preserving archaeological collections of human remains in order to understand human history. While these principles assume that human bones can and will be treated with dignity while in scientists' custody, Walker (In press) points out that they contain an inherent contradiction between the rights of descendants and the preservation ethic.

At the heart of the matter are two widely divergent understandings of the practice of respect:

> To a scientist, respectful treatment of human remains includes taking measures to insure the physical integrity of the remains and the documentation associated with them, avoiding treatments that will contaminate or degrade their organic and inorganic constituents, and so on. These convoluted academic arguments about the definition of and justification for treating human remains with respect, of course, seem bizarre to indigenous people who view ancestral remains, not as inanimate objects devoid of life but instead as living entities that are imbued with ancestral spirits [Walker, In press].

Walker (In press) notes that skeletal biologists are increasingly being forced to adapt their activities to the value systems of the descendants of the people they study, and yet their own values differ dramatically, since surveys have shown that anthropologists are less likely than most Americans to believe that individual beings continue to exist in an afterlife. To Native Americans, bones in a sense have a soul. To scientists, they are bodies of knowledge that can be deciphered if one learns the language. It is therefore no surprise that George Armelagos, past president of the American Association of Physical Anthropologists, has compared the repatriation of human remains to losing a wing of the Library of Congress and others have likened the burial of skeletal samples to the burning of single-copy manuscripts (White 1991).

Scientists mourn the loss of irreplaceable skeletal material: "Specimens of inestimable scientific value, such as the earliest known case of tuberculosis in the New World, are currently scheduled for reburial, and the fossil remains of the earliest hominids to reach the continent of Australia have already been returned to the ground" (Chamberlain 1994). Early on in the debate, Jane E. Buikstra (1981) detailed the problems introduced by reburial. She pointed out that unrealistic deadlines for reburial deny physical anthropologists the opportunity to recheck their results, allowing them to introduce errors into databases. She also called into question the possibility of later exhumation. The re-excavation of reburied bones would not only be costly, but would add the effects of the reburial on the bones to many other variables. "We are discussing here, in the question of reburial of prehistoric human skeletons, the important issue of direct control and limitation to the development of knowledge and advancement of science. That this knowledge can be of direct benefit to mankind must be recognized, as well as the fact that we risk severely limiting our ability to interpret the past" (Buikstra 1981).

Like the Native Americans, the archaeologists and anthropologists have organizations that are more confrontational in their approach to the issues. The mission statement of the American Committee for Preservation of Archaeological Collections (ACPAC) states, "We reconfirm the professional and ethical duty of scholars to observe their responsibility to preserve and maintain for study by qualified scholars all archaeological collections obtained in the course of field investigations. Archaeological collections are defined as including historic and prehistoric artifacts, skeletal remains, faunal and floral specimens, soil samples, and all other materials removed from archaeological sites for purposes of study and investigation." ACPAC urges individual archaeologists not to participate in projects where the collected material will be given up for destruction, urges teachers to instruct their students of the duty to preserve data for examination by others, and urge scholarly organizations in archaeology to enforce their statements of ethics and to expel professionals for complicity in acts of destruction. In this politically-charged climate in which Native Americans were making claims on human remains with which they were only loosely affiliated, museums began to protect their holdings fiercely. Their concerns were whether Native Americans without a proven direct lineal descent had legal standing (a direct, personal stake in the matter) to bring suit and whether deviating from their traditional method of handling claims against their collections would weaken their ability to defend against all other claims (Malari 1998). The policy of the American Association of Museums is to establish categories of repatriation cases based on circumstances of acquisition, age of the remains, and existence of living descendants. "All of these factors are considered and a balancing test is conducted to determine whether the religious and cultural interests of Native Americans outweigh the scientific interests of museums" (Ubelaker and Grant 1989).

Ethicists support case-by-case negotiations when implementing policies of repatriation. Lynne Goldstein and Keith Kintigh (1990) favor changes in the decision-making structure that will allow Native concerns to be equitably considered, but would like to put some limits on the legitimacy of the claims. They also lay out a prescription for ethical conduct, respect, sensitivity, and tolerance. They state that human remains should only be collected or retained by an institution if their preservation, study, and interpretation are called for as part of that institution's mission. They suggest consulting with relevant living cultural groups before undertaking projects that will result in the collection of human remains, whether or not it is legally mandated. They remind that such material should be interpreted accurately, sensitively, and with respect, and encourage involving the appropriate groups in the interpretation and dissemination of that information. In their opinion, institutions should complete inventories of their collections, despite the financial burden, and should share the information they have accumulated, even if it is limited. "In terms of what we have to do in the immediate future, giving back the bones would probably be the easiest immediate solution. But, what's easiest is not necessarily what's right or ethical," they write (Goldstein and Kintigh 1990), but they acknowledge that there is some material that should not be curated by museums and other institutions. In a contrasting viewpoint, Anthony L. Klesert and Shirley Powell (1993) argue that repatriation is not an infringement of academic freedom and that the study of the prehistoric past is not the exclusive domain of scientists: "Archaeologists have no intrinsic right to survey, excavate, or manipulate the material remains of the past, and their failure to understand this constraint is, we believe, the source of the current and continued contention between archaeologists and Native Americans." In their opinion, buried human remains should not be disturbed unless it is unavoidable, disposition of all excavated remains should be negotiated with descendant populations, and exceptions should be made on an individual basis only in the case of extraordinary scientific value (Klesert and Powell 1993).

In their defense, scientists attempt to rectify some of the misconceptions surrounding the collection of human skeletal material. Anthropologists correct the notion that Native American remains were singled out for curation and are disproportionately represented in skeletal collections: "Bioarchaeologists respond to this charge by pointing out the vast collections of non–Native American skeletal remains in European museums and arguing that it would be racist not to have collections of Native American remains in New World museums, since this would imply that knowledge of the history of the indigenous people of the New World had nothing to contribute to the understanding of our common past" (Ubelaker and Grant 1989). They explain that the composition of collections largely reflects the geographical setting and history of the areas in which they are located. North American collections contain representatives of blacks and whites, but the largest percentage comprises American Indians, Aleuts, and Eskimos, since these groups occupied North America for thousands of years before other groups arrived. Neither are American Indians the only group whose remains have been sought after by institutions outside their native country, as Mike Parker Pearson (1999) notes: "All around the world museums are full of cultural remains gathered far and wide over the last few centuries by antiquarians, archaeologists, adventurers and treasure hunters. Local communities and even national states have had the material remains of their past

and even their dead taken away for storage and exhibition in a faraway museum."

Physical anthropologists point out ways in which the study of Native American remains benefits contemporary Indians. From bones, scientists can establish several aspects of past cultures and many physical characteristics of past populations. Deciphering DNA from ancient remains may establish genetic links among past populations and lend insight into ancestral relationships. Studies of cemetery assemblages reveal not only the burial customs of an ancient society, but clues to social structure, demographic makeup, and health status. Such studies are motivated by sincerity — rather than the selfishness, personal advancement, and individual gain that researchers are sometimes accused of— and most scientists believe it would be wasteful and wrong not to take advantage of skeletal clues to past lives, as Stanley Rhine (1998) argues:

> The current desire of many native peoples to see the skeletons of their ancestors reburied out of reach of Anglo anthropologists is understandable on one level, but it deprives them of the opportunity to learn things about their ancestors that they can learn in no other way. It is sad if one believes that the remains of one's ancestors are being studied by outsiders primarily to burnish their own reputations and only secondarily to add to our store of knowledge, but it is sadder still to think that those ancestral voices will be forever muted by reburial. It is through research on skeletons that we come to understand something of what it was like to have been alive in a place and time other than our own. Not to conduct such research is to deprive ourselves (and others as yet unborn) of the opportunity to look through a unique window into the past — deliberately to choose ignorance over knowledge, a choice that flies in the face of what it means to be human.

The value of osteological research is also demonstrated by its use in prosecuting the looters and grave robbers of ancient Indian sites (Walker In press). And Native American remains are an integral part of large skeletal collections that have been used to devise forensic standards with which to identify the victims of mass disasters (Buikstra 1981).

In order for the research on human skeletal remains to have continued value, explain physical anthropologists, the evidence upon which the conclusions are based must remain available to future researchers. In this way, the studies may be repeated and refined (analyzing for any distortions, using new techniques, and applying fresh theoretical perspectives), making the field — like other sciences — self-correcting (Walker In press). This assumption has itself been studied. In 1981, Buikstra and Gordon examined 310 articles utilizing 724 skeletal series and found that a third of the series had been previously studied. Of this third, two thirds provided data for new research and the remaining third restudied earlier conclusions, reaching different conclusions and using newly available techniques in two out of three instances (Ubelaker and Grant 1989). "In other words," writes Buikstra (1981), "had the skeletal series not been available for re-study because they were reburied, our interpretation of the past would be incomplete or simply incorrect — given new scientific developments." The loss of skeletal collections is looked at in terms of the future of science and its practitioners:

> As scientists, we are aware that the loss of collections may hamper the continuation of research that we consider vital to the Native American community and to society at large. To prevent such a loss, it is our view that professional curation and study should precede the repatriation process. Otherwise, the education of future generations, full of questions, will be limited to our present store of knowledge and restricted by our inaccuracies and omissions. Although possessed of more advanced technological skills, they will

not have the opportunity to investigate these issues and validate these observations firsthand. Gaining a better understanding of the Native American and European-American past through the study of skeletal remains and burial artifacts is a highly valued enterprise [Owsley and Jantz 1994].

In addition to piecing together the past, collections of human remains are necessary to train forensic anthropologists to carry out identification procedures (Buikstra 1981). Permanent curation is supported by the American Association of Physical Anthropologists, the American Society of Forensic Sciences, the American Committee for Preservation of Archaeological Collections, the Ethnic Minority Council of America, the Paleopathology Association, and the Canadian Association for Physical Anthropology (Ubelaker and Grant 1989).

In cases where skeletal remains can be identified as those of a known individual or can be proven to have specific biological descendants, scientists agree that the closest living relatives should determine their fate. In the case of indigenous remains, however, even determining which relative is the closest (spouse, children, parents, then siblings) imposes the Western kinship system of the dominant society (Walker In Press). But disagreement about when and to whom to repatriate is magnified when the relationship to the living is distant. The more distant an ancestor is from a descendant, the more descendants there are sharing a genetic relationship to that ancestor. This would certainly include great numbers of people who are unaware of that relationship and uninvolved in the decisions based upon it. But many modern indigenous people do not accept the idea that the ancestor-descendant relationship becomes attenuated with time, nor do they see themselves as closely related to the rest of humanity (Walker In press). Ancestral remains may become a symbol of survival to Indian groups with dwindling numbers, despite a tenuous genetic link. The leeway allowed in assessing cultural continuity and tribal affiliation may also lead to conflicting claims for a single skeletal collection. Anthropologists argue, on the other hand, that ancient bones belong not to one group or another, but both. C. Turner pleads, "I explicitly assume that no living culture, religion, interest group, or biological population has any moral or legal right to the exclusive use or regulation of ancient human skeletons since all humans are members of a single species, and ancient skeletons are the remnants of unduplicable evolutionary events which all living and future peoples have the right to know about and understand. In other words, ancient human skeletons belong to everyone" (Ubelaker and Grant 1989).

The issues surrounding repatriation are fraught with contradictions. Some Native Americans object to the scientific study of the bones, and yet the determination of cultural affiliation necessitates their analysis so that they can be returned to the appropriate tribe. Native Americans believe that they are spiritually linked to all other Native American people, living and dead, and yet show concern that the repatriated bones of their tribespeople may include the bones of some of their ancestors' traditional enemies and are fearful of burying non-group members in their cemeteries. Native Americans may cherish the idea that their past lives on in the present and reject the notion that the remains of their people who lived in the past may provide the means to advance the lives of those who are alive today. Anthropologists are educated to respect other cultures, but to honor Native American beliefs (and to abide by the law) they must give up the material upon which they base their scholarship and their livelihood. And anthropologists continue to study cultural variation among Indian populations at a time when contemporary Native Americans are cultivating a growing sense of unified identity.

LEGISLATION

National Museum of the American Indian (NMAI) Act

Repatriation in the U.S. began at the Smithsonian Institution with the passage of the National Museum of the American Indian (NMAI) Act in 1989. NMAI established a National Museum of the American Indian that was intended to receive the Aboriginal collections of the Heye Foundation of New York, which were to be placed in a new facility in Washington, D.C. The new museum would also process repatriation requests. The act required that all human remains in the Smithsonian's collections be inventoried, documented, and returned — if requested — to culturally-affiliated, federally recognized Native American groups. Final inventories were due in June 1998, but no deadlines were established for claims. In 1991, the Smithsonian established a Repatriation Office at the National Museum of Natural History. The primary task of the Repatriation Office is to determine cultural affiliation (through analysis of biological, geographical, historical, genealogical, archaeological, linguistic, folkloric, ethnological, and archival information) and to summarize and report their findings. In the laboratory established as part of the Repatriation Office, osteologists, skeletal biologists, a dentist-radiographer, and a photographer document the remains using a protocol implemented in 1993. The protocol evaluates information obtained through physical examination; archaeological, anthropological, and museum records; and other means to form a permanent record that includes a list of skeletal remains present, photographs, x-rays, estimates of age and sex of each individual, information on health and diet, and descriptions of the bones' conditions, differences in shape, and any intentional modifications. The act requires that the museum offer to return the remains of any Native American individuals whose identity is known — which, along with honoring requests for any illegally acquired material, has long been a policy of the Smithsonian — and any Native remains determined to be demonstrably related to a present-day tribe. Claims may be made by lineal descendants of named individuals or representatives of the approximately 250 federally recognized Native American, Native Alaskan, and Native Hawaiian tribes or groups. Claims falling outside the stated guidelines are considered on a case by case basis, according to the website (www.nmnh.si.edu/anthro/repatriation/page1.htm) for the National Museum of Narural History.

Since 1991, the Repatriation Office has documented a growing percentage of the more than 16,000 sets of remains in the collections. Repatriation reports are available (online in summary and in writing in full) for dozens of tribes, including the Apache, Arapaho, Blackfeet, Cheyenne, Chippewa, Comanche, Cree, Crow, Iroquois, Mohegan, Mashantucket Pequot, Osage, Paiute, Pawnee, Shoshone, and Sioux. The Smithsonian also encourages alternatives to repatriation, including long-term loans, secured storage, transfer of the remains to regional or native museums, or retention by the museum under the joint care of the institution and the tribe.

Native American Graves Protection and Repatriation Act (NAGPRA)

The Native American Graves Protection and Repatriation Act (NAGPRA) was signed into law by President George Bush in November 1990. Excepting the Smithsonian Institution, which is governed by the National Museum of the American Indian Act, NAGPRA applies to museums that function as a department, agency, or instrumentality of the U.S.; any state or local government; and any institution that receives federal funds (Malari 1998). These muse-

ums, institutions, and agencies were obliged to provide to the National Park Service and all federally recognized Native American groups a summary of their holdings by November 1993. By November 1995, they were to have completed inventories of their collections, indicating cultural affiliations when determined (Malari 1998). Cultural affiliation is defined as a shared identity that can be reasonably traced between an identifiable earlier group and an identifiable present-day tribe or group. The statute applies to Native American human remains, whether or not they came from a burial site. Failure to comply puts a museum's federal funding in jeopardy.

While the law clearly attempts to redress the grievances of Native Americans, they and non–Native Americans find fault with it for a number of reasons. Museums, universities, and other institutions maintaining collections of human remains have had to devote resources that would otherwise have been spent on research and education to documentation of their skeletal collections, communication with Native American groups, and development of new policy (Ubelaker and Grant 1989). Claimants under NAGPRA must belong to a federally recognized tribe, which excludes authentic descendant groups that have either failed to receive or have rejected federal tribal recognition and the many people of Native American descent who lack any tribal affiliation. The law is therefore derided by some Native Americans who see it as the latest in a long history of attempts to define tribes in ways that facilitate their control and manipulation by oppressive governmental agencies (Walker In press). Another objection to the legislation is couched in terms of religious freedom: "The Constitution was supposed to treat all religions equally ... but under NAGPRA, Indians find themselves forced to defend their faith publicly against an array of scientific evidence marshaled by museum directors, archaeologists, National Park Service personnel, and state historians" (Thomas 2000). In fact, Native American obligations toward the dead are experienced as much through spiritual bonds, symbolic identifications, and psychological relationships as through genetic or ethnic ties (Davidson 1991). Spiritual beliefs, though, do not constitute a valid argument for the repatriation of human remains. According to Ubelaker and Grant (1989), the Supreme Court holds that the retention of materials does not infringe upon the right to religious freedom and not a single lawsuit has been brought in the U.S. against a repository of Native American skeletal remains under the First Amendment.

An especially contentious area is the disposition of "culturally unidentifiable" human remains, which include those associated with a tribe that is not federally recognized, those for which no present-day tribe exists, cases where there is insufficient evidence to make a determination of affiliation, and remains for which no information exists. NAGPRA urges speedy repatriation of such remains as "the most reasonable and consistent choice" since they have "little educational, historical or scientific value," an assumption that the American Association of Physical Anthropologists (AAPA) takes issue with, pointing out in a position statement (http://physanth.org/Positions.htm) the value of remains even when they do not retain contextual information and urging that choices other than repatriation be negotiated between the institutions and the groups that have an interest in collections of culturally unidentifiable remains. They urge a more balanced approach, since much can be learned from these bones. The AAPA also objects to giving groups that have been consulted as a courtesy the right to determine the fate of unaffiliated remains, since testing on them may only be performed if all the parties consulted agree to it. Determining cultural affiliation is a difficult business and is in part based on the territories of ancient and current tribes. When ancient human remains are discovered in the U.S., they are often assigned to a tribe on a purely geographical basis. But basing claims to the remains of hunter-gatherers on their geographic location is more likely to repatriate those remains to tribes that displaced them (Walker In press). Even when tribes weren't displaced, their territories often overlapped, and yet a modern counterpart must be chosen and notified before the remains may be examined to assess cultural affinities.

One of the benefits of NAGPRA, explained Eve Cockburn in her welcoming remarks during an August 1998 meeting of the European members of the Paleopathology Association, is that it has prompted the scientific community to realize just how valuable collections of human skeletons are for the knowledge of our biological history and to draw up detailed standards for skeletal examination. In addition, the crisis atmosphere has stimulated the funding and conducting of research on threatened collections that until recently had been studied only minimally (Ubelaker and Grant 1989). The National Science Foundation, the University of Tennessee, and the Smithsonian Institution, for instance, sponsored a major interdisciplinary effort organized by Douglas Owsley to study the W.H. Over collection prior to its repatriation (Ubelaker 1994). The only available response to the growing concern over the curation of human skeletal remains, Aboriginal and otherwise, is to take advantage of every opportunity to document and study them within the confines of federal legislation, state law, institutional policy, and the politically charged climate in which researchers find themselves. The results of their research will survive the specimens if it fails to convince their descendants and the public of the scientific value of their preservation.

State Laws

> *For the archaeologist the human skeleton is sometimes an awkward "find" that may seem time-consuming and complicated to record and excavate. Unlike that of most other finds, the legal status of buried skeletons can be uncertain, and the excavator also needs to be aware of the sensibilities of local communities. The opportunity to research the skeletal biology of past populations is nevertheless a valuable one, even when the remains are ultimately destined for reburial.*
> *— Andrew Chamberlain [1994].*

The unexpected discovery of human remains during an excavation immediately raises red flags. The appropriate next step depends upon the location of the remains (whether on federal, state, tribal, local, or private land) and the age of the burial (and therefore whether it falls under the responsibility of the medical examiner or the state archaeologist). Most state laws require that when remains are discovered, the excavation cease immediately and local law enforcement officials be notified. Typically, if remains are determined to be more than 100 years old, the state archaeologist is charged with determining whether they are Native American (Ubelaker and Grant 1989). Increasingly, however, states have attempted to legislate collections of remains previously recovered and have patterned new laws or modified laws on NAGPRA. In some cases, the laws have an even wider reach than NAGPRA, covering not just Native American remains but all human remains — even those in private collections, and establishing prohibitions against excavating, exhibiting, and curating them. In Delaware, for instance, all human remains within the state that were above ground as of June 1987 were to be reinterred within one year. New discoveries of Native American remains that were not of medicolegal significance were to be reinterred within 90 days based on the recommention of the Native American Skeletal Remains Committee. The strict,

retroactive statutes in Delaware were a response to lobbying by the local Nanticoke tribe against a 20-year-old in situ exhibit of the remains of 127 skeletons in a prehistoric cemetery at the Island Field Museum in South Bowers. The remains from all of the state's museums and repositories were reburied in 1988 in airtight containers, which allows the possibility of future research, but it and the testing of samples taken before reburial will have to have the consent of the committee (Ubelaker and Grant 1989, Price 1991). In 1989, Minnesota gave title to all affiliated and unaffiliated human remains to the newly formed Minnesota Indian Affairs Council. The council thus became responsible for determining the fate of approximately 2,000 skeletons — including a couple nearly 10,000 years old — gathered over the last century and curated by the University of Minnesota, the Minnesota Historical Society, the Science Museum, and other agencies. The bones are first examined by an osteologist at Hamline University, but the majority have already been turned over to the Minnesota Sioux for reburial.

The majority of states allow the study of native remains before they are reinterred, but often that window of opportunity is considered too short. Iowa's law precludes long-term, problem-oriented research by requiring reburial of prehistoric skeletal remains and by allowing excavation only when burials are already accidentally exposed (Buikstra 1981). Maine's Indian Bones Law requires that from October 1973 onward all publicly and privately held Native American skeletal material must be transferred to appropriate tribes in Maine for reburial after the scientific study of the remains by anthropologists or archaeologists for a period of one year (Price 1991). In other states, by law or negotiation, longer periods are allowed for study. H. Marcus Price III (1991) writes of Hawaii, "A number of burial treatment/reinterment plans have been worked out to all parties' satisfaction. All cases except one [because it was too fragmentary] have undergone osteological analysis, one of which was done at the request of the lineal descendants." The University of Kentucky Museum of Anthropology accepts excavated remains for curation and attempts to identify affiliated Indian groups for advice on disposition of the remains following scientific analysis (Price 1991). The Cleveland Museum of Natural History recommended in 1982 that remains removed through salvage archaeology be curated for a four-year period, during which they were to be identified if possible and curated permanently if they could not be proven to relate to a particular group. South Dakota allows five years for scientific study before remains are reburied (Ubelaker and Grant 1989).

Some states allow permanent curation in an appropriate facility as an alternative to reburial. Washington State prohibits disturbance of a burial unless destined for reburial or perpetual preservation in a duly recognized archaeological repository (Ubelaker and Grant 1989). The State of Illinois has designated the Illinois State Museum as a human skeletal repository and does not mandate reinterment (Price 1991). The Illinois Human Skeletal Remains Protection Act adopted in 1992 establishes guidelines for excavation and for the disposition of recovered bones. Archaeological remains excavated under permit and unclaimed remain the property of the state and are curated by the museum, which makes them available for scientific inquiry by qualified researchers and lends them to other educational institutions. Non-compliance with the act results in the assessment of civil damages, the forfeiture of equipment, and the reimbursement of the costs involved in restoring the site, including the curation or reinterment of skeletal remains.

Included in some of the state laws are sanctions against displaying human remains. In Delaware, the display of human remains is absolutely forbidden (Ubelaker and Grant 1989). In the State of Montana, display of human remains is legally prohibited (Price 1991). In Oregon, public display of remains or burial goods is a felony offense. Other states maintain a more tolerant view. Florida's law mandated the development of guidelines for display that do not restrict legal, medical, or educational use (Ubelaker and Grant 1989). The Illinois Human Skeletal Remains Protection Act includes a clause explicitly setting out the conditions under which display of human remains is justified and acceptable: "Human remains will be exhibited only in exceptional cases where the exhibit conveys an understanding of the lives of past peoples and insofar as the human remains are an integral part of the evidence of the past and contribute to an understanding of human culture." When the exhibit of human remains is not prohibited by state law, it is often discouraged as part of institutional policy. In some cases, plastic models have replaced natural bones in anatomical displays. The University of Kentucky Museum of Anthropology will only publicly display human skeletons in specific educational exhibits on human biology and paleopathology (Price 1991). In the 1980s, policies prohibiting the display of human remains were implemented by the U.S. Department of the Interior, the Department of Agriculture, and the U.S. Army Corps of Engineers. The Cleveland Museum of Natural History has had since 1987 a policy against public exhibition of human remains. The trend against displaying human skeletons to the public extends far beyond American borders, as a quote from the 1986 Code of Ethics of the International Council on Museums (Ubelaker and Grant 1989) shows: "Where a museum maintains and or is developing collections of human remains and sacred objects these should be securely housed and carefully maintained as archival collections in scholarly institutions, and should always be available to qualified researchers and educators, but not to the morbidly curious...."

LOSS OF COLLECTIONS IN THE UNITED STATES

However complex the underlying mechanisms, a sense of pan–Indian community persists and has taken on an international scope, as indigenous populations in areas colonized by foreign powers now look to the American aboriginal experience as a model.
— *H. Marcus Price III [1991]*

The estimated number of Native American remains in repositories in the United States varies depending on the source, but the number is dropping as the conditions of federal and state legislation are carried out. In the early 1990s, the Native American Rights Fund claimed that 600,000 specimens were located in museums, historical societies, universities, and private collections. The estimates by other Native groups were even higher, while the totals suggested by anthropologists were much more conservative. "It is certainly true that thousands of Indian skeletons were curated in America's natural history museums, virtually all of them obtained without consent of their Native American descendants. Indian people were justifiably horrified when they learned the scale of the museum holdings and the sometimes shocking circumstances under which the skeletons were acquired," writes David Hurst Thomas (2000). Of the total, some 100,000 to 200,000 remains were said to be eligible for return to native tribes under the law. Between 1990 and 1997, more than 5,300 human skeletons were repatriated. By January 1998, 264 public notices had appeared in the *Federal Register* announcing the willingness or intent by institutions to repatriate 10,000 sets of culturally affiliated human remains. For the Peabody Museum at Harvard University, which deaccessioned some of its skeletons in 1972 and 1976 in advance of the legal requirement to do so, the process of examining their collections revealed that they had in fact been underestimated. Assistant Director Barbara Isaac (1995) explains, "The collections at the Peabody are gargantuan. One of the byproducts of the NAGPRA inventory process has been to clarify the numbers of North American items in our care (themselves a fraction of the whole). Under our eyes these have increased, in the case of human remains, from an estimated 7,000 to about 10,000...."

In an effort to redress past wrongs, NAGPRA has tipped the scales in favor of Native Americans, mandating repatriation in all cases where cultural affiliation can be determined and encouraging it even when affiliation cannot be established. In one of the largest repatriations under this act, the University of Nebraska agreed in 1998 to turn over the remains of 1,702 Native Americans that had been excavated over several decades. The agreement was reached after representatives from tribes in Nebraska, Kansas, Iowa, Oklahoma, North Dakota, and South Dakota protested the discovery of 23 Indian skeletons in a laboratory in 1997 rather than a special storage building for native remains. More than 1,000 skeletons were to be returned to the Ponca, Pawnee, and Omaha tribes, and a memorial was to be built on campus. But university officials also agreed to release the 673 culturally unaffiliated skeletons for burial on the Omaha reservation in northeast Nebraska. Oklahoma Pawnees had to go through legal channels for access to another collection in Nebraska, this time at the State Historical Society. Despite orders issued by the state attorney general, the society sued the tribe to prevent them from researching the records indicating that the remains were procured without permits. After the passage of a state repatriation bill, more than 400

Pawnee remains were released and reburied in 1990. An enormous effort by the State of South Dakota in 1986 divested it of hundreds of Native American remains that formed most of a contentious collection of skeletal materials held at the Archaeological Research Center at Fort Meade. In this case, the bones underwent years of intensive study under the supervision of Arikara tribe elders prior to reburial (Price 1991).

In many cases, especially when remains are discovered during construction, some analysis is allowed before they are repatriated. When 450 Hohokam gravesites were found during the building of the Papago Freeway in Phoenix in 1989, a group of Gila River residents and others tracing their lineage to the Hohokam tribe agreed to allow Arizona State University to conduct limited non-destructive analysis provided the bones were reburied afterward. Curation and study was allowed to continue beyond the initial 90 days as the Gila River residents searched for a suitable reburial location. The remains were returned to the community in 1993 and reburied later that year. In contrast, 90 protohistoric skeletons from the Stoeser Site on the grounds of the Pierre Indian Learning Center were buried in 1989 by the Bureau of Land Management without even a cursory analysis (Willey 1990). Further examination of several particularly ancient American skeletons is being precluded by repatriation. Minnesota Woman (7,840 years old), Browns Valley Man (8,900 years old), and Saulk Valley Man (4,000 years old) have been returned to a coalition of Minnesota Sioux tribes who plan to rebury them. Buhl Woman (10,700 years old) from Idaho was reburied in 1992. The disposition of skeletons from Wizards Beach (9,200 years old) and Spirit Cave (9,400 years old) in Nevada is pending.

Not all Native American remains are lost to science through repatriation. Some, tossed aside by relic hunters, have been recovered and then reburied with or without adequate scientific analysis. Looting and amateur excavation have caused incalculable damage to certain prehistoric American sites. The Slack Farm site in western Kentucky is one of these. The site, which dates from about 1450 to 1650 A.D., is marked with holes where objects were removed in the mid–1980s. They had been located by probing the ground, in the process damaging many of the human remains, which were left scattered over the area. "You make all those probes because you're looking for the soft feel of bones," explains relic hunter Ed Hastings (who now only collects from the surface). "If you find bones, chances are you're going to find grave goods too. That's where the money is. The only bones they usually take are the whole skulls — people buy 'em as candle holders" (Arden 1989). In all, more than 450 holes had been dug and at least 650 graves disturbed. Human bones found at the site included jaws, legs, fingers, and teeth. The remains were studied at the State Medical Examiner's Office (for criminal evidence), the University of Kentucky (for scientific analysis), and then boxed and returned to Native Americans of the Six Nations Iroquois Confederacy — who had claimed them under a "friend of the deceased" provision of state law — for ceremonial reburial (Arden 1989). Tim D. White (1991) makes the point that the controversy surrounding repatriation overshadows the need to protect and preserve prehistoric sites: "In the face of this catastrophic decimation of the past's only record, the reburial issue could prove to be a costly diversion for all parties. The scientific community and native groups need to redirect their energies in a concerted effort to save and protect the heritage of the past before it disappears."

Kennewick Man, Kennewick, Washington

We didn't go digging for this man. He fell out— he was actually a volunteer. I think it would be wrong to stick him back in the

ground without waiting to hear the story he has to tell. We need to look at things as human beings, not as one race or another. The message this man brings to us is one of unification: there may be some commonality in our past that will bring us together.
— *James Chatters quoted by D. Preston [1997]*

It was luck, good or bad, that brought the remains of an ancient skeleton to light in Kennewick, Washington, in July 1996. Boat traffic and changes in the water level of a pooled part of the Columbia River caused the erosion that exposed the bones. Two college students then stumbled upon the skull and notified the police. The skull was turned over to Benton County Coroner Floyd Johnson, who enlisted the help of forensic anthropologist James Chatters, owner of the local consulting firm Applied Paleoscience. Johnson and Chatters recovered most of the rest of the skeleton from the river bank that evening. Only the sternum, a few rib fragments, and some of the small bones of the hands, wrists, and feet were missing from among the 380 bones and fragments, making the skeleton 80 to 90 percent complete (Gugliotta 1999). Chatters assessed the gender as male, height as 5'8" or 5'9", and age as 40 to 55 years. Features of the skull pointed to the remains of a Caucasoid, possibly a European settler, but a gray object lodged in the right ilium soon challenged that notion. The object was not visible in an x-ray, but a CT-scan revealed it to be a stone spearpoint that compares with the Cascade projectile points of the Pacific Northwest. Recurring infections from this wound may have caused death and Chatters speculated that the body may have been swept away in a flood during a fishing trip. Isotopic-carbon studies indicated that the man's diet was rich in marine food.

Chatters made a cast of the skull with the idea of having the face reconstructed. He was asked by the U.S. Army Corps of Engineers (COE), which controls the stretch of the Columbia River where the bones were found, to get a second opinion. He drove the remains to Ellensburg, Washington, where they were examined by Catherine J. MacMillan of the Bone-Apart Agency. She concurred that the skeleton belonged to a Caucasian male. With the permission of the coroner and the COE, Chatters sent the left fifth metacarpal bone to the University of California at Riverside for radiocarbon dating. In late August, the lab reported that the remains were between 9,300 and 9,600 years old, which made the find extremely important, newsworthy, and — as it turned out — contentious. Minutes after the Kennewick remains were examined by a third anthropologist, Grover S. Krantz of Washington State University, on August 30th, Chatters was ordered by Johnson to cease study of the bones at the insistence of the COE. Chatters regretted not having photographed the post-cranial skeleton, although he quickly made a videotaped record of the skeleton before relinquishing custody. "Am I going to be the last scientist to see those bones?" he wondered (Preston 1997).

The Kennewick area is generally recognized to have been used by many tribes. Claimants of Kennewick Man's remains — the Confederated Tribes of the Colville, the Nez Perce Tribe, the Confederated Tribes of the Umatilla, the Wanapum Band, and the Confederated Tribes and Bands of the Yakama Indian Nation — mirror this diversity, but were united in their outrage. The Native Americans submitted their formal claim under NAGPRA on September 9th, announcing their intention to bury the skeleton secretly and their anger that the remains had undergone scientific study. The COE capitulated immediately, running the required public notice of its intent to repatriate and observing the 30–day waiting period. Three prominent scientists wrote letters to the Corps stating that the loss to science would be incalculable if Kennewick

Man were reburied before being studied. Their pleas were ignored and similar requests by four congressmen were rebuffed. The COE was prevented from allowing reburial of the skeleton by a court order in 1997. But in defiance of Congress and with the flimsy excuse of halting further erosion, the COE covered the Kennewick site on April 6, 1998, with 600 tons of boulders, gravel, logs, and backdirt, on top of which they planted thousands of closely spaced trees (Thomas 2000).

The conflicting desires of scientists and the Native Americans have been brought into sharp focus during the controversy surrounding Kennewick Man. The Native Americans involved believe that the scientists have desecrated the bones by studying them. Conversely, the scientists believe that the Native Americans have tainted the remains by bringing them into contact with damaging materials during the ceremonies they have been allowed to conduct. They placed cedar boughs in the box with the bones and exposed them to contaminants including moisture, oils, pesticides, and bacteria. The scientists also take issue with the COE about the improper storage of the skeletal remains in uncushioned, unsupported plastic bags and fault them for field notes about the recovery of the remains that are characterized as difficult to decipher and incomplete. Scientists feel so strongly that their rights regarding the Kennewick remains have been trampled in favor of an overinterpretation of NAGPRA that they have sued to obtain access. In *Bonnichsen et al. v. United States of America*, eight archaeologists and physical anthropologists claim that Kennewick Man may not fall under the NAGPRA definition of "Native American" and the remains must be studied to determine cultural affiliation. They also argue that the freedom of expression protected by the U.S. Constitution also incorporates the right to gather and receive information (Thomas 2000). They are pursuing the suit

as individuals, since their academic institutions are reluctant to get involved in such a controversial lawsuit at a time when most of them are negotiating with tribes over their own collections (Preston 1997). The case of Kennewick Man may lead to changes in the existing law. A bill has already been introduced to modify NAGPRA with regard to the disposition of remains whose cultural affiliation cannot be determined (Pearson 1999).

Temporarily secured in the county sheriff's evidence locker, the Kennewick remains had been turned over in September 1996 to the COE, which directed that they be placed in a vault at the Pacific Northwest National Laboratory in Richland, Washington. The bones were transferred to the Burke Museum in Seattle in October 1998. In March of that year, the Department of the Interior had been charged with determining whether the bones meet the definition of "Native American" under NAGPRA and, based on their conclusions, determining their disposition. A team was convened to analyze the Kennewick skeleton and included scientists, conservators, and personnel from the U.S. Army Corps of Engineers. The team met with five tribal groups to outline current investigations and continued study. To accommodate tribal objections to destructive testing, nondestructive investigations were carried out, including physical examination, modification of the existing inventory of the bones to indicate the disappearance of portions of both femora, recording of metric traits and comparison to nearly 300 other skeletal populations, and observing nonmetric traits and pathologies, including trauma and dental wear.

In September 1999, a federal judge ordered testing of the Kennewick remains to determine their age. Bone samples of the man Native Americans refer to as the "Ancient One" were sent to three laboratories for radiocarbon dating. Results similar to the date obtained in an earlier test would preclude establishing a relationship of lineal descent between the Kennewick remains and contemporary Native American tribes. Kennewick Man would join other ancient skeletons found in Nevada, Colorado, Idaho, Texas, California, and Minnesota as part of a growing body of contradictory and controversial evidence that the earliest inhabitants of the New World may have been a Caucasoid people, possibly from Europe (Preston 1997), although classification of race is a tricky business. James Chatters believes that the skull of Kennewick Man, like those of other ancient American skulls, predates modern craniofacial categories (Malcolmson 2000). In January 2000, federal officials announced that Kennewick Man was Native American, but that his tribal affiliation has yet to be determined. The results of radiocarbon dating indicated that he lived between 9,320 and 9,510 years ago. DNA testing began in April, and should further illuminate — rather than complicate — the situation of these bones that mean so much to so many.

Mount Vernon Mound, Mount Vernon, Indiana

In another example of poorly handled repatriation, Native American remains from an important site in Indiana were reburied after years of looting but before qualified scientists were given an opportunity to examine them. The Mount Vernon Mound was discovered on the property of the General Electric Company in Posey County in 1988. Local and state law enforcement agencies investigated allegations of looting and the F.B.I. entered the case because it involved interstate trafficking. The investigators found that a worker had uncovered artifacts at the site when about six meters of mound fill was removed during county highway construction. Rather than bring them to the attention of the authorities, he

concealed their presence and later sold them to local dealer Art Gerber for $6,000. Gerber and three other men returned to the site several times to recover additional artifacts, but were finally caught by a security guard. They pled guilty in 1992. Gerber was sentenced to a year in federal prison, fined $5,000, and barred from artifact trading for three years. His appeals were unsuccessful.

Gerber and his associates were not the only people to loot the Mount Vernon site, as Thomas C. Beard (1997) laments: "Information which can be obtained only through skilled, controlled excavation was blown through by the frenzied looters who are reported to have been so numerous as to have had a soft drink concession on the site. The mound was reported to have been littered with five-gallon buckets used to carry out the plunder." Ironically, a two-week scientific test and salvage excavation allowed by the Indiana Department of Transportation was limited only to disturbed areas and soil that had been backfilled by the looters. The extent of the material remaining in the mound is unknown and the extent of the theft remains undetermined. The F.B.I. recovered material from 17 individuals and, again ironically, the human remains that are of such value to physical anthropologists were of no value to the looters. As Beard (1997) describes, "Human remains were stripped of their silver and pearl adornments, their bones crushed by the shovel and tossed aside." When they were no longer required by the F.B.I. for evidence, the looted artifacts and human remains from the Mount Vernon Mound were returned to the landowner, General Electric Plastics, in February 1994. The additional material recovered during the test excavations was also returned at G.E.'s request. G.E. repatriated the bones and burial goods to Native American tribal leaders, who reburied them in a circular pit on the property in May. The ceremony, which involved offerings of tobacco and food, was attended by representatives of more than 25 tribes. The Mound has been entered into the National Register of Historic Places and the reburial site is marked and maintained by G.E.

What has been learned from the Mount Vernon Mound pales compared to the site's potential. The Mound is representative of the Middle Woodland (Hopewell) culture and — with a volume estimated at 11,000 cubic meters — it is among the five largest such sites in North America. It was constructed about the first century A.D. and was originally approximately 400 feet (122 meters) long, 170 feet (52 meters) wide, and 20 feet (6 meters) high. The human remains were analyzed by Stephen P. Nawrocki of the University of Indianapolis during a total of 26 hours of firsthand examination. Nawrocki (1997) inventoried the bones and bone fragments, conducted nondestructive examinations, and recorded as much data as possible about them within this time frame. The "looted collection" consisted of 33 mandibles, 41 teeth, and five miscellaneous bones. The assemblage from the test excavation included six mandibles, five teeth, and 15 miscellaneous bones. Nawrocki cleaned the remains by brushing or with water, glued loose teeth into their sockets, and numbered each specimen with a pencil. Nawrocki's work was made more difficult by the treatment to which the looted remains had been subjected. He explains, "Many of the human mandible sections had been covered with a clear preservative that sealed in the soil and grime on uncleaned surfaces" (Nawrocki 1997). Nevertheless, he was able to observe blackening and calcination that indicated exposure to fire, dark green staining that pointed to direct contact with copper artifacts, and the adherence of red ocher, mica, and an unidentified white powder to some of the bones.

Nawrocki's inventory includes 42 fragments of worked human mandibles charac-teristic of Hopewell sites, five of which could be conjoined into two larger fragments, reducing the total number to 39. A fraction of these are documented on a compact disk that is distributed with a report published by General Electric (1997) about the site. Nawrocki (1997) was able to estimate the minimum number of individuals represented by the jaws to be 13, but was unable to determine sex because all morphological indicators had been erased by extensive modifications. Marks including grinding, scratching, perforations, and polishing also obscured any signs of dismemberment or defleshing. Bone fragments that had not been modified consisted of a right pubic ramus and symphysis, an ilium fragment, a right talus, a left fourth metacarpal, and parts of a right scapula, humeral head, tibia shaft, radial shaft, calcaneus, frontal bone, and cranial vault (Nawrocki 1997).

Cheryl Johnston, who is studying Hopewellian culturally modified remains, laments that the Hopewellian scholars who would have been able to make the most of the short time allowed for the study of the Mount Vernon material were never given the chance to examine it. "I never got to look at the modified remains," she writes (personal correspondence, January 19, 1999), "yet I had already studied in some detail many of the other examples of Hopewellian modified remains from a number of classic Hopewell sites. My situation was nothing compared to what other people who have devoted their careers to Hopewellian studies must have gone through.... The way something is studied and by whom it is studied are critical to the outcome of the research. Lots of observations were made but nobody put anything into a bigger framework. So we are left with more questions than before and not much new information about Hopewell. I'm afraid that the scientific robusticity of the studies done by those in my discipline will suffer from situations like Mount Vernon Mound."

Johnston collaborated with Nawrocki after his analysis of the Mount Vernon remains to match his firsthand observations to her familiarity with similar finds from other Hopewell sites.

LOSS OF COLLECTIONS
WORLDWIDE

There is no denying that to watch parts of collections that we value destroyed diminishes us, and future generations, both Aboriginal and non–Aboriginal may condemn us for having allowed it to happen.
— *Colin Pardoe [1995b]*

Around the world, indigenous people are making claims for the skeletal remains of the populations from which they have descended. Institutions are responding to those claims whether or not they are supported by changes in the law. In fact, many international museums have developed professional guidelines and practices regarding indigenous remains in the hope of avoiding government legislation. Nevertheless, the indigenous populations of many countries, following the success of the Native Americans, have succeeded in having new laws passed that make responding to their claims mandatory. The cause was taken up by the Inter-American Commission on Human Rights of the Organization of American States in 1995, which drafted a declaration on the rights of indigenous peoples that states that sacred graves and relics that have been appropriated by state institutions shall be returned to them (Walker In press). The U.S. and Canada signed an agreement in 1997 restricting the import into the U.S. of archaeological and ethnological material representing Aboriginal cultural groups in Canada. Not all indigenous Americans feel as strongly as the North American Indians, however. In Latin America, members of the Indian population have varied opinions about reburial and have not organized

themselves, so human remains are excavated and exhibited in museums without opposition. A sense of their contribution to the past has been integrated into the national identity and their remains are displayed as a symbol of the region's history (Ubelaker and Grant 1989).

In the United Kingdom, remains have been repatriated from a number of museums. Edinburgh University returned 304 Australian Aboriginal specimens in 1991 and the Glasgow Museums returned four Aboriginal skulls. The Pitt Rivers Museum in Oxford removed several artificially deformed crania from display and returned five of them and a complete skeleton to Australia. Tibetan religious and skeletal artifacts have been repatriated by the Museums of Exeter and the Cambridge University Museum of Archaeology and Anthropology. Some museums in the U.K. are less willing to part with their collections. The Royal College of Surgeons of England refused to hand over 53 contested human skulls. The National Museums of Scotland refused to turn over seven skulls in 1990. In the case of the Museum of Natural History in London (formerly the British Museum), English law forbids them to deaccession anything unless there is a perfect duplicate in the collection, which is of course impossible with human remains. Their consequent refusal to repatriate has caused tension between the museum scholars and individuals culturally linked to material in the collections (Ubelaker and Grant 1989).

In some international cases, the issue of control over the remains does not preclude their continued study, but instead calls for the bones to be transferred to an institution in their country of origin or a museum devoted to their culture. In other cases, indigenous remains continue to be exhibited without objection, as they are in Latin America. In instances where human remains are neither repatriated nor proudly displayed, they are often housed in separate storage areas to which there is restricted access and the documentation about them is carefully guarded. By taking indigenous skeletal remains off display, museums not only remove from public view the material symbolic of mortality in general, but bones that have been used in some situations to keep a specific group in its place. The strongest voices heard outside of the United States are those of the indigenous populations of Australia and South Africa, who have succeeded in curtailing archaeological excavation and analysis of skeletal remains (White 1991).

Another powerful group with religious reasons for objecting to the excavation and study of human remains is Orthodox Jews. After years of campaigning to prevent archaeological excavation of human remains rabbis were given legal authority in 1983 to intervene if remains of likely Jewish origin were found. After this law was rescinded, the political right — including Orthodox Jews — succeeded in lobbying the government to issue a new interpretation of the Antiquities Act, leading to the reburial of all human remains younger than 5,000 years (Pearson 1999). In response, the Department of Antiquities and Museums of the State of Israel issued a position paper outlining guidelines for excavations that include study of the remains, followed by transfer to appointed religious authorities (Ubelaker and Grant 1989). A minority of ultra–Orthodox Jews (about 8 percent of Israel's population) insists that any excavation of ancient graves violates Jewish religious law and harms the souls of those interred. Despite Attorney General Michael Ben-Yair's ruling in 1995 that human remains are not considered "antiquities" under existing law and should be turned over to the Ministry of Religion for immediate reburial, the ultra–Orthodox Jews continue to press for a sweeping prohibition that would forbid not only research on human bones, but even the opening of a grave to

view and document its structure and contents. Leading the fight against excavation is an organization called Atra Kadisha, whose ultra–Orthodox members have protested at many sites, throwing stones and carting bones away for reburial. Archaeologists maintain that they are protecting the graves through proper and orderly documentation followed by respectful delivery of human bones to the Ministry of Religion. Since many of the digs carried out in Israel are rescue excavations by the Israel Antiquities Authority, the academicians believe it would be a desecration to leave the sometimes pillaged graves in place and allow housing developments and roads to be built over and around them. Another group, the Conference of Academicians for the Protection of Jewish Cemeteries, does not condone the violent behavior of some activists, but is opposed to the violation of graves under any circumstances and believes that when bones are uncovered, the grave should be closed quickly with as little handling as possible. "For us, rescuing the grave means leaving it where it is," explains member David Schaps, chair of the classics department at Bar-Ilan University (Watzman 1996). Jews have been successful in their efforts not only in Israel, but in England, where the Chief Rabbi of London succeeded in curtailing the analysis of 496 remains excavated from a thirteenth-century cemetery in York in advance of building construction. The bones recovered from the Jewbury cemetery, which were believed — but not conclusively determined — to have belonged to the Jews who lived in the area in the Middle Ages, were reburied on orders of the Home Office in 1984 (Pearson 1999).

Australian Aboriginal Remains

It would indeed be mistaken to assume, as unsympathetic commentators would have it, that indigenous Australian demands only became an issue in the wake of such developments as the publicity generated by the demands of the first nations of North America for the repatriation of remains and grave goods. Far from it — Paul Turnbull [n.d.]

In Australia, Aboriginal demands have resulted in repatriations of human remains from institutions inside and outside the country. The Archeological and Aboriginal Relics Preservation Act of the state of Victoria was amended in 1984 to make it unlawful for anyone in the country to hold Aboriginal remains without government consent. The University of Melbourne transferred its collection of more than 800 Aboriginal skeletal remains to the Victoria Museums, where they were to be stored until a state-appointed committee of Aboriginal people decided their fate, which ultimately was to be reburied (Ubelaker and Grant 1989). The Australian Archaeological Association demanded in the early 1980s that the Tasmanian state government return the William L. Crowther collection to the Aborigines, but stated that it would only support reburial of remains when they belonged to an individual of known identity who had expressed a desire not to be used for scientific purposes, or when it was the wish of an appropriate community that remains be buried (Turnbull n.d.). In the U.K., the most frequent repatriation requests are for Aboriginal Australian and Maori remains collected in the nineteenth and early twentieth centuries. In 1991, the University of Edinburgh returned approximately 300 osteological specimens to representatives of the Aboriginal people. Some researchers in Australia are working toward compromise between scientists and Aboriginal people. Leading prehistorian John Mulvaney encourages preservation and respect for Aboriginal material culture, but is critical of politically motivated demands for repatriation. He believes that support for land rights might provide grounds for reconciling scientific aspirations with indigenous demands (Turnbull n.d.).

The debate about the repatriation of one skeletal assemblage — the remains found at Kow Swamp — was particularly heated. The remains of between 22 and 40 individuals as many as 10,000 years old had been excavated in the late 1960s by Alan Thorne, who found that they compared morphologically with ancient fossils from Java. Discussion continues about whether these Australian hominids are representative of late *Homo erectus*, archaic *Homo sapiens*, or the result of interbreeding between them. In 1990, P.H. Piggott, former chairman of a government committee of inquiry on museums and national collections, condemned demands for the reburial of the Kow Swamp remains, arguing that anyone in favor of the destruction of the material was of the same mentality as those who persecuted witches or burned books (Turnbull n.d.). The Kow Swamp remains were reburied by the Aboriginal community that year and the remains of more than 100 individuals found by Thorne near Lake Mungo were returned to Aboriginal custody in 1992. Although these and other bones have much to offer in the study of Australian prehistory, some Aborigines reject the need for continued curation and analysis and may be reluctant to allow the study of newly-discovered remains for fear that the research will go on indefinitely. Most Aboriginal people, though, are very interested in their heritage, including the knowledge that can be gained from their skeletons. But there is still some ambivalence about the institutions that represent the establishment. As Colin Pardoe (1995b) explains, some Aboriginal people value the diversity that is found only in museums and others see museums as representing a dominant class and take offense at the sequestering of their heritage.

The skeletal remains of Aboriginals became the object of collectors in the mid-eighteenth century, when they were seen as evidence of physical and intellectual deterioration brought on by the rigors of their savage lives. In the nineteenth century, they were prized by phrenologists and later by craniologists as representative of primitive types in human evolution (Turnbull n.d.). Local amateur phrenologist Alexander Berry excavated and sent to England the skull of Arawarra (d. 1825), an Elder of the Shoal-haven people, only a few years after his death, from his grave in sand dunes near the township of Cooloomgatta. When a woman named Truganini died in 1876, she was certain that her body would be prized after death, since she was believed to be the last pure-blooded Tasmanian, and so specified that her body be cremated. Although a petition by the Royal Society of Tasmania to preserve her remains was denied, her wishes were not honored. She was buried and predictably exhumed two years later. Truganini's skeleton was sent to Melbourne and London for study, afterward remaining on display at the Tasmanian Museum. Lobbying by the Australian Institute for Aboriginal Studies finally resulted in the remains being cremated and scattered at sea (Pearson 1999).

Grave-robbing forced Aboriginal communities to become secretive about where they buried their dead. This in turn caused friendships with ulterior motives to develop in order to learn their locations, led doctors in rural districts to rob their Aboriginal patients of their skeletons before or after burial, and — in the case of German naturalist Amalie Dietrich — prompted (unsuccessful) inquiries into the possibility of having an Aborigine shot to obtain the skin and skeleton. In 1891, A.D. Goodwin, who had arrived in Australia 15 years earlier, befriended a Paikalyug man dying of tuberculosis, took his portrait for later comparison with the skull, secretly excavated his remains from the Lismore town cemetery after his death, and included the skeleton in a collection of ethnographic objects sold to the Peabody Museum (Turnbull n.d.). In the twentieth century, living and dead Aboriginal peoples were studied as populations little affected by European genes. Skeletal material continued to be gathered and examined to chart the chronology and spread of human occupation of the continent. "Much of this century has seen the quiet deposition in Australia's museum of remains unearthed by erosion or the bulldozer," writes Turnbull (n.d.). Most of the skeletal material was (and in some cases still is) stored in museum collections in capital cities separated by bone type. The few complete skeletons are often missing elements and typically articulated with wires (Webb 1995).

As Aboriginal populations make their desires known, museums attempt to accommodate them, although sometimes lacking the necessary resources. Important collections are being returned for reburial, which has prompted publication of research gathered to date from Aboriginal remains. Of his survey of the pre- and post-contact health status of Aboriginal Australians, Stephen Webb (1995) writes:

> The continuing return of whole skeletal collections to Aboriginal communities for reburial has added further impetus to the production of this book. Because of these events many of the remains used in this survey are no longer available for study. Under these circumstances I felt that it was important to make available much of the palaeopathological data that I have gathered from all Australian collections for over a decade. Unfortunately, the sudden demise of such scientifically important collections has prevented further and much needed study of many pathologies, including rare and unique examples; it has also meant the loss of other important palaeobiological information. Moratoria prevented many collections from being studied for several years before burials took place. Reassessment and further study of certain pathological conditions which I would like to have undertaken has not, therefore, been possible in the interim.

Webb's study confirmed the general good health of earlier Aboriginals everywhere in

Australia through the comparison of remains in a number of skeletal collections, the history, condition, and status of which he describes:

- Murray Black Collection: This collection of more than 1,700 prehistoric skeletal remains was excavated between 1929 and 1951 from traditional burial places by George Murray Black. It formed the largest single sample of Aboriginal skeletal remains and included 70 carbonate-encrusted crania excavated from the Coobool Creek site in 1949 and 1950; 60 burials of certain provenance excavated from two adjacent sites, including 50 to 100 skulls from Baratta and 70 from Tulla; 139 mineral-stained skeletons from Lake Poon, and more than 400 individuals excavated from the Robinvale-Euston area in 1946. The collection was held jointly by the Anatomy Department of the University of Melbourne and the Australian Institute of Anatomy in Canberra until 1938, when the entire collection was transferred to Canberra. In 1984, the Murray Black collection became the focus of Aboriginal concerns over the curation and continued study of ancestral remains. Moves by the Aboriginal community to have the collection repatriated received legislative support from both state and federal governments and the bulk of this collection has now been reburied (Webb 1995).

- Broadbeach Collection: The Broadbeach collection consisted of 140 remains from southeastern Queensland that dated to about 660 A.D. and were heavily biased toward males and subadults. Though fragmentary and poorly preserved, the remains included a number of pathologies. This collection was reburied in 1985 (Webb 1995).

- Swanport Collection: This assemblage accidentally exposed during the building of a levee at the turn of the twentieth century represents a single tribe or close group. The site contains between 90 and 160 individuals and was thought to have resulted from an epidemic (Pardoe 1988). Although the burials are undated, the majority are believed to span the 400 years prior to European settlement and preservation of the remains is excellent. This collection, a mainstay of osteological and physical anthropological research in Australia for years, has been set aside for reburial (Webb 1995).

- Roonka Collection: Though dated, the remains in this collection are fragmentary, poorly preserved, and severely eroded (Webb 1995). They consist of 165 individuals determined to have a mean age of 24, including 60 children and subadults, 58 males, and 47 females. The remains were analyzed by Miroslav Prokopec and Graeme L. Pretty (1991) to determine demographical structure, health status, genetics, culture, and probable way of life 7,000 years before the arrival of the first Europeans.

- Willandra Lakes Hominid Series: This skeletal series was exposed by natural erosion from sand dunes in Western New South Wales that date from 14,000 to 40,000 years ago. The series consists of 135 individuals, many of which are represented by fragments. Almost all of the articular ends of the major long bones are missing (Webb 1995).

Webb made use of the skeletal material still available, radiographing 1,002 tibiae at Australian National University to study the frequency of Harris' lines. He examined trephinations in the skulls of three adult females and two examples of amputation above the knee. Over 40 types of bony tumor were observed, but were poorly preserved and fragmentary. Webb documented pathologies including multiple myeloma, nasopharyngeal carcinoma, metastatic carcinoma, osteoma, spina bifida, meningocele, scaphocephaly, achondroplasia, cleft palate, and supernumary digits. Webb's survey found that arthritis affected males more than females, elbows more than knees, and Murray people more than anyone else. He found that female crania from all parts of the continent display more head trauma than males, possible due to attacks by males, arguments among themselves, or self-inflicted injury (since it was common practice for women in mourning to deliberately strike or beat their foreheads with stones or sharpened instruments). He inferred from the presence of congenital conditions, pathological diseases, and trauma that there was a great tolerance in Aboriginal society of malformed and badly injured individuals and a willingness to look after them (Web 1995). Webb regrets the time that has been lost to study the collections, which are now themselves being lost. He explains that systematic assessment of museum collections did not begin until the mid–1960s, due to the lack of properly trained physical anthropologists in Australia. The one exception was Cecil Hackett, who began studying treponematosis in the 1920s and examined more than 9,000 Aboriginal skulls and bones between 1967 and 1968 (Webb 1995).

Colin Pardoe is a contemporary researcher who is familiar with Australian Aboriginal biology and burial practices through the examination and interpretation of human skeletal material. Until about 7,000 years ago, the dead were buried near rivers, which changed course at about that time. Multivariate analysis and other techniques used by Pardoe indicate that the riverine groups were biologically diverse, but the similarities in their burial practices indicate religious and social cohesion (Pardoe 1994). Formal graveyards were used and differential treatment of the bodies of men and women was the norm. The cemeteries

span centuries and even millennia and the varied mortuary practices include extended, flexed, and cremated burials. After 7,000 B.P., cemetery usage was territorial and bundle burial was practiced. He has found that the dating of the material is inconsistent and, in general, overestimated. "Although there has been great interest by Aboriginal people in the study of their ancestral remains (contrary to some views), it is the case that direct dating of bone is a delicately negotiated process," he writes (Pardoe 1995a). At about 7,000 years ago, however, it has been shown that the Aboriginal people decreased in size by as much as 15 to 20 percent of their body mass, a dramatic change attributed to adaptation to higher temperatures (Pardoe 1995a). The teeth also show more wear (from abrasives such as ash consumed with food) and the skulls exhibit more signs of violence.

Until 1998, Colin Pardoe was the curator of human biology and archaeology at the South Australian Museum, which curates the only major Australian collection of human remains that has not been repatriated and reburied. "I may well be the last curator of this collection," Pardoe (1995b) told participants at a symposium. He had completely reorganized the museum's collection by region and relevant social groupings to allow consultation with Aboriginal communities about the long-term future of the bones. Of his work with Aboriginal skeletal material, he writes (personal correspondence, August 11, 1999), "I've spent a lot of time trying to put forward the values of these studies by appealing to the knowledge that is locked in the bones." He explains that Aboriginal people must sift through competing world views in which bones are at the same time religious reminders, symbols of oppression, and repositories of knowledge about their past. Participating in archaeology helps Aboriginal people make sense of these multiple meanings as they read their history from the bones: "Past patterns of human social behaviour are carved on the skeleton as holes, bony bridges, accessory bones and suture lines and as shape and size" (Pardoe 1994). To establish patterns of individual variation and in the biological relations between and within groups of people requires the examination of samples spanning long periods of time. One site that fills just such a need, but has not yet been fully excavated, is a cemetery located at the southern end of Lake Victoria estimated to contain 10,000 burials and believed to have been in use for 6,000 years. More than 570 remains from the area reside in Australian museums, including 200 crania sent by Black to the Australian Institute of Anatomy in 1938 and skeletons sent to the University of Melbourne in the 1940s (Pardoe 1988).

Another particularly important group of human remains is that of the Tasmanians, who may have experienced the longest period of isolation of any human group. Multivariate analysis and studies of metric and nonmetric traits are being used to determine whether they originated in Australia or outside the continent. If the latter is true and yet the Tasmanians and Aboriginal Australians are so similar morphologically, it points to a need to reinterpret the evolutionary constraints and factors responsible for variation (Pardoe 1991). Despite their importance in unraveling prehistory, the remaining Tasmanian skeletal collections are in jeopardy. N.J.B. Plomley of Tasmania's Queen Victoria Museum and Art Gallery makes the point strongly:

> Attention must be drawn to the fact that any further studies of the Tasmanian skull will be limited because much of the material previously in collections has been destroyed. This is a consequence of legislation that has compelled holders of skeletal material relating to the Tasmanian Aborigines, both full-blooded and hybrid, to hand it over to some people in Tasmania calling themselves Tasmanian Aborigines, who have destroyed it. The museums in Tasmania have been stripped, and collections elsewhere in Australia have been handed over to these people as well. They are now trying to gain possession of collections in Europe, America, and elsewhere, and if they succeed there will be fewer remains of the Tasmanian Aborigines than feathers of the dodo (Pardoe 1991).

Although the South Australia Museum displays modeled skulls from New Guinea in the Pacific exhibition and daggers carved from human bone, it does not exhibit the skeletons of Aborigines even though these make up the bulk of their skeletal collections. The Aboriginal remains have come to the museum through the coroner, the public, land developers, and — less often — archaeological excavations. Most are from the densely populated areas of the Adelaide Plains and the River Murray, with some from the Northern Territory. About 10 percent of the skeletons lack provenance. Pardoe is now working to determine their origin using the methods of biological anthropology and quantitative skeletal analysis. This is especially necessary in cases where remains identified only as Aboriginal are returned by museums from overseas, in which case they are compared to the extensive holdings of well-provenanced remains to place them geographically and so return them to the appropriate group. Pardoe (1995b) notes the irony of demonstrating the value of the skeletal collection by assisting in the reburial process.

One skeleton that is not in jeopardy is that of "Max" at the South Australian Museum. Johann David Max Dreyssig, who was not an Australian native but an immigrant from Saxony, was born in 1850. After serving gallantly in the Prussian Army and visiting Australia twice, he sailed to Adelaide in 1885 and never left. Max broke his leg at age 39 in 1889. Even though he spent 33 days in Adelaide Hospital recuperating,

Pages 230–231: The skeleton of Max Dreyssig at the South Australian Museum, with a close-up of his fractured leg. Photos courtesy of Jasmine Day.

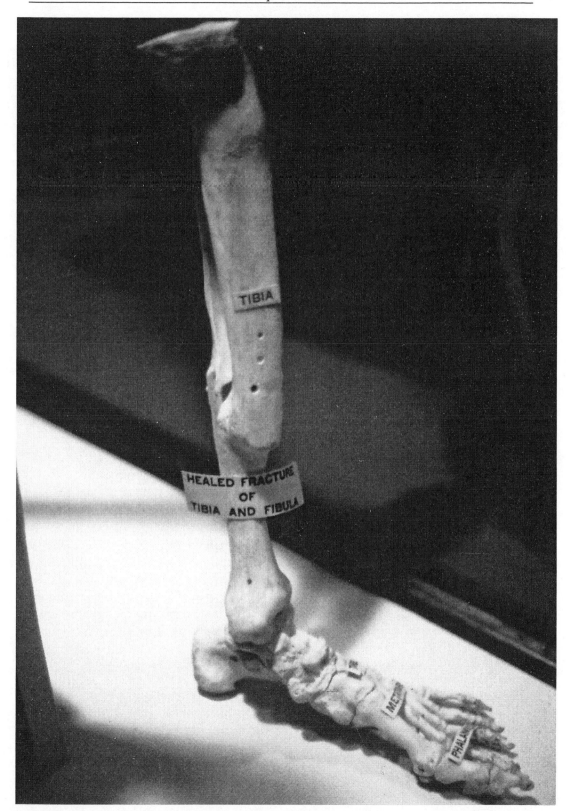

the fracture to the left tibia and fibula knitted poorly, with the ends overlapping by about two centimeters, which would have caused him to walk with a considerable limp. Two months of lumbago and severe indigestion in July 1913 drove Max to seek help from Dr. Archibald Watson, a professor of anatomy at the University of Adelaide Medical School. Dr. Watson's diagnosis of stomach cancer was confirmed when he operated in August, but the disease was too advanced to remove the tumor and the incision was closed up. Max was medicated, but must have known the seriousness of his condition. Two days earlier, he had mortgaged his house and land. He took advantage of surviving the surgery to make a will which left most of his small estate to his sister in Germany. He died a week later at age 62 and was autopsied the following day. Max's longest-lasting bequest was that of his body to the Medical School for the sum of ten pounds. Dr. Watson brought the body to Joe Rau, taxidermist at the South Australian Museum. Rau flensed it out behind the main building and prepared and articulated the skeleton. The Iron Cross Max had been awarded was attached to the bones, but later disappeared. The skeleton was used as a demonstration model in the Anatomy Department for years. In 1942, Max's skeleton was accessioned by the Anthropology Department of the Museum, to which Max had earlier donated a penguin specimen and a locust. The taxidermist then at the museum, Rau's son Alan, mounted the skeleton on a small chair. The museum has a photograph of Max in his army uniform that bears his signature and the later inscription "Portrait of the individual represented by mounted skeleton No. A34494 in S.A. Museum" (Thurmer 1996). Max is still seated inside a glass case in one of the visitor galleries. His bones are labeled, his left leg shows a severe fracture, and he is missing several teeth.

South African Indigenous Remains

In the nineteenth century, the remains of the natives of South Africa suffered much the same fate as those of the natives of North America. Graves were robbed not long after they had been dug and the highly prized skulls and skeletons of the San ("Bushmen") and the Khoikhoi were shipped to museums inside and outside the country. Since 1990, questions about the treatment of these remains have been raised by the descendants of both indigenous groups, collectively known as the Khoisan. At issue are thousands of skeletons, since most South African museums curate indigenous remains. The South African Museum in Cape Town has at least 788 specimens, the National Museum Bloemfontein has 403, the University of Witwatersrand Department of Anatomy has 365, the University of Cape Town Department of Anatomy has 239, the Albany Museum Grahamstown has 168, and the McGregor Museum in Kimberley has 150, according to a master catalog compiled by Alan Morris in the early 1990s (Legassick and Rassool 1999). The collection of native skulls began among the colonizers of the country after the Khoisan had been neutralized as a military threat. Rather than collecting their skulls as trophies of war, the Europeans collected them to form statistical samples of significant size for craniometric research. The size of institutional collections grew rapidly, as historical records from the South African Museum show. In 1905, the museum curated eighteen skulls. Two years later another six had been procured. In 1917, the museum had 163 Khoisan specimens, of which 106 were complete skulls. And by 1922, the specimens totaled 217 (Legassick and Rassool 1999).

At the turn of the twentieth century, there was such rivalry among museums to procure skeletons that they not only disinterred the recently deceased, but made arrangements with living Khoisans to secure their remains after death. In the first decade of the 1900s, Maria Wilman, an employee of the South African Museum, was sent to the Northern Cape and Southern Rhodesia to look for rock art and skeletons. She reported to F. Peringuey on a number of Korana and Bushmen burials, but said that the missionaries declined to touch them for fear of angering the natives. She told him that the bones of a dying Bushwoman had already been spoken for by Professor Von Luschan. The correspondence holds ominous inferences for researchers Martin Legassick and Ciraj Rasool (1999): "By 1906 it seems that, while religious objections persisted, the government might already have been supporting the exhumation of human remains. Moreover from the fact that it is written so openly, clearly neither Miss Wilman nor Peringuey had compunctions about competing with a foreign professor for the skeleton of a person who had not yet died." Worse still were the methods of George St. Leger Lennox ("Scotty Smith"), a procurer of human skeletons who was rumored to shoot Bushmen to obtain them.

A rivalry soon began between Peringuey at the South African Museum and Wilman, who took over directorship of the McGregor Museum. Peringuey appealed to the dealers not to export native skeletons, but to sell them within the country so that their race could be studied even if the Khoisan people died off like the natives of Tasmania (Legassick and Rassool 1999). Peringuey complained in 1909 about the number of skulls being sent to Austria and England. Maria Wilman, on the other hand, cultivated a relationship with Dr. Rudolf Pöch of the Imperial Academy of Sciences in Vienna. She sent specimens to him for analysis and he bolstered two institutional collections with specimens from South Africa. At Austria's Museum of Natural History, the African skeletons joined 35,000 other skeletons in the attic with

their skulls separately stored. At the academy, the African bones were stored in boxes said to line the walls from floor to ceiling. Pöch dispatched an assistant named Mehnarto to South Africa to obtain even greater quantities of skeletons. When it came to the attention of police officials that Mehnarto had shipped out some 150 skeletons between 1907 and 1909, he was questioned but said he had acted under local police authority. Pöch afterward paid him per specimen rather than the salary he had been receiving, but the police continued their investigation. They collected statements from people who had assisted Mehnarto, including a wagon driver named Cornelius Goliath who described Mehnarto's actions. At Gamopedi, Mehnarto excavated five skeletons, reburying one that had not skeletonized and returning for it later, at which time he severed the joints, boiled the bones, and packed them in a box in the wagon. He also exhumed two San servants, Klaas and Trooi Pienaar (d. 1909), despite the objections of their former employer, placing the remains into a large barrel filled with salt and loading it on the wagon. At Kuie pan, with the assistance of a local farmer, Mehnarto excavated an old man, an old woman, and a young man, defleshed them, and packed their bones on the wagon. His actions were witnessed by the widow of the old man, who had died of malaria in 1909. Mehnarto conducted similar excavations at Rooiwal, Gamesup, Steinbok Kloof, Lupanen, Oorlengs Kloof, and Douglas. Martin Legassick and Ciraj Rassool (1999) point out that of the more than 30 skeletons Mehnarto procured during this expedition, at least five were recently deceased, but this violation was excused at the time because "a Bushman death was the death of a living relic, a fossil of natural history, and not the death of a human being." Legally, exhumations were supposed to require the sanction of the Minister of Health and the cemetery authorities, but Khoisan remains fell outside the protection of the law because they were not buried in "consecrated ground." In any case, Mehnarto had received enough support from the government in his illegal activities that the attorney-general declined to press any charges.

In 1910, Lennox — who was also procuring skeletons for Pöch at a price of £7 to £10 each — ran into trouble at Port Elizabeth. Customs officials impounded a case of human remains being sent to Vienna and learned from Peringuey that this was only one of about 36 cases sent to Pöch in that year alone. Because the bones were said to have been gathered from the surface of the ground, and in several instances from a location outside their jurisdiction, authorities did not prosecute. Later that year, however, officials seized two more cases containing human skulls and bones that were being shipped by Lennox to the Royal College of Surgeons. To prevent further trouble, Lennox applied to the Ministry of Health for permission to procure skeletons of "Kalahari Bushmen" for the McGregor Museum, but was questioned. At Lennox's request, Peringuey applied for and was granted a permit. He tried to persuade Lennox to work only for the South African Museum, which was unable to pay the going rate per skeleton. Instead, Lennox supplied 14 of the 16 skeletons acquired by the McGregor Museum in 1911. There are no records of sales after 1912 and Lennox died in 1919 (Legassick and Rassool 1999).

Peringuey made other arrangements. In 1911, he sent James Drury to Namaqualand. Drury returned with life models of Bushmen and 13 of their skeletons. In 1912, Peringuey himself excavated at Coldstream, recovering four complete skeletons and two skulls. In 1913, Peringuey put the word out to freelancers, authorizing J. S. Henkel, Conservator of Forests at Knysna, to pay 25 shillings in labor for each skeleton procured, plus an additional gratuity of £2 for each

three skeletons. When a Major Gage at Karibib suggested that he may be able to obtain a quantity of remains from a native cemetery, Peringuey suggested 25 skulls and a single complete skeleton. When Gage's exhumation request was denied, he received the following communication from Peringuey: "To say that I was not somewhat disappointed at the non realization of an increase in our human skull collection would not be saying the whole truth, but perhaps someone not officially connected with the Administration might undertake the task for a small remuneration." Peringuey was at this time offering 5 shillings for each good skull with lower jaw and 10 shillings for the whole body (Legassick and Rassool 1999).

The contemporary Khoisan object to the continued display of human remains that were so unethically obtained, particularly those of known identity. The skull of Koos Sas, a San murderer who was shot in Namaqualand in 1922, was exhibited at the Montagu museum between 1975 and 1993. In at least one case, requests have resulted in indigenous South African remains being returned to the country from museums in Europe. Philip Tobias of the University of the Witwatersrand lobbied successfully for the return of Saartjie Baartman from the Musée de l'Homme in Paris, although the bones have not yet been reburied (Legassick and Rassool 1999). Repatriation is not mandated by South African law except in "special cases" where remains may be returned to those who can be traced as descendants. The use of human remains for scientific purposes is regulated by the 1911 Anatomy Act and its successor, which control the disposal of unclaimed bodies. Exhumations are overseen by the National Monuments Council. The National Museum Bloemfontein is now in the process of reorganizing its human skeletal collections, reports J.S. Brink (personal correspondence, September 15, 1999). A computer database is being used to record the information about the specimens, which include historic and proto-historic Khoisan skeletons collected by T.F. Dreyer and A.C. Hoffman. "Institutionally, only the South African Museum has developed a partial policy on human remains," write Legassick and Rassool (1999), who conclude from their research, "We submit that there is no conceivable scientific value in the preservation by museums of these remains which outweighs the ethical need for their reburial."

7

The Future of
Existing Collections

Bones in quantity are collections and assemblages, notable for a particular bias or for a size that allows generalizations to be made about the human skeleton. They are teaching aids and clues to murder. They are the remains of ancient predecessors or earlier generations to which some feel strong spiritual attachment and others see as an opportunity to learn about their lives and ours. Skeletal remains are sometimes untapped reservoirs of information, as in cases of speedy repatriation, unexcavated sites, or failing funds. In many cases, both time and money are at issue. Most labs would welcome the opportunity to digitize the bones in their collections, but can't afford the equipment and — in the case of Native American remains — don't have time. Instead, many institutions are taking advantage of less expensive options to create computer databases describing their skeletal collections that can then be shared with researchers worldwide. The creation of these databases and collection of standardized data may be the lasting byproducts of collections that have been buried. These include repatriated bones and the remains of homicide victims, interred skeleton by skeleton as they are identified. The information compiled from such bones allows research limited by current predictions of future needs. Curation of the bones themselves allows skulls and skeletons to be looked at with new eyes, examined with fresh sets of hands, and analyzed with newly-trained minds, allowing less limited analyses and encouraging the testing of new theories. Maintaining collections of human skeletal remains and collections of data about them takes best advantage of current (affordable) technologies, allowing remote access of data, but still offering the opportunity for researchers to study the specimens firsthand. A computerized inventory of specimens — in a museum or the museums of an entire country — guards against their loss, underscores their value to scientists in many fields, and allows researchers to share what has become in some countries a dwindling resource.

MAKING COMPROMISES

Whether they are stacked neatly in dark crypts, stored carefully in museum facilities, or lying underground, collections of human bones are imbued with meaning, with potential, and with attachment to people of the past, present, and future. For native populations, this attachment is spiritual and is served by protecting the bones from the desecration represented by scientific study. For the casual visitor to an

The author in the catacombs of Paris, April 1999. Photo courtesy of Cris Hastings.

ossuary, the attachment is symbolic, reminding the viewer of the destiny he or she shares with the original owners of the bones. For osteologists, physical anthropologists, paleopathologists, and others, the bones are connections to humans, recent and ancient. Because they study the bones with objectivity, the scientists' relationship to them may be misinterpreted as detachment. "Although it is true that, for most skeletal biologists, human remains are viewed as depersonalized and de-sanctified, there is still general agreement that they are nevertheless highly meaningful and should be treated with dignity and respect," writes Phillip L. Walker (In press). Unlike their earlier counterparts, today's collectors, curators, and researchers are guided by respect for both the bones themselves and the living cultures that look upon them so differently.

When members of these living cultures allow skeletal collections to be analyzed before being repatriated, they ameliorate the loss of scientifically obtained knowledge about ourselves that accompanies their reburial. Even so, the loss of curated bone collections and the curtailing of skeletal excavations will leave significant gaps in the historic and prehistoric record that is being pieced together. It is clear that NAGPRA cannot redress centuries of injustice in a few years, and it has caused resentment on both sides of the debate, but it has also forged new alliances. The Chumash Indians, for instance, have allowed their ancestral remains to be housed in a specially constructed subterranean ossuary at the University of Southern California-Santa Barbara, a campus located near the center of the area historically occupied by the tribe. Tribal members participated in the design of the ossuary and are actively involved in the research on the remains, conducted under their supervision. The facility meets the needs of the descendants, protects the bones, and provides a mutually agreeable destination for Chumash remains repatriated from other museums and universities (Walker In press).

Other compromises have been reached that do not preclude indefinite curation. Skeletal collections have been transferred to ethnically appropriate museums or institutions, for instance the repatriation of Native Alaskan remains collected by Ales Hrdlička to a museum in that state. Human skeletal remains have been removed from public display and replaced with replicas, as was done at Kolomoki Mounds in Blakely, Georgia. Transformation of some — especially in situ — skeletal collections from tourist attractions to purposeful anthropological libraries is applauded by some, but not all of the tourists drawn by such displays should be characterized as merely "morbidly curious." Exposure of human bones to those without scientific credentials should not be considered obscene, although it is reasonable to insist that the remains be displayed tastefully and in an educational context. In today's careful climate, admission into some of the existing exhibits of human bones — including those at the Wellcome Museum of the Royal College of Surgeons — is limited to students and professionals. But exposure to natural bone may lead laypersons to study osteology, physical anthropology, or skeletal biology. Or it may point out to the uninitiated by way of an authentic example the importance of such study to better our knowledge of the past and improve our lives today. The skeletons in the display cases are not being ogled at, but considered, compared, and in a sense congratulated for providing us with research opportunities that would otherwise be locked underground.

When human remains resulting from modern genocide or a contemporary murder are excavated, scientists are obliged to study them to determine how they died.

This same obligation is felt toward ancient remains, including those of Native Americans and Aboriginal Australians, but to determine how they lived. Some assemblages are ideal for answering certain questions, but are no longer available for examination. The Native Hawaiian remains from Mokapu represent a pre-contact breeding isolate, revealing clues to heredity and variation. The natives of Tasmania were also isolated, but so similar morphologically to the native Australians that study of the remains of both groups may shed light on human evolution. Study of paleopathology in Native North and South American remains may dispel long-standing assumptions that certain diseases arrived in the New World with its colonizers. Analysis of each assemblage of bones represents a unique window of opportunity through which to gain insight about an often confusing past. Repatriation closes and locks that window, with the keys in the hands of native groups. Reburial effectively walls up the window or, at the very least, paints over the glass.

Bones dozens of generations removed from living descendants of the same ethnic group are claimed by many in the scientific community to belong to all of us. Legally, if repatriation claims have been made and honored, Native American remains belong to those descendants. Ways have been found to reconcile the obligations culturally-affiliated groups feel toward their ancestors with the requests of scientists to scrutinize the remains and thereby add to our common body of knowledge. These include a limited period of study prior to reburial, sometimes with the participation of those affiliated with the bones; curation in a facility considered to be more appropriate because of its mission and focus, such as the analysis of African-American remains found in New York at traditionally black Howard University; and modification of an existing facility to meet the needs of both the native groups and the scientists, who are then allowed an extended or indefinite time frame in which to analyze the bones. Negotiations have also convinced some ethnic groups to allow small samples of bone to be taken for DNA and other analysis, while in other cases researchers honor Native American or institutional prohibitions against any destructive testing.

The bones of the skeleton have been manipulated as part of the disposition process by many cultures. Native Americans, Greeks, Austrians and other Europeans, and the Capuchin monks practiced secondary burial for centuries, some believing that skeletonization freed the soul of the earthly remains. Scientists are among the most recent to occupy themselves with the bones of the dead, and do so not to comfort dead souls but without intent to harm them. Rather, they attempt to make the best use of the remains of those who can no longer speak for themselves except through their physical legacy. While some consider this legacy to be their distant descendants, others believe it to be their bones.

ENCOURAGING DONATION

Because excavations of historic cemeteries are usually followed by reburial, the surest way to supplement the existing documented skeletal collections is by harvesting the bones of donated bodies. As the collections grow, this method will ensure sizable contemporary samples on which to base studies and statistical analyses. If the need for such collections had been realized two hundred years ago, great numbers of documented remains would now be curated, rather than the anomalies or representative pathologies that were kept as specimens. Phillip L. Walker (In press) explains:

> Although the increase in dissections [after the passage of "anatomical acts" to allow

dissection of suicides and unclaimed bodies] opened the possibility of increasing the scope of skeletal collections, this potential was not fully realized. Collections were made of specimens with interesting anomalies and pathological conditions but, as a rule, the rest of the dissected person's skeleton was disposed of.... From what can be discerned from the remnants of nineteenth-century medical school collections that survive today, little effort was made to create carefully documented skeletal collections of known age and sex for use in assessing the normal range of human variation. The failure to create such systematic collections probably stems in part from the prevalence of racist views that minimized the importance of variation within groups and exaggerated the significance of population differences.

Documented historic collections are therefore cultivated from places less likely than museums. Like cemetery assemblages, the remains deposited in church crypts are often accompanied by coffin plates or other identifiers. Such existing caches of skeletal material are easier to access than remains that must be excavated and, like them, can be researched in the official records for additional demographic information. T. Sjøvold (1993) took advantage of existing records, including their recorded identities, to study the skulls at Hallstatt. Fornaciari and Gamba (1993) studied the skulls in the Church of S. Maria Della Grazia in Comiso, Sicily. Although the time agreed upon for analysis of the remains in a private or municipal crypt or ossuary may be limited, it is usually followed by replacement rather than reburial of the remains, so studies could potentially be replicated at a later time.

The fact that bones from overcrowded cemeteries are now being sought out by scientists with a lack of curated skeletal material is ironic. So are the premortem arrangements to procure human skeletons: yesterday's coerced minorities and rightfully paranoid "freaks" are today's willing body

donors — welcomed whether they are anomalous or average. Another irony lies in the
institutional accession of some trophy
skulls, originally obtained without consent
and then donated by the families of veterans 50 years later. Solicitation of donated
remains has its own history: dispatches from
the founder of Florence's Museo di Antropologia ed Etnologia requesting skeletal material from Italian doctors and dignitaries
abroad, orders from the surgeon-general
during the American Civil War to collect
and submit specimens. These may in the
future be matched by requests from academic institutions like the Forensic Anthropology Center at the University of Tennessee and the Maxwell Museum, both of
which are actively calling for donations. The
Hyrtls, Huntingtons, Terrys, and Todds of
yesterday have their contemporary counterparts.

COLLECTING DATA

Though the skeleton and its components are physically durable, their strength
lies in their numbers. Statistical surveys and
comparisons of bones yield not a seamless
but a solid basis for theories about migration, development, and cultural relationships. To preserve the knowledge gained
from the bones — especially in the absence
of the bones themselves — physical and
forensic anthropologists have standardized
their data collection techniques and paleoanthropologists have recognized the need
to do the same. At the same time, inven to-
ries of institutional collections conducted
voluntarily or in compliance with legislation have revealed the extent of the world's
holdings of skeletal remains and how they
are being put to use. By studying skeletal
populations that are not subject to repatriation, researchers will continue to shed light
on their questions and refine their techniques — with limitations. The limitations

of availability require careful curation of
current skeletal resources to preserve bones
that, if lost, could or would not be replaced.

Much of the research on human skeletal remains involves comparison between
them, which necessitates standardized observations. Measurements of an assemblage
are therefore best taken by a single specialist rather than a team (Pearson 1999). But
the lack of comparability mounts when the
specimens deviate from the norm. Donald
Ortner (1991) points out the lack of a consistent protocol for the collection of paleopathological information, a handicap in a
field where data is collected from original
specimens spread out across many collections. Arthur Aufderheide (1991) concurs:
"While paleopathology is often labeled a
'young science' ... it is old enough to have
developed an area of vulnerability suffi-
ciently serious to threaten its potential for
flourishing growth: lack of methodological
standardization. Since most skeletal collections are of small or modest size, prevalence
data can only be computed for many conditions by combining multiple, independent reports." C. Roberts (1991) suggests
that the standardized information based on
these surveys will be tomorrow's need:
"There will always be a special place in the
literature for unusual and isolated pathological conditions, but in the future there
will be an increasing demand for more
wider ranging analyses of human skeletal
data. It will no longer be deemed acceptable
to consider skeletons as a single entity, un-
responsive to their surroundings. The use
of modern clinical data in paleopathology
will further help to broaden our horizons
and help interpretation go further than mere
diagnoses of cases."

In paleopathology, as in many fields,
large numbers of specimens are needed to
make sense of the health and other patterns
they represent. While many substantial collections in the U.S. have been divested, others around the world remain permanently

available to researchers and still more assemblages are exposed by erosion or construction activities and are available for limited or long-term analysis. Many collections of human remains have a particular bias: the African-American remains in the Cobb collection, the disaster victims at Pompeii, the war casualties of the Battle of Little Bighorn, the homicide victims in identification laboratories, the victims of plague or genocide buried in mass graves. Bias during the collection process over the centuries has left museums with a prevalence of skulls, some of them examples of artificial cranial deformation, others examples of racial or other types collected by craniologists and phrenologists and occasionally identified by name. These biases are generally used to their best advantage, for instance the bones of Custer's men have revealed volumes about the lives and deaths of nineteenth-century cavalrymen. And what appears to be bias may be beneficial to researchers, though of course devastating to the victims, such as the sudden events at Crow Creek and Pompeii that have captured osteologically a large cross-section of the population.

While legislation has robbed researchers of the opportunity to analyze (or reanalyze) some Aboriginal remains, it has been a catalyst in many instances, prompting more thorough examination of collections that had not received sufficient attention. Even from remains that are slated for return to NAGPRA claimants without analysis, measurements can be recorded to add to appropriate databases. Published guidelines for the collection of data—*Standards for Data Collection from Human Skeletal Remains* (Buikstra and Ubelaker 1994) and *Data Collection Procedures for Forensic Skeletal Material* (Moore-Jansen, Ousley, and Jantz 1994)—ensure consistency, whether the information is shared internally or internationally. Institutional inventories provide the opportunity for that information to be computerized. The records associated with the Hamann-Todd collection in Cleveland are now available in electronic format, the Museo di Antropologia ed Etnologia in Florence has computerized its catalog, and the National Museum Bloemfontein in South Africa is reorganizing its collections and creating a database. Collections at other institutions—the Belgian Natural History Museum, the University of Leeds, and the University of Helsinki—are also in the process of being reorganized and recataloged. Some of these inventories are country-wide. While Denmark is ahead of the game, having published a several-volume survey of skeletal material curated in that country (Sellevold, Hansen and Jørgensen 1984), Holland is following suit with a combined and computerized inventory of the collections at its five major universities.

It seems to be a time of regrouping and reassessing the extant human skeletal collections around the world. The bones are being inventoried and cleaned, deaccessioned in some cases and reanalyzed in others. Scientists of many disciplines are sharing the bones, using them to their best advantage in rounding out our picture of human life and health. Curated collections that are subject to repatriation are being examined as efficiently as possible. Databases are being compiled and shared via the Web. Donated collections of skeletons are being built up to ensure that physical anthropologists of the future have more than mere measurements to work with. Bones have maintained their utility, but at the same time they have retained their symbolism and when gathered together inevitably have a meaning. They are trophies or relics or ancestors or specimens. Their importance as the latter is marked by the historic landmark status conferred on the collections at the National Museum of Health and Medicine, making them national treasures. International treasures (that have not been so designated) include the bone churches of

Rome, Portugal, and the Czech Republic. Abundance sometimes results in anonymity, but singularly the death's-head stares at us mockingly, more so if the individual is named and described. And yet identification adds value to remains from which as many details as possible are being culled to complete a demographic picture. The information obtained from the bones is organized into patterns like the bones themselves on the chapel walls. It is hoped that bones can be honored in the manner in which that word is understood in each culture and that those various definitions can be reconciled in ways that allow osteological secrets to be told.

Appendix: Addresses

Æbelholt Museum
Frederiksværkvejen
3400 Hillerød, Denmark

American Committee for
  Preservation of Archaeo
  logical Collections
P.O. Box 1171
Whittier, CA 90609-1171
www.acpac.org

Anthropologische Rudolf-
  Virchow-Sammlung
Medizinische Fakultät der
  Humboldt-Universität zu
  Berlin
Tucholskystrasse 2
D10117 Berlin, Germany

Anthropologische Staatssamm-
  lung
Karolinenpl. 2a
80333 München, Germany

Beinhaus
St. Michael's
Kircherweg 40
Hallstatt, Austria

The Bone Room
1569 Solano Avenue
Berkeley, CA 94707
www.boneroom.com

Carolina Biological Supply
  Company
2700 York Road
Burlington, NC 27215
www.carolina.com

Catacombes
1, place Denfert-Rochereau
75014 Paris, France

Cleveland Museum of Natural
  History
1 Wade Oval Drive
University Circle
Cleveland, OH 44106-1767
www.cmnh.org/research/
  physanth/skeletons/skeletons.
  html

Dickson Mounds Museum
10956 N. Dickson Mounds
  Road
Lewiston, IL 61542

Domkirche St. Stephan
Kirchenmeisteramt
A-1010 Wien
Stephansplatz 3
Vienna, Austria

Forensic Anthropology Center
Dept. of Anthropology
Univ. of Tennessee
252 S. Stadium Hall
Knoxville, TN 37996-0720

Golden Chariot Productions
270 Adelaide St. West
Toronto, Ont. M5H 1X6,
  Canada
www.head-hunter.com/

Goldene Kammer
Basilica of St. Ursula
Ursulaplatz, Cologne,
  Germany

Phoebe Hearst Museum
Univ. of California at Berkeley
103 Kroeber Hall #3712
Berkeley, CA 94720-3712
www.qal.berkeley.edu/~hearst/

Hrobka Kapucínského Klástera
Kapucínské nám. 5
Brno, Czech Republic

Kolomoki Mounds State Park
Blakely, GA 31723

Kostnice Sedlec
Zamecka 127
Kutna Hora — Sedlec
284 03, Czech Republic
www.kostnice.cz

Landesmuseum für
  Vorgeschichte
Richard Wagner-Str. 9/10
06114 Halle, Germany

Little Bighorn Battlefield
  National Monument
P.O. Box 39
Crow Agency, MT 59022
www.nps.gov/libi/

Maxilla and Mandible Ltd.
451 Columbus Avenue
New York, NY 10024
www.maxillaandmandible.com

Maxwell Museum of
  Anthropology
Univ. of New Mexico
University & Ash, N.E.
Albuquerque, NM 87131-1201
www.unm.edu/~maxwell/

Morbid Curiosity
Automatism Press
P.O. Box 170277
San Francisco, CA 94117
www.charnel.com/automatism

Musée de l'Homme
Palais de Chaillot

pl. du Trocadéro
75016 Paris, France

Musée Dupuytren
Hospital St. Antoine
184 Foubourg St.-Antoine
75571 Paris Cedex 12, France

Museo Archeologico e
Paleontologico
Corso Alfieri, 357
14100 Asti, Italy

Mütter Museum
College of Physicians of
Philadelphia
19 S. 22nd St.
Philadelphia, PA 19103
www.collphyphil.org/
muttpg1.shtml

National Museum of Health
and Medicine
Armed Forces Inst. of
Pathology
Walter Reed Army Medical
Center
Building 54
Washington, D.C. 20306-6000
www.natmedmuse.afip.org

National Museum of Natural
History
Smithsonian Institution
10th St. & Constitution Ave.,
N.W.
Washington, D.C. 20560-0112
www.mnh.si.edu

National Park Service
P.O. Box 37127
Washington, D.C. 20013-7127
www.nps.gov

Natural History Museum
London WC1B 3DG, U.K.
www.nhm.ac.uk/

Øm Kloster Museum

Munkevej 8
8660 Skanderborg, Denmark

Osteologische Sammlung des
Landesdenkmalamtes Baden-
Württemberg
Gartenstr. 70
72108 Rottenburg, Germany

Paleopathology Association
18655 Parkside
Detroit, MI 48221

The Panum Institute
Laboratory of Biological
Anthropology
Blegdamsvej 3
2200 N. Copenhagen, Den-
mark

The Parish of St. Leonard
Hythe Vicarage
Oak Walk
Hythe, Kent CT215DN, U.K.

Peabody Museum
Harvard University
11 Divinity Avenue
Cambridge, MA 02138
www.peabody.harvard.edu

C.A. Pound Human
Identification Laboratory
Dept. of Anthropology
P.O. Box 112545
Gainesville, FL 32611
http://web.anthro.ufl.edu/
c.a.poundlab/poundlab.htm

Ripley's Believe It or Not!
5728 Major Blvd.
Suite 700
Orlando, FL 32819

Rollettmuseum
Städtische
Sammlungen/Stadtarchiv

Weikersdorfer Pl 1
2500 Baden, Austria

Royal College of Surgeons of
Edinburgh
Nicolson St.
Edinburgh EH8 9DW, U.K.

Royal College of Surgeons of
England Hunterian Museum
Lincoln's Inn Fields
London WC2A 3PN, U.K.

Saints Alive Relics/ICHRusa
P.O. Box 0471
Temple City, CA 91780
www.ichrusa.com/saintsalive/

San Diego Museum of Man
1350 El Prado
Balboa Park
San Diego, CA 92101

Santa Maria della Concezione
Veneto 27
Rome, Italy

Skulls Unlimited International
10313 South Sunnylane
Oklahoma City, OK 73160
www.skullsunlimited.com

South Australian Museum
North Terrace
Adelaide, S.A. 5000, Australia

Staatliches Museum für
Völkerkunde
Palaispl. 11
Japanisches Palais
01097 Dresden, Germany

University of Pennsylvania
Museum of Archaeology and
Anthropology
33rd & Spruce Sts.
Philadelphia, PA 19104-6324

Glossary

Aboriginal. *adj.* Indigenous to a region; native.—**Aborigine**, *n.*

acetabulum. *n, pl.* **acetabula.** The socket in the innominate into which the femur head fits.

acrocephalic. also **acrocephalous.** *adj.* Tower-skulled; having a peaked or pointed head due to premature suture closure.—**acrocephaly**, *n.*

alveolus. *n., pl.* **alveoli.** A tooth socket.

anatomy. *n.* The science dealing with the structure of animals and plants; dissection of an animal in whole or in part to study its structure; a skeleton.—**anatomic, anatomical**, *adj.*

ankylosis. *n.* Complete fusion of a joint due to pathological changes, such as the degenerative inflammatory disease ankylosing spondylitis.—**ankylotic**, *adj.*, **ankylose**, *v.*

anthropology. *n.* The science of human origins, physical and cultural development, social beliefs, and biological characteristics; the study of the similarities and differences between humans and other animals.—**anthropologic, anthropological**, *adj.* **anthropologist**, *n.*

anthropometry. *n.* The measurement of the size and proportion of the human body and its parts.—**anthropometric, anthropometrical**, *adj.* **anthropometrist**, *n.*

appendicular skeleton. *n. phr.* The bones of the limbs, including the shoulder girdle.

archaeology. also **archeology.** *n.* The scientific study of historic or prehistoric peoples and cultures by analysis of their artifacts, esp. through excavation of ancient sites.—**archaeologic, archaeological**, *adj.* **archaeologist**, *n.*

articular. *adj.* Relating to the normal points of contact between adjacent bones; of the joints.

articular facet. *n. phr.* A plane on the bone that occurs where two bones meet.

articulation. *n.* An area in which adjacent bones are in contact at a joint; assembly of the separate components of a skeleton in correct anatomical position.—**articulate**, *v.*

assemblage. *n.* The complete collection of artifacts or remains found at a particular site.

astragalus. *n.* Ankle bone; talus.—**astragalar**, *adj.*

atlas. *n.* The first cervical vertebra, which supports the head.

axial skeleton. *n. phr.* The bones of the head and trunk, including the vertebrae, pelvis, ribs, and sternum.

axis. *n.* The second cervical vertebra.

B.P. *n.* Before present day.

basicranium. *n.* The base of the skull.

biological identity. *n. phr.* The basic characteristics of a person, such as age, sex, race, race, and stature, that may be determined from skeletal remains.

bone *n.* One of the structural components of the skeleton of a vertebrate; the hard connective tissue that forms the skeleton.

bone bed. *n. phr.* A layer of skeletal material encountered in an excavation.

bone board. *n. phr.* Osteometric board.

bone house. *n. phr.* Ossuary.

boss. *n.* A protuberance or broad, round growth on bone.

brachycephalic. also **brachycephalous.** *adj.* Having a broad, short skull.—**brachycephaly, brachycephalism**, *n.*

bundle burial. *n. phr.* A group of defleshed and disarticulated bones tied or wrapped together for burial.

burial bundle *see* **bundle burial**

calcaneus. *n., pl.* **calcanei.** The largest tarsal bone, forming the prominence of the heel; heel bone.

calcification. *n.* The process of the formation of bones and teeth.—**calcify**, *v.*

callus. *n*. The hard tissue that grows at the site of a fracture to unite the break during the healing process.

calotte. *n*. The calvarium without the base; skullcap.

calvarium. *n., pl.* **calvaria**. The dome of the skull; a skull that is missing the bones of the face and mandible.

canal. *n*. A tunnel-like opening or cavity in a bone.

cancellous bone. also **cancellate bone**. *n. phr.* Porous, spongy bone inside a solid casing of compact bone. *See* **trabecular**.

carpal bone. *n. phr.* One of the bones of the wrist.

carpus. *n., pl.* **carpi**. The group of bones forming the wrist.

catacomb. also **catacombs**. *n*. An underground cemetery, esp. one that consists of tunnels and chambers with hollows in the walls to contain remains.—**catacumbal**, *adj*.

caudal vertebrae. *n. phr.* The fused vertebrae below the sacrum; tailbone.

center of ossification. *n. phr.* An area of the body in which a skeletal element initially forms.

cephalic index. *n. phr.* The ratio of the breadth to the length of the skull, multiplied by 100.

cervical vertebrae. *n. phr.* The bones of the neck, consisting of the top seven vertebra.

charnel, *n*. also **charnel house**, *n. phr.* A repository for the bodies or bones of the dead.

clavicle. *n*. The collar bone.—**clavicular**, **claviculate**, *adj*.

coarse fiber bone. *n. phr.* Bone which is permeated microscopically by large channels containing fat, blood vessels, and connective tissue.

coccyx. *n., pl.* **coccyges**. The tailbone, consisting of the caudal vertebrae.—**coccygeal**, *adj*.

coffin wear. *n. phr.* A flattening of the side of the skull that develops over long periods of time from small movements of the bone against a hard surface.

collagen. *n*. A fibrous insoluble protein found in the skin, ligaments, cartilage, and bone.—**collagenous**, *adj*.

commingled. *p. part.* Of bone assemblages containing the physical remains of two or more individuals whose skeletons are mixed together and often incomplete.

comminuted fracture. *n. phr.* Breakage of a bone resulting in splintering or crushing.

compact bone. *n. phr.* The hard, dense outer layer of bone. *See* **cortical bone**.

comparative osteology. *n. phr.* Study of the similarity and differences within and between the bones of different species.

condyle. *n*. A rounded projection on the end of a bone, usually for articulation with another bone.—**condylar**, *adj*.

corpus. *n*. The body of a bone.

cortex. *n*. The outer portion of a bone.

cortical bone. *n. phr.* The solid outer layer of bone, thickest on the shafts of the long bones and thinner on their ends and on the surface of irregular bones.

costa. *n*. A rib.—**costal**, *adj*.

cranial deformation. *n. phr.* The alteration of the normal shape of the skull by applying external forces, intentionally or unintentionally.

cranial index. *n. phr.* Cephalic index.

craniography. *n*. Examination of the skull as depicted by drawings, photographs, and charts.—**craniographic**, *adj*.

craniology. *n*. The science of the size, shape, and other characteristics of the skull.—**craniological**, *adj*. **craniologist**, *n*.

craniometry. *n*. The measurement of the skull and its contents.—**craniometric**, **craniometrical**, *adj*. **craniometrist**, *n*.

craniostenosis. also **craniosynostosis**, *n*. Premature closure of the sutures of the skull.

cranium. *n., pl.* **crania**, **craniums**. The skull without the lower jaw; the braincase.—**cranial**, *adj*.

crest. *n*. A prominent, usually sharp and thin ridge of bone.

cribra crania. *n. phr.* An abnormality involving perforations or porosities in the inner skull, usually in the frontal region.

cribra orbitalia. *n. phr.* An abnormality involving pitting of the orbital part of the frontal bone.

crural index. *n. phr.* Ratio of the length of the tibia divided by the length of the femur, multiplied by 100.

crypt. *n*. An underground burial chamber, esp. beneath a church.

cuneiform. *n*. One of the three wedge-shaped bones of the ankle.

curate. *v*. To manage and attend to a collection.—**curatorial**, *adj*. **curator**, **curatorship**, *n*.

dentocranial. *adj*. Pertaining to the teeth and cranium.

dermal bone. *n. phr.* The facial bones and the bones forming the roof and sides of the skull.

diagenesis. *n*. The chemical, physical, and biological changes that occur in a bone after initial deposition, with the exception of weathering.—**diagenetic**, *adj.*

diaphysis. *n.* The long, straight section between the ends of a long bone; shaft.—**diaphysial**, **diaphyseal**, *adj.*

diploë. *n.* Cancellous bone between the inner and outer compact layers of the flat cranial bones.—**diploic, diploetic**, *adj.*

disarticulation. *n.* Separation, as of the loose bones of a skeleton; the state of being out of their natural order.—**disarticulate**, *v.*

discrete trait. *n. phr.* Nonmetric trait.

distal. *adj.* Of the part of a bone that is furthest from the center of the body.

documented skeletal collection. *n. phr.* A group of skeletons from individuals whose identities, and other information that may include age, sex, race, stature, cause and manner of death, and medical history, are known.

dolichocephalic. also **dolichocephalous**. *adj.* Long-skulled.—**dolichocephalism, dolichocephaly**, *n.*

dry bone. *n. phr.* Bone that is not flesh-covered; skeletal material that has lost its organic components.

eburnation. *n.* The smooth, polished surface of exposed subchondral bone produced when destruction of the intervening cartilage allows the bones in a joint to rub together.

ectocranial. *adj.* On the outer surface of the skull.

edentulous. *adj.* Without teeth.

element. *n.* A single kind of bone.

eminence. *n.* A bony projection, usually smaller than a prominence.

endocranial. *adj.* On the inside of the skull.

epiphysis. *n., pl.* **epiphyses**. The extremity of a bone separated from the shaft by a cartilaginous disk during development, and subsequently uniting with the shaft through continued ossification.—**epiphysial, epiphyseal**, *adj.*

erosion. *n.* Wearing away of the external surface of a bone.—**erosional**, *adj.*

ethnography . *n.* A branch of anthropology dealing with the study and scientific description of individual cultures.—**ethnographic, ethnographical**, *adj.* **ethnographer**, *n.*

ethnology. *n.* A branch of anthropology dealing with the analysis and comparison of cultures and their historical development, formerly focusing on the origin, distribution, and distinguishing characteristics of the human races.—**ethnologic, ethnological**, *adj.* **ethnologist**, *n.*

evolution. *n.* The continuous genetic adapta-

tion of organisms or species to the environment by the integrating agencies of selection, hybridization, inbreeding, and mutation.

excarnation. *n.* The practice of allowing the flesh of a corpse to decay so that the bones may be collected and deposited.

excavation. *n.* The process of unearthing or exposing by digging.

exostosis. *n.* A growth from the surface of a bone, often involving the ossification of muscular attachments and characteristically capped by cartilage. **exostosed, exostotic**, *adj.*

extrasutural bone. *n. phr.* Wormian bone.

facet. *n.* A small articular surface on a bone.

facial reconstruction. *n. phr.* The build-up of clay or other material on the skull or a cast of it to restore a likeness of the individual, esp. based on average thickness of the flesh.

facial reproduction *see* **facial reconstruction**

femur. *n., pl.* **femora, femurs**. The thigh bone.—**femoral**, *adj.*

fibula. *n., pl.* **fibulae, fibulas**. The outer and thinner of the two bones in each lower leg.—**fibular**, *adj.*

fine-fiber bone. *n. phr.* Lamellar bone.

flat bone. *n. phr.* A bone with a large surface area, such as a scapula.

foramen. *n., pl.* **foramina**. A natural opening or orifice in a bone.—**foraminal**, *adj.*

foramen magnum. *n. phr.* The opening at the base of the skull through which the brain stem connects with the spinal column.

forensic anthropology. *n. phr.* The application of osteology and physical anthropology to medicolegal matters.

forensic osteology. *n. phr.* Medicolegal investigation based on examination and interpretation of skeletal material.

fossa. *n.* A pit, cavity, or depression in a bone.

fossilization. *n.* Mineralization of the organic components of bone.—**fossilize**, *v.*

fovea. *n.* A pit or depression in a bone, usually smaller than a fossa.

fracture. *n.* Breakage of bone or cartilage.

Frankfurt plane. also **Frankfurt horizontal**. *n. phr.* A standard orientation of the skull to allow valid comparisons and to approximate the position of the head during life.

fresh bone. *n. phr.* Bone that is flesh-covered; skeletal material that retains its organic components.

friable. *adj.* Brittle; likely to crumble.

frontal. *adj.* Of a skull bone that forms the forehead and upper eye sockets.

fusion. *n.* The replacement of soft tissue with bone, resulting in a solid union between two skeletal elements.

gracile. *adj.* Delicate; characteristic of a female skeleton.—**gracility, gracileness**, *adj.*

green bone. *n. phr.* Fresh bone; bone that is flesh-covered.

growth arrest lines *see* **Harris' lines**

hard tissue. *n. phr.* The bones and teeth.

Harris' lines. *pl. n. phr.* Zones of lamellar bone that appear as lines on an x-ray and indicate temporary growth arrest.

Haversian canals. *pl. n. phr.* Microscopic channels in the compact tissue of bone that contain blood vessels, lymph vessels, nerves, and marrow.

head. *n.* The large, rounded, usually articular end of a bone.

headhunter. *n.* One who removes and preserves the heads of enemies as trophies.—**headhunting**, *v.*

hominid. *n.* A member of the family *Hominidae* consisting of all modern or extinct species of the genera *Homo* and *Australopithecus* and characterized by bipedalism.

humerus. *n., pl.* **humeri**. The bone of the upper arm.

hyoid. *n.* The U-shaped bone at the root of the tongue.

hyperostosis. *n., pl.* **hyperostoses**. Development of bridges of bone due to excessive growth.—**hyperostotic**, *adj.*

hypogeum. *n., pl.* **hypogea**. A subterranean burial chamber.—**hypogeal, hypogeous**, *adj.*

hypostosis. *n., pl.* **hypostoses**. Abnormal development of bony tissue.—**hypostotic**, *adj.*

ileum. *n., pl.* **ilia**. The thin, bladelike section of the innominate above the hip socket.—**ileal**, *adj.*

in situ. *adj.* Situated in its original position.

inca bone. *n. phr.* A small bone occurring in the suture between the parietal bones of the skull.

individualization. *n.* The identification of an individual through comparison of the bones and teeth with premortem records.

innominate. *n.* One of the paired, fused bones forming the pelvis and consisting of the ilium, ischium, and pubis.

interosseous. *adj.* Occurring between bones.

intrusive burial. *n. phr.* Interment in earlier strata that may hamper the dating of an excavated skeleton.

involucrum. *n., pl.* **involucra**. A sheath of bone that grows to surround a sequestrum.

irregular bone. *n. phr.* A bone with a complex shape, such as a vertebra.

ischium. *n., pl.* **ischia**. The thick lower portion of the hip bone.

jacket. *v.* To cover an exposed bone with a layer of plaster to protect it when removed from the excavation site.

joint-mice. *pl. n. phr.* Small irregular bones in the cranial sutures; wormian bones.

lacuna. *n., pl.* **lacunae, lacunas**. A small hollow space in a bone.—**lacunal, lacunary**, *adj.*

lamella. *n., pl.* **lamellae, lamellas**. A thin plate of bone.—**lamellar**, *adj.*

lamellar bone. *n. phr.* Bone in which collagen fibers are organized microscopically in layers or sheets around Haversian canals.

landmark. *n.* Standard reference point for taking anthropometric measurements.

lipping. *pres. part.* Projecting of bone beyond the normal margins.

long bone. *n. phr.* A large, cylindrical bone containing marrow and consisting of a shaft and two extremities; a femur, tibia, fibula, humerus, radius, or ulna.

lumbar vertebrae. *n. phr.* The bones of the lower back, consisting of the five lowest and strongest vertebrae.

maceration. *n.* Removal of flesh from a body during preparation of the skeleton.—**macerate**, *v.*

macrocephalic. also **macrocephalous**. *adj.* Large-skulled.—**macrocephaly**, *n.*

malar bone. *n. phr.* Zygomatic arch.

mandible. *n.* The bone of the lower jaw.—**mandibular**, *adj.*

mastoid process. *n. phr.* A projection on the skull behind and below the opening for the ear, to which the muscles of the neck attach.

matrix. *n.* The intercellular material of bone, made of of collagen; the substance, such as soil or clay, from which human remains are excavated.

maxilla. *n., pl.* **maxillae, maxillas**. The upper jawbone.—**maxillary**, *adj.*

meatus. *n.* An opening or short canal in bone, such as the opening of the ear.—**meatal**, *adj.*

medullary cavity. *n. phr.* The marrow-filled hollow inside a long bone.

mesocephalic *adj.* Having a skull of medium size.—**mesocephaly**, *n.*

metacarpal. *n.* One of the bones of the hand between the fingers and the wrist.

metacarpus. *n.* The group of bones between the phalanges and the wrist.

metaphysis. *n*. The wider part at the end of the shaft of a long bone, where the bone growth that joins it to the epiphysis occurs.

metatarsal. *n*. One of the bones of the foot between the toes and the ankle.

metatarsus. *n*. The group of bones between the phalanges and the ankle.

metric trait. *n. phr*. A characteristic of bone, such as length, that can be measured.

metrical analysis. *n. phr*. The comparison of standardized measurements of bones with reference sets of figures.

microcephaly. *n*. Having an unusually small head.—**microcephalic**, *adj*.

MNI. *abbrev*. Minimum number of individuals represented in a sample.

monostotic. *adj*. Pertaining to a single bone.

morphology. *n*. The study of the form, structure, and appearance of skeletal elements.—**morphological**, *adj*.

muscle marking. *n. phr*. A line on a bone indicating where the muscle attached.

NAGPRA. *abbrev*. The Native American Graves Protection and Repatriation Act.

nasal spine. *n. phr*. The thin projection of bone from the midline of the lower nasal margin that holds the cartilaginous center of the nose.

nearthrosis. *n*. A false joint formed between parts of a fractured bone that have not united.

neck. *n*. The section of a bone between the head and the shaft.

neurocranial vault. *n. phr*. The portion of the skull that houses and protects the brain; braincase.

neurocranium *see* **neurocranial vault**

nonmetric trait. *n. phr*. A characteristic of bone, such as shape, that can be described and compared, but not measured; variations of skeletal elements than can best be classified as present or absent.

nuchal crest. *n. phr*. The bony ridge at the back of the skull to which the neck muscles attach.

occipital. *adj*. Of the bone in the skull at the back of the head.

orbit. *n*. The bony socket that contains the eye.

os coxae. *n*. The bony pelvis consisting of the ilium, the ischium, and pubis; innominate.

osseous. *adj*. Composed of or resembling bone.

ossicle. also **ossiculum**. *n*. A very small bone.—**ossicular**, **ossiculate**, *adj*.

ossification. *n*. The fusion of bones which are segmented in subadult skeletons.—**ossify**, *v*.

ossuary. also **ossuarium**. *n., pl*. **ossuaries**, **ossuaria**. A place or receptacle for the bones of the dead; a communal grave containing the remains of individuals initially stored elsewhere.

osteitis. *n*. Inflammation of bone due to infection or injury.

osteoarchaeology. *n*. The recovery and study of excavated skeletal material.—**osteoarchaeological**, *adj*.

osteoarthritis. *n*. Inflammation of a joint characterized by destruction of articular cartilage, outgrowth of bone, lipping, and spur formation.

osteobiography. *n*. The story of an individual's life as documented in his or her skeleton.

osteoblast. *n*. A specialized cell that produces bone.

osteoclast. *n*. A specialized cell that destroys bone.

osteogenesis. *n*. The formation and development of bone.—**osteogenic**, **osteogenous**, *adj*.

osteoid. *adj*. Resembling bone; having a skeleton of bones.

osteology. *n*. A branch of anatomy dealing with the study of the skeleton.—**osteologic**, **osteological**, *adj*. **osteologist**, *n*.

osteolysis. *n*. The softening and destruction of bone, especially due to lack or loss of calcium.

osteoma. *n*. A benign osseous tumor that develops on bone, particularly of the skull.

osteomalacia. *n*. Softening of the bones due to a vitamin deficiency.

osteometric board. *n. phr*. A device used to measure long bones and other skeletal materials.

osteometry. *n*. The standardized measurement of the bones of the human skeleton for description and comparison.—**osteometric**, **osteometrical**, *adj*.

osteomyelitis. *n*. Inflammation of the bone and marrow usually caused by a bacterial infection.

osteon. *n*. The basic structural unit of compact bone, consisting of a Haversian canal and the lamellae that surround it.

osteopathology. *n*. The study of diseases of the bone.—**osteopathologic**, **osteopathological**, *adj*. **osteopathologist**, *n*.

osteopenia. *n*. Loss of bone; cortical thinning.

osteoperiostitis. *n*. Inflammation of a bone and its protective periosteum.

osteophyte. *n*. A small osseous outgrowth on the surface of a bone.

osteoporosis. *n*. Increased porosity of bone due to lack of mineralization.—**osteoporotic**, *adj*.

osteosarcoma. *n*. A malignant tumor of the bone.

osteosclerosis. *n*. Hardening and increased density of the bone as a result of chronic inflammation or stimulation of bone cells.

oxycephalic *see* **acrocephalic palate**. *n*. The bones of the skull that support the roof of the mouth.

paleoanthropology. *n*. The study of human origins, esp. based on fossil remains.—**paleoanthropological**, *adj*. **paleoanthropologist**, *n*.

paleodemography. *n*. The study of the vital statistics of past populations, including population size and structure, life expectancy, and birth and death rates, esp. as reconstructed through analysis of skeletal remains.

paleopathology. *n*. The study of human biological history, esp. through the examination of ancient remains.—**paleopathologist**, *n*.

parietal. *adj*. Of the bones of the skull that support the side of the head.

patella. *n*., *pl*. **patellae**, **patellas**. The knee cap.—**patellar**, *adj*.

pathology. *n*. The study of the origin, nature, and course of disease; deviation from a healthy or normal condition.—**pathologic**, **pathological**, *adj*. **pathologist**, *n*.

pelvis. *n*. The bony structure composed of the sacrum, ilium, ischium, and pubis.

periosteum. *n*. The membrane of connective tissue that covers all surfaces of bones except the areas of articulation.—**periosteal**, **periosteous**, *adj*.

periostitis. *n*. Inflammation of the periosteal layer of a bone.

periostosis. *n*. Abnormal bone formation on the periosteal layer of a bone.

phalanx. *n*., *pl*. **phalanges**, **phalanxes**. Any of the bones of the fingers or toes.

phrenology. *n*. The study of the shape of the skull in the belief that it indicates character and mental capacity.—**phrenologic**, **phrenological**, *adj*. **phrenologist**, *n*.

physical anthropology. *n. phr*. The branch of anthropology dealing with the biological study of humans to record and explain diversity within the context of human culture and behavior.

physiologic age. *n. phr*. The estimated age of an individual based on comparison of the degree of physical maturity of the skeleton with the majority of the population.

polyostotic. *adj*. Affecting several bones.

porosis. *n*. A condition of bone marked by the formation of pores or cavities.

porotic hyperostosis. *n. phr*. The thickening and pitting of the skull.

post-cranial. *adj*. Of the bones below the skull.

primary burial. *n. phr*. An articulated skeleton buried in the flesh.

primary ossification center. *n. phr*. The site where bone first begins to form during its growth.

process. *n*. A bony prominence or outgrowth.

provenance. also **provenience**. *n*. The exact relation of a specimen to the deposit in which it is found; place of origin.

proximal. *adj*. Of the part of a bone that is closest to the center of the body.

pseudoarthrosis. *n*. A false joint formed between parts of a fractured bone that have not united.

pseudo-articulation. *n*. Nearthrosis.

pubic symphysis. *n. phr*. The mid-line at the front of the pelvis where the pubic bones meet.

pubis. *n*. The part of the hipbone that forms the front of the pelvis.

pyriform aperture. *n. phr*. The nasal opening of the skull.

radius. *n*., *pl*. **radii**, **radiuses**. One of the two bones in the lower arm.

ramus. *n*. The portion of a bone that is at an angle to the body.

reactive bone. *n. phr*. Bone that is in the process of being formed, lost, or modified, usually in response to a pathological condition.

reconstruction *see* **facial reconstruction**, **skull reconstruction**

relic. *n*. A venerated object associated with a holy person, esp. part of his or her bodily remains.

reliquary. *n*. A container in which a relic is enshrined.

remodelling. *pr. part*. The process through which bone tissue is constantly removed and replaced in response to changing stresses on the body.—**remodel**, *v*.

repatriation. *n*. The return of curated human skeletal remains to the groups with which they are culturally affiliated, usually for reburial.—**repatriate**, *v*.

resorption. *n*. The biological process of the destruction of bone.

robust. *adj*. Heavy, large, and muscularly developed; characteristic of a male skeleton.—**robusticity**, *adj*.

sacrum. *n., pl.* **sacra.** The fused vertebrae at the back of the pelvis.—**sacral,** *adj.*

salvage osteology. *n. phr.* Excavation of human remains necessitated by development and usually carried out hurriedly before the site is destroyed.

scaphocephalic. also **scaphocephalous.** *adj.* Having an elongated, keel-shaped skull.—**scaphocephaly,** *n.*

scapula. *n., pl.* **scapulae, scapulas.** The shoulder blade.—**scapular,** *adj.*

scoliosis. *n.* Abnormal lateral curvature of the spine.—**scoliotic,** *adj.*

secondary burial. *n. phr.* Burial of an individual's bones following temporary disposition during which the flesh has decomposed or been removed; interment of disarticulated bones.

sequestrum. *n., pl.* **sequestra.** An isolated piece of dead bone, usually resulting from disease or trauma.

sesamoid. *n.* A small bone located within a tendon or cartilage.

shaft. *n.* The long, straight section between the ends of a long bone.

short bone. *n. phr.* A small bone consisting of a shaft and two extremities, such as a metacarpal.

side *v.* To determine whether a bone is from the left or right side of the body, based on the observation of bilateral symmetry.

sinus. *n.* An air-filled cavity within a cranial bone.

skeletal age. *n. phr.* The estimated age of a person at death as determined by developmental and other markers.

skeletal biology. *n. phr.* The study of demographics and other characteristics through examination of bones.

skeleton. *n.* The set of bones that form the framework of a vertebrate body.—**skeletal,** *adj.*

skeletonize. *v.* The reduction of a human body to its skeletal elements, usually by natural processes.—**skeletonization,** *n.*

skull. *n.* The skeletal components of the head, including the lower jaw.

skullcap. *n.* The dome of the skull.

skull reconstruction. *n. phr.* The reassembly of a fragmented cranium.

skull vault. *n. phr.* The braincase.

splanchnocranium. *n.* The bones of the face.

spondylitis. *n.* Inflammation of the vertebrae.—**spondylitic,** *adj.*

squama. *n., pl.* **squamae.** The flat portion of a cranial bone.

sternum. *n., pl.* **sternums** or **sterna.** The breast bone.—**sternal,** *adj.*

subchondral bone. *n. phr.* Bone underlying cartilage.

sulcus. *n.* A groove or fissure in a bone.

suture. *n.* The irregular line formed by the meeting of two or more bones of the skull.

sutureal bones. *pl. n. phr.* Small irregular bones in the cranial sutures.

symphysis. *n., pl.* **symphyses.** A point of junction between two paired bones.—**symphyseal,** *adj.*

talus. *n., pl.* **tali.** The ankle bone.

taphonomy. *n.* The study of changes in human remains caused by environmental conditions.—**taphonomic,** *adj.* **taphonomist,** *n.*

tarsal. *n.* One of the bones of the ankle or foot.

tarsus. *n.* The group of bones making up the ankle.

temporal. *adj.* Of the bone forming the lower sides of the skull.

thoracic vertebrae. *pl. n. phr.* The bones of the middle back, consisting of the twelve vertebrae to which the ribs are attached.

tibia. *n., pl.* **tibias, tibiae.** The inner of the two bones in the lower leg.—**tibial,** *adj.*

torus. *n., pl.* **tori.** A thickening, protuberance, or round ridge of bone.

trabecular bone. *n. phr.* The porous, lightweight bone found in the interior of bones, including the ends of the long bones and the vertebrae.

translation. *n.* Transfer of the relics of a saint from one location to another.

trepanation *see* **trephination**

trephination. *n.* The surgical removal of a disk of bone, usually from the skull.

tubercle. *n.* A small, rough projection of bone, often at the site of a tendon or ligament attachment.

tuberosity. *n.* A large, rough projection of bone, often at the site of a tendon or ligament attachment.

ulna. *n., pl.* **ulnae, ulnas.** One of the two bones in the lower arm.—**ulnar,** *adj.*

vertebra. *n., pl.* **vertebrae, vertebras.** The bones of the spine.—**vertebral,** *adj.*

vitrification. *n.* The heating of bone to temperatures of 800° C. or more, resulting in a hard, porcelain-like quality.—**vitrify,** *v.*

wet bone. *n. phr.* Bone that retains its organic components.

wormian bones. *pl. n. phr.* Small irregular bones in the cranial sutures.

woven bone. *n. phr.* Bone which is microscopically permeated by large channels containing fat, blood vessels, and connective tissue.

zygomatic arch. *n. phr.* The cheek bone.

Bibliography

Adams, W.H. 1972. *Famous Caves and Catacombs.* 1886. Reprint, Freeport, N.Y.: Books for Libraries.

Anthropological Survey in Alaska. 1930. Wash., D.C.: Government Printing Office.

Arden, H. 1989. Who owns our past? *National Geographic* 175, no. 3 (March): 376–393.

Ariès, P. 1982. *The Hour of Our Death.* Translated by H. Weaver. N.Y.: Vintage.

Armelagos, G.J., D.S. Carlson, and D.P. Van Gerven. 1982. The theoretical foundations and development of skeletal biology. In *A History of American Physical Anthropology 1930–1980*, ed. F. Spencer, 305–328. N.Y.: Academic Press.

Auchard, J. 1999. Tyrants' day out. *Washington Post*, May 2.

Aufderheide, A.C. and D.J. Ortner. 1991. Synthesis and conclusions. In *Human Paleopathology*, ed. D.J. Ortner and A.C. Aufderheide. Wash., D.C.: Smithsonian Institution Press.

Bahn, P.G. 1991. The face of Mozart. *Archaeology* March/April: 38–41.

Barber, P. 1988. *Vampires, Burial, and Death: Folklore and Reality.* New Haven: Yale Univ. Press.

Barker, J.F. 1998. *A Study of the Crypt of St. Leonard's Church, Hythe: Being all the Available Evidence Concerning the Bones Examined and Explained.* Hythe: Chaucer Technology School.

Bass, W.M. 1983. The occurrence of Japanese trophy skulls in the United States. *Journal of Forensic Sciences* 28, no. 3 (July): 800–803.

_____. 1984. Time interval since death. In *Human Identification*, ed. T.A. Rathbun and J.E. Buikstra. Springfield, Ill.: C.C. Thomas.

_____. 1987. *Human Osteology: A Laboratory and Field Manual, 3rd ed.* Columbia: Missouri Archaeological Society.

Beard, T.C. 1997. The mound. In *Hopewell in Mt. Vernon*. Ed. General Electric. N.P.: G.E. Co.

Bennike, P. 1991. Epidemiological aspects of paleopathology in Denmark. In *Human Paleopathology*, ed. D.J. Ortner and A.C. Aufderheide. Wash., D.C.: Smithsonian.

Bentley, J. 1985. *Restless Bones: The Story of Relics.* London: Constable.

Binford, L.R. 1981. *Bones: Ancient Men and Modern Myths.* San Diego: Academic Press.

Blakey, M.L. 1996. Skull doctors revisited. In *Race and Other Misadventures: Essays in Honor of Ashley Montagu in his Ninetieth Year*, ed. L.T. Reynolds and L. Lieberman. Dix Hills, N.Y.: General Hall.

Boddington, A. 1987. From bones to population: The problem of numbers. In *Death, Decay and Reconstruction*, ed. A. Boddington, A.N. Garland, and R.C. Janaway. Manchester: Manchester Univ. Press.

_____. A.N. Garland, and R.C. Janaway, eds. 1987. *Death, Decay and Reconstruction: Approaches to Archaeology and Forensic Science.* Manchester, England: Manchester Univ. Press.

Bondeson, J. 1997. *A Cabinet of Medical Curiosities.* N.Y.: W.W. Norton.

Brace, C.L. 1982. The roots of the race concept in American physical anthropology. In *A History of American Physical Anthropology 1930–1980*, ed. F. Spencer. N.Y.: Academic Press.

Brew, J.O. 1966a. *People and Projects of the Peabody Museum 1866–1966.* Cambridge, Mass.: Peabody Museum of Harvard University.

_____. 1966b. *Early Days of the Peabody Museum at Harvard University.* Cambridge, Mass.: Peabody Museum of Harvard University:

Brothwell, D.R. 1981. *Digging Up Bones: The Excavation, Treatment and Study of Human*

Skeletal Remains. San Diego: Academic Press.

Browne, M.W. 1991. Scientist tells silent victims' tales of terror. *New York Times*, April 9: C1.

Buckland, F. 1873. *Curiosities of Natural History*. 4 vols. London: Richard Bentley & Son.

Buckley, J.T. 1999. Ripley's warehouse of the weird. *USA Today*, Jan. 15.

Buikstra, J.E. 1981. A specialist in ancient cemetery studies looks at the reburial issue. *Early Man* 3: 26–27.

_____. and G.R. Milner. 1989. *The Dickson Mounds Site: An Annotated Bibliography*. Springfield: Illinois State Museum.

_____. and D.H. Ubelaker, eds. 1994. *Standards for Data Collection from Human Skeletal Remains*. Fayetteville: Arkansas Archeological Survey.

Butler, J. 1995. *The Quest for Becket's Bones*. New Haven, Conn.: Yale.

Carmichael, B. 1971. *Incredible Collectors, Weird Antiques, and Odd Hobbies*. New Jersey: Prentice-Hall.

Chamberlain, A. 1994. *Human Remains*. Berkeley: Univ. of California Press.

Ciarallo, A. and E. De Carolis, eds. 1999 *Pompeii: Life in a Roman Town*. Milan: Electa.

Clarke, R.J. 1998. First ever discovery of a well-preserved skull and associated skeleton of Australopithecus. *South African Journal of Science* 94, no. 10 (Oct.).

Cobb, W.M. 1936. *The Laboratory of Anatomy and Physical Anthropology of Howard University*. Wash., D.C.: Howard Univ.

_____. 1939. Thomas Wingate Todd: An appreciation. *American Journal of Physical Anthropology* 25 (Supp): 5–7.

_____. 1959. Thomas Wingate Todd. *Journal of the National Medical Assoc.* 51, no. 3: 233–246.

Colbert, C. 1997. *A Measure of Perfection: Phrenology and the Fine Arts In America*. Chapel Hill: Univ. of North Carolina Press.

Cooperthwaite, D.R. 1978. *Ripley's Believe It or Not! A Guide to the Collection of Oddities and Curiosities*. Ripley International.

Crist, T.A.J. 1995. Bone chemistry analysis and documentary archaeology: Dietary patterns of enslaved African Americans in the South Carolina low country. In *Bodies of Evidence*, ed. A.L. Grauer. N.Y.: Wiley-Liss.

Cruz, J.C. 1984. *Relics*. Huntington, Ind.: Our Sunday Visitor.

Culbertson, J. and T. Randall. 1986. *Permanent Parisians: An Illustrated Guide to the Cemeteries of Paris*. Chelsea, Vt.: Chelsea Green.

Curry, D.C. 1999. *Feast of the Dead: Aboriginal Ossuaries in Maryland*. Crownsville, Md.: Archeological Society of Maryland and Maryland Historical Trust Press.

Danforth, L.M. 1982. *The Death Rituals of Rural Greece*. Princeton, N.J.: Princeton Univ. Press.

Davidson, G.W. 1991. The human remains controversies. *Caduceus* 7, no. 1 (Spring): 18–33.

Davies, J.D. 1971. *Phrenology: Fad and Science, a Nineteenth-Century American Crusade*. Hamden, Conn.: Archon Books.

de Montclos, B. and J.-P. Willesme. 1994. *Catacombes: General Guide*. Translated by C. Taylor-Bouché. Paris: Paris-Musées.

Drexler, M. 1986. The secrets of the skeletons: Bone collection chronicles life, death in another era. *The Plain Dealer Magazine* (Oct. 26).

Dvorchak, R.J. and L. Holewa. 1991. *Milwaukee Massacre: Jeffrey Dahmer and the Milwaukee Murders*. N.Y.: Dell.

Echo-Hawk, R.C. and W.R. Echo-Hawk. 1994. *Battlefields and Burial Grounds: The Indian Struggle to Protect Ancestral Graves in the United States*. Minneapolis: Lerner.

El-Najjar, M.Y. 1977. The distribution of human skeletal material in the continental U.S. *American Journal of Physical Anthropology* 46: 507–512.

Emerson, E. 1998. Remains of the day. *Los Angeles Times*, Oct. 18: L10.

Ericksen, M.F. 1982. How 'representative' is the Terry Collection? Evidence from the proximal femur. *American Journal of Physical Anthropology* 59: 345–350.

Fagan, B.M., ed. 1996. *Eyewitness to Discovery*. Oxford: Oxford Univ. Press.

Federal Register. 1998. Vol. 63, no. 77: April 22.

Florence, R. 1996. *City of the Dead: A Journey Through St. Louis Cemetery #1, New Orleans, Louisiana*. Lafayette: Center for Louisiana Studies, Univ. of Southwestern Louisiana.

Folsom, F. and M.E. Folsom. 1994. *America's Ancient Treasures*. Albuquerque: Univ. of New Mexico Press.

Fornaciari, G. and S. Gamba. 1993. The mummies of the church of S. Maria Della Grazia in Comiso, Sicily. *Paleopathology Newsletter* 81 (March): 7–10.

Gardiner, R. 1991. Edgar orders burial site to be closed. *Daily Ledger* (Canton, Ill.). Nov. 25.

Geary, P.J. 1978. *Furta Sacra: Thefts of Relics in the Central Middle Ages*. Princeton, N.J.: Princeton Univ. Press.

General Electric Company, ed. 1997. *Hopewell*

in Mt. Vernon: A Study of the Mt. Vernon Site (12-PO-885). N.P.: General Electric Co.

Gill, G.W. 1984. A forensic test case for a new method of geographical race determination. In *Human Identification*, ed. T.A. Rathbun and J.E. Buikstra. Springfield, Ill.: C.C. Thomas.

_____. 1994. Skeletal injuries of pioneers. In *Skeletal Biology in the Great Plains*, ed. D.W. Owsley and R.L. Jantz. Wash., D.C.: Smithsonian.

Gladykowska-Rzeczycka, J. 1991. Tumors in antiquity in east and middle Europe. In *Human Paleopathology*, ed. D.J. Ortner and A.C. Aufderheide. Wash., D.C.: Smithsonian.

Goldstein, L. and K. Kintigh. 1990. Ethics and the reburial controversy. *American Antiquity* 55, No. 3: 585–591.

Gottlieb, M. 1982. Skeletons in the closet: Who was Dr. T. Wingate Todd and what was he doing with all those bones? *Northern Ohio Live Magazine.*

Gould, S.J. 1996. *The Mismeasure of Man.* N.Y.: W.W. Norton.

Grauer, A.L., ed. 1995. *Bodies of Evidence: Reconstructing History Through Skeletal Analysis.* N.Y.: Wiley-Liss.

Gugliotta, G. 1999. Unearthed skeleton launches a debate on first Americans: Tribes vie for custody of 'Kennewick Man.' *Washington Post*, July 25: A3.

Gup, T. 2000. Empire of the dead. *Smithsonian* 31, no. 1 (April):106–113.

Habenstein, R.W. and W.M. Lamers. 1994. *Funeral Customs the World Over.* Milwaukee, Wis.: Bulfin Printers.

Haestier, R. 1934. *Dead Men Tell Tales: A Survey of Exhumations, from Earliest Antiquity to the Present Day.* London: John Long Ltd.

Haglund, W.D. and M.H. Sorg, eds. 1997. *Forensic Taphonomy: The Postmortem Fate of Human Remains.* Boca Raton: CRC Press.

Harn, A.D. 1980. *The Prehistory of Dickson Mounds.* Springfield: Illinois State Museum.

Harper, K. 1986. *Give Me My Father's Body: The Life of Minik, the N.Y. Eskimo.* Iqaluit, Canada: Blackhead Books.

Harrington, J.M. and R.L. Blakely. 1995. Bones in the basement: Bioarchaeology of historic remains in nonmortuary contexts. In *Bodies of Evidence*, ed. Anne L. Grauer. N.Y.: Wiley-Liss.

Hartshorne, A. 1841. *Hanging in Chains.* London: T. Fisher Unwin.

Havill, L.M., A.A. White, and K.A. Murphy. 1998. Skeletal biology and cemetery use at the Albee Mound, Bucci, Shaffer, and Shepherd sites. Paper presented at Annual Midwest Archaeological Conference in Muncie, Indiana.

Henneberg, M. and R.J. Henneberg. 1999a. Human skeletal material from Pompeii. In *Pompeii: Life in a Roman Town*, ed. A. Ciarallo and E. De Carolis (Milan: Electa).

_____. 1999b. Variation in the closure of the sacral canal in the skeletal sample from Pompeii, Italy. *Perspectives in Human Biology* 4, No. 1: 177–188.

_____. and A. Ciarallo. 1996. Skeletal material from the house of C Iulius Polybius in Pompeii, 79 AD. *Human Evolution* 11, no. 3–4: 249–259.

Henry, R.S. 1964. *The Armed Forces Institute of Pathology: Its First Century, 1862–1962.* Wash., D.C.: Office of the Surgeon General, Dept. of the Army.

Henschen, F. 1965. *The Human Skull: A Cultural History.* N.Y.: Frederick A. Praeger.

Hertling, S.J., L. and E. Kirschbaum, S.J. 1956. *The Roman Catacombs and their Martyrs.* Translated by M.J. Costelloe, S.J. Milwaukee: Bruce Publishing Co.

Higgins, R.L. and J.E. Sirianni. 1995. An assessment of health and mortality of nineteenth century Rochester, New York using historic records and the Highland Park skeletal collection. In *Bodies of Evidence*, ed. A.L. Grauer. N.Y.: Wiley-Liss.

Holland, T.D., B.E. Anderson, and R.W. Mann. Human variables in the postmortem alteration of human bone: Examples from U.S. war casualities. In *Forensic Taphonomy*, ed. W.D. Haglund and M.H. Sorg. Boca Raton: CRC Press.

Huntington, R. and P. Metcalf. 1979. *Celebrations of Death: The Anthropology of Mortuary Ritual.* Cambridge: Cambridge Univ. Press.

Indians continue to protest display at Dickson Mounds. 1990. *Times-Republic* (Watseka, Ill.). Sept. 18.

Isaac, B. 1995. An epimethean view of the future at the Peabody Museum of Archaeology and Ethnology at Harvard University. *Federal Archeology,* Fall/Winter.

Iserson, K.V. 1994. *Death to Dust: What Happens to Dead Bodies?* Tucson: Galen.

Jantz, R.L. and D.W. Owsley. 1994. White traders in the Upper Missouri: Evidence from the Swan Creek site. In *Skeletal Biology in the Great Plains*, ed. D.W. Owsley and R.L. Jantz. Wash., D.C.: Smithsonian.

Janus, C.G. with W. Brashler. 1975. *The Search for Peking Man*. N.Y.: Macmillan.

Johnston, C.A., S. Nawrocki, C. Schmidt, and M. Williamson. 1997. An interregional comparison of culturally-modified Hopewellian human remains. Paper presented at the 62nd meeting of the Society for American Archaeology. Nashville, Tenn., April 4–6.

Jones-Kern, K.F. 1997. *T. Wingate Todd and the Development of Modern American Physical Anthropology, 1900–1940*. Ph.D. diss., Graduate College, Bowling Green State Univ.

Jones-Kern, K.and B. Latimer. 1996. Skeletons out of the closet. *Explorer* 38 (Spring), no. 1 + 2.

Joyce, C. and E. Stover. 1991. *Witnesses from the Grave: The Stories Bones Tell*. Boston: Little, Brown and Co.

Kanowski, M. 1987. *Old Bones*. Melbourne, Australia: Longman Chesire.

Katzenberg, M.A. and S.R. Saunders, eds. In press. *Skeletal Biology of Past Peoples: Research Methods, 2nd ed*. N.Y.: John Wiley and Sons.

Kerley, E.R. 1984. Microscopic aging of human bone. In *Human Identification*, ed. T.A. Rathbun and J.E. Buikstra. Springfield, Ill.: C.C. Thomas.

Kerrigan, J. 1990. Dickson Mounds dispute pits logic against religion. *Journal Star* (Peoria, Ill.), Jan. 6: A14.

Key, P.J. 1994. Relationships of the Woodland Period on the northern and central plains: The craniometric evidence. In *Skeletal Biology in the Great Plains*, ed. D.W. Owsley and R.L. Jantz. Wash., D.C.: Smithsonian.

Klesart, A.L. and S. Powell. 1993. A perspective on ethics and the reburial controversy. *American Antiquity* 58, no. 2: 348–354.

Kobler, J. 1999. *The Reluctant Surgeon: A Biography of John Hunter*. N.Y.: Akadine.

Krogman, W.M. and M.Y. Işcan. 1986. *The Human Skeleton in Forensic Medicine, 2nd Ed*. Springfield, Ill.: Charles C. Thomas.

Krohe, J., Jr., 1992. Skeletons in our closet. *Reader: Chicago's Free Weekly* 21, no. 19: Feb. 14.

Lawson, K. and A.Rufus. 1999. *Weird Europe*. N.Y.: St. Martin's Press.

Leaton, C. 1991. Who owns the past? The Dickson Mounds Museum controversy. *Illinois History* 45, no. 1 (Oct.).

Legassick, M. and C.Rassool. 1999. Skeletons in the cupboard: Museums and the incipient trade in human remains, 1907–1917. Paper presented at the conference of the South African Historical Society, July 11–14, at the University of the Western Cape.

Lewin, R. 1993. *The Origin of Modern Humans*. N.Y.: Scientific American Library.

_____. 1997. *Bones of Contention: Controversies in the Search for Human Origins, 2nd ed*. Chicago: Univ. of Chicago Press.

Little, J. 1998. Motherhouse holds bodies of seven early saints. Posted on Saints Alive Relics/ I.C.H.R. website http://home.earthlink.net/ ~saintsalive/, May 10.

López-Bueis, I., R. Robledo, D. Campillo, and G.J. Trancho. 1994. Tibial exostosis: Ambiental stress indicator in a medieval population. In *Biología de Poblaciones Humanas*, ed. C. Bernis et al. Madrid: Univ. Autonoma de Madrid.

_____. A. Fernández-Salvador, B. Robledo, and G.J. Trancho. 1996. Ulnar osteoarthrosis in a medieval Spanish population. Paper presented at the first Conferenza Internazionale di Antopologia e Storia della Salute e delle Malattie in Genoa, Italy (May/June).

_____. and G. Trancho. 1999. Paleopathology in a medieval Spanish ossuary (Wamba, Valladolid). Paper presented at the 26th Annual Meeting of the Paleopathology Assoc., April 27–28, in Columbus, Ohio.

Lorz, K. 1986. So ist's recht, da liegt der Meister bei seinem Knecht. *Frau and Mutter* 7/8: 48.

Luyendijk-Elshout, A.M. 1970. Death enlightened: A study of Frederik Ruysch. *Journal of the American Medical Assoc*. 212, no. 1: April 6.

Lynnerup, N. 1998. *The Greenland Norse: A Biological-Anthropological Study*. Copenhagen: Commission for Scientific Research in Greenland.

Malari, M.C. 1998. *A Legal Primer on Managing Museum Collections*. Wash., D.C.: Smithsonian.

Malcolmson, S.L. 2000. The color of bones. *New York Times Magazine*, April 2.

Mancinelli, F. 1981. *Catacombs and Basilicas*. Firenze: Scala Books.

Mann, G. 1964. The anatomical collections of Frederik Ruysch at Leningrad. *Bulletin of the Cleveland Medical Library* 11 (Jan.): 10–13.

Mann, R.W. and T.D. Holland. 1998. Three taels of gold: Bone dealers in Vietnam. Paper posted on website www.thehistorynet.com/ Vietnam/articles/1998/12982_text.htm.

Maples, W.R. and M. Browning. 1994. *Dead Men Do Tell Tales*. N.Y.: Doubleday.

Mays, S. 1998. *The Archaeology of Human Bones.* London: Routledge.

McCarthy, P. 1994. American headhunters. *Omni* 16: 14.

McGregor, L. 1898. A crypt of skulls. *The Royal Magazine* 1 (Nov. 1898–April 1899). London: C. Arthur Pearson Ltd.

McManamon, F.P. 1994. Changing relationships between Native Americans and archaeologists. *Historic Preservation Forum* 8, no. 2: 15–20.

_____. 1995. The reality of repatriation. *Federal Archeology.* Fall/Winter.

The Medical and Surgical History of the Civil War. 1991. 1879, reprint Wilmington, NC: Broadfoot Publishing Co.

Mensforth, R.P. and C.O. Lovejoy. 1985. Anatomical, physiological, and epidemiological correlates of the aging process: A confirmation of multifactorial age determination in the Libben skeletal population. *American Journal of Physical Anthropology* 68: 87–106.

Merbs, C.F. 1980. *Catalogue of the Hrdlička Paleopathology Collection.* ed. R.A. Tyson and E.S. Dyer Alcauskas. San Diego: San Diego Museum of Man.

_____. 1995. The ossuary at Kutná Hora. *Newsletter of the Assoc. of Gravestone Studies* 19:2 (Spring).

Micozzi, M.S., F.M. Townsend, and C.E. Koop. 1990. From Army Medical Museum to National Museum of Health and Medicine. *Archives of Pathology and Laboratory Medicine* 114 (Dec.).

Mikelbank, P. 1988. Unearthing the unearthly. *Washington Post,* Oct. 30: E1.

"Missing Link" in New York. 1999. *Fortean Times* 129 (December): 18–19.

Montgomery, D. 1999. William Bass wants your body. *Washington Post,* July 4: F1.

Moore, M. 1998. To Guatemalan scientists, dead men do tell tales. *Washington Post,* July 19: A22.

Moore-Jansen, P., S.D. Ousley, and R.L. Jantz. 1994. *Data Collection Procedures for Forensic Skeletal Material: Report of Investigations No. 48.* Knoxville: Univ. of Tenn. Dept. of Anthropology.

Morley, J. 1971. *Death, Heaven and the Victorians.* Pittsburgh: Univ. of Pittsburgh Press.

Mould, R.F. 1984. *Mould's Medical Anecdotes.* Bristol, England: Adam Hilger Ltd.

Murphy, E. 1995. *After the Funeral.* N.Y.: Citadel.

Murray, E.A. and A.J. Perzigian. 1995. A glimpse of early nineteenth century Cincinnati as viewed from potter's field. In *Bodies of Evidence,* ed. A.L. Grauer. N.Y.: Wiley-Liss.

Nawrocki, S.P. 1995. Taphonomic processes in historic cemeteries. In *Bodies of Evidence,* ed. A.L. Grauer. N.Y.: Wiley-Liss.

_____. 1997. Analysis of the human remains. In *Hopewell in Mt. Vernon.* Ed. General Electric. N.P.: G.E. Co.

Neves, W.A., J.F. Powell, A.Prous, E.G. Ozolins, and M. Blum. 1999. Lapa Vermelha IV Hominid 1. *Genetics and Molecular Biology* 22, no. 4: 1–5.

Norfleet, B.P. 1993. *Looking at Death.* Boston: David R. Godine.

Ortner, D.J. 1991. Theoretical and methodological issues in paleopathology. In *Human Paleopathology,* ed. D.J. Ortner and A.C. Aufderheide. Wash., D.C.: Smithsonian.

_____. 1994. Descriptive methodology in paleopathology. In *Skeletal Biology in the Great Plains,* ed. D.W. Owsley and R.L. Jantz. Wash., D.C.: Smithsonian.

_____. and A.C. Aufderheide, eds. 1991. *Human Paleopathology: Current Syntheses and Future Options.* Wash., D.C.: Smithsonian.

Owsley, D.W. and R.L. Jantz. 1994. An integrative approach to Great Plains skeletal biology. In *Skeletal Biology in the Great Plains,* ed. D.W. Owsley and R.L. Jantz. Wash., D.C.: Smithsonian.

_____. eds. 1994. *Skeletal Biology in the Great Plains: Migration, Warfare, Health, and Subsistence.* Wash., D.C.: Smithsonian.

_____. R.W. Mann, and T.G. Baugh. 1994. Culturally modified human bones from the Edwards I site. In *Skeletal Biology in the Great Plains,* ed. D.W. Owsley and R.L. Jantz. Wash., D.C.: Smithsonian.

Pardoe, C. 1988. The Cemetery as symbol: The distribution of prehistoric Aboriginal burial grounds in southeastern Australia. *Archaeol. Oceania* 23: 1–16.

_____. 1991. Isolation and evolution in Tasmania. *Current Anthropology* 32, no. 1 (Feb.).

_____. 1994. Bioscapes: Evolutionary landscape of Australia. *Archaeol. Oceania* 29: 182–190.

_____. 1995a. Riverine, biological and cultural evolution in southeastern Australia. *Antiquity* 69: 696–713.

_____. 1995b. Where is A38235? Paper presented at the Tindale Symposium held by the South Australian Anthropological Society and the South Australian Museum at the University of Adelaide.

Le Paris Souterrain de Félix Nadar, 1861. 1982. Paris: Caisse Nationale des Monuments Historiques et des Sites.

Parrington, M. and D.G. Roberts. 1984. The First African Baptist Church Cemetery. *Archaeology* 37, no. 6: 26–32.

Parsons, T.J. and V.W. Weedn. 1997. Preservation and recovery of DNA in postmortem specimens and trace samples. In *Forensic Taphonomy*, ed. W.D. Haglund and M.H. Sorg. Boca Raton: CRC Press.

Pearson, M.P. 1999. *The Archaeology of Death and Burial.* College Station: Texas A&M Univ. Press.

Peters, H.A. 1995. Cambodian history through Cambodian museums. *Expedition* 37: 52–62.

Pfeiffer, S. 1991. Is paleopathology a relevant predictor of contemporary health patterns? In *Human Paleopathology*, ed. D.J. Ortner and A.C. Aufderheide. Wash., D.C.: Smithsonian.

Powell, M.L. 1991. Endemic treponematosis and tuberculosis in the prehistoric southeastern United States. In *Human Paleopathology*, ed. D.J. Ortner and A.C. Aufderheide. Wash., D.C.: Smithsonian.

Prag, J. and R. Neave. 1997. *Making Faces.* College Station: Texas A&M Univ. Press.

Preston, D. 1997. The lost man. *New Yorker* 73 (June 16): 70–80.

Price III, H.M. 1991. *Disputing the Dead: U.S. Law on Aboriginal Remains and Grave Goods.* Columbia: Univ. of Missouri Press.

Pridmore, J. 1992. Dickson Mounds: Closing a window on the dead. *Archaeology*, July/August.

Prokopec, M. and G.L. Pretty. 1991. Observations on health, genetics, and culture from analysis of skeletal remains from Roonka, South Australia. In *Human Paleopathology*, ed. D.J. Ortner and A.C. Aufderheide. Wash., D.C.: Smithsonian.

Ragon, M. 1983. *The Space of Death: A Study of Funerary Architecture, Decoration, and Urbanism.* Translated by A. Sheridan. Charlottesville: Univ. Press of Virginia.

Rankin-Hill, L.M. and M.L. Blakey. 1994. W. Montague Cobb. *American Anthropologist* 96: 74–96.

Rathbun, T.A. and J.E. Buikstra, eds. 1984. *Human Identification: Case Studies in Forensic Anthropology.* Springfield, Ill.: C.C. Thomas.

Reich, C. 1995. Cemeteries I have known: Europe. In *Death's Garden: Relationships with Cemeteries.* San Francisco: Automatism Press.

Rhine, S. 1984. Forensic anthropology in New Mexico. In *Human Identification*, ed. T.A. Rathbun and J.E. Buikstra. Springfield, Ill.: C.C. Thomas.

_____. 1998. *Bone Voyage.* Albuquerque: Univ. of New Mexico Press.

Rhoads, L. 1999. So shall you be. *Morbid Curiosity* 3: 31–34.

Roberts, C. 1991. Trauma and treatment in the British Isles in the historic period. In *Human Paleopathology*, ed. D.J. Ortner and A.C. Aufderheide. Wash., D.C.: Smithsonian.

Roberts, K.B. and J.D.W. Tomlinson. 1992. *The Fabric of the Body: European Traditions of Anatomical Illustration.* N.Y.: Oxford Univ. Press.

Robinson, M.B. 1998. Museum inventories Indian remains before turnover. Associated Press, March 9.

Rothschild, N.A. 1979. Mortuary behavior and social organization at Indian Knoll and Dickson Mounds. *American Antiquity* 44: 658–675.

Roylance, F.D. 1999. Old bones a source of insights, mystery. *Baltimore Sun*, May 2: 10F.

Rufus, A. 1999. *Magnificent Corpses.* N.Y.: Marlowe & Company.

Sabbatini, R.M.E. 1997. Phrenology: The history of brain localization. *Brain and Mind* (March).

Sandford, M.K. 1992. A reconsideration of trace element analysis in prehistoric bone. In *Skeletal Biology of Past Peoples*, ed. S.R. Saunders and M.A. Katzenberg. N.Y.: Wiley-Liss.

Santos, A.L. 2000. *A Skeletal Picture of Tuberculosis: Macroscopic, Radiological, Biomolecular, and Historical Evidence from the Coimbra Identified Skeletal Collection.* Ph.D. diss., Dept. Antropología, Univ. de Coimbra.

Sargent, W. 1976. *My Life with the Headhunters.* St. Albans, Hertfordshire, England: Panther.

Saunders, S.R. and M.A. Katzenberg, eds. 1992. "*Skeletal Biology of Past Peoples: Research Methods.* N.Y.: Wiley-Liss.

_____. and R.D. Hoppa. 1997. Sex allocation from long bone measurements using logistic regression. *Canadian Society of Forensic Science Journal* 30, no. 2: 49–60.

_____. C. DeVito, and M.A. Katzenberg. 1997. Dental caries in nineteenth century upper Canada. *American Journal of Physical Anthropology* 104: 71–87.

_____. C. DeVito, A. Herring, R. Southern, and R. Hoppa. 1993. Accuracy tests of tooth formation age estimations for human skeletal remains. *American Journal of Physical Anthropology* 92: 173–188.

Schermer, S.J., A.K. Fisher, and D.C. Hodges. 1994. Endemic treponematosis in prehistoric western Iowa. In *Skeletal Biology in the Great Plains*, ed. D.W. Owsley and R.L. Jantz. Wash., D.C.: Smithsonian.

Schultz, Michael. 1997. Microscopic investigation of excavated skeletal remains. In *Forensic Taphonomy*, ed. W.D. Haglund and M.H. Sorg. Boca Raton: CRC Press.

Schwartz, J.H. 1998. *What the Bones Tell Us.* Tucson: Univ. of Arizona Press.

Scott, D.D., P. Willey, and M.A. Connor. 1998. *They Died With Custer: Soldiers' Bones from the Battle of the Little Bighorn.* Norman: Univ. of Oklahoma Press.

Sears, W.H. 1956. *Excavations at Kolomoki: Final Report.* Athens: Univ. of Georgia Press.

Sellevold, B.J., U.L. Hansen, and J.B. Jørgensen. 1984. *Iron Age Man in Denmark: Prehistoric Man in Denmark, Vol. 3.* Copenhagen: Det Kongelige Nordiske Oldskriftselskab.

Serafin, T.J. 1998. *Relics: The Forgotten Sacramental.* Temple City, Calif.: Thomas J. Serafin and International Crusade for Holy Relics.

Shields, T. 1999. Native American remains prompt emotional debate. *Washington Post*, April 25: C1.

Shreeve, J. 1996. *The Neandertal Enigma.* N.Y.: William Morrow.

Shufeldt, R.W. 1910. Personal adventures of a human skull collector. *Medical Council* 15, no. 4: 123–27.

Sjøvold, T. 1993. Testing assumptions for skeletal studies by means of identified skulls from Hallstatt, Austria. *American Journal of Physical Anthropology.* 16 (supp.): 181.

Skinner, M. and R.A. Lazenby. 1983. *Found! Human Remains: A Field Manual for the Recovery of the Recent Human Skeleton.* Burnaby, B.P.: Archaeology Press/Simon Fraser Univ.

Sledzik, P.S. and S. Ousley. 1991. Analysis of six Vietnamese trophy skulls. *Journal of Forensic Sciences* 36, no. 2 (March): 520–530.

Smith, G. 1999. The body farm. *Science*, Jan./Feb.: 60–63.

Smith, Sir S.A. 1939. *Studies in Identification* 3: 19–27.

Snow, C.E. 1974. *Early Hawaiians.* Lexington, Ky: Univ. Press of Kentucky.

Spencer, F., ed. 1982. *A History of American Physical Anthropology 1930–1980.* N.Y.: Academic Press.

_____. 1997. *History of Physical Anthropology: An Encyclopedia.* N.Y.: Academic Press.

Starrs, J.E., ed. 1999. *The Harewood Cemetery Excavations.* Wash., D.C.: Scientific Sleuthing.

Stephens, J.L. 1970. *Incidents of Travel in Egypt, Arabia, Petraea, and the Holy Land.* 1837, reprint N.Y.: Dover Publications.

Stevenson, J. 1978. *The Catacombs.* London: Thames and Hudson.

Stone, A. 1995. High-tech grave diggers solve history's mysteries. *USA Today*, Oct. 26: 6A.

Suchey, J.M., P.A. Owings, D.V. Wiseley, and T.T. Noguchi. 1984. Skeletal aging of unidentified persons. In *Human Identification*, ed. T.A. Rathbun and J.E. Buikstra. Springfield, Ill.: C.C. Thomas.

Sundick, R.I. Ashes to ashes, dust to dust or Where did the skeleton go? In *Human Identification*, ed. T.A. Rathbun and J.E. Buikstra. Springfield, Ill.: C.C. Thomas.

Suzuki, T. 1991. Paleopathological study on infectious diseases in Japan. In *Human Paleopathology*, ed. D.J. Ortner and A.C. Aufderheide. Wash., D.C.: Smithsonian.

Talbott, J.H. 1970. *A Biographical History of Medicine.* N.Y.: Grune & Stratton.

Tansey, V. and D.E.C. Mekie. 1982. *The Museum of the Royal College of Surgeons of Edinburgh.* Edinburgh: Royal College of Surgeons.

Tattersall, I. 1995. *The Fossil Trail.* Oxford: Oxford Univ. Press.

Thomas, D.H. 2000. *Skull Wars: Kennewick Man, Archaeology, and the Battle for Native American Identity.* N.Y.: Basic Books.

Thompson, C.J.S. 1968. *Giants, Dwarfs and Other Oddities.* N.Y.: Citadel.

Thompson, D.D. Forensic anthropology. In *A History of American Physical Anthropology 1930–1980*, ed. F. Spencer. N.Y.: Academic Press.

Thompson, M.D. 1988. *The Illinois State Museum.* Springfield: The Illinois State Museum.

Thurmer, J. 1996. The story behind the skeleton. *FOSAM: Friends of the South Australian Museum* 26, No. 1 + 2 (Jan.–June): 1–2.

Tobias, P.V. 1991. On the scientific, medical, dental and educational value of collections of human skeletons. *International Journal of Anthropology* 6, no. 3: 277–280.

Trancho, G.J., B. Robledo, and I. López de los Bueis. 1994. Sexual differences in coxa bone of European populations. In *Biología de Poblaciones Humanas*, ed. C. Bernis et al. Madrid: Univ. Autonoma de Madrid.

Turnbull, P. n.d. Ancestors, not specimens: Reflections on the controversy over the remains of Aboriginal people in European scientific collections. *Electronic Journal of Australian and New Zealand History.*

Twain, M. 1980. *The Innocents Abroad or The New Pilgrims Progress.* 1869, Reprint, N.Y.: Signet.

Ubelaker, D.H. 1982. The development of American paleopathology. In *A History of American Physical Anthropology 1930–1980,* ed. F. Spencer. N.Y.: Academic Press.

_____. 1984. Positive identification from the radiographic comparison of frontal sinus patterns. In *Human Identification,* ed. T.A. Rathbun and J.E. Buikstra. Springfield, Ill.: C.C. Thomas.

_____. 1989. *Human Skeletal Remains: Excavation, Analysis, Interpretation, 2nd ed.* Wash., D.C.: Taraxacum.

_____. 1994. An overview of Great Plains human skeletal biology. In *Skeletal Biology in the Great Plains,* ed. D.W. Owsley and R.L. Jantz. Wash., D.C.: Smithsonian.

_____. 1995. Historic cemetery analysis. In *Bodies of Evidence,* ed. A.L. Grauer. N.Y.: Wiley-Liss.

_____. Ubelaker, D.H. and L.G. Grant. 1989. Human skeletal remains: Preservation or reburial? *Yearbook of Physical Anthropology* 32: 249–287.

Ubelaker, D. and H. Scammell. 1992. *Bones: A Forensic Detective's Casebook.* N.Y.: Edward Burlingame Books.

Uhlman, M. 2000. College of Physicians sees past as its future. *(Philadelphia) Inquirer,* Jan. 10.

Waldron, T. 1994. *Counting the Dead: The Epidemiology of Skeletal Populations.* Chichester, England: John Wiley & Sons.

Walker, A. and P. Shipman. 1996. *The Wisdom of Bones.* London: Weidenfeld and Nicolson.

Walker, P.L. In press. Is the battered-child syndrome a modern phenomenon? In *Proceedings of the Xth European Meeting of the Paleopathology Assoc.*

_____. In press. Bioarchaeological ethics. In *Skeletal Biology of Past Peoples: Research Methods, 2nd ed.,* ed. M.A. Katzenberg and S.R. Saunders. N.Y.: John Wiley and Sons.

Watzman, H. 1996. Religion, politics, and archaeology. *Chronicle of Higher Education* 42: A31.

Webb, S. 1995. *Palaeopathology of Aboriginal Australians.* Cambridge: Cambridge Univ. Press.

Weil, T. 1992. *The Cemetery Book.* N.Y.: Hippocrene Books.

Werner, P. and R. Werner. 1985. Bemalte totenschädel: Besonderheiten der sekundärbestatttung im süddeutschen sprachraum. In *Jahrbuch der Bayrischen Denkmalpflege* 39: 246–271.

White, T.D. 1991. *Human Osteology.* Illustrated by P.A. Folkens. San Diego: Academic Press.

Wilkins, R. 1991. *The Bedside Book of Death.* N.Y.: Citadel.

Willey, P. 1981. Another view by one of the Crow Creek researchers. *Early Man* 3, no.26.

_____. 1990. Prehistoric warfare on the Great Plains: Skeletal analysis of the Crow Creek massacre victims. N.Y.: Garland Publishing.

_____. and D.D. Scott. 1999. Who's buried in Custer's grave? *Journal of Forensic Sciences* 44, no. 3: 656–665.

Wolpoff, M.H. 1996. *Human Evolution.* N.Y.: McGraw Hill.

Zeiger, L. with J.H. Byrd and P.R. Stubblefield. 1999. Five crypts and a chapel — postmortem style. *NEST* (Summer).

Zimmerman, L. and R. Alex. 1981. How the Crow Creek archaeologists view the question of reburial. *Early Man* 3, no. 3: 3–10, 25–27.

Index